APPLIED ANTHROPOLOGY IN AMERICA

APPLIED ANTHROPOLOGY IN AMERICA

Elizabeth M. Eddy and
William L. Partridge,
Editors

WITHDRAWN

Columbia University Press • New York • 1978

Library of Congress Cataloging in Publication Data
Main entry under title:

Applied anthropology in America.

Bibliography: p.
1. Applied anthropology—United States.
2. United States—Social conditions.   3. United States
—Social policy.   I. Eddy, Elizabeth M.   II. Partridge,
William L.
GN397.7.U6A66   309.1'73   78-6386
ISBN 0-231-04466-6
ISBN 0-231-04467-4 pbk.

Columbia University Press
New York   Guildford, Surrey
Copyright © 1978 Columbia University Press
Printed in the United States of America

TO SOLON T. KIMBALL

Who teaches that the study
of human behavior should
be of service to people

CONTENTS

ACKNOWLEDGMENTS

The preparation of this volume was made possible by the continuous support of a number of people. These especially include the contributors themselves, who unstintingly gave of their time to the initial preparation and subsequent revisions of essays for inclusion. They were a remarkably conscientious group with whom the editors found it a privilege to work.

Several contributors played an important role beyond that represented here. Jacquetta Hill-Burnett and Gwen Kennedy Neville were particularly important in the early days of the entire effort and contributed ideas which substantially shaped the content of the volume. Amidst an extraordinarily busy schedule, Margaret Mead found time to contribute her knowledge about the history of applied anthropology and to criticize the first draft of the first essay. In a telephone conversation with one of the editors, Frederick L. W. Richardson provided suggestions which significantly altered the focus of Part I. Throughout the development of the volume, Solon T. Kimball provided previously unknown factual knowledge and wise advice about a myriad of practical problems which arose in the course of bringing the volume to a conclusion.

In addition to the contributors, several other persons gave generously of their time and experience. Eliot D. Chapple responded to the first draft of essay 1 and furnished data which considerably expanded our knowledge about the early days of applied anthropology. George Spindler read an entire first draft of the volume and made several constructive suggestions for improvement. G. Alexander

Moore, Jr., and Antoinette B. Brown read early versions of selected essays and gave us editorial advice. Dr. Lambros Comitas read two drafts of the volume and was a key person in the final editorial process.

Finally, Charlotte Bannister served as a careful and interested typist who made innumerable corrections and minor editorial changes which improved the text. Lydia Deakin, Barbara Wubbell, Melody Melian, and Mark Hoover patiently transferred individual bibliographies to cards so that the final bibliography could be prepared.

PREFACE

This book of contributed essays is about applied anthropology in American society. It is written for students, professionals, and others who are curious about the relevance of anthropological training and knowledge to contemporary American social problems. Our purpose here is to provide an overview of some of the contributions of anthropology to major policy issues which confront our nation, the experiences of anthropologists who have chosen to work in nonacademic settings for part or all of their careers, and the ways in which applied work in the United States contributes to the development of anthropology itself as well as matters of public concern.

The reasons for this focus should be stated at the outset. First, since America today plays a critical and leading role in world affairs, anthropologists will do well to seriously address themselves to an understanding of the complex American institutions, values, and patterns of relationships with others which increasingly touch and influence the rest of the world. Second, during the last decade, growing numbers of anthropologists have questioned the traditional orientation of the discipline to foreign area studies and the exclusion of the United States as a legitimate area for anthropological research and activity. This trend has been bolstered by the objections of foreign peoples to being studied by outsiders who fail to establish mutually beneficial relationships with them. In addition, the twin demands of students for anthropology to become relevant to American social problems and of governmental agencies for research related to national needs have resulted in a reexamination of the role of anthropologists within our own society. Finally, the recent halcyon era of rapid and extensive growth of academic anthropology departments is at an end for the foreseeable future for reasons set forth in essay 1. A major consequence is that many anthropologists will need to find employment outside of academe in situations which demand that they apply their knowledge and skills to practical problems.

Anthropology traditionally embraces the four major subfields of archeology, physical anthropology, ethnology, and linguistics. Their common purpose—to study the origins, persistence, and modifications of human beings and the cultures they create—holds the branches together as a single discipline. Yet, the topical branches of anthropology are only one way in which the field has evolved in recent years. Today there are scientists in each branch who are concerned with the consequences of their investigations for the problems of contemporary peoples and societies.

For example, there are linguists who eschew the study of glottochronology and protolanguage and focus instead upon analyses and descriptions of unwritten contemporary languages in order to develop lexicons in which health manuals can be written, or who concentrate on the sociolinguistic behavior of specific groups in complex societies so as to discover cognitive patterns of use to educators. In physical anthropology, some specialists engage in research on human nutrition, the epidemiology of disease, or forensic analysis of victims of violent death, rather than on the physical characteristics of extinct human ancestors. Similarly, some archeologists specialize in reclaiming the heritage of contemporary peoples rather than in reconstructing civilizations of lost continents. Among ethnologists, some study education and socialization, drug use and abuse, health care, economics and development, and a host of other current concerns.

While a number of archeologists, linguists, and physical anthropologists are making significant contributions to the application of anthropology to social problems in America today, their work is beyond our purview here. In an area as broad as applied anthropology in American society, selectivity is both necessary and inevitable. This volume is limited to a consideration of the application of ethnological theories and methods derived from social and cultural anthropology. Moreover, the topics and contributors included herein partially reflect the state of the art in applying anthropology within the United States, the willingness and ability of those invited to participate in a volume of this kind, our own interests, and a conscious effort to include anthropologists with varying levels of formal preparation in anthropology, and young anthropologists as well as those with long experience.

The fact that the volume is dedicated to Solon T. Kimball, one of the foremost leaders in anthropological studies of American communities and institutions, means that the majority of contributors are persons who have been professionally associated with him in one way or another. Though they do not always share his orientation to applied anthropology, they represent a cluster of people who do share his conviction that anthropologists must cross the disciplinary boundaries which have traditionally prevented them from coming to grips with the modern world, if anthropology is to continue as a viable and productive endeavor in the future. The chapters which follow give expression to this conviction from a number of different vantage points.

The contributors to this volume have specialized in contemporary America or, to state it more accurately, in one or more of the many subcultures, institutional complexes, and communities which comprise the blend of diverse elements which constitute American society today. Their contributions are a direct result of their personal experiences in applying anthropological knowledge and insights to the development of better solutions for the amelioration of some of our nation's most urgent problems. Though the contributors do not represent all aspects of applied work which engage anthropologists in the United States, they all have been pioneers in what they have done. They document the significant differences between what F. S. C. Northrup (1953) has called the naturalistic logic of anthropological science and the deterministic logic of mathematics and engineering. From our contributors, therefore, we can learn much that is important to the rethinking of both anthropology and our society if problems of mutual concern are to be redefined in ways that permit better solutions to emerge than those now extant.

APPLIED ANTHROPOLOGY IN AMERICA

INTRODUCTION

1

THE DEVELOPMENT OF APPLIED ANTHROPOLOGY IN AMERICA

William L. Partridge and Elizabeth M. Eddy

During the last fifty years, anthropology has changed from an esoteric taxonomy of primitive customs into a systematic, comparative, and holistic science of man. Its methods of study are derived from natural science, yet its subject matter is humanity. As both science and humanism, it keeps pace with changes in the conditions of human life which now engulf peoples all over the world. The most significant changes which have affected anthropology are the massing of humanity in new urban settlement forms; a technology with the potential to feed the world or destroy industrial civilization; human consciousness of the limits of natural resources; a revolution in public health which brings the paradox of increased life expectancy and

William L. Partridge (Ph.D., Florida) is assistant professor of anthropology at the University of Southern California. His research has been among the Oto and Ponca Indians of eastern Oklahoma, the American hippie subculture, and an agro-pastoral community on the north coast of Colombia, South America. Currently, he is a consultant to the World Health Organization, and is codirecting an interdisciplinary study of the long-range consequences of development planning in the Papaloapan River Basin of Mexico.

Elizabeth M. Eddy (Ph.D., Columbia) is chairperson and professor of anthropology at the University of Florida. She is a specialist in educational anthropology and has conducted fieldwork in hospital and school systems in the United States. She has served as associate project director of research at the New York School of Social Work, project director of research at Hunter College in the City University of New York, and director of the Urban Studies Bureau of the University of Florida. Dr. Eddy is a past president of the Council on Anthropology and Education, and is currently editor of applied anthropology for the *American Anthropologist*. She has been a consultant to the National Assessment of Educational Progress Project and to ABT Associates.

overpopulation; the rise to power of new nations with hungry people, the most modern armaments, and few resources; and systems of communication which bring battlefield body counts and rising expectations into the home.

Problems of food production, ethnic relations, urban planning, health care services, population, education, aging, and many others which stem from these changes have produced the response which we call applied anthropology. Together with the growth of university programs in anthropology to create knowledge and train people to use it, increased specialization and interdisciplinary collaboration, the emerging awareness of professional responsibility to subjects of study, and a focus upon contemporary peoples and practical problems, applied anthropology is a recent development.

In this essay, we describe this development and devote attention to the following questions: What is applied anthropology? How do applied anthropologists differ from other anthropologists?

What Is Applied Anthropology?

There is no genuine theoretical or methodological distinction between "pure" and "applied" science. In popular thought, scientists engaged in pure research have little concern with potential uses of the results of their labor, and applied scientists are not concerned with making theoretical contributions. Yet, as any physician or biologist will testify, this neat distinction does not exist in actual scientific work. Physicians use theory daily in order to diagnose and treat clinical cases, and the results they obtain alter both theory and clinical practice. If this were not the case, they would still be using unicorn horn, leeches, and extract of human skull. Similarly, biologists utilize theory to develop pesticides permitting the control of fruit flies, and must modify theory when fruit flies multiply in the laboratory.

In science, the basic dialogue between theory and application is at the heart of any progress. Applications are in part determined by the adequacy of theory, and theory is accepted or rejected over the long run in relation to its utility in successive applications (Kuhn 1962). What is true of science generally is also true of the science of anthropology. The distinction between "applied" and "pure" anthropology is largely a fiction of popular culture. Both draw upon the same body of theory and methods that are commonly recognized as anthropological (Foster 1969: Clifton 1970; Naylor 1973; Bastide 1973).

However, there is an important differentiation to be made between "abstract" and "applied" anthropology, and it was first noted by Conrad M. Arensberg (1947) in one of the early editorial statements of the Society for Applied Anthropology. Three features distinguish applied from abstract anthropology. The first is that applied anthropologists study living cultures and contemporary people. The kinds of data they seek cannot be excavated in historical ruins, discovered in archives, or prodded from the memories of the aged. Insights gained from history or selective memories of the past may lead to important suggestions for applied research, but they tell us little of how people today form social groups, accomplish tasks, survive in an environment, or solve problems.

In addition to research among living peoples—a type of research which engages increasing numbers of anthropologists who are not "applied"—applied anthropologists conduct research oriented toward the problems of those they study. Their research stems from the needs of the people themselves, and these might range from such problems as drug abuse or food shortage, to such unconscious needs as dietary deficiency. In contrast, the problems posed for scientific investigation in abstract anthropology may or may not bear any relationship to the needs of living people. For example, the rage with which academic professionals attack one another over the diffusion of pottery in the first millennium B.C., the religion of the Cheyenne in the late nineteenth century, or the origins of Caribbean mortuary customs, all may bear little relation to the immediate problems of contemporary Hopi craftsmen, Cheyenne Baptists, or the laborers from St. Kitts who migrate to Galveston, Texas.

Finally, applied anthropologists seek applications of their findings, data, and analyses beyond anthropology. Abstract anthropologists, on the other hand, find significance for their work in the debates which stimulated their forebears in the eighteenth and nineteenth centuries. The ideas of these scholars define and give meaning to abstractions, define the procedures by which data are selected and collected, and restrict the focus of research within the bounds of historical tradition. Applied anthropologists utilize the same process of scientific abstraction, or theory building, but these abstractions derive their significance from their contemporary implications for living people. As a consequence, applied anthropologists commonly cross disciplinary boundaries, investigate problems which are novel to anthropological traditions, and select data for analysis on the basis of their relevance for current issues rather than ancient precept.

The following essays extend and clarify the above characteristics of applied anthropology as they appear in the present. Before turning to them, however, it is necessary to examine the past and to trace the development of the distinction between abstract and applied anthropology in America and the phases through which it has passed. In doing so, we will further illustrate the contrast posed here and illuminate the varied responses of anthropologists to contemporary problems and issues.

We begin with a consideration of early American anthropology and the emergence of modern anthropology in America before examining the history of applied anthropology and the contemporary position of this subfield within anthropology and our society. Even if it were possible to do so, it would not serve the purpose of this summary to describe all the details that are germane to the development of American anthropology, nor all the instances of work by American applied anthropologists. Rather, our purpose here is to illustrate the major differences between abstract and applied anthropologists, to indicate the range of activities of applied anthropologists, and to present the current dilemmas of relating the science of anthropology to the problems of our times.

Early American Anthropology

When Lewis Henry Morgan, a lawyer from Rochester, N.Y., made his first field trip to the Kansas and Nebraska Territory to study Indian kinship in 1859, the first white child born in the Territory was not quite thirty-one years old. John C. Frémont had explored the region only seventeen years earlier; the railroad would not arrive for another six years; Topeka was a mere cluster of houses. As it did in Europe, anthropology in America began to develop as a profession only after decades of colonial expansion. On both continents, anthropology represented a new science of man and a consolidation of research interests in prehistory, paleontology, comparative anatomy, and geology directed toward the integration of the study of man before the dawn of written history (Voget 1975).

The doctrine of progress, with the concomitant belief in the moral superiority of Western culture, was virtually unquestioned when anthropology was born in America. Throughout centuries of progress, the modern, "superior," "moral," social life of nineteenth-century industrialism was believed to have developed from "primitive," "immoral," "childlike" societies. Whether rooted in the Judeo-Christian belief of a divine plan of the creator or the newer belief in the power of human reason to direct human advancement that emerged from eighteenth-century European developmentalism, the doctrine of progress guided scientific inquiry and held the attention of a nation expanding westward. European social theorists were progenitors of many of the issues posed during that time. They included Comte, Spencer, Millar, Kames, Bachofen, Fustel de Coulanges, Sumner, Nietzsche, and others (Voget 1975; Harris 1968). None of these theorists had studied alien peoples firsthand for any extended period of time. Speculations about societies outside of the literate civilizations of Europe and Asia were generally without empirical foundation.

More fortunate than their European counterparts, American anthropologists found at their doorstep a living laboratory in which to study the postulated early stages of human evolution. American Indians, surviving on the outskirts of civilization's towns and cities and camped in the path of industrial expansion, provided important clues to the discovery of the invariant and determinant laws of both the divine plan for progress from "inferior" to "superior" moral ethics and the mental stages of developmentalism through which "inferior" social institutions such as hordes, communal property, and "primitive" promiscuity evolved into democracy, private property, and monogamous marriage. The tools, foods, tribal laws, and words of American Indians were all signposts along the unilineal road of human progress, which only had to be generalized into stages by means of which all societies could be ranked. This was the purpose that drew Lewis Henry Morgan into the Kansas and Nebraska territories (White 1951, 1959a).

Morgan was the most outstanding but not the first early American anthropologist. The American Ethnological Society had been founded in 1842 in New York City. Composed of members of local historical and literary societies, it drew together professionals interested in geography, archaeology, philology, history, travelogue, and sometimes literary criticism. While a few members, such as E. G. Squier and H. R. Schoolcraft, carried out field research, most had no experience of this nature. Some, such as the Reverend Francis Hawkes, used the meetings to further racial determinism theories. The lack of coherent, explicit scientific criteria for defining the field of interest led to the demise of the society in 1870 (Bieder and Tax 1976).

The geologist and explorer Major John W. Powell, leader of the first United States Geological Survey of the western states and the first director of the Bureau of American Ethnology (founded in 1879 at the Smithsonian Institution), is probably the clearest example of the generalized, global, evolutionary nature of anthropology in nineteenth-century America. American Indian word lists, rainfall records, geological features, arrowheads, and anything else which could be recorded on paper or carried back to Washington, were collected and stored by the Bureau. Although untrained in anthropology as we know it today, Powell and his staff were the first professional proto-anthropologists in America to initiate ethnological studies of Indian cultures for use by the U.S. government's Bureau of Indian Affairs. As physical scientists, they hoped to contribute useful knowledge in what they foresaw would be the conflicts between native Americans and incoming Europeans. However, their preoccupation with reconstructing the earlier ways of life of Indians and evolution resulted in little use of their work by governmental administrators (Kennard and Macgregor 1953). Moreover, their lack of explicit social scientific criteria for evaluating their collected evidence contributed to the decline of the Bureau as the focal point of American anthropology (Hinsley 1976).

Among the early American anthropologists, only Morgan achieved the objective of a synthetic, global schema of human evolution. His original interest in law led to study of law, politics, and social organization of the nearby Seneca Indians (1851) and the discovery that kinship systems in North America and elsewhere displayed basic uniformities which crossed linguistic and cultural barriers (1871). Through his own fieldwork and a widespread network of correspondents, who were missionaries and others who lived among American Indians, Morgan gathered data to demonstrate that jural aspects of relations in "primitive" society were based on kinship, whereas those of modern society were established on property relations (1877). He described the transition from one organizational form to the other in terms of three stages of human progress: savagery, barbarism, and civilization.

Morgan's theory became one of the leading nineteenth-century concepts of unilineal evolution. He was the first American ethnologist to undertake field research in terms of specific theoretical problems. Yet he was not so much a pioneering leader in the development of American anthropology as he was its finest expression. For several decades, Jesuit priests, frontier missionaries, educated travelers, and learned professional men from eastern cities had written numerous treatises about native Americans, human nature, and progress. To counter Morgan's deterministic theory of evolution through a series of "ethnical periods," there were other equally deterministic theories which deduced conclusions about native Americans on the basis of assumptions about the racial inferiority of "primitives," divine intervention, and the like. A member of the group to which Morgan read his scientific papers "could see nothing in it [the Iroquois kinship nomenclature] but the total depravity and perversity of the Indian mind—that it could ever have thought of such utterly absurd ways of characterizing relationships" (White 1959a). The period abounds with "armchair anthropologists" who had nothing to contribute to scientific debate other than inaccurate and secondhand impressions bolstered by deterministic theories grounded in the doctrine of unilineal progress from the ways of life of American Indians to those of the white man.

The deductive logic and determinism of late nineteenth century anthropologists did not come under scientific scrutiny until Franz Boas came to the United States from Germany in 1889. More than any other person, Boas deserves recognition as "the central figure in the emergence of American cultural anthropology" (Voget 1975:319). His influence was no less seminal in physical anthropology and linguistics (Brace and Montagu 1965; Lowie 1937b). As Voget (1975:320) notes, estimates of Boas' influence sometimes overlook the fact that he was part of a new intellectual movement in the social sciences, stemming from German inductive empiricism. Having earned a doctorate in physics, with extensive training in geography and ethnology as taught in Germany, Boas represented the radical empiricists who placed faith entirely in the inductive method and tolerated only those generalizations which were supported by assemblages of data. It was not social theorists such as Durkheim or Simmel who inspired Boas, but natural scientists and geographers such as Alexander von Humbolt, Adolf Bastian, Theobald Fisher, and Karl Ritter (Kluckhohn and Prufer 1959; Smith 1959).

Through a lifelong dedication to empirical data collection and taxonomic classification, Boas challenged deterministic theories. His own extensive and intensive fieldwork and that of his students loosened the grip of theories of racial determinism, mental determinism, geographical determinism, and unilineal evolution upon American anthropology (Harris 1968:250–289). For nearly half a century, from 1896 until his death in 1942, Boas taught at Columbia University in New York City and during this time he transformed anthropology from a part-time occupation of untrained theorists to a scientific profession. Through his leadership, the American Ethnological Society was reactivated at the turn of the century, and the American Anthropological Association was founded in 1902 (Lesser 1976). He trained some of the most influential American anthropologists of this century: Alfred Kroeber, Robert Lowie, Melville Herskovits, Edward Sapir, Paul Radin, Irving Hallowell, Clark Wissler, Leslie Spier, Alexander Goldenweiser, E. Adamson Hoebel, Ruth Benedict, Margaret Mead, Ruth Bunzel, Ashley Montagu, Jules Henry, and Frank Speck (Harris 1968:251).

Franz Boas' major contribution was to map out the scientific field of anthropology as we know it today (Mead 1959). Dismissing generalization based on deductive assumptions as premature, he trained students as collectors of the ethnographic details of linguistics, physical anthropology, and ethnology, from which he hoped that generalizations would emerge. Faced with the expansion of industrialism, the steady decrease in the numbers of American Indians, and the threat that much of pre-European life would be lost, Boas launched a huge concerted salvage operation to record the "vanishing" cultures of North America. This was "to be done with almost no money, very few trained people, and no time to spare" (Mead 1959:30). As Murray Wax (1956) has pointed out, the price paid for such exhaustive data collection was that Boas was prevented from developing any major, integrated, theoretical synthesis based on the mountains of data collected. In the 1880s, the aim of his work was the search for cultural "laws," but by the 1930s he had abandoned this goal (Kluckhohn and Prufer 1959:24). Rather, his "function became that of critic," the watchdog of a young science empirically too lean to support the weight of theory building (Wax 1956:63). The voluminous data are still mined today by anthropologists such as Claude Lévi-Strauss, who are specialists in the synthesis Boas anticipated.

The distinction between abstract and applied anthropology did not exist in Boas' time. Application of scientific knowledge as a distinct pursuit and objective within the field only emerged later. Yet, even before Boas began his attack upon determinism and deduction, American anthropologists were periodically finding practical applications of their knowledge. But it was Boas himself who demonstrated that anthropological evidence could contribute to the solution of practical problems.

Episodic Attention to Practical Problems

The relevancy of anthropologists' intellectual concern to practical issues of their time is normally quite tenuous. Nevertheless, events can give previously esoteric knowledge wider dissemination, and anthropologists who are disposed to do so can have significant impact upon popular and official thought about practical matters at particular moments in history.

In the early days of anthropology, for example, Henry R. Schoolcraft, a founder of the American Ethnological Society, married an Indian woman and spent years living among native Americans. Formerly the superintendent of Indian Affairs in Michigan, Schoolcraft was commissioned by the State of New York to carry out a census of Indians, after having spent nine years in New York intellectual circles (Bieder and Tax 1976:19). He was later appointed by the United States Congress to prepare a comprehensive statistical history of American Indians. *Information Respecting the History, Condition and Prospects of the Indian Tribes of the United States,* published between 1852 and 1857 in six volumes, was presented to President James Buchanan. It was the author's hope that public presentation of the facts "neither overrated by exaggeration nor underrated by prejudice" would lead to a less cruel policy toward native Americans (Schoolcraft 1857:vii).

Similarly, James Mooney, a Bureau of American Ethnology fieldworker, testified before Congress in 1890 on behalf of American Indians involved in the Ghost Dance, which was widely interpreted as preparation for war, and defended this indigenous response to forced acculturation (Wallace 1965:vi). Lewis H. Morgan, while primarily motivated by purely scholarly interest, published in popular magazines a defense of Indians against the "hue and cry" for their extermination following the Civil War and the westward surge of immigrant Americans (White 1959a:12, 18).

None of these scholars considered themselves applied anthropologists, nor is it likely that their colleagues thought of them as such. Practical application was not the objective of their scholarly interests but rather a result of the accumulation of anthropological knowledge which, due to circumstances of the day, became politically, ethically, or intellectually relevant to practical issues. Episodic applications to practical issues were largely the expression of personal commitments of individual scientists who functioned as knowledgeable experts in a field of public policy normally removed from the course of their daily work. These anthropologists were clearly a minority among their colleagues.

Franz Boas is another striking example of an anthropologist whose personal humanitarian beliefs and scientific knowledge found expression in his day. His humanism has been described as one of the primary factors that stimulated his thinking (Kroeber 1959:vii). Throughout his career, Boas was ardently committed to the promotion of human equality. He himself was a German immigrant who lived in New York during the early decades of this century at a time when racial prejudice against most immigrants, black Americans, and American Indians was virulently alive. Moreover, his lifetime spanned two world wars which evoked strong attacks on German-Americans.

Although Boas generally rejected deterministic theories as an explanation of sociocultural differences, those based on race provided a special focus for his scholarly endeavors. As early as 1898, in a report of the United States Commissioner of Education, he related the results of a study of the growth curves of Toronto children and an attempt to develop a standardized methodology for assessing the impact of culture in biological maturation. Physical measurements of nearly 18,000 immigrants representing five nationalities and eight occupational groups were reported in a second government report published in 1910. By documenting changes in the bodily shapes of the children of immigrants, Boas' study called attention to environmental influences on physical characteristics.

His book, *The Mind of Primitive Man* (1911) has been called the "Magna Carta of race equality" (Kardiner and Preble 1961:155). In *Anthropology and Modern Life* (1928), Boas attacked various forms of the belief that heredity determined behavior by devoting chapters to such topics as the myth of racial superiority, eugenics, and the inheritance of criminal traits. Towards the end of his life, he worked tirelessly and militantly on a range of anti-Nazi activities (Mead 1959:38–39). A month before he died, he spoke to the American Ethnological Society and urged it to "continue its active participation in anthropological work and contribute by the researches of its members and by its more popular activities to the difficult social problems of our times" (quoted in Mead 1959:35).

The implications of Boas' research to practical problems were and continue to be multiple. Yet, like Schoolcraft, Mooney, and Morgan, Boas was not an applied anthropologist. Useful applications of his knowledge were episodic, and the practical implications of his scientific work were implicit and largely the product of controversial issues which brought his research to public attention and personal convictions which encouraged him to address contemporary social problems. Nonetheless, the major portion of Boas' energy was devoted to abstract anthropology, and his fame is based on his methodological and substantive contributions to the profession and discipline of anthropology as an abstract rather than an applied science.

The Emergence of Modern Anthropology

Anthropology in the United States matured only when it was brought "out of the museums and into the mainstream of the social sciences" (Linton and Wagley 1971). This transition occurred between the mid-1920s and the mid-1950s. It was facilitated by the work of Ruth Benedict, Margaret Mead, Robert Redfield, W. Lloyd Warner, Melville Herskovits, Ralph Linton, and many others, as well as the very substantial contribution that such Britsh social anthropologists as A. R. Radcliffe-Brown and Bronislaw Malinowski made to American intellectual thought and development.

By 1925, the exhaustive task of documenting the historical diffusion of culture traits among "vanishing" American Indians had reached a stage of development which permitted attention to be devoted to other problems. During the following decades, the taxonomic studies of early Boasian students were complemented by intensive systematic studies of single societies and cultures whose objective was that of explaining the functional relationships among various elements of social life. Boas himself pointed the way towards analyses of cultures as integrated functioning wholes, when he sent Ruth Bunzel to study the role of the individual artist at Zuni Pueblo in New Mexico in 1924, and Margaret Mead to study adolescents in Polynesia in 1925 (Mead, personal communication).

There were still other influences upon anthropology in America during the 1920s. The most significant came from Great Britain and the school of anthropologists known today as functionalists. Bronislaw Malinowski and A. R. Radcliffe-Brown were among the first British anthropologists to carry out extended face-to-face research among "primitive" people in the language of the people themselves. Whereas previous studies in British colonies had been conducted for short periods through interpreters, both Malinowski and Radcliffe-Brown immersed themselves for several years in the collection of empirical evidence using the language of their informants. After their fieldwork studies were published, the ivory tower seemed a dull and irrelevant home for the science of anthropology.

Malinowski's *Argonauts of the Western Pacific* and Radcliffe Brown's *Andaman Islanders* both appeared in 1922. Each explicitly rejected the search for origins, the taxonomic studies of trait distributions, and historical reconstructions. Instead, they focused upon the behavior of living people and the systematic interconnections among social structure, economics, religion, and politics through which primitive societies survived as a unified whole. The focus upon functional interdependencies between the various spheres of human experience in a culture made possible a systematic analysis of the traits which European and American scholars had heretofore merely collected. The question was no longer, "What is the origin and/or distribution of the mortuary rite?" but rather, "What function does the mortuary rite perform in this society which encourages its origin, persistence, and modification?" Moreover, extended fieldwork conducted in the language of the people provided anthropologists with more reliable data, a more comprehensive perspective on social customs, and an understanding of the meaning of human behavior in its natural context. The contributions of Malinowski and Radcliffe-Brown were unique in comparison to anything else going on in America at the time.

During the early 1920s, Margaret Mead was studying psychology at Barnard, where she took a course in anthropology from Boas in which Ruth Benedict was assisting. In 1923, she began her studies in anthropology under Boas at Columbia after completing a master's essay in psychology which had relevance for anthropological problems. After completing her dissertation, she won his support to begin fieldwork in 1925 (Mead 1972a: 111–128). Boas encouraged her to study adolescence among American Indians, while Mead argued for a study of culture change in Polynesia. They compromised on a study of adolescent girls in Samoa (Mead 1972a:127–129).

When she left for Samoa, Mead was already convinced that anthropologists must study contemporary problems using contemporary tools while there still were "primitive" peoples among whom anthropologists could work. But she did not go to Samoa "to record the memories of old people." Rather, she went "to find out more about human beings like ourselves in everything except their culture" (Mead 1972a:292–293). She returned from Samoa in 1926 and wrote *Coming of Age in Samoa* (1928), which quickly became a best seller. By relating anthropology to psychology and including two chapters comparing the adolescent Samoan girl with her counterpart in the United States, Mead clearly emerged as a major leader in both modern American anthropology and in the relationship of anthropology to contemporary American problems.

While Margaret Mead was in the process of beginning a lifelong career of scientific endeavor to bring anthropology into the modern world, W. Lloyd Warner was a student of Lowie at Berkeley. Malinowski taught there during the summer of 1926 and contributed significantly to Warner's eventual intellectual development (Lowie 1937a:xix). However, Warner was probably more influenced by Radcliffe-Brown than he was by Malinowski. Both Malinowski and Radcliffe-Brown lectured in the United States—the former at Berkeley, Chicago, and Columbia between 1920 and 1929 and subsequently at the New School for Social Research, Cornell, and Yale from 1929 until his death in 1942. Radcliffe-Brown lectured at Chicago from 1931 to 1937.

Deciding that he would study contemporary Australian aborigines, Warner, with the help of Radcliffe-Brown secured support from the Australian National Research Council. As a result, in 1926, he began three years of fieldwork among the Murngin. Though Lowie continued as Warner's American sponsor, Radcliffe-Brown directed his work on the kinship, economics, and religion of the Murngin. Warner emerged from the experience dedicated to the study of modern peoples and the methods of functional analysis. As he wrote a few years later:

When I went to Australia, I told my friends, Professor Robert H. Lowie and Professor Alfred Radcliffe-Brown, that my fundamental purpose in studying primitive man was to know modern man better; that some day I proposed to investigate (just how I did not then know) the social life of modern man with the hope of ultimately placing the researches in a larger framework of comparison which would include the other societies of the world (Warner and Lunt 1941:3).

Warner returned from Australia to accept a position as instructor at Harvard. There he met Elton Mayo, a friend of Malinowski and Radcliffe-Brown. Together with L. J. Henderson the physiologist, Mayo was one of the founders of the Committee on Industrial Physiology. His interests were in what he considered to be the deleterious effects of modern industrial society (Chapple 1953a:819). Mayo was convinced that much of what was then called "fatigue" among factory workers was not physiological at all, but rather the result of social and psychological factors (Chapple 1953a:820). Mayo brought Warner into the Committee, with an appointment in the School of Business and the Department of Anthropology, and together they generated the famous Bank Wiring Observation Room study.

A segment of a work department in the Hawthorne Plant of the Western Electric Company of Chicago was set aside for intensive observation and recording of social interaction among workers. Warner utilized for this study the techniques with which he had recorded Murngin funeral rites, marriage ceremonies, gathering expeditions,

and hunting (Warner 1941). The systematic analysis of human in-
tereaction patterns pioneered by Malinowski and Radcliffe-Brown
were applied to the least primitive aspect of modern society, to the
very heart of industrial society (Chapple 1953a:820; Arensberg and
Kimball 1965:218). The results demonstrated that fatigue could be
reduced through manipulation of interactional variables, and became
classic contributions to the field of human relations in industrial organization and business administration (Roethlisberger and Dickson
1939).

Within anthropology, these findings sparked a new branch of
scientific investigation which is given the label "interaction analysis"
(Chapple and Arensberg 1940). Exact techniques of micro-observa-
tion, classification, and recording of the periodicity, frequency, intensity, and duration of interaction sequences were developed as an
outgrowth of functionalism and the recognition of functional interdependencies among elements of behavior. These techniques permitted observation of how minute changes in one element produce adjustments throughout the system.

Following his work at the Hawthorne Plant, Warner turned his
attention to the utilization of anthropological methods for the study of
modern American communities. The first study of this type in
America had been undertaken by Robert and Helen Lynd in *Middletown* (1929), and Robert Redfield had already published *Tepoztlán*
(1930), a study of folklife in a Mexican village. Warner's study,
however, was and remains the most comprehensive of its kind to be
undertaken in American society. His purpose was to explore the interconnections between family, work, and other systems of organization within the setting of community. An understanding of these
functional interconnections was necessary in order to interpret the
findings of the Hawthorne Study (Warner and Lunt 1941).

In a small New England town, Warner deployed Conrad Arensberg, Eliot Chapple, Allison Davis, Burleigh Gardner, Solon Kimball, and other Harvard anthropology students to undertake the study.
The work began in 1931 and culminated in 1936 when Warner
moved to the University of Chicago. Building upon the earlier work
of the Lynds (1929) in Middletown, Warner and his students in-
novated technical tools such as the *Index of Evaluated Participation*.
Rejecting *a priori* formulations based on income, housing, and level
of education for determining social class, they analyzed social behav-

ior, how groups were formed, who interacted with whom, and what the people of Yankee City felt were the significant divisions and groupings among them. The findings indicated that beyond the family, two significant social forms could be described which distinguished American community and culture: the corporation and the voluntary association (Warner and Lunt 1941; Warner and Low 1947). Individuals, families, and ethnic categories and groupings were articulated one to another through such institutions, and the importance of these organizational forms distinguished American culture as clearly as the Kula distinguished Melanesian culture.

Upon the completion of the Yankee City study, Warner's students, other colleagues, and Warner himself engaged in similar studies elsewhere. Arensberg and Kimball (1938) employed Warner's methods in their study of County Clare, Ireland, where, for the first time, they mapped out the social anthropological concept of community. Through analysis of ongoing behavior of peasants, shopkeepers, tinkers, laborers, and others, they delineated a constellation of enduring social relationships in Irish rural culture and found these to be localized and perpetuated through community level social processes. Within the United States, Warner's influence was evident in a number of studies. These include John Dollard's study of *Caste and Class in a Southern Town* (1937); Davis, Gardner, and Gardner's study of family and racial divisions in *Deep South* (1941) and the differential access to human and nonhuman resources which characterized that community; Davis' (1948) comparative study of child-rearing which revealed the social and cultural bias in IQ testing; and Whyte's (1943) analysis of *Street Corner Society*.

During the years that Warner was undertaking his research in Australia, the Hawthorne Plant, and Yankee City, Ralph Linton was at the University of Wisconsin. While there, he established contacts with colleagues in sociology, social psychology, and psychology as well as with fellow anthropologists at Chicago. At Chicago, he met Radcliffe-Brown who introduced him to the functional approach and greatly influenced his intellectual development (Linton and Wagley 1971:37–38). Though he differed from both Radcliffe-Brown and Malinowski in many of his basic concepts, Linton developed a conceptual framework for viewing the social and cultural system as a response to the biological, psychological, and social needs of man and a lifelong interest in the problems of culture contact, diffusion, and acculturation. His textbook, *The Study of Man* (1936), was unlike any other available at the time (Linton and Wagley 1971:50) and it brought him into the forefront of anthropology. In 1937, Linton became visiting professor of anthropology at Columbia and then Boas' successor as chairman of the department. His new status gave expression to the increasingly important role that anthropology would assume not only at Columbia but elsewhere in the modern world.

The events set in motion by the work of Mead, Malinowski, Radcliffe-Brown, Warner, Linton, and many others during the 1930s mark this period as a distinct one in the development of modern anthropology. The overemphasis on historical reconstruction yielded to studies of people within the context of the cultures in which they lived. There was increased concern with contemporary problems and closer relationships with colleagues in the social sciences—especially sociology, social psychology, and psychology. The rise of social anthropology was accompanied by a functional approach to the understanding of cultural systems and attention to social structure and social organization.

For our purpose here, however, the significance of this decade is that the florescence of research and theory which related anthropology to contemporary peoples laid much of the theoretical and methodological groundwork for the development of applied anthropology. Yet, the work itself was primarily concentrated upon theoretical problems. The objective was to develop the knowledge necessary to understand society and culture, and most anthropologists still viewed the study of "primitive peoples" as a key to comprehending modern societies. Nevertheless, the pioneering work of Warner and those he influenced had extended anthropology to include ourselves, and Chapple and Coon's textbook, *Principles of Anthropology* (1942), encompassed all peoples, not only "primitives." Both "functional" and "historical" in outlook, it regarded anthropology as a science of human relations and interaction within social groups based on the natural science method of observing human beings within their environments and the use of the time scale to examine change. It foreshadowed a new anthropology in which contemporary peoples belonged.

Precursors of Applied Anthropology

We noted earlier that events external to anthropology can arouse interest in the application of anthropology to practical problems and also can result in significant episodic attention to social policy issues on the part of anthropologists whose primary commitment remains with abstract work within academe. In similar fashion, external events can also bring about a demand for anthropologists to become employees of governmental agencies, foundations, or other organizations and to become engaged in the task of applying their skills to the amelioration or solution of social problems.

During the 1930s, both in America and in other countries, governmental interest in the use of anthropologists and their data grew in strength. The crisis of colonialism created conditions which opened up opportunities for anthropologists as aides to administrators of native peoples. Jobs were suddenly available for anthropologists who were interested in social problems of living peoples and the formulation and implementation of policy. As Forde (1953:843–848) noted, government administrators in Africa were uninterested in information about tribal society until taxation and other compulsory schemes produced rebellion. In America, the situation was similar. The failure of colonial policy had been dramatically documented by a joint committee of Congress in 1867, which reported that native Americans were dying out, reservations were constantly being invaded by whites, and disease and starvation were a way of life (Officer 1971:27). No actions in defense of native Americans followed the report. In 1928, four years after American Indians were granted citizenship, the Meriam Report, commissioned by the Congress, documented the same conditions which were reported in 1867 (Officer 1971:41–42).

Following the election of Franklin Roosevelt as President in 1932, John Collier was appointed commissioner of the Bureau of Indian Affairs. Collier had been active in the defense of Pueblo land from white squatters in the 1920s. In his new position, he pushed through the Indian Reorganization Act or the Wheeler-Howard Act of 1934. This legislation has been the basis for Indian policy up to the present (Officer 1971:43–44). It provided that Indian lands would not be allotted any further, that land lost would be restored, that tribal governments would be formed, that loans would be made available to reservations, that the Bureau of Indian Affairs would hire Indians, but that the Department of Interior would retain control over reservation timber, soil, minerals, and tribal budgets (Officer 1971:43; Jorgensen 1971). The first intensive application of modern cultural anthropological concepts and methods to the problems of governmental administration was introduced by Collier when he employed anthropologists to aid in the implementation of these policies. During the same period, other anthropologists were hired in the Human Dependency Unit of the Technical Cooperation Group of the Soil Conservation Service. This unit was also linked to the Bureau of Indian Affairs and was assigned to the study of Indian lands with special attention to economic development, resources, social organization, education, and administrative policies (Kennard and Macgregor 1953:832–833).

It was logical to seek anthropologists to study American Indians and to make policy recommendations, since many of them had specialized knowledge about native Americans. However, most anthropologists at the time were ill-prepared to be of much service to either Indians or the government. Their interests were primarily with abstract problems and the past. As Malinowski (1929:note 4) remarked: "Even in the study of the fully detribalized and yankified Indian, our United States colleagues persistently ignore the Indian as he is and study the Indian-as-he-must-have-been some century or two back." Despite the fact that not all Indians were 'detribalized," Malinowski accurately described the focus of the majority of American anthropologists. Tax (1937), Lowie (1922, 1935), Steward (1933, 1938), Swanton (1922), Densmore (1929), Murdock (1936), Benedict (1935), White (1932), and other acknowledged experts on American Indians did not study the relationship between contemporary native Americans and the larger society into which they were systematically integrated. Rather, the focus of their analyses was the nonchanging aspects of indigenous cultures and the past. As one example, we will describe the interests of Robert H. Lowie, one of Boas' early students. His work on the Crow (Lowie 1912, 1922, 1935) provides a glimpse of the difference between abstract anthropology, to which Lowie's intellectual gifts were devoted, and the kinds of questions an applied anthropologist might have asked.

Although Lowie studied among living people, he did not study the contemporary cultural experiences of living people. The Crow were a seminomadic hunting people living in close symbiosis with sedentary maize agriculturalists previous to European contact. It was this period of Crow history which interested Lowie. He attempted to trace the diffusion of culture elements present among the Crow, to find out what the Crow had adopted from whom and what came out of their Hidatsa origins (e.g., the hot dance). He questioned old people about their childhood, and their memories became the vehicle for answers to abstract questions he had inherited from anthropological lore. He did not question them about their contemporary culture, although the reservation Crow carried a new culture quite different from that of their parents and grandparents—one which was partially comprised of elements contributed by traders, agents, missionaries, white settlers, the United States Congress, and the War Department. Had Lowie been an applied anthropologist, he would have given attention to this culture of the living people by examining similar theoretical issues (i.e., the diffusion of culture elements) within the contemporary context. His work would have examined the ideas, traits, and institutions in the day-to-day experiences of the generation that was then reaching maturity in a pluralistic society as members of a subordinate and confined subculture.

Moreover, Lowie's work was not oriented to immediate problems of consequence to the Crow or other parties to the reservation relationship. Among the tribes of the northern plains, the Crow were remarkable for their acceptance of allotment policies whereby plots of land were assigned to the heads of families for farming. Most tribes of seminomadic hunters rejected farming and, like the Sioux, ignored governmental orders to build European-style houses and plant European crops. In contrast, Department of Interior Reports during the 1880s reveal that the Crow cut hundreds of logs for building European-style houses on plots which they had already marked out and planted to European crops (Keller 1881; Armstrong 1882, 1883, 1884, 1885). Indeed, the Crow were so enthusiastic that their agents complained of insufficient technical personnel to show them how to build these new houses and that the Crow suspected the government of bad faith (Armstrong 1884:154). At the time of agent Armstrong's 1885 report, logs for 125 European-style houses had been cut, and the Crow were awaiting further instructions (Armstrong 1885:345). Elsewhere in the United States, the allotment of Indian land and the attempts to instill European farming were spectacular failures and had disastrous consequences (Wallace 1969; Mead 1966). However, the important and different response of the Crow and its consequences did not interest Lowie at the time he worked among them. An applied anthropologist could hardly have ignored a problem of such central significance to the Crow, other Indians, the government, and other parties to the reservation relationship.

Finally, the uses of knowledge sought by Lowie were solely within the circles of professional anthropology. The diffusion of moccasin designs, age societies, and the hot dance from one group to another in prereservation days could not have been of interest to the Crow or others concerned with reservation life. That such audiences should find his work of interest was not one of Lowie's considerations. Much more compelling was the interest of Clark Wissler, Alfred Kroeber, and other anthropologists who were concerned with reconstructing native life as if Europeans had never crossed the Atlantic Ocean.

In his choice of people, problems, and application for his studies, Lowie represented the mainstream of abstract anthropology. Nothing of immediate, practical value came out of his work for those he studied. This is not to say that Lowie's work and abstract anthropology are without value, for students of abstract problems have found, and will continue to find, a wealth of insights into the nature of religions, art, kinship, economics, and political processes in Lowie's work. From his contributions, there emerged important understandings of the nature of man, society, and culture, as the insights of Maine, Morgan, Smith, Frazer, Tylor, and other early anthropologists were put to the test of scholarship. Eventually, if conditions permit, other uses may develop for the insights gained by Lowie. But this was not the case in early twentieth-century America.

The few anthropologists who did focus upon contemporary peoples stand out as notable exceptions. Margaret Mead (1966) conducted the first reservation-wide, household-by-household study of an Indian reservation in 1930, and painted a vivid picture of alienation and demoralization instilled by the reservation relationship, although it was personally a devastating experience for her (Mead 1972a:189–190). Robert Redfield, Ralph Linton, and Melville Herskovits (1936) attempted to summarize the anthropological knowledge of acculturation and the culture change which results from continuous face-to-face contact among alien peoples. Even in the best anthropological studies of previous years, the focus was essentially upon native cultures or ethnographic areas. Relatively little was known of the structure of relationships which provided the conditions of contact between traditional Indians, progressive Indians, white ranchers, mining companies, farmers, land companies, the Department of Interior, the Public Health Service, missionaries, volunteer service workers, and other parties to the reservation relationship. Rather than descriptions and analyses of existing social relationships through which goods, services, and personnel moved on a reservation, anthropologists had concentrated upon only selected elements in a complex system.

When the government first hired anthropologists, therefore, there was little precedent for study of contemporary problems. Those who were hired were a minority willing to carry out innovative work. For example, Scudder MeKeel (1936) worked for the Bureau of Indian Affairs on problems of indigenous economic and political organization among the Sioux; and several others, including Gordon Macgregor (1946), worked in the Education Division of the Bureau on problems of socialization, child rearing, and enculturation among the Sioux. Morris Opler (1952) discovered that traditional leaders among the Creek of Oklahoma vigorously resisted implementation of the provision of the Indian Reorganization Act requiring political centralization. His recommendation that the revolving loan funds be decentralized and administered by traditional community leaders was initially rejected. When the centralization program failed, however, Opler's recommendation was finally adopted. John Provinse (1942) and Solon Kimball (Kimball and Provinse 1942; Kimball 1946) carried out land use and socioeconomic studies of resource interdependency among Navajo. They discovered a unit of socioeconomic organization among the Navajo, the ''outfit,'' which was a natural social unit by which the livestock enterprise was organized, and recommended that political and economic programs among the Navajo be organized along these lines. John Collier felt that the Provinse–Kimball discovery of natural social units which could form the basis of genuine cooperation among Navajo and government workers was extremely valuable. Of all anthropological research for the BIA, this discovery most fulfilled Collier's dream of preserving cultural integrity while building economically and politically viable Indian societies (Kelly 1977).

But the Provinse–Kimball advice went unheeded. The BIA lawyers and other government employees, having already created havoc several years earlier in the sheep reduction program, were committed to an existing policy and administrative structure. Not even Collier's enthusiasm for the recommendations could sway lower level employees. As Kimball (1946:16) reported:

It proved impossible to gain assent to proposals which would make the Navajos full participants in building and carrying through the program. If this was the situation under liberal policy and wise leadership, one can appreciate how much more difficult the problem will be elsewhere.

Kennard and Macgregor (1953:834) described the general response to anthropological perspectives as follows some years later:

From the anthropologists' insistence that functioning Indian life be recognized as a real force to be reckoned with, there arose a curious opposition on the part of the administrators to anthropologists themselves. The administrators, failing to understand the significance of expressions of traditional ways of behavior by Indian groups, assumed that anthropologists, in insisting on recognizing these, were arguing for the preservation of aboriginal Indian life. . . . This stems from one of the major tenets of the American people which underlies the idea of the American "melting pot," namely, that distinct behavioral differences cannot be tolerated.

Congressional budget cuts insured that anthropologists' services would be terminated. Opposition to anthropological work continued, and a few years later when Laura Thompson (1951), in collaboration with Collier and W. Lloyd Warner, undertook a massive interdisciplinary study of educational programs on twelve Indian reservations, interpreted the findings, and formulated policy recommendations, the response of the BIA was to ignore these findings and recommendations completely.

If anthropologists failed to be heard in administrative circles, the reasons lie partly with administrative prejudices and preference for familiar policy recommendations of BIA lawyers and career staff personnel. But they also lie within the narrow tradition of abstract anthropology. From this experience, it became clear that narrowly conceived, piecemeal studies of only one element in a complex human relationship were inadequate. Anthropologists had too often concentrated on the past, and were vulnerable to the misperception of "arguing for the preservation of aboriginal Indian life." Anthropological holism, the approach which encompasses the total structural relationships among elements of an ongoing system of human interaction, revealed that the studies of natives in isolation from colonial administrative superstructures and the surrounding white society were not fruitful. Kimball (1946:8) summarized the lesson to be drawn from this period:

Students of the science of human relations know that understanding, not of battles fought and won, but of reasons why colonial peoples are today in ferment, must come first from knowledge of the history and culture of the native groups, something of administrative organization and philosophy of the colonial powers, but basically there is need to examine the system of relations from which agreement or conflict arise as two peoples impinge upon each other.

The governmental work of anthropologists during the 1930s was instrumental in bringing a handful of anthropologists into direct contact with some of the major institutionalized patterns of American society which directly affected native Americans. It provided methodological and theoretical approaches whereby the processes of culture contact and social change could be more fully understood within the context of the crisis of colonialism. But applied anthropology as a distinct branch of anthropology had not yet emerged. Important foundations were laid, but it was not until 1941 that the climate of scholarly opinion brought the early precursers of applied anthropology together to form the Society for Applied Anthropology, in order to give voice to the professional goals of those concerned with specific problems of consequence to living peoples and the relevance of anthropology for policies and programs which affected them.

The Birth of Applied Anthropology

World War II marked a major turning point in the development of anthropological concern for contemporary human problems. Ever since the mid-1930s, anthropology had been undergoing a differentiation of specializations within the field. By the time the United States entered the war in 1941, subdisciplines within the field of anthropology had emerged. Ethnology had become clearly defined as the study of the living cultures of people in contrast with archaeology which dealt with the study of cultures which are now extinct, and physical anthropology which was concerned with the study of humans as one of many mammalian species. Moreover, ethnologists had begun to give attention not only to "primitive" peoples who lived outside the range of "civilization" but also to cultures in transition and complex societies. Their aim and interests had become aligned with those in other social sciences, and cooperative efforts between anthropology, psychology, and sociology were well established. Anthropology was envisaged by some as the nucleus of a new Science of Man which would be "broad enough in its scope to include all aspects of human existence" and to ascertain "the processes and continuities involved in the phenomena with which it deals with the view to the prediction of events and ultimately to their control" (Linton 1945:17).

While John Collier had hired a few anthropologists during the depression years, the crisis of war provided unprecedented opportunities for anthropologists to participate in efforts related to war activities. During and following the war, spectacular technological advances such as the transformation of modern agriculture to the point where it could potentially feed the world, the threat of nuclear warfare, and heightened American involvement in world affairs, all contributed to an optimistic belief that many of mankind's perennial problems could be solved. The spirit of the time is well articulated in a book, *The Science of Man in the World Crisis,* edited by Ralph Linton in 1945. The book brought together articles by prominent anthropologists and other social scientists who discussed the application of their scholarly work to world problems in such areas as population, race and minority relations, the control of natural resources, international relations, the adjustment of indigenous peoples to modernization and colonial administration. It was a report from the "frontiers" of research which aimed to bring knowledge from the social sciences into the cognizance of other scientists and planners.

This period set the stage for our own, and an understanding of the responses of anthropologists to the new conditions of American life imposed by the war and its aftermath is essential if we are to appreciate later developments in applied anthropology (Mead 1964a:13-15; Mead and Metraux 1965). It was an era in which America moved from an isolationist position to one of intense involvement in international affairs. Economic development, improved public health, the spread of democratic institutions, and sufficient food for everyone were believed to be attainable goals. Together with others, a number of anthropologists dedicated themselves to the reconstruction of the world in ways that would hopefully prevent the reappearance of the virulent racism of Nazi Germany and the nuclear holocaust which inevitably would follow should World War III ever begin. While the war-related activities of anthropologists are too numerous to fully describe here, a summary of some of the more significant ones will provide an understanding of the diversities of contributions made by anthropologists and the ways in which the experiences of the war years contributed to the birth of applied anthropology.

As early as 1939, a small Committee for National Morale was organized to consider the ways in which anthropology and psychology could be applied to the improvement of national morale during wartime. Committee members included Gregory Bateson, Eliot Chapple, Lawrence K. Frank, and Margaret Mead. Bateson (1935) had been one of the earliest to call attention to the systematic aspects of relationships whereby conflicts were inevitably escalated, a process he called "schismogenesis." Chapple (1942) was a pioneer of interaction analysis in industry. Frank had instigated the Lynds' study of Middletown (1929), one of the earliest studies of an American community, and Dollard's work at Yale, which led to his study (1937) of race relations in the American South. Mead had returned to New York after a brief trip to Bali. After seventeen years of work among "primitive" contemporary people, she "came home to a world on the brink of war, convinced that the next task was to apply what we knew, as best we could, to the problems of our own society" (Mead 1942a:3).

The Committee began to develop methods for interviewing highly educated members of other cultures about their own lives (Mead 1972a). The purpose was to elicit data on basic theories relevant to a better understanding of cultural differences germane to the problems of building and sustaining morale during wartime. The problem was an important one. Ignorance of cultural differences obscured an understanding of the actions of alien peoples, and misconstrued information exacerbated tensions among allies as well as between allies and enemies.

In 1940, M. L. Wilson, director of extension work in the Department of Agriculture, became chairman of a federal task force charged with coordinating the nutrition programs of all federal agencies for the imminent war effort. In the same year, the Committee on

Food Habits was formed by the National Research Council in an effort to mobilize scientific contributions for this effort. The Committee met once a month for two days, and leaders of the food programs in Washington, economists, and community organizers, together with anthropologists, addressed the problems introduced by Dr. Wilson. Ruth Benedict, Allison Davis, W. Lloyd Warner, and Margaret Mead were the anthropological participants (Mead 1964b). Out of their work came "The Problem of Changing Food Habits" and a "Manual for the Study of Food Habits" in 1943 and 1945, respectively (National Research Council).

The bombing of Pearl Harbor in December of 1941 and the entry of the United States into the war interrupted the academic and research activities of most anthropologists. One of the first to go to Washington was Geoffrey Gorer, who joined the Office of War Information. He was soon followed by Ruth Benedict. By 1943, anthropologists in and out of government included Clyde Kluckhohn, Margaret Mead, Ruth Benedict, Rhoda Metreaux, Gregory Bateson, Gorer, and others who had joined in the study of "culture at a distance" or national character studies of parties to the conflict (Mead 1953a; Mead and Metreaux 1965). One result was the recommendation by Gorer, in a memorandum prepared for the Committee for National Morale in 1942, that the surrender and occupation terms for Japan be different from those to be imposed upon Nazi Germany. It was felt that faith in the Emperor and the divine way of life he symbolized indicated that abolition of the prewar government in Japan would only guarantee strong resistance. This recommendation was adopted. When the end of the war came in 1945, the emperor was not deposed but instead personally issued the surrender terms to his people (Mead, personal communication).

One of the domestic tragedies of World War II was the evacuation and relocation of 110,000 West Coast Japanese-Americans. Their impoundment in camps located in inland areas of the West remains today as one of the most dramatic examples of the violation of civil rights in our nation's history. The human distress this mass incarceration caused, was made even more acute by administrative traditions and policies which failed to bring Japanese-Americans into responsible policy-making positions in the governing of the War Relocation Centers. John Collier, who was still Commissioner of Indian Affairs at this time, recognized the importance of documenting and analyzing what was happening to both the evacuees and the administrators in this situation. He conceived the idea of establishing a Bureau of Sociological Research at the Poston center for which the Bureau of Indian Affairs had initial responsibility. During the early summer of 1942, Alexander H. Leighton went to Poston as director of the new bureau and initiated research to help solve the administrative and human problems there. Edward H. Spicer worked with Leighton in developing research for this purpose.

At this time, John Embree had already joined the Washington staff of the WRA as an advisor on Japanese culture, and Solon T. Kimball had begun to assist in the organization of community government in the various relocation centers. Subsequently, after riots had occurred at the Poston and Manzanar centers in late 1942, it became clear that better understanding of the cultural aspects of Japanese behavior was needed. A decision was made to establish a Community Analysis Section under the direction of John H. Provinse, who was Chief of Community Services for WRA at that time. In early 1943, Spicer went to Washington as head of the Community Analysis Section. Katherine Luomala, Asael T. Hansen, Marvin K. Opler, and Gordon Brown were among the anthropologists who were hired to undertake community analysis of the centers, to trace the outcome of administrative policy, and to evaluate the human and social consequences of policy for the evacuees (Arensberg 1942; Embree 1943; Leighton 1945; Provinse and Kimball 1946; Spicer 1946; Kimball 1946; Spicer et al. 1969). Their studies complemented those of anthropologists working on Indian reservations which had been described earlier. They reaffirmed the importance of examining the culture of those governed within the context of administrative policy and the society which was expressed by it.

During the war years, anthropologists became intensively engaged in training officers for military government duties overseas. At Columbia University, for example, a School of Military Government and Administration for the United States Navy was formed. The curriculum included courses in languages, history, government, and ethnography of countries in the Pacific and Asia itself. Ralph Linton was involved in the school from its beginning and taught classes. The teaching of anthropology was expanded by the addition of John Whiting and George P. Murdock, both of whom were naval officers at the time, and by anthropologically trained linguists who taught unwritten languages through informant techniques (Linton and Wagley 1971:61). Similarly, the School of Naval Administration at Stanford relied heavily upon anthropologists as advisers in preparing navy personnel for work in Micronesia (Kennard and Macgregor 1953:837). After the war, under the Coordinated Investigation of Micronesian Anthropology Project, forty-two scientists, of whom thirty-five were anthropologists, carried on basic research of Micronesian peoples between 1947 and 1949. This work was sponsored and partially financed by the navy during its civil administration of the United States Trust Territory of the Pacific Islands. In 1945, the navy proposed that an anthropologist be appointed to the Trust headquarters and three others to district staffs. This number was increased to six in 1950. In these positions, anthropologists worked as advisers to administrators and research specialists who provided analyses which could be used in policy implementation (Barnett 1956).

Under the United States Scientific and Cultural Cooperation Program, the Smithsonian Institution established the Institute of Social Anthropology in 1943. This Institute worked in collaboration with the Institute of Inter-American Affairs, which had been founded in 1942 as part of the Good Neighbor Policy between the United States and Latin America. Anthropologists were sent to Latin American countries to train students there in anthropology and to work with local anthropologists and students in making community studies and undertaking research related to United States technical assistance programs (Kennard and Macgregor 1953:839; Foster 1969:24). A series of important studies about Latin American cultures resulted (Beals 1945; Foster 1948; Gillin 1947; Wagley 1941, 1949).

Beginning in 1942, the Institute of Inter-American Affairs initiated cooperative developmental programs with Latin American governments in the fields of public health, agriculture, and education. However, it was nearly a decade before the government sought anthropological advice in evaluating or administering these programs. During the early 1950s, the United States Public Health Service undertook a major six-month evaluation of the cooperative health work. Five of the Smithsonian anthropologists became members of the team which examined the social and cultural problems encountered when new medical and health practices were brought into traditional communities. The public health programs were not working as well as expected, and administrators wanted to know why efforts in sanitation, health education, control of disease, and preventive medicine were failing. The evaluations of the Institute anthropologists were included in reports detailing progress, and resulted in modifications in planning and programming for the future (Oberg and Rios 1955; Oberg 1956; Foster 1969).

The work of anthropologists in the Committee for National Morale, the National Research Committee on Food Habits, the Office of War Information, the War Relocation Authority, the training of military officers, the United States Trust Territory of the Pacific Islands, and the Institute of Social Anthropology, all provide significant examples of the governmental employment of anthropologists in matters related to domestic and foreign policy during and after World War II. The use of anthropologically based scientific research in policy formulation and implementation reflected the maturation of anthropology to a point which permitted anthropological contributions to be made. In addition, there was a core group of distinguished anthropologists who accepted the public policy role of anthropology and were concerned with the applied implications of anthropology for an America which was emerging as a world power but had little knowledge of, or experience with, many of the peoples among whom it would find itself increasingly involved in both war and peace in the years to come.

The war crystallized efforts of the precursors of applied anthropology to utilize scientific procedures in the study of contemporary problems, and it was within this context that the Society for Applied Anthropology was founded at Harvard in 1941. A meeting for this purpose was called by Eliot Chapple and Conrad Arensberg. An invitation sent from Chapple to Kimball, who was working for the Soil Conservation Service in Window Rock, Ariz., at that time, shows that they had received the support of M. L. Wilson, director of Extension Services of the Department of Agriculture, John D. Black, professor of agricultural economics at Harvard, and Alfred V. Kidder, director of the Carnegie Institution Divison of Historical Research in Cambridge, Mass.

The meeting was held on May 2 and 3, and the papers read included C. M. Arensberg, "Application of Anthropology to Industry"; E. D. Chapple, "Organization Problems in Industry"; R. S. Harris, "Scientific Diet"; M. L. Wilson, "Work of Food Habits Committee, Department of Agriculture"; D. L. Oliver, "The Problem of Changing Food Habits''; C. P. Loomis, ''Administrative Problems in Resettlement Community''; F. L. W. Richardson, ''Rehabilitation vs. Resettlement''; R. Underhill, ''Anthropology in the Indian Service''; F. Rainey, ''Native Economy and Survival in Arctic Alaska''; L. Thompson, ''Anthropology in the British Colonial Service''; J. Gillin, ''Work of the Committee on Latin American Anthropology''; M. Field, ''Behavioral Factors in Mental Health Disease''; W. F. Whyte, ''The Social Role of the Settlement House''; M. Mead, ''Anthropology and the Social Workers''; G. Bateson, ''National Morale and the Social Sciences''; and R. Benedict, ''Personality and Culture'' (Kimball, personal communication).

Clearly, this was a new kind of anthropology that did not find expression in existing professional journals. At the meeting, George P. Murdock moved that a journal devoted to applied anthropology be established, and, with the approval of the fifty-six members present, *Applied Anthropology*—later to be renamed *Human Organization*—was founded. During the next several years, the articles which appeared in the journal provided evidence that a variety of human problems drew the attention of scientists devoted to the aims of the society—''the principles controlling the relations of human beings to one another . . . and the wide application of these principles to practical problems.'' The major problem areas investigated at the time were Social Psychiatry and Health Services, Rehabilitation and Community Development, Administered Peoples, and Industrial Relations (Arensberg 1947:2-7).

Most American anthropologists at that time were not involved in the work of the Society. Nonetheless, many who professed little interest in policy research or program development were affected by the events which had given rise to the Society. Beginning in the mid-1940s, there was a discernible shift from the study of ancient societies and past cultures to the study of contemporary ones. This new focus on the present necessarily entailed attention to problems of social and cultural change among living peoples. As Mead (1946a:13) has observed, the evolutionary theories of culture as professed by Leslie White (1943, 1959b) did not spark much interest at the time they were formulated. Even Julian Steward (1955), who had contributed an important reconceptualization of classical evolutionary theory, applied his research tools to the contemporary people of Puerto Rico (1956). Charles Wagley (1941, 1949, 1953) devoted his skills to analyzing the changes which were transforming the economies and societies of Guatemalan and Amazonian peoples, and Sol Tax (1942, 1951) began his work on ethnic and economic relations in Guatemala. Morton Fried (1953) and Martin Yang (1945) studied cultural change in Chinese society. Edward Spicer (1940, 1954) concentrated upon the modern Yaqui, both in their homeland and in migrant communities in the United States. Robert Redfield (1950) initiated the Yucatan Project, building upon earlier work with Villa Rojas (Redfield and Villa Rojas 1934) and focused upon the relationship of Mayan peasants to the urban civilization of which they were a part (Hansen 1976; Singer 1976). Numerous other examples could be cited, but it is clear from the above that the conditions of the 1940s and the leadership of Warner, Mead, Malinowski, and other precursors had redirected American anthropology. Contemporary plantation laborers, peasant farmers, and urban laborers, who were quickly becoming the majority of the world's people, were now the subject of study.

Empirical studies were accompanied by a series of theoretical and methodological statements addressed to contemporary societies and cultures. Steward (1950) pointed to the possibility of a comparative sociology of the modern peoples of the world. Arensberg (1955), Wagley and Harris (1955), Wolf (1955), and others proposed theoretical schemes for a much needed taxonomy of contemporary new world societies and subcultures. Arensberg and Kimball (1965) proposed that the community be considered as the basic unit of analysis and minimal sample for the study of primitive, peasant, plantation, and metropolitan societies of the world. Redfield (1955) formalized his concept of the folk-urban continuum, and with Singer (Redfield and Singer 1954) proposed a theory of the development of civilization.

The transformation of anthropology and the birth of applied anthropology were completed by the 1950s. The inductive empiricism of Boas, the systematic study of ongoing cultures by Malinowski, Radcliffe-Brown, Mead, and Warner, interaction analysis as an empirical method for discovery of behavioral patterns and definition of social units, and the holistic method of problem identification and study were all now firmly established. The optimism which followed the war about the possibilities for ameliorating social problems throughout the world as well as in the United States, together with the knowledge that anthropologists had made positive contributions to policy and program implementation, created an atmosphere in which applied anthropology could grow.

The Postwar Period: Retreat from The Challenge

Following World War II, the discipline and profession of anthropology expanded on an unprecendented scale. This expansion was part of the phenomenal growth of higher education during the late 1950s and the 1960s and the general burst of scientific endeavor in the United States after the Russian launching of Sputnik in 1957. Returning veterans eager to get on with their civilian careers, and subsequently, the products of the wartime baby boom, filled lecture halls to overflowing. Old departments were enlarged, and new departments were created where none had existed previously. In 1947–48, anthropology bachelor's, master's, and doctoral degrees numbered 139, 26, and 24, respectively. In striking contrast, these totaled an impressive 6,008, 1,078, and 445, respectively in 1975–76 (American Anthropological Association 1976b). Research monies flowed from both governmental and private foundation sources and were available as never before to support anthropological training and research.

There were several results of this florescence. They include energetic efforts to discover new facts and theories through specialization, the rise of new subdisciplines to research particular variables, the forging of new links to other disciplines and professions, and a consequent fragmentation of the field of anthropology as a whole. In addition, the great increase in governmental expenditures for research and postsecondary education affected the nature and direction of academic research and teaching in ways that were heretofore unknown. The manpower shortage in academe during much of the postwar period meant that attention was almost exclusively given to the training of anthropologists for college and university positions. There was an exodus of anthropologists from government jobs as the war ended and academic opportunities beckoned. Most importantly for our discussion here, the concern of anthropologists with the applied uses of their findings declined as they turned to abstract problems.

The evolutionary theories of Morgan, Spencer, Tylor, White, and Steward were revived, and issues such as Morgan's concept of "ethnical stages" of evolution, Lowie's notion of "incorporeal property," and the like became foci of heated polemics (Harris 1968; Posposil 1963). The origins of cross-cousin marriage as interpreted by Lévi-Strauss (1969) arose as a major issue in college classrooms and evoked scholarly debate (Homans and Schneider 1955). Major advances were made in linguistics (Hymes 1964, 1972) and stimulated the creation of structuralism, cognitive anthropology, and componential analysis (Goodenough 1956; Lévi-Strauss 1963; Tyler 1969). The hope of achieving greater exactitude through the use of statistical models stimulated some to further distributional studies of cultural traits (Naroll and Sipes 1973). Important work took place in general systems theory which was focused on man's role in the physical and biotic environment (Rappaport 1968; Vayda 1969). The biological basis of social life received fresh attention in behavioral anthropology (Chapple 1970). Van Gennep's 1908 formulation of rites of passage was given new significance by Turner (1969).

Concern with abstract problems during this period elicited fruitful insights which in many ways recast classical anthropology. Most anthropologists were primarily attracted to these traditional problems and disdained collaborative activities with those outside of academic circles who were concerned with practical problems of public policy and programs. Even in areas such as economics and development problems, abstract anthropologists ignored the data and theory of postcolonial, ongoing, economic change in favor of classical problems (Dobyns 1971). Paradoxically, though the number of studies of modern peoples multiplied, fewer anthropologists sought practical uses for this newly gained knowledge. As Mead (1975a:15) reports, in reference to anthropologists who were asked to teach Peace Corps volunteers going to Nigeria in the 1960s:

Most of them had not done any thinking about the wider scene for ten years; they did not think about broader issues. . . . So what did they do? They have a course on primitive rites among the Ibo or initiation ceremonies of the Yoruba. And Nigerian students who had come over here to study international affairs picketed the course and protested. Our anthropologists were absolutely myopic and did not take anything into account except nice little bits of ethnology. . . . As anthropologists withdrew from the world scene, they more or less withdrew from anything having to do with government.

. . . They went into deciding how many cross-cousins could dance on the head of a pin.

The withdrawal of American anthropologists from the relevant problems of the world scene was not unanimous. In 1952, for example, Allan Holmberg and his associates at Cornell University, in collaboration with the Peruvian Indian Institute, embarked on a five-year experimental program of induced technical and social change in Vicos, which was directed toward the problem of transforming a highly dependent manor system into a productive modern self-governing community adapted to the modern Peruvian State. The Cornell-Peru Project still stands as a landmark endeavor to blend social science knowledge with action (Holmberg 1958; Holmberg et al. 1962; Dobyns, Doughty, and Laswell 1971).

Though earlier opposed to applied anthropology, Sol Tax began to advocate an action anthropology to cope with the situation of the Fox Indians in the 1950s. Viewing the Fox as trapped in a political, social, and economic situation which prevented them from acting in their own self-interest, Tax and his students began to provide and suggest opportunities for such things as crafts and scholarships which allowed alternatives for decisions whereby the Fox could implement new goals (Tax 1958; Peattie 1958; Gearing 1970).

Many other anthropologists made significant contributions to applied work in areas such as the practical problems encountered in technical and economic development (Niehoff 1966; Spicer 1952; Mead 1953b and 1956b; Goodenough 1963; Eramus 1961; Foster 1962; Arensberg and Niehoff 1964); improvement of health and health care delivery (Paul 1955; Niehoff 1966; Kimball and Pearsall 1954; Foster 1952; Caudill 1953); and education and child-rearing (Kimball 1960; Spindler 1955 and 1963; Macgregor 1946).

Developments in both medical and educational anthropology attracted sufficient interest and activities among anthropologists that the Society for Medical Anthropology was founded in 1967 and the Council on Anthropology and Education in 1968. Yet, even in these organizations and in the Society for Applied Anthropology itself, interest in abstract problems was high in comparison with applied problems. Governmental and other patrons of applied anthropology frequently complained—and with some justification—that applied anthropologists were unable to relate their work to the political realities and operational problems that agencies were confronted with or to conform to existing administrative requirements. Anthropologists, on the other hand, complained—with similar justification—that their findings were often ignored in the formulation of official policy.

Contemporary difficulties in relating anthropology to practical problems have been exacerbated by the emergence of a vastly expanded and centralized federal governmental structure. Warner (1962:30) has documented the growth of centralized administration in Washington, noting that of the thirty largest independent administrative and regulatory agencies in existence in the 1960s, twelve appeared between 1920 and 1940, and eleven more between 1940 and 1960. During the Civil War, there were 36,000 civilian employees in the entire Executive Branch and only 950 in the War Department. By 1940, the number had risen to over 1,000,000 in the Executive Branch and more than 250,000 in the War Department. By 1960, over 2,500,000 civilians worked in the Executive Branch, and Defense (formerly War) Department civilian employees numbered over 1,000,000. The power and influence of these giant agencies continues to be enormous.

For example, the Pentagon, unlike the earlier Department of War, is a permanent military establishment which can affect the entire range of economic, social, and ideological behavior of our society. It can create entire industries and support major portions of others. It offers to millions the opportunities to achieve the upward mobility of American mythology. The ideological symbols at its command can direct the attention of the vast majority of Americans to an obscure pinpoint on the global map of its interests and convince many that the pinpoint is an essential element of national destiny. Its immense number of personnel represents a constant bleeding of national wealth, which in time of crisis becomes an arterial lesion.

While the provenance of activity and the absolute amounts of power differ between bureaus and departments, the scale of the bureaucracy is similar in education, health, agriculture, and most of the fields in which applied research is undertaken. Decision making in these vast corporate hierarchies seems at times mysterious, but Mulhauser (1975) has provided a useful summary of some of the reasons the holistic, systematic, and comparative perspective of anthropologists is often incompatible with bureaucratic perspectives.

The policy maker wants immediate action in reaction to troubles which arise, and in his or her view the complexity of a situation must be ignored in favor of *ad hoc* compromises within a bureaucratic agency. Moreover, fractionation of tasks within and between agencies means that questions are never phrased holistically; short-run solutions are sought in a continuing process of negotiation between the involved agencies, legislative committees and staffs, interest groups, and so on. Despite the numbers of employees in any given agency, since no single unit handles a problem by itself, staff shortages result from work overloads. As Mulhauser's (1975:313) personal experience indicates, lengthy consideration of scientific data can hardly be a factor:

In the Congressional subcommittee where I worked, the four professionals on the staff were involved in new or renewal legislation and administrative overseeing in the following areas: child abuse, nutrition and employment of the elderly, vocational rehabilitation, educational research, support for museums and libraries, the National Endowment for the Arts and Humanities, education for the handicapped, comprehensive child development, environmental and drug-abuse education, educational technology, accreditation of schools and state agencies for the blind, regulation of state social service agencies, a national institute for film, and still more.

Mulhauser concludes that the only way scientists can be heard amidst these pressures of time, work overlap and overload, is through "politically viable levers of action." Individuals and organized groups in and out of government who are receptive to anthropological theory and data must exist in order for information to flow effectively from research scientists to policy makers. When this occurs, as in the flow of information regarding surrender terms for the Japanese during the war or the case of potential epidemics today, the massive bureaus and agencies respond quickly. When such levers of action do not exist, the information flow is blocked.

During the crisis of World War II, vital links between anthropological research and policy applications existed, but as the crisis subsided the linkage was broken; Mead (1975a:13–14) describes it:

We only do applied anthropology if somebody is going to apply it. We have to have a consumer. What happened in World War II is that we had, in every government agency, people who were prepared to use what those of us who were outside or in another agency were producing. We organized that. We assembled a group of people, prepared them, and sent them to Washington, where they were put into government agencies. . . .

When the end of the war came, of course everybody was a little tired and anxious to go home. There was still a fair number of people in Washington who were willing to go on and work in this field. A great deal of the very best work was done right after the war. Then came the Joseph McCarthy era and the Korean War, when everybody inside the government who could have used the new material or insights that anthropologists could have produced went home or got fired. By 1952, there was no one in the government to ask for information of the sort anthropologists would have provided or to use it if it had been provided. We began to have boners of the kind that were not made in World War II.

A major indication of the break is that, according to the U.S. Civil Service Commission, there were only 55 full-time anthropologists employed by the government as of October 31, 1973. At the same time, in startling contrast, there were 4,638 economists, 2,492 psychologists, 2,200 psychiatrists, 69 sociologists, and 48 archeologists (Maday 1977:89).

The growth and proliferation of government agencies, the severe lack of skilled anthropologists within them, and the retreat of most anthropologists to departmental and disciplinary cocoons combined in the mid-1960s to create a situation of extreme distrust of the federal government on the part of anthropologists and heated debates about the ethical responsibilities of anthropologists engaged in applied work. Within the profession, two events were particularly instrumental in precipitating these attitudes. The first was Project Camelot, a proposal sponsored by the Office of Research Development in the United States Army and oriented toward Latin America. The aim was to utilize social science data and analysis "to predict and influence politically significant aspects of social change in the developing nations of the world" (Horowitz 1974:5). The second was the involvement of anthropologists in research sponsored by the Department of Defense and the Agency for International Development in Southeast Asia, especially Thailand. The details of these debates and the issues entailed have been described elsewhere and will not be repeated here (Belshaw 1976: 255–274; Beals 1969; Sjoberg 1967; Horowitz 1965 and 1974; Jones 1971; Wolf and Jorgenson 1970).

For our purpose, the important contribution of the controversies is that they revealed a basic lack of understanding of the nature of social scientific research in powerful governmental agencies and naïveté on the part of both governmental officials and social scientists, as well as raising ethical issues inherent in applied work. In these instances, at least, it became clear that social scientists were being used merely as technicians who would supply information to governmental patrons who already had formulated prior assumptions about the nature of the problems to be investigated and the policies to be defended. The outrage expressed by social scientists reflected not only a reaction against the reduction of the social scientist to a technician who collects and processes data, but also raised a genuine doubt about the purposes for which the data were to be used.

If the quality of social research, its methods, theory, analytical techniques, and data collection procedures are to be determined by governmental patrons who are untrained in methods of scientific inquiry, unknowledgeable about the types of research needed to advance theory, and perhaps even unsympathetic to scientific development, there can be no applied *science*. Moreover, there can be no anthropology worthy of the name, if the social purpose of a project is accepted as an excuse for relaxing the criteria by which data and theory are judged for scientific reliability, accuracy, cohesiveness, and completeness, and a consideration of the potential consequences of the research for human beings.

The ethical crisis of these years produced debate, but few commentators agreed about the proper "applications" of anthropology. Some took the position that application consisted in teaching or telling powerless people how to achieve power (Stavenhagen 1971), while others concluded that only the people who were being studied could teach the anthropologist proper applications of research results (Hessler and New 1972), ignoring the fact that such people are often ill-informed about forces affecting their lives (Gonzalez 1972). Still others concluded that the applied anthropologist must concede scientific definition of problems and research techniques to an employer, ignoring the lesson of Project Camelot (Clinton 1975). There were those, also, who argued that some form of individual commitment to the political beliefs of the people studied was the essential element of anthropology (Jacobs 1974), while a few claimed there could be no research during troubled times and the best an anthropologist could do would be to cook meals or gather firewood for a chosen faction (Talbert 1974). But by far the most common response was avoidance of the issues and retreat into abstract problems and academic career building.

Little of the debate illuminated two central issues raised during the 1960s: What contribution can an anthropologist make which distinguishes his or her action from that of any other citizen with an opinion? What should be the responsibility of the applied anthropologist to the people he or she studies? Answers to these questions must be forthcoming if we are to understand the nature of our role in America today.

Applied Anthropology in America Today

Reflection upon the place of applied anthropology within the overall field of anthropology and upon the crisis of the postwar period permits us to provide answers to the questions posed above, and these will serve well as themes to guide our consideration of applied anthropology today. First, the contribution of the applied anthropologist as distinct from other kinds of contributions will be considered. Second, the ethical considerations which shape our profession today will be summarized. Together these two aspects of the subject will set the stage for a brief introduction to the chapters which follow.

The vital essense of applied anthropology is the scientific analysis of the nature of human problems amidst changing technological, environmental, and social conditions. The nature of human problems is best discovered through the empirical study of the interplay between their macrocosmic context and the microcosmic contexts in which human beings live out their daily lives. Macrocosmic technological, economic, political, and social changes today link the microcosmic units of human behavior and interaction to regional, national, and multinational organizational structures in extraordinarily complex ways. As a consequence, peoples all over the world are confronting rapidly changing conditions which now demand innovative adaptive strategies so as to design organizational systems which take the welfare of human beings into account. The application of a holistic view to the understanding of human problems, and the analysis of social systems in terms of their interdependence, are unique contributions which can be made by applied anthropologists to the new types of organizational problems which confront all of us.

The contribution of applied anthropologists must be based on an ethical commitment to our science, our fellow men and women, the communities and institutions being served, and our employers or sponsors. We take as our guide the ethics code of the Society for Applied Anthropology, the product of a continuing effort dating from 1949 to formulate ethical guidelines. The cornerstone of that code is commitment to the freedom to inductively describe and analyze the empirical realities of human social life, to not be constrained by the assumptions of logico-deductive ways of thinking, whether they be embodied in preexisting policy, administrative procedure, or contemporary fashion. To the extent that inquiry is governed by commitments other than that of scientific validity, we no longer function as applied anthropologists. If commitments are personal and stem from our own ideologies, social classes, religion, and the like, we are private citizens acting on private beliefs. Moreover, if these commitments stem from the ideologies, social classes, religions, and so on, of our employers, sponsors, or the community served, we are technicians acting on the beliefs of others. In either case we are no longer applied anthropologists and should not be distinguished from any other person with an opinion. A value-free science does not exist, nor do value-free scientists. Private values and those of our employers, sponsors, and the community being served partially determine when and where research takes place, the choice of problems, and the uses to which results may be put. Ultimately, we as individual investigators must bear responsibility for the impact of our work upon the lives of the people for and with whom we work. But in the processes of research and data analysis, the influence of private values has no place, nor is there a role for those of our clients. Scientific criteria for data identification and collection, analysis and theory building, and professional debate and criticism are the principles which at once constitute our unique contribution to the world of practical problems and our ethical guidelines which safeguard against the intrusion of values other than scientific ones.

The nature of the corporate society in which we live, the shrinking need for professionals trained in abstract problem solution, the opening up of new opportunities for applied anthropology both within and outside of academe, and the ethical challenges of today are the conditions in which our profession will grow in the future. These conditions give new importance to the themes discussed above, raising a series of issues explored in the following contributed essays. We have divided them into four parts that reflect our understanding of the major issues, areas of opportunity and challenge, which confront contemporary applied anthropology in the United States.

Part I brings together contributors who have propounded theory in anthropology through their work in applied anthropology, thereby demonstrating the significance of a continuing dialogue between theory and practice. Theory is abstraction from empirical evidence serving the purpose of illuminating regularities and complex patterns, and demonstrating relationships which may be obscure. The testing of the validity of theoretical abstractions through empirical research is neither new nor unique to applied anthropology. But the creation of theory out of analysis of human problems is worthy of special attention, for this is at the heart of applied anthropology. Constant modification of the conditions of human life in which contemporary problems are given shape and meaning demands that theory be built out of analysis of primary data gathered in specific settings. Change in contemporary societies is multilineal, and relationships among variables are predicated on numerous contingencies and alternatives. Adequate theory must be built out of empirical evidence, and subsequently tested in application where the consequences of theoretical assumptions can be observed. If we would understand cultures as organic, changing entities which are part and product of the adaptive strength of our species, rather than as constructs composed of categories manipulated in the minds of abstract theoreticians, the dialogue between theory and practice described by the contributors should guide our efforts.

Part II reports the experiences of anthropologists who have taken actions based on analysis of situations in the roles of administrator, employee, advocate, researcher, consultant, and expert witness. In each case, we learn something of the obstacles to effective action found in specific institutional settings: universities, Indian reservations, communities, hospitals, prisons, business corporations, and courtrooms. Moreover, we learn that application does not necessarily proceed according to rigid steps, nor can we devise a cookbook formula which certifies that success will be forthcoming. The empirical nature of anthropological analysis precludes any such uniformity. For the constraints on application are the product of institutional goals, procedures, and organization, the conditions in which institutionalized groups interact with one another, and the situational strategies utilized by actors in these groups to achieve goals, manipulate procedures, and shape the organization. These vary between settings among groups, and over time. The analysis of these variations is a necessary first step in the process of devising appropriate actions. Beyond that, the applied anthropologist must devise situational strategies for taking action. Like the actions of other participants in the institution, these strategies must be varied, multiplex, and tailored to the institutional setting.

Part III examines some of the areas of application which have been explored in recent years under the rubric of policy studies. As Kimball points out, policy recommendations must stem from scientific research just as in the case of other kinds of action. In each of the areas explored here, we are discovering limits to the uses of applied anthropological research which lie in the social and cultural environment in which policy decisions are made. Administrators trained to think in the logico-deductive models of mathematics and derivative models of engineering have difficulty understanding more complex contingency-alternative models derived from natural science (Northup 1953). The strictures of time and personnel shortage and overload favor the use of familiar binary logics. Anthropologists who are sensitive to this fact will work hard to learn the language of policy makers. They will make recommendations in meaningful ways that decision makers can understand, as opportunities increase for policy research and recommendation. To the extent that current policy formulation is removed from the realm of empirical data analysis, the applied anthropologist has a great deal to contribute.

Finally, Part IV addresses the issue of the necessary but as yet insufficient training provided by classical abstract anthropology and the issue of ethics. The conditions of today demand novel approaches to the manpower problems of our society. A vocational orientation to anthropological training is needed, and students of anthropology must be provided with additional tools if they are to work in applied settings. Concomitant with these new conditions and novel approaches must come a rethinking of the ethics which inevitably will shape the emerging relationships between our science and our society.

placing
anthro in
context of
colonialism

AA. as
computerizing +
fulfilling needs
of research areas
+ that fundamentals provide
paradigm ground-
But still unserved. I downed
group while I continued
sympathies out of subordinate
group concerns.
WWII. emphasis changing to
war effort and spreading benefits
of Westfam. to technology
advances → to non-west areas.

Effect of an. col. will power.
Rise + spreading of
AP and changes
forms in anthro.
geared from study
of past cultures to
contemporary ones.

# of AA.
during WWII +
post. Gov't.
opportunities on
anthro swelled
# of anthro.
producing growth of
shrinking possible
job opp. for anthro.
in acad. terms →
shifting anthro.
interest back to
applied areas +
non-acad. demand
jobs.

Part I

THE DIALOGUE BETWEEN THEORY
AND APPLICATION

Like applied scientists in all fields of science, applied anthropologists systematically use theory in formulating problems for study and in developing new knowledge in the course of their work on practical problems. The contributed essays of Part I describe specific instances of the ways in which the dialogue between theory and application develops in nonacademic settings. They provide rare glimpses into what is entailed in the interweaving of discoveries made about processes of human organization, adaptation, and change into both theoretical and practical concerns.

Taken together, these essays are a case study of the dialogue between theory and application as it has emerged in the field of organizational behavior. Other fields might have been selected, but there are several reasons for having chosen the field we did. Within American society and beginning in the early 1930s, organizational behavior was the first field to attract a visible group of anthropologists who were concerned with the application of anthropological methods to an understanding of American organizations as social systems. Some of these early pioneers are still active in the field today, and they can review the diachronic development of their work over a period of nearly fifty years. The articles by Arensberg, Richardson, and Whyte represent reports of this nature and reveal the changes that occur in the theoretical formulations of applied anthropologists over time. The articles by Goodenough and Hill-Burnett are reports from applied anthropologists who have built on past theoretical contributions but who also bring new perspectives into the field as a consequence of their own experiences and new theoretical perspectives in anthropology generally.

Finally, we have chosen this field for special attention in this volume because the social systems which we label as organizations are the settings in which most people today spend most of their time. There is evidence to suggest that present organizational forms of social structure and human interaction are woefully failing to meet the needs of large segments of populations both at home and abroad. We believe that there is no doubt of the need for inquiries of the type described here, and we agree with Whyte (article 6) that the time is right for a new generation of applied anthropologists to work on both the theoretical and practical problems of organizational behavior.

2

THEORETICAL CONTRIBUTIONS OF INDUSTRIAL AND DEVELOPMENT STUDIES

Conrad M. Arensberg

Too often those who write about complex societies and the institutions within them assume that they are the same or in the process of becoming so. They argue that such factors as scale, industrialization, economic development, technology, and mass communications operate so as to standardize and homogenize family structures, settlement patterns, community forms and functions, and other expressions of cultural patterns. In his review of the theoretical contributions of industrial and development anthropology, Conrad M. Arensberg presents a quite different point of view.

Arensberg's central theme is that complex social systems, founded in multiple asymmetrical relationships among members, are as varied and unique as the cultural traditions from which they evolve. Empirical evidence of applied and other anthropologists reveal that the structure of social interaction results in a variety of elaborate, coordinate patterns of initiation and response. There are cultural variations in these interactional sequences which are found in the variety of institutionalized hierarchical relationships which comprise complex societies. These variations may be observed in the domains of religion, politics, economics, and other settings, and in the decision-making patterns of ongoing social

Conrad M. Arensberg (Ph.D., Harvard), professor of anthropology at Columbia University, is a social anthropologist who has done research in the areas of industrial and community studies, and in both economic and applied anthropology. His fieldwork has been in the United States, rural Ireland, Germany, and India. Dr. Arensberg has served as a consultant and researcher with the United States Departments of Agriculture, Interior, and State, the Rockefeller Foundation, UNESCO, the University of Münster, Germany, and the Institute for the Social Sciences in Cologne, Germany. He was a founder of the Society for Applied Anthropology, president of the Society from 1945 to 1946, and editor of its journal from 1946 to 1951.

life. Within American culture, the significance of these distinctive patterned interactional sequences in asymmetrical relationships is evident in hierarchical organizations as diverse as schools, prisons, hospitals, churches, communities, and governments.

The situations in which applied anthropologists normally work usually involve social change within the context of hierarchical structures. Successful planning, administration, intervention, advocacy, evaluation, and other applied activities flow from the discovery of effective actions in such settings. The elaborate ballet of behavioral sequences which Arensberg describes are the content in which novel behaviors are accepted or rejected. We learn from applied anthropology that change cannot be coerced, programmed, or legislated. Rather, it comes about when new behaviors are "naturalized" by all parties to the institutionalized hierarchical relationships and when the new pattern is incorporated into the interactional sequences considered proper, ethical, right, and rewarding by powerless and powerful alike.

MUCH HAS BEEN written about the practical successes and failures of applied anthropology. Equally important, though less well known, are its contributions to behavioral, social, and cultural anthropological theories. Here I discuss such feedback as it has already appeared in two substantive fields, and the possibilities for applying it to solve an insistent problem in social science theory: the nature of decision making in the context of hierarchical organization and leadership. This problem is not only insistent in the modern world of ever-increasing organizational complexity, but it is also central to anthropology's perennial concern with cultural evolution and institutional growth. In the two fields I shall report on, the use of anthropology has led to discoveries which show the ineluctable force of the emergence of regular social processes from personal and interpersonal behaviors and their assumption of hierarchic form. But a report of the feedback of field experience would be incomplete without an example of one of the many resultant theoretical advances. In this essay, I have chosen to present the advance into a processual understanding of the dynamics of communication, social interaction, and coordination in hierarchic decision-making. Other examples closer to historical anthropological concerns, such as the evolution of other organizational forms (e.g., monarchy, civil-religious "cargo" systems, "hydraulic empires," etc.) are left for later work.[1]

This essay then, will report on two fields and one extension of theory emanating from both of them. The first field is that of industrial behavior and relations. There, an early "industrial anthropology" worked beside industrial sociology and social psychology in "human relations" and "organizational behavior" in researches in factories, hospitals, and businesses (Mayo 1940; Roethlisberger and Dickson 1939; Barnard 1938; Richardson 1961). The second is the field of transcultural transfer of innovations, or, as more recently described, "development research" and development project "evaluation." In this field, anthropology's effort has become known as "development anthropology" (Cochrane 1971; Rubin 1961).

As mentioned in the editors' introductory essay, industrial anthropology took the science into small groups and personal networks within large institutions. Anthropology's methods of natural history observation, inductive generalization from participant observation and open-ended interviews, and its use of sociometric measures of interaction among live human beings in real events, lately expanded into network and event analysis, made new and telling contributions (Arensberg and Kimball 1965; Chapple 1970; Horsfall and Arensberg 1949; Guest 1962; Boissevain and Mitchell 1973). Fieldwork penetration of the relatively autonomous "informal" groups and networks of the diverse institutional personnel (workers, unionists, managers, engineers; doctors, nurses, patients, and so on) and cultural awareness of their differences gave scope for anthropology's special skills.

The field of development also provided useful employment of anthropological method and experience. It plunged anthropologists into working with the human subjects of current social and cultural change. As spectators of the "natural" worldwide transformations overtaking traditional cultures everywhere, anthropologists were pulled into direct observation of the planned local and "induced"

---

[1] For application of processual and systems-analysis to the problems of the emergencies of shamanism, prophetic leadership, and the state, see the forthcoming volume on the Springhill-Minnesota October 1976 conference on the state of anthropology, particularly the chapter "The Recovery of Holism" by Conrad Arsenberg. For parallel observation, see Richardson's essay in this volume.

social and cultural change involved in the political and economic modernizations of our time. They were especially close to the cultural innovations and the transfers of technology visited upon the recipients of the planned and programmed projects of regional and community development that marked national and international modernizaton efforts around the world and reached again and again into the very countrysides in which anthropologists worked.

Anthropology shared observation of development with the other social sciences: economics, sociology, and political science. From the 1930s up to the present, they have all turned to the world scene and the developing countries beyond metropolitan societies. But anthropology's vantage point was unique. Its experience with grassroots cultures and its fieldwork outside national capitals and project planning headquarters gave it a special advantage.

The fortunate position of anthropology in the study of development was a concomitant of its evolutionary trends. First, fieldwork expanded out from tribal and antiquarian into community and village studies. Attention turned from the "primitive" (preliterate) to the peasant and "post peasant" worlds and to comparisons of the other great urban civilizations with the European one in which anthropology already had crystallized. Second, the science awoke, with new fossil evidence, to the huge antiquity of Man. It rediscovered human evolution, adaptive ecology, comparative mammalian and human ethology, and "sociobiology." It turned back again to concern with the emergence of successive stages of culture and the levels of complexity of behavior in men and animals. It came to accept empirical but controlled cross-cultural comparisons based on the worldwide evidence, compiled now in such compendia as the Human Relations Area File and the World Ethnographic Atlas. Documenting questions as to what was various and what was universal in the cultures of mankind, it could again ask evolutionary and nomothetic questions. What are the lawful processes of change? After the end of peasantry (Mendras 1970; Franklin 1969), what next?

These trends propelled anthropology into a confrontation with the two kinds of modern culture change already cited, "the natural" (adaptive and evolutionary) and the "induced" (planned). Appraisal of change and development became inescapable. New experience called for reexamination of older theories of culture contact and culture growth, to be tested now in the interaction between the culture bearers of the new ways and those of the old.

Developers' projects and the reactions of those served by them were lively theatres of that interaction. The former came to be called "change agents" and "donors" by the analysts, though they stoutly called themselves "experts"; the latter came to be called "donees." The observed dramas taking place between these two sides called for further theory of the processes of change itself and the roles of individual and groups in behavior, attitude, social organization, and cultural values in change and contact situations.

Experience with industry had already discovered workplaces to be exactly such dramas of human relations, clashes of motives, adjustments of interests to larger institutional pressures and in wider economic and technical trends. Now old places of residence and subsistence in planned and project-engulfed villages became new stages of similar dramas of contact, power and pressure, and change. The feedback into theory that rose (and continues to rise) from watching these dramas will occupy us here.

The Feedback from Industrial and Organizational Studies[2]

Critics of anthropological research into industrial shops, business, and hospital organizations during the 1930s and 1940s often state that the observation undertaken was only small group research. They hold that the study of small closed groups was too limited to yield results which could readily be transferable to larger settings of human social behavior and culture. Yet, we did not think of ourselves at that time as doing small group study. Instead, we treated observations of human beings in offices and workshops as studies in a laboratory of rapid social and cultural change where general processes of human organization and cultural interaction might be explored, for both grand trends and the dynamisms of relatively closed social systems.

The laboratory was not a setting of controlled experiment; we ourselves did not impose the changes we watched. Rather, it was a

[2] This section paraphrases sections of "Discussion" of C. Stewart Sheppard, "The Role of Anthropology in Business Administration" (Arensberg 1975).

field of direct observation which provided a comparative microcosm of rapidly changing human events. These showed many variations in social organization and in cultural understandings and misunderstandings; they also showed misunderstandings which were analogous to larger movements outside. It was a laboratory of palpably and continually shifting parameters of human action and motivation—shifting from organizational plan to plan, from production drive to drive, from machine-process innovation to innovation, and from incentive scheme or interest negotiation to new scheme and new negotiation. In this respect, the early in-plant industrial and organizational research setting was similar to the changing tribal, village, and slum settings of contemporary studies of social and cultural change and modernization. To the extent that current anthropology is moving from studies of static social structure to newer treatments of social and cultural change, and is also working its way through to delineations of social strategies and emergent processes in social and cultural life, it is largely due to the experience gained in the early years of applied anthropology. It was then that the science first turned professional attention to scenes in American business, community, and institutional life.

In the case of both earlier industrial-interaction studies at home and modern studies of personal networks or development processes abroad, more is to be learned than the immediately useful practicalities for the businessman or national developer. In the industrial studies, there was more to be recorded and understood than the rooting of motivation for workshop morale and productivity in the informal organization. Likewise, in the current peasant and urban-immigrant studies, there is more to be learned about agricultural modernization than the dangers of wiping out peasant-villagers' traditional cultural supports. In both cases, there are the dynamics of human systems to be unraveled.

During the 1930s and 1940s, it was discovered that industrial unrest, dissatisfaction, and alienation on the job in factory or office were much like the current anomie, resistance to innovation, and conflict in agrarian countrysides among contemporary ex-peasants torn between pressures of the new market and planning entrepreneurs and their own remaining (or newly lost) peasant life and local subsistence. The problems of industry were not to be cured simply by an easy, purely local revival of informal organization among workers or by solely personal collective or community securities. As with the once closed peasant villages, now disrupted and torn by modern agro-technics and world market demands, the workrooms and the offices studied were only relatively closable at best. They were remarkably sensitive and reactive to processes derived from managerial purposes and business imperatives, from engineering strictures and controls, and from the vagaries of economic and political worlds far outside the workroom but still influencing factory and business as larger wholes.

The informal organization of the work place, like the peasant securities of an earlier agrarian day, was protective and responsive. It reflected workers' universal human needs and fluctuated according to the pressures of the business institution and current culture. Teamwork and team support bolstered workers against their isolation and disciplined containment, the impersonal and arbitrary controls of standardized production, and the atomizing incentive pay schemes of the day. Nevertheless, teamwork efficacy fluctuated according to the extent that it provided workers with mediating remoter relationships, through informal and formal grievance reporting and workload adjustments in shop and in union representation. The informal organization gave workers both a work life with workmates and a voice in the larger organization which embraced all the levels of business personnel—supervisors, managers, engineers, and so on. Hence, social science discovered in that early anthropological fieldwork of modern culture not only some psychology of industrial morale, incentive, and productivity (or alienation and impersonalization, if you prefer) but also important dynamics of large-scale human organization.

The lesson of the workroom studies went far beyond the mere managerial practicalities of learning that "human relations" support of workers made better producers and happier employees. This trivial though salutary reading of the evidence eventually discredited the movement of social science study of work behavior. However, the more significant lesson was that, if workers were to be more productive and committed ("less alienated"), some initiative and responsible spontaneity must be returned to them; some initiative of theirs must be channeled into the larger, hierarchical social system of the factory, the business, and the corporation. Today, events such as the revolt against the assembly-line pressures in the Lordstown plant of Chevrolet have showed us a new generation of better educated factory workers who are no longer passive under the old disciplines of factory work. There is also the current recasting at Volvo in Sweden of the assembly line itself into teams, each completing a car of its own, from frame to fittings. With such examples before us, the lesson of local initiative is revived once more.

The lesson is an old one, presented from many disciplines—history, politics, and our own cultural anthropology and sociology. Culture as shared meaning and organization as ordered behavior, together leading to cooperative result, are not merely planned and commanded; they are always partially spontaneous, responsive, both self-realized and socially sanctioned and inspired. Even in the hierarchical settings of the larger-scaled organizations of our present world, the rank and file are evolving a morale and organization of their own. There always will be a grapevine, at least, and usually more. Shared feeling and organization among workers can work either for or against their hierarchs, their pace-setters, and direction-givers. The "for" or "against" felt by workers depends inevitably on both their immediate satisfactions and their more extended participations.

Social science has still more than this to learn about large-scale organization and its dynamics, not only in general terms but specifically about business and the corporation in our civilization. Such knowledge is needed both at the rank and file level of workers and consumers, alienated or committed, and at higher levels. We need more insight into the dynamics of large-scale business organization for many reasons: for managing it; for teaching management to manage it; for efficiency; for taming business organizations for human use and social responsibilities; and for coming to terms with the powerful force and the steady growth shown by large-scale business organizations in national and international life.

Even in the early studies, the track of organizational dynamics led from a concern with the morale, motivation, and productivity of the worker on the assembly line or in the records office to interest in the broader relationships among the levels and kinds of personnel. Each of these often had, and continues to have, its own professional subcultural tradition. Moreover, each level and kind of personnel was cross-tied to the others. In order to trace relationships among diverse groups and through hierarchical ties in those settings, it is necessary to reveal the dynamics of grievances and of shop representational systems with their links to better productivity and freer participation. It is equally necessary to trace the connections from department to department, from specialty to specialty, or from profession to profession in the staff-line contacts, as well as in the other complexities of the organizational activity of modern multiplex bureaucracies and "plural societies." Large-scale hierarchical organization perforce builds structure putting persons of diverse traditions into harness together. A way must be found to identify, and to reconcile if not satisfy, such diverse and opposed traditions.

The way was pointed out long ago. Veblen, for one, marked it in his *Engineers and the Price System* (1921). He was the first to study the clash of values and traditions in a single power system (manufacturing) and to foreshadow the concept of the "segmentary opposition." Segmentary opposition is a staple of anthropological study of lineages, plural societies, caste systems, and the ethnic mosaics of the stratified diversities in complex civilization. Veblen accurately observed that the engineers of the artisan tradition, valuing efficiency and serviceability in products, did not always see eye to eye with the businessman of merchant and countinghouse tradition who was moved by profitability, quick turnover, and "planned obsolescence" (a later word).

More recently, we have had further studies which tell of clash and differences of value and custom in the professions and of the difficulties of accommodation between scientist and businessman. As corporations have increasingly taken over occupations, they have come to dominate the once lone inventor's work with teams and laboratories of their own. They have pushed technology forward by harnessing scientists to their businesses, just as they have harnessed designers, publicists, salesmen, and artist-advertisers. The recruitment and engulfment of nonbusiness occupations into the corporation, in its search for newer lines of profit and for wider and more stable coordinate and conglomerate diversity, show no sign of abatement.

Scientists, we learn in particular from Livingston and Milberg (1957), Marcson (1960), and others, have a tradition of their own which differs from that of the engineer and the businessman. They are restive under fixed-period budgets and programmed results; they need freer wheeling to follow up unexpected openings. They are more responsive to collegial review and to publication notice than to superiors' program audits and balance sheets. Organizational tinkering is required for them to find a place in corporation and department plans.

We need to watch such acculturations and to follow plural societies as they unite various internal traditions both in our own and in other cultures. Ours is an age in which private or public bureaucratic corporations continually increase in size, complexity, and spread, as one dominant new social form within our own nation and between nations, whether as native enterprises or as multinationals. We need to observe these developments in order to teach and train the business and organizational personnel of our age, to balance their connections with the unincluded classes, and to gain scientific understanding of the signal cases that corporations present of the worldwide cultural fusings and the modernizing institutional evolutions which our age unfolds. It is both of anthropological interest and of use to business and administration to record the acclimatization in the outer world of business and the corporation which were originally social inventions of northwest Europe.

James Abegglen (1958), student and successor of W. Lloyd Warner, first explored the unexpected evolution in Japan after World War II. There, the factory organized machines and labor very much like, or even better than, European models. However, hiring practices, employee/employer relationships, and corporate lifelong careers were ordered in quite different ways than the European and Anglo-Saxon model which emerged from a medieval past of hiring fairs, short-term employment contracts, and layoffs for slack seasons between market sales. The cultural backgrounds of British industrialization were such ubiquitous concomitants of industrial enterprise that economists in our own country thought them indispensible to it. Yet the Japanese evolution, with a feudal past and an earlier imperial and Tokugawa centralization, retained quite other hiring practices and market-competitive interfirm relationships. The Japanese did not hire "at the gate," but rather for life; they did not "lay off" but instead they fed and nurtured firm-bound workers even through the ruin of World War II; they mounted research and operations research and development in pools of technicians and scientists who were permanently employed in their own corporations but temporarily pooled with others until the job was done, at which time they were sent home. As another anthropologist, Nakane (1970), later found, the factory and the firm in Japan replicate the *ie,* or kindreds of their family system, rather than the mobile small families of ours.

There are similar preliminary and instructive lessons from the experience of the corporation and its European and American cohesions of custom and practice in Brazil, the Middle East, India, and the Chinese Overseas (*Nanyang*) World of South and Island Asia. The evidence reveals that rationalized production—the machine, the assembly line, automation, production, and market planning, basic techniques of civilization and of business enterprise—managed, developed, and elaborated by our businessmen and our corporations, all need rethinking. We learn that large-scale organization can be analyzed, parts and processes separated, and institutions understood beyond traditional and untested acceptance of them. For example, the Chinese of Singapore and Hong Kong do very well with both nepotism and industry. The businesses of the private sector of India continue to grow, not by abandoning the caste system but by naturalizing it in part and moving it inside the factory walls and the office space. The Brazilian great families, *parentelas,* move from the fazendas of earlier years to incorporating as family corporations. The Arabs and the Greeks enter world commerce again without western stewardship ideals and impersonal relationships but as authoritative families and undissolved lineages.

In summary, the evidence mounts, from older as well as newer social science, that it is important for both practical life and the active professions such as business, the social sciences, and cultural anthropology, that study of business and the corporation not fall away but be carried onward. It is clear, too, that anthropological study of business, like that of the workroom, is not trivial piecemeal observation. Science always looks for the general in the particular, the great in the small, as well as the small in the great. The same attention to both observation and inference is still needed before our view of modern processes in our civilization, ones in which our lives are caught, firms into useful and generalizing science.

The Feedback from Studies of Transcultural Transfer of Innovations[3]

The second field in which applied anthropology has made major contributions to anthropological theory is that of "development." In par-

[3] This section reprints, with permission and modification, the text of Conrad M. Arensberg (1967) "Upgrading Peasant Agriculture: Is Tradition the Snag?"

ticular, event analysis has had considerable and fruitful use during recent decades. Event analysis is a technique for the analysis of ongoing cultural and social process and is associated with the names of Solon T. Kimball and myself. I review its use in the applied anthropology of development projects and give attention to its part in the identification of a common process which unfolds in a minimal sequence structure of interpersonal relations and is capable of modeling and thus of explaining the successful and unsuccessful transfer of skills between people of a "donor" culture and those of another "donee" culture.

I call the process of directed social change to be reported here the Reciprocal Accommodation Process.[4] It is built on older theories of culture contact and generalized from the accumulated experience of projects of planned innovation for the transfer of the skills, tools, seeds, and other items of modern technology to peoples all over the world. The Reciprocal Accommodation Process seems capable of predicting the outcome of these transfer efforts from the sequence of interpersonal events through which the transferred item of culture is proffered, received, and incorporated. Modeling the transactions between donors and donees in successful and unsuccessful transfers reveals more than an adaptive strategy for donor and donee (cf. current social anthropological analyses of participants in many political or economic structures). It suggests the existence of a specific sequence or flow of adaptive actions in and between the members of the donor and donee groups who are in contact with each other. Without the specific occurrence of this sequence and flow of actions, successful transfer fails. In other words, transfer seems to depend

---

[4] This model of successful incorporation of skills transferred from one culture to another through planned projects of social change arose in the time of the development efforts running from Point Four and the Community Development movement down to the Green Revolution. I have previously (Arensberg 1967) made a limited statement about the Reciprocal Accommodation Process model. I have also alluded to it elsewhere as follows:

"Whether in work productivity, role maintenance, or acceptance of innovations, as in factory workrooms or hospital offices or peasant villages in transfer of technique efforts, documented and analyzed by William Whyte, Frederick Richardson, Conrad Arensberg, Solon Kimball, Robert Guest, these covariances (between interpersonal equilibria and performances) were demonstrated during the heyday of "in-plant research," "human research," "human relations research," and "applied anthropology" of the 1950s" (Arensberg 1972:7).

The data on the acceptance or the rejection of transfers of skills have already appeared in a factorial correlation exploration in the work of Arthur Niehoff (1966). But a codification of the process by which the factors combine to move a project of directed social change has not yet been presented. The model has been used to good effect in a doctoral thesis, generalizing East African development data (Campbell 1971).

upon the unfolding of a social process, and progress can be made toward delineating its exact form and rate of development. Before turning to the details, I will discuss some common assumptions that are often made about the introduction of new agricultural technologies in the developing world.

Prevailing opinion has it that agriculture in the newly emerging Third World will continue to limp and stumble so long as its backbone is the peasant. Everything is wrong with peasants, or so it is said. Their values and customs frustrate acceptance of necessary technical innovations; their religious observances block progress; their motives and purposes are out of step with the needs of a nation for modernity.

Some plans call for sweeping aside peasants and the impediments of their ways, values, and beliefs, and turning them as quickly as possible into more amenable kinds of persons and members of society: commercial farmers, salaried rural proletarians, or members of a commune that is both agricultural and industrial. Other schemes would clear them off to cities, just as the enclosure movement during the eighteenth century once cleared the land in Great Britain; or as the Negro in the southern United States is "tractored out" into northward, city-bound emigration; or as the serrano leaves Andean Peru for Lima and makes room for cattle in the high valleys. These efforts look for other chemical, mechanical, and agronomic food makers, and they assert the futility of establishing continuity with, or building upon, the ancient rural pattern of subsistence farming now dominant in most "have-not nations." They fail to take into account either the realities of the present world, especially of the developing nations, or the current record of successes in transforming the peasantry into farmers capable of expanding food production in the crowded nations over and beyond the advance in population growth.

Today, it is clear that the developing nations have both vast numbers of peasants in their increasing populations (the proportion is over half) and lagging food production. Moreover, plans for clearing out the peasants or for proletarianizing them on the land are not associated with past notable increases in food production. On the contrary, both historically and in the present, it has been shown that peasants have greatly increased productivity without having to abandon either all of their customs or all of their lands—their base for being.

European countries, such as Denmark, and Asian ones, such as first Japan and now Taiwan (Formosa), have pushed forward with their peasantries undissolved. Old ways have not been obliterated but rather have been productively combined with new ones. Even the spectacular American agricultural revolution of the twentieth century did not move directly from folk subsistence to chemurgical manufacture on the land but instead it traveled through decades of upgrading family farming. American scientific advance and its movement to agricultural engineering on a corporate scale, with corporate capitalization, came very late. It came after and not before industralization and the transformation of the peasantry.

As with us, perhaps so with others. Perhaps an increase in food production in the developing world must come from a peasantry that slowly learns to combine entrenched customs and generations-old local know-how with new scientific knowledge. The application of science to new conditions of climate, terrain, and endemic disease may turn out to be a two-way process, a dialogue of research at the farm and village level, reminiscent of the earlier similar dialogue in industry, where shop practice preceded engineering advance, and scientists codified what the skilled artisan already knew.

The tradition-tested peasants of the underdeveloped world have long coped with the practical and special local realities of desert, tropics, and jungle which agronomic science has barely begun to explore despite its knowledge of European and American conditions. In the developed world, a thousand years of peasant experience lie behind current scientific agriculture, refined and distilled from the best practices of peasants long forgotten and superseded. In the underdeveloped world, the dialogue has just begun.

Far from being only unreasoned resistance, peasant custom may embody economies and techniques that today's scientists and planners can either adapt to their purposes or ignore at their peril. Many a project has introduced fine new herds into a village to replace scrawny ones, only to have the animals die the next time drought or disease struck the area. Many economies of scale in farming have failed to promote production and have eventually destroyed incentive, because they were introduced before the management skill needed to cope with them had been grafted onto the old inventory of traditional techniques.

The proposition that durable progress in agriculture depends on blending peasant know-how with scientific techniques is, therefore, not idly posed. It is based on a knowledge of successes and failures of a few projects of technical innovation that can be fully evaluated and on the insights that scholars are gaining into the true histories of agricultural progress in both western and nonwestern countries. The details are given below.

Generalization about Innovation

It is remarkable that so little generalization of the experience of technical assistance and other efforts directed at the transfer of know-how from one culture to another has been undertaken. In a summary of international technical assistance evaluation, Cyril Belshaw reported in 1966 that there is no continuous development of ideas, that very few attempts at evaluation have been coordinated, and that no bibliography of evaluation reports yet exists. Evaluation efforts of international and bilateral aid agencies are often made without cross-contact, and the agencies even appear to lose track of what they themselves have done before. Knowledge of the process of transfer in technical assistance, even in agriculture, where new methods, seeds, and other innovations are central, is minimal and the growth of technique and conceptualization slow.

In summarizing initial research on the experience of technical experts of the United Nations, AID, and others, Belshaw (1966:22) states that the "contribution of technical assistance to overall development cannot be judged finally without some fairly specific assumptions about the strategy of development in the circumstances of the country." If technical assistance is to win enduring acceptance and contribute to further growth, it must mesh with the preexisting wants of the people of the recipient country and not merely with government plans and aspirations for them. Aid must supplement indigenous resouces rather than merely replace them; it must be "institution building," as the current phrase aptly describes it, but the building has to be done on the existing base, not as new edifices on a *tabula rasa*. New techniques and new institutions cannot be effective engines of development unless they are naturalized and interlinked with older, more established practices. This naturalization takes time, effort, and habituation to the local scene. What is needed is the training of local trainers who will take over and complete the process of interlacing the old and the new.

The experience of "development" anthropology corroborates

and expands these conclusions, which are drawn from the few evaluations of technical assistance now extant. In recent years, both anthropologists and developers have evaluated programs and projects of directed innovation, technical assistance, and planned development. They have looked at these both as observers from the outside and as partial participants. At times, they have been asked to look into the real impact and the true fate of the programs or projects designed for their human subjects; more often they have come upon the scene by chance, gathering data on ways of life about to disappear under modernization.

As ersatz locals, anthropologists have had a different vantage point from that of the technical expert, the economist, or indeed any other developer, even the public health expert and the epidemiologist. They have lived in the village, learned the local language, and participated in the institutions of village and peasant and tribal life as part of their professional commitment to field work; in many cases, they have been on the scene before, during, or after such projects. They have seen the planning office goals for these projects, or the home office reports, and they have observed their real impact on the people themselves, their acceptance or rejection by village families, and their contribution—enduring or ephemeral—to local knowledge and resources.

The projects of planners and innovators, whether in agriculture, medicine, or any other professional domain, are of interest to the anthropologist, not only because they affect for good or ill the lives of villagers, but because they are modern instances of an age-old dynamic of culture trait, or bit of human knowledge, and the receivers of the same. What the village does with the bit of transmitted lore, or what the villagers do in reaction to the innovators and their pressure, is grist for the anthropologist's mill as scientist of culture. The growth of civilization has always proceeded by just such transfer and reworkings of cultural material as villagers now undertake before the anthropologist's eyes. There is as much to learn from the new transfers that carry penicillin or hybrid corn or birth control to the village as from the older ones such as writing from the Egyptians to the Phoenicians, or gunpowder and paper money from the Mongols to the Europeans, or Christianity and metallurgy from the Spaniards to the Indians, or tobacco, chocolate, and the fateful potato from the Indians back to Europe.

To learn the process by which cultures change when acted upon by outside forces, and for the purposes of agency and project planners and directors who want to know more of the successes and failures of their innovations, anthropologists have compiled cases so as to draw comparative conclusions from them. The compilation is not easy. Equally difficult is the empirical distillation of the factors responsible for the success or failure in transmitting techniques, the process of contact and transmission, and the reworking and adapting by which one outcome or the other develops.

Compilation, assessment, and identification of process and final effect require a long, continuous, and thorough record. This record must document the needs and problems before the project, the plans and their implementation during the project, and the response of the recipients to the innovation and to the innovators. It must also include the details of how the local people worked out the "bugs," with or without the help of the innovators; how they fitted the amended technique into the other knowledge, resources, habits, and concurrent changes of their way of life; and finally, after the project, the ways in which the technique was incorporated into their culture—something that comes only when the receivers can pass the technique on to their neighbors and their children, in short, among themselves.

Such complete records, rare but usable, disclose, with event analysis and reduction to flows of interpersonal action between donor and donee personnel, a Reciprocal Accommodation Process in successful transfer. This process, a dialogue of donor and donee which grows to include them both in a common social structure, is the successful process of transfer. Unless it unfolds to follow the order of events described below, it seems that acceptance of innovation does not occur.

Arthur Niehoff (1964, 1966) has compiled 203 histories of efforts to introduce new techniques into peasant communities of developing countries. By means of factorial analysis, he established the primary variables leading either to success or to failure in the case histories. Using these variables, I have analyzed the processual structures of the events of the cases, sequenced the occurrences of the factors Niehoff finds significant, and modeled the flows of social interaction among the donor and donee personnel and in the two-way communication between them. I believe I have discovered in each case of transfer the same process at work, unfolding to acceptance ("success"), aborting to abandonment ("failure") where impeded or derailed.

In no case were peasants and others not yet modernized willing to give up their accustomed way of life, with its traditional techniques, merely on the promise of technical or economic advantage. In every case of success, there was a continuing dialogue of initiative and reaction between innovator and recipient, which moved forward until the new techniques became an integral part of the lives of the people.

In a feedback of experiences to theory, the cases validated the cherished maxims of experienced developers. A self-declared conscious need, they say, is better than imposed betterment; enlisting local leadership and self-help is better than paternalism; concrete and specific demonstration is better than proof in theory and tables; follow-up, feedback, and continuing attention are better than quick solutions; immediately perceived benefits and tangible gains in crop, health, convenience, or security are more effective than are vague long-term gains; peasants prove ready to innovate when they can personally experience any improvement they themselves can value, etc. Such maxims are hard-won half-truths which social science can reorder and verify.

It is clear, moreover, that these experts' maxims, now grossly empirical, can be generalized. They are examples of the theoretically statable process that I have named the Reciprocal Accommodation Process. The process, generalizing the experts' maxims of project experience, is the same kind of flow of initiative and localization of plans that can sometimes run upward from workers in the shops and production lines of industry, through worker participation and their unions into the decisions of managers and top brass. In industry this upward flow, though often too small, is the two-way communication necessary to create motivated and constructive hierarchical relationships as already attested in the literature of the industrial experience cited earlier. My (1972) social-interactional processual analysis gives a common minimal-sequence model of that same flow in development—another human and equally hierarchical setting.

As already noted, innovations presented in culture contacts, especially in settings of differential power and expertise, do not win acceptance on their merits alone. Both in industry and development, they are accepted or rejected on the basis of a social process of two-way communication. Nor are they accepted at once and exactly as initially presented. Reworking, localization, removal of the "bugs" are all part of the process of the mutual accommodation of donors and donees and the building of a new social system inclusive of the representatives of the two cultures.

The history of cultural innovations especially documents the failure of donors and developers when they do not respond to the peasants' reworking and naturalizing of their plans. They fail when they do not help the peasants, at peasant request, to remove unforeseen obstacles to their plans and when they do not continue to rework, on their side, the necessary adjustments to local experience the peasants know and face, as they, the donors and developers, do not. On the other hand, donors succeed when they do so respond and help donees to their pay-off.

This mutual accommodation is a social process. It is a sequence of human interactions that must unfold to have its result. In other words, accepted, successful change or "development" is a synergetic outcome of donor and donee actions moving themselves and one another in a proper order, a systematic process and a predictable result. As such, it can take its place in social science and in anthropology with other theories of system, process, decision, and hierarchy that are coming to be proffered (Goodenough 1963; Haskell 1972).

Mechanisms of Agricultural Advance

The science of anthropology, then, with its evolution-long view of past cultural, economic, and social changes (both historical and archeological) and its processual analysis of human interactive sequences, has something to say about the most effective mechanisms of agricultural progress.

If the problem is to raise food production in the developing world, anthropology, and perhaps even the other social sciences as well, would bet on the present rural inhabitants of the villages of the tropics, the desert, and the mountain terrains. These people currently support (or nearly support) themselves and their city-based fellow nationals. Anthropologists would vote for upgrading these inhabitants *in situ*, both as the most practical course and as the historically correct one to pursue. They would argue that the absence of research into innovation and the agronomic realities of local terrain and climate is the bottleneck or the missing ingredient as it were, rather than the paucity of fertilizer or new seeds.

John P. Lewis (1964) has argued that, historically and realistically, scientific advances in agriculture are the most difficult to achieve and come last because such advances must be made in the face of incredible diversities of microclimates, microsoils, and microtechnical supports—the very conditions that make it difficult to transfer techniques from the successful to the less successful. He uses the experience of Japan, Taiwan (Formosa), and India to show that success is based not on paternalism and central direction but upon peasant naturalization of new information. He notes that new science meets real competition: the fact that peasants now have subsistence security, but little more, and no margin for error or experiment. This rigorous competition must be won not in the laboratory but in the village itself. The high yielding rices of Japan do not yet produce equally well in tropical, semi-drought-ridden India; the tractors of America are too big and heavy for German field plots or South Asian rice fields. Fertilizers are needed, but so are new inventions and ways of getting them into farmers' hands.

John W. Mellor (1962) develops a different but parallel reasoning from history. He appeals to wide experience in the developing world and the comparative history of agricultural economics. He uses the instructive histories of the United States, Denmark, Japan, Greece, and Taiwan (Formosa)—countries that have been successful in making big advances in food production. He says:

A commonly recommended alternative to the evolutionary process of training the mass of farmers to make their own decisions is to institute a form of large-scale farming using specialized management. Unfortunately, economies of scale in farming do not continue . . . as in other industries, particularly if labor is cheap and the opportunity cost . . . of large-scale machinery is relatively high (1962:712).

Regarding research and education of peasants, along with the provision of necessary agricultural inputs, Mellor concludes that increased productivity, especially a Rostovian take-off into full development and great increase, depends less on any one input than on a complementarity among several modern inputs. "In practically all underdeveloped countries," he states, "there has been continuous conscious effort by government . . . some of the nontraditional factors of production have been made available in a quantity out of proportion to other complements . . . additional amounts . . . may have very low short-run returns, while a small addition of others would provide extremely large [ones].'' He goes on to cite developments in Denmark, Japan, and Taiwan (Formosa), and the early phases of American growth (through the ''agricultural extension'' service of American land-grant colleges and other local stations) to show that: (1) a very small number of missing inputs curtails advance in many countries; (2) these missing inputs are by no means the same from region to region; and (3) there are substantial short-run returns when the missing inputs are plugged in (1962:714).

Mellor then gives an evolutionary, history-tested phasing of agricultural development that encompasses but does not bypass the upgrading of the peasants. This phasing strikes the anthropologist as promising real success, because it reflects the true process of culture contact, culture change, and the steps necessary to the successful transfer of the techniques we have already discussed. His comparative analysis of the sequence of stages America and Denmark went through some time ago, that Japan has just passed through, that Taiwan (Formosa) is already in, and that India perhaps has just barely entered, is especially instructive. Phase I is a ''stagnant phase,'' in which production increase, if any, is achieved largely from increased application of traditional inputs—more sweat and labor from an expanding, traditional population. This phase can only lead to change if the preconditions for advance evolve—namely, changes in land tenure and in political power. These changes are not in themselves sufficient conditions, but they create a ''decision-making environment in which farmers accept the possibility of personal gain from improvements'' (Mellor 1962:712).

Phase II is the crucial stage: agriculture is still a large proportion of the economy, capital is scarce, new land is limited, and machines are too costly. Traditional forms of labor, land, and capital are abundant but as yet relatively unproductive. Only the peasants with larger holdings have any security. Increase is likely to be achieved through the growing acceptance of even a few technical changes in perhaps only a few areas of the country. These include insecticides, rodent controls, farm-to-market roads, seeds, fertilizers—in short, some of the innovations that our projects have striven to transfer. Later, a larger number of further changes builds on these: Land consolidation, marketing facilities, storage, credit, and other institutions succeed the initial, recognizable gains that have been experienced. Once more, it is research and the transfer process that are the bottlenecks. To quote Mellor again: "The requisite research in this phase is of the applied type often involving no more than regionally decentralized comparative testing of variability in traditional [cultural] practices. The major input . . . is personnel of the level of training that can be provided in large quantity in a . . . few years' time" (1962:714). If Phase II is successfully passed, the result is a dynamic process of continuing increase.

Phase III is the final emergence of chemurgical, scientific agriculture, the factories-in-the-field. Japan, after ninety years of intensive development, is just entering it. We ourselves went fully into it only in the 1930s, long after our industrialization. Mellor, like the anthropologists, believes that evolution moves through its own phases and has its own laws. Perhaps upgrading the peasants before industrializing them is just such a law. If the developing world is to grow the food it must have, this is the route it may be compelled to take.

New Models of Behavior, Social Process Leadership, and Hierarchy

Finally, let us consider the feedback of industrial and development anthropology into theories of organization and organizational behavior itself. What does the theory of process necessary for successful change and rewarding hierarchical relationships have to say about organization and about the behavior of the individuals involved in it?

The feedback from applied anthropological research into the theory of organizational behavior and innovation process has led to new models of interpersonal interaction, social process, emergent structure, and, most widely, to a new look at organization and hierarchy theory. The experience of the two fields of applied anthropology just reviewed has also illuminated current theories of leadership, organization, and social hierarchy from interactional and behavioral anthropology (Arensberg 1972; Collins and Collins 1973).

William Foote Whyte, a fellow contributor to this book, reminds us that in recent years we have seen a boom in organizational and interorganizational studies. He points out that "we have come to recognize that civilizations advance through increasing division of labor and specialization, which means, among other things, the creation of more and more organizations to perform specialized functions." He calls for a better meshing of individual and shared human problems as they are experienced within organizations by the individuals manning them and those they serve. Our knowledge of organization as social process and cultural form must be improved if we are to develop the "organizational forms and strategies that coordinate specialized services and resources (that) people need. This means particularly studying the coordination and cooperation among organizations, or, more generally, interorganizational relations." This is, of course, a modern problem of biology as well, where organization also takes hierarchical form. In addition, it is an aspect of general systems theory and what Herbert Simon (1973) has recently called an intersystems interlocking "cross-coupling" of hierarchies.

Whyte feels that, while organization and hierarchy and the cross-coupling of organizations are fields of rapidly growing inquiry, we have as yet no theoretical framework adequate to deal with the phenomena. I hope here to suggest some aspects of more adequate theory and I am glad to see that Whyte himself, along with Leonard Sayles, Chapple and Coon, Kimball and I, and still other anthropologists, applied or not, have provided pieces of that theory. Indeed, applied anthropology of earlier years now provides specific pieces of theory directly applicable to the problem. One of these pieces is worth reviewing here. It is a behavioral, social-interactional, sequential-process model of leadership or "decision making" in large-scale hierarchies.

Leadership and "Decision-Making" Theory

There are excellent summaries of current inquiry into decision making from social psychology, political science, and writings on administration. Their only omission is that class of studies of ongoing organization and the leadership and decision making within organizations made by observational methods. They completely omit studies made by field work and natural history ("ethological") methods. These studies come into social science from social and cultural anthropology, where leadership is treated from the point of view of leaders as diverse as shamans, chiefs, sheikhs, and prophets, and from applied anthropology (and small group sociology) which seeks out natural and informal leaders, culture-brokers, and community influentials.

The nonanthropological studies of leadership, organization, and administration provide formal deductive models, schemata and tables of organization, generalizing observations, historical summaries and biographies, and even some laboratory experiments. They treat decisions as part of organizational behavior in a general and often static way. The natural place of decisions in the flow of organizational events in which they are only one kind of action is not precisely explored. Excellent as they are for their purpose, these studies abstract the matter of decision processes out of context. The "process" is studied for itself, but not for its relations or functions within the overall context of organizational activity.

Suggestions for a different look at decisioning are to be found where naturalistic and participant-observational studies have been made. These can be found in the tradition of the field worker in anthropology or the applied anthropologist who comes into a factory, project, or tribe with no prior knowledge of what is going on or what he or she shall find. Anthropologists in these situations treat organizational and institutional behavior whole, making comparisons not only from people to people but from organization to organization—for example, from business, to church, to army, or to Algonquin village. They follow, as best they can, the canons of depicting a culture as an integrated whole system of observed behaviors and of placing that culture in the spectral range of the crosscultural variation of all mankind, and of placing a culture's subsystems in a spectral, comparative range.

The anthropologist thus places the acts of decision-making leaders—whether chiefs or high priests or generals or businessmen—in the full context of the other behaviors and activities of the persons they decide for and among. Hence, naturalistic studies of ongoing situations treat decision making as one regular kind of action which is less an art or a skill than a necessary and regular role which most persons—once their awe of the responsibility and honor which surrounds decisioning is overcome—could well be taught to fill. It is a natural role, and has become a regular part of organizational life. As such, it is to be understood as a data processing and data checking function where education and science may, indeed must, be part of the individual decision maker's equipment. But leadership is also, and importantly, a regular procedure of social action which is related to the other kinds of action which make up organization. And like them, it is capable of being ultimately reduced to technique.

It is possible to remove the mystery from decision making: by treating it as one kind of action among many in a human social system; and by following it as a sequence of interpersonal actions having a natural place among like sequences of actions carried out by other personnel. This approach requires that organizations be viewed as a field of persons among whom the actions of the events in the life of the organization or social system flow in several directions or lines of persons (and their offices) which can be observationally recorded and statistically compared. By doing so, it is possible to establish a naturalistic matrix of contacts and relationships among the personnel and to define and separate activities of every organizational function, leadership included, in terms of the involvement with and initiatives upon other personnel. Functions can be stated not so much in terms of what is done as in terms of with whom and at what rate of interpersonal contacts such functions are done. Decision making, like the other activities in this interpersonal mapping of the human events of organization, becomes an activity clearly defined in context and quantifiable in the relative directions and frequencies of contacts in which it occurs. It is comparable and contrastable with the other activities of the human system.

By quantifying them in context, decisions can be related to various occurrences of human relations and company activity within an organization, as well as to the balance sheet of sales and purchases outside it. When we perfect techniques for reducing the events of action within organization to a ledger of flows and pressures of action and interaction among the personnel, the possibility arises that the rightness or wrongness of one or several decisions can eventually be checked against the human track record of timely interactions performed or necessary actions missed, as well as the record of dollars and cents.

Treating decisions in context, as they are made in the ongoing flow of human action and interaction making up the life of a group, company, or other institution, means that they must be viewed not merely as judgments of persons, however bold or skilled, but also as events which have a necessary fit, in time occurrence, within a matrix of other events. Looked at as an element of a pattern of action, even the most abstract model of decision making takes on new dimensions. The model one must use is no longer limited to the decisions themselves or to the data-gathering, shifting, and testing processes which the decider himself goes through. Necessary as these processes are, decisions are also events in a field of interpersonal action within an ongoing organization. Their field and their place in it take abstract minimal form as Diagram 1 shows:

Diagram 1 Simple Decisioning: Pair and Set Events

(The structure of action)

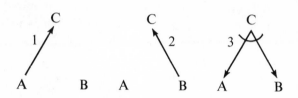

Lineal decisioning in
unit organization

In minimal definitional terms of social action, a decision arises when three events occur in order over time and involve a unit organization of three persons in a set of relationships uniting them all. The relationships entail all three persons acting upon one another within a field of common experience and concern and within limits of custom, consent, and right, though not necessarily for a common goal. The sequence is as follows:

Act 1. A pair event in which A informs, etc., C, who delays response and does not immediately intiate new action.
Act 2. A pair event in which B informs, etc., C, who delays as above.
Act 3. A set event in which C responds or acts, having collated information, etc. C originates a new action in which B and A respond alike, together or in coordination or unison. (The ligature of the arrows from C to A and B indicates this "set event" of joint response.)

A system of leadership of decision making arises in minimal terms when a repetitive sequence of some frequency (at least greater than events of alternate form and sequence) arises in which decisioning repeats itself among the same personnel, in the same order of their interpersonal action upon one another, with the same alternation of pair events and set events (dyadic and triadic relationships). The comparative regularity establishes roles: leadership in C, follower-ships in A and B (Diagram 2).

Diagram 2

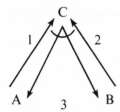 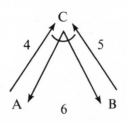 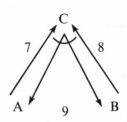

We thus have three decisions in nine consecutive interpersonal acts (interactions) and a system of action; a unit organization with decision making attributes and leadership/followership roles has emerged. A, B, and C now cooperate, but in a structured way reflect-ing decision making or leadership. Each act, relationship, role, and decision has measurable, comparable, predictable relative frequencies of occurrence, operational definition, and interdependent qualifica-tion.

Organizational decisioning in organizations having line organi-zation, hierarchical, and pyramidal form merely combines through levels and linked units such acts and events of decisioning into fur-ther concatenated sequences and orders of progression. It thus es-tablishes—again in operational defintion—lines or flows of action in interpersonal and intergroup relationships through the entire organiza-tional population (Diagram 3).

Diagram 3 Complex or Organizational Decisioning: Flows of Action

(The structure of organizational action and decision)

Hierarchical decision-making in linked units, making up pyramidal or hierarchical organization

Units: triangles

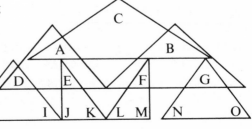

For example, CAD H is such a flow of action, of common direction, in direction and levels of progression comparable to CBG O. Both are operationally definable "line authority," as chains of pair events, comparable again to set events A/HIJK or C/DEFG in direction but not in level, definable likewise as "line action." Similar operational defintions, which are measurable, quantifiable, and comparable, can express all and any other parts or elements of organization and the decisions taken within it.

Each combined sequence has its own frequency of the occurrence of events flowing down it ("commands") or up it ("reports"). One can matrix these, of course, or otherwise summarize them as rates (acts per time periods), and so on. A model of hierarchical decisioning as a down-flow among other sequences of action can be sketched as in Digram 4.

In other words, decision making, is one flow of action among many in an ongoing organization. We are treating here only internal decisions—those that involve authority or "down-the-line action." Other decisions involve adjustment of the whole to the outside, for example, in interaction of the personnel at various levels with customers, the community, the state, suppliers, competitors, and so on. But internal processes can be treated apart from external interactions and relations and relationship. The internal decisions, such as have been modeled here, are not only judgments about such things as data, actions, and resources. Naturalistically seen as behavior in context, they are also steps or acts, where the actor-decider does the next thing required in the drama of continuing the balance of organizational relationships comprised of the interactions of the personnel of organization in their many flows.

When Barnard (1938:194) tells us, as we are told here again, that the decision-making art lies in "not deciding questions that are not now pertinent, in not deciding prematurely, in not making decisions that cannot be made effective [which the next fellow won't act out], and in not making decisions that others should make," he is telling us what the above diagrams tell us: There is an elaborate, necessary, closely timed minuet—a stately dance of many coordinate persons, of exquisite choreography, of figures now individual and now in unison. This choreography is what we lamely call "organization." This choreography, this rhythm may be under the baton of the

Diagram 4 Decisioning as Down-Flow among Other Sequences of Action

Hierarchical decisioning in
the matrix of organization
relationships as flows of
actions among all personnel
in the various directions of
most frequent occurrence

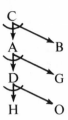

Note the flows: 1. C A D H etc. "down the line."

2. H   O "the flow of work."

3. O   H "against or out of the
flow of work," i.e.,
Informal Organization.

4. H D A C "up the line" (reporting)
"in channels."

5. O G B $\begin{smallmatrix}C\\A\end{smallmatrix}$ either

     a. staff-line ("advice").

     b. grievance, etc. "out
of channels, up."

Decisions: Note that only the barred arrow events, the down-the-line
flow, are treated as decisions.

All these flows: down-the-line (authority, decisions), the flow of work,
up-the-line reporting, informal organization, staff-line action, and
grievance channel, have their rates of occurrence. Any full picture of
decisions and their effects must set them in the ongoing streams of
these flows.

"manager," C, our top decider and our captain, but he can only lead
or, failing to lead, rearrange again.

Good decisions, then, are not only those which show the right
science of materials, the market, the economic cycle, or other skills
that have nothing to do with management or organization *per se*.
Rather, they are those that act out the right steps and lead the right

rhythm in organization itself, based on a sure knowledge of what organization is and what makes people work in it. We are only now just beginning to incorporate this knowledge of organization, men, and their orchestration into the social and psychological sciences of today. The experience of applied anthropology will continue to feed back into the mastery of this knowledge.

3

MULTICULTURALISM AS THE NORMAL
HUMAN EXPERIENCE

Ward H. Goodenough

Understanding of the structure of action between individuals requires analysis of the ongoing behavior of the actors themselves rather than the aggregate categories of statistical data. This theme, already discussed by Arensberg, is further elaborated by Ward H. Goodenough. The elaborate patterns of initiation and response highlighted by Arensberg are here approached from the standpoint of patterns of cognition and individual perception. These cognitive "microcultures" attach ideas of what is good, proper, satisfying, and the like, to patterns of interaction. They constitute varied expectations among the people of complex societies.

The differential social power which is characteristic of asymmetrical relationships has the effect of legitimizing or denying the validity of cognitive perceptions. Powerful and powerless alike display contrasting microcultures which act as barriers to communication insofar as they are exclusive or singular in nature. Multiculturalism is the normal experience of most individuals in the world today, for they are perforce drawn into the microcultures of administrators, physicians, teachers, and others who have power over them. Skill in multicultural situations is thus a basic requirement of life in modern societies, especially for the powerless.

Ward H. Goodenough (Ph.D., Yale) is professor of anthropology at the University of Pennsylvania. His fieldwork has been in Micronesia and Melanesia, with a primary focus on the theory of culture change and linguistics. Dr. Goodenough has been especially interested in community development. He was president of the Society for Applied Anthropology from 1963 to 1964.

This essay was presented in substantially its present form as a paper at the seventy-fourth Annual Meeting of the American Anthropological Association in the symposium entitled "Toward a Definition of Multiculturalism in Education." Subsequently, the paper presented there has been published in the CAE Quarterly 7(4):4–6.

An important question raised by Goodenough is whether the narrowly trained and highly specialized professional has sufficient normal life experiences to permit the development of interactional skills in multicultural situations. To the extent that enforced isolation and administrative layers separate professionals from each other and from those they serve, the work of the applied anthropologist can be extremely important in the "naturalization" processes of new behaviors described by Arensberg.

THE VIEW OF culture and the individual which I present here is one I have arrived at in the context of thinking about the contributions anthropology can make to programs for social and cultural change (Goodenough 1963). A major problem in the course of all such programs is the emotional investment of individual persons in preserving or changing existing customs and institutions. Why is the same individual distressed at one kind of change and unconcerned about another? Why do individuals in the same community differ so markedly in their feelings about the same situations? Why do some segments of a population, for example, express little interest in having their children learn to read and write, while other segments are distressed that their children are not learning to read and write better? Applied anthropology's recognition of the crucial importance of wants and felt needs—of the role of motivation—in social and cultural process inevitably forces theory to come to terms with how individual, purposeful, human beings relate to that process.

Anthropologists traditionally have acted on the assumption that most societies are not multicultural, that for each society there is one culture. They have seen multicultural societies as developing only in the wake of urbanism, economic specialization, social stratification, and conquest states.

The view of culture as characterizing societies or subsocieties as wholes is appropriate to problems that involve comparing societies as organized human systems or that call for the classification of societies according to one or another taxonomic scheme. For these purposes, minor cultural differences from household to household, such as reported for the Navajo by Roberts (1951), or even from village to village, can often be conveniently ignored. But such a macroview of culture, if I may call it that, is inappropriate for the theory of culture, for any theory of something necessarily considers the processes of which that something is a product and that account for the way it changes over time. If, by culture, we have reference to the understandings about things and the expectations of one another that the members of a society seem to share, then a theory of culture requires us to consider the processes by which the individual members arrive at such sharing. In this regard, the differences among individuals, their misunderstandings, the different ways of doing things from family to family and village to village, all become noteworthy.

When we look at process, then, we no longer look at societies only as wholes but at individual people as learners of culture in the context of social interaction, as they pursue their various interests and try to deal with their various problems of living—problems that involve the necessity of choosing among conflicting goals, competing wants, and long-range as against short-range concerns. From the standpoint of process, multiculturalism is no longer a feature of complex societies alone; it is to be found in simple societies as well. To say this is not to gainsay that multiculturalism plays an increasingly prominent role in the affairs of complex societies, but that the difference between complex and simple societies in this regard is one of degree and not of kind.

Anthropologists have always properly insisted that culture is learned. From the learner's point of view, the problem is to learn what the expectations are in terms of which others act. The understanding arrived at regarding the expectations of one's parents is applied to other adults. In the absence of feedback to the contrary, one assumes that these others have the same expectations as one's parents. Thus, one comes to attribute concepts, beliefs, and principles of action uniformly to a set of other people, finding that for one's own practical purposes one can successfully do so. What is thus attributed to that set of others becomes the culture of that set. I use the word "culture" advisedly here, for in anthropological practice the culture of any society is made up of the concepts, beliefs, and principles of action and organization that an ethnographer has found could be attributed successfully to the members of that society in the context of his dealings with them.

From this point of view, the sharing of culture by the members of a group is a matter of attribution. The apparent validity of this attribution is measured by its practical utility for dealing effectively with members of the group in situations in which one deals with them. The process is that of stereotyping. The very limited purposes and situations in which a plantation manager in the Solomon Islands interacts with his Melanesian workers may result in very crude stereotyping of them by him and of him by them, stereotyping that serves its very limited purposes but is found entirely wanting when the bases for interaction are expanded. There is a difference between this kind of limited stereotyping and the kind that occurs in ethnography. Good ethnography requires us to test the adequacy of our stereotypes within the full range of contexts in which the people to whom we attribute them deal with one another. By direct participation, if we can, and by various forms of vicarious participation, we test our stereotypes, in the same way the society's members individually test the adequacy of their own individual stereotypes of their fellow members.

What does all this have to do with multiculturalism? In the learning process, people inevitably find that they cannot generalize the same expectations to everyone. Children learn that the expectations of their parents and other adults are not the same in many respects as the expectations of their playmates. They find that the expectations of their mother and father's sister are different, and so on. There are different role-expectations that go with different social relationships and different social situations. Each of these different expectations constitutes a different culture to be learned. Because such cultures are situation-bound and thus ordered with respect to other situation-bound cultures, we may choose to think of them as subcultures or microcultures, reserving the term "culture" for the larger, ordered system of which these are a part; in this sense, culture ceases to refer to a generic phenomenon of study and refers instead only to some level of organization of that phenomenon. From a theoretical viewpoint, the process of learning a society's culture or macroculture, as I would rather call it, is one of learning a number of different or partially different microcultures and their subcultural variants and how to discern the situations in which they are appropriate and the kinds of others to whom to attribute them.

All human beings, then, live in what for them is a multicultural world in which they are aware of different sets of others to whom different cultural attributions must be made, and of different contexts in which the different cultures of which they are aware are expected to be operative. Their competence in any one of these is indicated by their ability to interact effectively in its terms with others who are acknowledged as already competent. Everyone develops varying degrees of multicultural competence in relation to at least some microcultures. Moreover, intersocietal contacts make at least some people minimally competent in some aspects of different macrocultures. The range of cultural diversity increases in complex societies, where multicultural competence at the macrocultural as well as the microcultural level may play an important role in the conduct of affairs and in differential access to privilege and power. I shall come back to this in a moment.

Before I do, I wish to summarize what I have been implying in the foregoing discussion of culture by observing that it is analytically and conceptually useful to distinguish among the following: (1) culture as a phenomenon, arising out of learning in the context of interaction, the expectations people attribute to others; in this regard akin to G. H. Mead's (1934:152–163) concept of the "generalized other"; (2) the specific micro- or macrocultures individuals attribute to specific sets of others as the ones that are appropriately operative in social situations; (3) the range of variance in what the individual members of an interaction network or group attribute to the membership of the network or group as the group's culture; (4) the number of such interaction networks and groups in a social unit under consideration, the degree to which they overlap in membership or come together in larger networks or groups, and the subject matter with respect to which they function as networks or groups; and (5) the total range of knowledge of, and competence in, various microcultures and macrocultures that is possessed by the members of a given social unit, whether or not they are appropriately operative in interactions within that unit, and that compose what can be called the "cultural pool" or "reservoir" of the membership of that unit (Goodenough 1971:41–44).

Several of those considerations are of obvious interest for the study of process and change. What, for example, are the specific processes by which the variance in cultural attributions individuals make to their networks or group (3) is kept within workable bounds? Whatever these processes are, they clearly have to do with the rates and kinds of interaction that take place among members of the network or group. Of interest, too, are the processes by which elements in a group's cultural pool (5) achieve or lose status as part of a specific microculture that is expected to be operative in some context (2). Also of interest are the processes that increase or reduce the number of networks or groups within a society (4) and that affect the extent of overlap in their memberships. All of these processes involve people pursuing their various and competing interests, a consideration that brings us back to privilege and power.

Real social power, as distinct from jural authority, is a function of two variables. One is the extent and intensity of people's wants, and the other is the extent to which people are in a position to facilitate or impede the gratification of one another's wants. If nothing matters to me, even whether I live or die or whether I am free of pain or not, then no one is in a position to affect my behavior, and no one has any social power in relation to me. If, on the other hand, others are unable to gratify any of their wants without my cooperation, then I have enormous power in relation to them. In no human society is real social power evenly distributed. The greater dependency of the young, the old, the sick, and the infirm on others for the gratification of their wants and the relative lack of dependency of others on them, guarantee unequal power relationships everywhere. Such inequalities are compounded by individual differences in knowledge and skills and in physical and personal attractiveness. The cultural definition of jural relationships and the different rights and duties that attach to different social identities in their dealings with one another inevitably reflect these inequalities in real power, and also reflect the kinds of trade-offs that people in their past dealings have been able to achieve as the basis for present cultural expectations.

Among the resources to which access is of paramount importance in power relationships are the various microcultures that make up a macrocultural system. Growth in the number of specialized skills and bodies of knowledge creates more power in the social system to be distributed and managed and increases the consequent possibilities for inequalities in power. The amount of power in a social field of relationsips, it appears, increases directly as the complexity of the field increases, and its management becomes a problem of increasing importance and difficulty for the people involved.

Even in the relatively uncomplicated societies of Melanesia and Micronesia, with which I am personally familiar, control of specialized forms of knowledge is perceived as a source of social power generally and of political power in particular. Validation of claims to land and political office rests on a public display of a kind of knowledge that only those in line of succession are given access to. For those not in line of succession to aspire to such knowledge is to presume to something they are not entitled to. I suspect that it was no accident that in 1964, in the little community of Romonum on Truk in Micronesia, all four of the government salaried positions under the American administration (medical assistant, local judge, and principal and teacher in the local school) were monopolized by the highest ranking men in the two chiefly lineages. Even more significant was the fact that only the children of chiefly rank had qualified for education beyond the elementary level, in accordance with an apparently impartially administered examination system. Access to the kinds of alien cultural knowledge and skills which the schools afforded seems to have been perceived in the same way as access to important forms of traditional knowledge, ie., as appropriate for persons of high social rank only, and inappropriate for those without such rank. I do not think that this was a matter of which people were necessarily conscious; rather, it resulted largely from what each individual felt somehow to be appropriate to his or her own sense of social self.[1]

If the management of social power involves, among other things, the manipulation of access to knowledge and skills, the obvious targets of such manipulation are the conditions necessary for acquiring knowledge and skills. These may be briefly summarized as: (1) mental and physical aptitudes needed to develop the indicated skills and to acquire the necessary level of comprehension; (2) a perception of self and self-goals that make developing the skills and acquiring the comprehension seem appropriate or desirable; (3) freedom from emotional blocks in relation to the skills and knowledge in question (partly related to 2 above); and (4) access to situations in which there is opportunity to rehearse the skills and work at getting the knowledge, as well as opportunity to acquire helpful feedback (guidance), until the desired proficiency is achieved.

In complex societies, the great number of micro- and even macrocultures they comprise are inevitably the subject matter of social and political manipulation. Access to the cultures and subcultures in

---

[1] In the twelve years since these observations were made, children of commoners have begun to succeed in school.

which competence must be demonstrated in order to establish eligibility for positions of privilege becomes a major matter to which social organization is geared and is at the same time a prime target for political maneuvering. The social rules that serve to control such access, usually multiple and mutually reinforcing, become a prime target for reform in times of change, with accompanying changes in personal aspirations. Today, we are witnessing this phenomenon in connection with the concerns with women's liberation and education for minorities.

The problems of multiculturalism, then, arise as aspects of the processes I have been discussing, as does human concern with them. Multiculturalism is present to some degree in every human society. Differential access to and knowledge of the various microcultures in macrocultural systems is a significant aspect of power relationships in all societies. As multiculturalism becomes more pronounced and elaborated and the field of power becomes greater with increasing social complexity, multiculturalism becomes an ever more important consideration in the management of power relationships. As such, it also becomes an increasingly serious problem in the politics, education, and other institutions which are the instruments by which people control access to more specialized microcultures and to the power and privilege they confer.

In conclusion, practical considerations both in social action and in social theory continually invite us to deal with our fellow humans as aggregates rather than as individuals. The practical necessity to do so helps account for the stereotyping process of which the important phenomenon we call culture is a consequence. But practical considerations should not lure us into the false expedient of forgetting to look for relevant individual and small group differences. Nor should we allow our ideals for our fellow human beings lead us to forget the stuff of which social power is made and to forget that in pursuing those ideals we are seeking to alter or reinforce existing distributions of power. The arena of education is no exception. The design and implementation of learning programs in a world in which multiculturalism is the natural condition requires that these considerations have our close attention.

4

THE ELUSIVE NATURE OF COOPERATION AND LEADERSHIP: DISCOVERING A PRIMITIVE PROCESS THAT REGULATES HUMAN BEHAVIOR

Frederick L. W. Richardson

Differential social power is characteristic of all societies, and conflict between superiors and subordinates has been documented throughout history. At the same time, human survival and productivity require cooperative relationships between superiors and subordinates. What are the processes whereby these adversary relationships are transformed into mutual collaboration?

Here Frederick L. W. Richardson summarizes several decades of applied anthropological research into this basic and critical question. From the work of applied anthropologists in industry, we have learned that interactional sequences of behavior between managers and workers are a key factor in productivity. The early discoveries of applied anthropologists about the nature of superior-subordinate relationships in factories and other institutions must be augmented in light of what we know about the significance of the cognitive patterns described by Goodenough. Richardson adds still another dimension to these behavioral subtleties based on the work of those who have discovered the importance of sensory and nonintellectual processes in interactional behavior among humans and other mammals.

Frederick L. W. Richardson (Ph.D., Harvard) is professor of business administration in the Colgate Darden Graduate School of Business Administration at the University of Virginia. Dr. Richardson has worked as research associate in the Harvard Business School, the Labor and Management Center of Yale University, and was professor of business administration at the University of Pittsburgh. He has been a consultant in the area of organizational improvement and human problems in organization for American business corporations, the United States Department of Agriculture, and the Massachusetts General Hospital. He has written extensively about human organization in industrial and other work settings. He was one of the founders of the Society for Applied Anthropology and served as president from 1952 to 1953.

In contemporary, complex societies, specialization usually results in people who are either intellectually intelligent or behaviorally intelligent. Successful leadership today, however, requires a comprehensive intelligence which encompasses both dimensions of organizational life. Thus, Richardson echoes Goodenough in calling for novel learning experiences so that leaders and others may become better able to respond to the interactional patterns of the diverse groups and individuals in contemporary competitive hierarchical structures.

THIS ESSAY PRESENTS the results of several decades of trial and error in the systematic study of work organizations to comprehend how to help members transform adversary or rebellious actions into productive collaboration. The work began in the mid-1920s, and by the late 1920s several anthropologists and psychologists had been recruited for pioneer, long-term projects to develop a new profession concerned with worker problems and later focusing on administration and leadership, especially that of business management. Up until that time, the problem of how to run an organization to ensure the cooperation of members had consistently eluded intellectual comprehension.

These pioneer projects were financed for over a decade by grants to the Harvard Business School for research directed by Elton Mayo, one of the earliest psychologists working in industry. Mayo collaborated closely with a number of anthropologists, especially with W. Lloyd Warner. The projects also served as a training ground for several professionals who later continued to make important contributions to the field.

During this pioneering period, two different but complementary general strategies and methods were launched and developed. One was the individual interviewing of informants away from their jobs with a special emphasis on their personal concerns; the other was the observation and recording of what workers did while with their co-workers both on the job and occasionally in experimental situations.

The former was used and developed by psychologists, and the major results were reported by Mayo (1940 and 1945) and Roethlisberger and Dickson (1939). Observation, in contrast, was principally developed by anthropologists. In particular, W. Lloyd Warner promoted the generalized method of participant observation (Roethlisberger and Dickson 1939:389), and Eliot D. Chapple introduced and developed a method of precise quantitative recording. In turn, Chapple and Arensberg (1940) emphasized that the social and psychobiological study of man must be based not on verbal symbols of what persons say they do or feel, but rather on visible and audible behavioral data that can be unambiguously and clearly defined. Contrary to the conviction overwhelmingly prevalent at the time, these researchers believed that the painstaking and laborious effort such observations required would in the end provide the foundation for a science of human behavior that no analysis of the spoken word could obtain.

This essay focuses on major contributions to our understanding of transforming adversary into collaborative relationships resulting from primary reliance on observation, with special attention to the contributions made by four different observational strategies. These strategies represent different methods used to discover and evaluate the critical variables by which people induce one another to cooperate and, in particular, to identify the leadership traits responsible for doing so. The first strategy, participant observation, is the well-recognized and essential method that provides researchers with a general understanding and firsthand familiarity with situations. The second, more technical and focused strategy of identifying and quantifying critical variables, necessarily follows from the first. As will be presently described, this second strategy has made possible the identification of an interactional process that apparently induces participants to cooperate.

The third and fourth strategies, the historical and ethological, provide comparative evidence from human and animal societies that strongly corroborates the interactional discoveries revealed by the second strategy. In summary, the evidence to be presented below shows that cooperation—and the leadership skill that induces it—is primarily neither verbal nor intellectual but rather a reciprocal process between and among interacting persons that involves, for example, the rhythmic interplay of actions and inactions and the decibel level and tone of vocal sounds.[1]

[1] See Guest (1962) for a particularly revealing and readable account, clearly differentiating skilled from inferior management.

Strategy 1: Participant Observation

In industrial settings, participant observation is the application of the same approach used by more traditional anthropologists. Extreme care must be taken to become as unobtrusive as possible in order to minimally disturb the normal activities of the subjects as they go about their daily affairs. The method requires being present, wherever one is allowed, when the subjects are engaging in their daily routines, and the observation and recording of what takes place. One must be prepared to act intuitively by paying particular attention to unusual or problem situations. As a field technique, participant observation holds an important place among other methodological strategies, for it provides an absolutely essential means of acquiring firsthand familiarity with situations that are othewise puzzling when more restrictive methods are used.

In industrial situations, some major discoveries resulting from participant observation, or combinations of interview and observation, have included: the importance of informal relationships as they influence cooperation for or against management (Roethlisberger and Dickson 1939); determining the dependence of sentiments on behavior (Richardson 1961); and recognizing job boredom and technological factors that strongly influence relationships (Walker 1962; Woodward 1965; Richardson and Walker 1948). In addition, participant observers have repeatedly described feuding and adversary activities, a subject which will be elaborated on below.

The Western Electric and Harvard Studies focused professional attention on the human problems of business and industry during a period when national attention was focused on these and related problems due to the depression of the 1930s. It was a period of great worker-management unrest, with government intervention providing unions with considerable legitimate power and, hence, a period of intensive labor organizing. During this time, intellectuals and sympathizers, personally unfamiliar with labor–management problems, began to penetrate industrial sanctuaries and to associate with and listen to the plights of working-class people.

To gain firsthand familiarity with worker–management relationships, whether unionized or not, required either the introduction of scholarly spies as workers into management's controlled territory, or the winning of approval from both labor and management protagonists to allow free access for and cooperation with an observer/interviewer. This latter step was difficult to achieve. Labor–management controversy was high, and considerable skills and tact were required to maintain objective neutrality and to be constantly alert against "playing favorites" by associating more with the members of one group rather than with another. Consequently, only a few dozen scholarly observers succeeded during the 1930s and 1940s (and rarely in serious conflict situations) in gaining acceptance and remaining for long periods of time within company-controlled buildings and territory. Several who did succeed, however, were anthropologists or those working closely with them. They included Burleigh Gardner, William F. Whyte, Melville Dalton, Conrad Arensberg, and myself.

Although these observer/interviewers gathered information in many work places not actually in open conflict, subtle kinds of suppressed hostility were evident everywhere. There was chronic feuding between company men struggling to get workers to increase their output, while at the same time workers were cleverly and covertly resisting these maneuvers (Whyte 1955). Management's principle weapon was to establish a minimum level of output, reward those who met or exceeded it, and punish those who failed. During this continual feuding, on the one hand to raise and on the other hand to withhold production, skirmishes between labor and company men were daily affairs, as were their partisan discussions of feuding and counterploys. When any union member's partisanship weakened, he or she was soon set upon to be forcibly reconverted by fellow workers. Supervisory and company men had similar experiences if the dominant "hard-line" members of management felt the former were "soft" on workers.

Unionized workers developed great skill in misleading company men, especially those establishing output standards. Through a system of warning signals, these workers slowed their pace whenever company men sallied forth with clipboard, pencil, paper, and stopwatch. More importantly, they rarely revealed to company men the shortcut methods they had devised to increase their daily output. Those who kept these treasured secrets to themselves were able to complete their daily quota of work in a fraction of the official time designated. Thereafter, if not too evident, they idled their time away by visiting and talking with their co-workers, organizing gambling pools, and disciplining rate-busters when necessary. Now and then, they occasionally even used remote corners of the shop for sleeping and clandestine rendezvous.

Simultaneously, in company offices, a superintendent might be bawling out a foreman for practicing the "soft" human relationship skills he had learned in an academic seminar. In a conference room, an aggressive, young, well-dressed, college-trained engineer, aspiring to high position, might be giving a pep talk to older and simply dressed working class foremen, demanding that they push for high production goals, assert their management prerogatives, and punish slackers, and finally finishing off with warnings against sabotage, troublemakers, and Communist infiltration.

Numerous studies revealed that however obvious hostility is to both parties during conflicts and feuds, many persons, particularly dominant ones, are often unaware of the frustration, annoyance, and anger they sometimes generate in others simply by their inadvertently obtuse or superior manner. Such a manner on the part of an organizational superior unconsciously provokes antiproductive responses among subordinates that are often far more automatic than conscious. Thus, supervisory relationships are closely related to the output of work groups.

When a superintendent or plant manager cockily strides about taking over in a curt and uncompromising manner, the response of his subordinate managers is usually to let him do so while they themselves withdraw from active supervision (Richardson 1961:69; 1965:17–19). Should the superintendent actively rebuff his subordinate managers as problems build up, he can further provoke them to angry rebellion. In contrast, there are supervisors who feel they must know every last detail, and in doing so they frustrate and annoy their subordinates through persistent quizzing and long-winded discussion. Even more destructive to cooperative endeavors are authoritative individuals who devote much time to fraternizing with some while ignoring others, and who busily walk around and glance about checking on those they distrust.

It is one thing to be deliberately hostile toward an enemy and even sometimes to be forceful, if not a bit hostile, toward intimates and companions to ensure an even sharing of privilege and chores. But why do organizational superiors so often unconsciously annoy and alienate their subordinates and thereby diminish their productivity? A second observational strategy, to be elaborated upon below has made possible the discovery of numerous behavioral subtleties by which interacting persons often unknowingly please or alienate each other.

Strategy 2: Identifying and Quantifying Critical Variables

As previously mentioned, the two anthropologists, Chapple and Arensberg (1940), set themselves the task of precisely defining what they determined would be critical behavioral units to observe, record, and quantify.

By the late 1930s, they had identified and defined two distinct classes of units. One was rather simple, namely, a *contact* or the period during which two or more persons first interacted, beginning when they greeted or acknowledged each other, and ending when they parted, ceased to interact, or were joined by one or more others. The other is a more elemental and complex unit that makes it possible to describe within seconds and fractions of a second the timing of the sounds and the motions by which, for example, conversants attract each other's attention and indicate that they respond. As the tempo of interchange is often rapid with nods, eye glances, and "hums" following in rapid succession, many subtleties are often missed by simple pencil and paper recording. To attain the necessary split-second accuracy requires special recording equipment. In addition, a specialized computer technology is required to analyze the deluge of quantified data.

These two methods of counting and timing—one simple and rough, the other complex and detailed—have yielded important quantified results clearly identifying leadership traits which an analysis of language has never revealed.

Interaction and Productivity
Considering first the simple pencil and paper method of recording and quantifying contact units only, one of the important advances has been a further simplification that made it possible to predict the work performance of groups by recording only the supervisor's contacts which lasted one minute or longer. The usefulness of this simplified

method was demonstrated in the early 1960s after I conducted a systematic study of nearly thirty design engineering sections in a large electronic laboratory (Richardson 1965; Richardson and White 1965). For a two- to four-week period, managers recorded all their contacts at work which were one minute or longer in duration. The findings provided a means for clearly differentiating high from mediocre and poorly performing groups.It was discovered, for example, that the managers of the high-production sections practiced what might be called *contact moderation*. This term is best defined as the balance between the extremes of interaction, between too much and too little, between contacts too numerous and too few, or too long and too short in duration. This ''golden mean'' would characteristically vary from situation to situation. The managers studied tended to devote not less than one-half nor more than three-quarters of their time to contacts with others. They also distributed their time among subordinates without favoring some and ignoring others. Moreover, the average length of their contacts was neither long-winded nor curt; the number per day was not less than fifteen nor more than thirty; and they did not resort to excessive proportions of group versus pair discussion. A rank ordering of the sections by the quality and quantity of work completed within allotted time periods was compared with a ranking of section managers according to the degree to which they conformed to the above mentioned interactional moderation or golden mean; there was more than a 90 percent correspondence.

By using a special electronic device and computer called an interaction chronograph, elemental interactional units within a contact were counted and timed accurately to fractions of a second (Chapple 1949). Using this equipment, Chapple and his associates were able to specify personality traits far too subtle to be revealed through interview data. To reach such conclusions with minimum recordings, Chapple (1953b) devised an experimental stress interview by subjecting his subjects on the one hand to a standardized manner of interrupting and on the other to the contrary stress of a uniform bland manner of nonresponsiveness.

The systematic use of this quantitative and experimental method soon yielded all kinds of unsuspected results. It became possible, for example, to establish that different interactional tempos are associated with different kinds of selling, such as retailing inexpensive and familiar items in contrast to the bulk selling of more expensive ones (Chapple and Donald 1947; Norman 1954; Chapple 1970:278–281, 284–285). It was also possible to detail the different tempos required for example, a patter of interjections of shorter duration for the first than the second, and the degree to which a salesperson should attempt to take over or keep silent and let the customer contemplate and ask questions.

In a similar fashion, Chapple (Chapple 1970:282–283; Chapple and Donald 1946) has compared low and high level supervisors and managers. He found that those in supervisory positions tend to have a higher activity rate (e.g., more talkative than silent), greater dominance (i.e., holding the floor despite interruptions), and greater interactional flexibility (more adaptive in varying the length of their talking and listening depending on such things as the idiosyncracies of other persons or on the situation). Additionally, it was determined that higher-level persons are less temperamental or "flappable." They do not react emotionally to a series of persistent stress-provoking interruptions or prolonged silences introduced by the interviewer. In contrast to their subordinates, they over- or underreact less to excessive talking or silence by more persistently maintaining their normal rhythm despite the stress introduced by others.

Interaction and Verbal Discussion

Supervisors or salespersons are judged not only on their ability to influence the productivity and purchasing of things but on their skill in verbal discussion. On the one hand, they must have skill to take over, control, and persuade, and on the other they must be able to learn from others and encourage them to inform, critique, and suggest. Interactional recordings provide a surprisingly useful, simple, and revealing method of judging these skills.

To make this possible, a simple paper and pencil recording method of intermediate exactitiude between the two mentioned above was devised to count and time to five-second accuracy all utterances or "talks" during a conversation or meeting. This method proved useful for evaluating a community resettlement program with the purpose of developing leadership and initiative among the so-called homesteaders (Richardson 1941:47–51). It provided, for example, one concrete piece of contrary evidence. Based on a systematic recording of seven management-homesteader meetings during a nine-month period, the few members of management consistently appropriated about 30 percent of the talks, while no single or small group of homesteaders increased their talking percentage.

To improve an understanding of committee skills and chairmen, and those of a moderator-chairman in particular, I organized a series of five-person, twenty minute, experimental committee meetings using students as subjects. A study of about twenty such committees (Richardson et al. 1972) revealed major interactional distinctions between good, poor, and mediocre committees, as judged by the number of ideas generated or the development of a practical plan. In the poorest committees, for example, considerable time, 50 percent or more than in the other committees, was consumed by monologues of one minute or longer, or "duologues" (the same two persons monopolizing at least two consecutive minutes). The poor committees were not mediated by active chairmen skillfully using their initiative and prerogative to encourage the reticent and to silence the garrulous.

In addition to committee discussion, leadership skills are critically important in two-person dialogues. A study was conducted of an able surgeon in a teaching hospital who revealed a number of interactional traits that he regularly practiced (Richardson 1966: 166–171). One was his control of conversations by continuing to talk despite interruption. However, with appropriate persons and times, this assertiveness was balanced by a parallel ability to listen more than he talked. He also displayed considerable skill in what might be called composing a conversation from beginning to end with a well-structured internal sequence. When reassuring patients, for example, he commonly talked twice as much as he listened at the beginning and end, but in the midst of the discussion, he reversed the proportion. When advising and persuading on one occasion, his pattern was more or less the reverse: when seeking information, his percentage of talking time progressively lessened from the beginning to almost the end.

Close familiarity with dozens of leaders and hundreds of their followers has revealed that in contrast to the poorer leaders having too much or too little contact, the better leaders won over their followers through a more moderate pattern of contacts. The more highly placed and successful leaders exhibited numerous interactional subtleties, such as greater flexibility in adapting their conversational tempo to others, and in controlling discussion by skillfully timing and directing their interruptions at appropriate persons.

Strategy 3: An Historical Approach to Superior–Subordinate Disassociation and Involvement

Firsthand familiarity with a number of work organizations repeatedly revealed that poor performance, conflict, and troublesome superior-subordinate relationships were often associated with leaders who had, for example, little or at best erratic contact with their subordinates (Richardson 1961: chapter 15; Richardson and Walker 1948: chapters 2 and 3) or a similar degree of contact neglect between members from two different but closely interdependent groups such as test and production (Sayles 1964: chapter 8). To check this general observation which had been reinforced by considerable quantitative evidence, I undertook a survey of the literature of past and present organizations—particularly large states and business organizations. This survey not only corroborated the above generalization, but also revealed several independently evolved institutional practices designed to promote a closer acquaintance between superior and subordinates. Some of these are briefly mentioned below.

Ancient Practices

It should first be emphasized that the long history of mankind amply documents superior–subordinate dissension, particularly in large states and class societies with minimal social mobility. Consider the struggles of peoples against enforced subservience, the striving of subordinates for more advantageous positions, and the violence which accompanies the rise and fall of rulers and dynasties, particularly in large states and empires. Those states that succeeded in converting strangers or enemies into working associates and cooperative subordinates gained competitive advantages over those less able to do so. Some of the practices which developed for this purpose have a long history.

One is trade, which, in contrast to military conquest and forced subjugation, provided a relatively peaceful means of meeting and penetrating into alien societies. A second is the development of an increasing number and kind of services and help that professionals supply to complete strangers or large numbers of persons they barely know. A third is joint consultation and negotiation among the leaders and representatives of constituent units to reach agreements essential for de-escalating a natural feuding and rivalry. With the emergence of large states, this latter practice required the shuttling back and forth by high level intermediaries between the capital and the provinces. Thus, in pre-nineteenth century Great Britain and Japan, the ruling provincial lords regularly alternated their residence between the capital center and their local territories in contrast to the metropolis-bound lords of Russia and France. In no small measure may the revolutions of the latter two nations be due to the nearly full-time metropolitan or palace involvement by their provincial elite and the growing estrangement from peasants, tenants, and serfs. As a comparable adaptation, large American industrial corporations, in recent decades, have reversed the practice of executives exclusively residing at the company center and occasionally commuting outward to confer with plant superintendents and low level supervisors at local factories. Instead, some of the executives have replaced the local superintendents as plant managers, and now usually reside near the branch plants and only occasionally do they visit the more distant home office.

In addition, there is a more recent means of forcing members of the elite to take greater cognizance of common people. This has increasingly come about, beginning with the Industrial Revolution, in response to the accelerating rate of discovery and invention by many persons of humble background who, in the recent past, have often been without much formal education. As a consequence, these inventive commoners were sought after, financed, and employed by persons of means, thus, in these instances, weakening interclass avoidance and status taboos. It should be noted, however, that while the Industrial Revolution may have forced a greater interaction between the elite and some commoners, it did not obliterate class distinctions or the actual wealth and power of the elite. On the contrary, the system frequently became more autocratic and the jobs of the workers even more rigidly proscribed.

The above practices provide means for unfamiliar persons to become better acquainted, and often lessen fears and uncertainties inherent in strangeness. By acquiring a familiarity, many not only came to accept one another, but also developed an actual liking or a cooperative and productive working relationship. With the progressive enlargement of business and other organizations during the past century, the difficulty of transforming superiors and subordinates, or rivals and strangers, into productive collaborators has continued to present a constant challenge and has given rise to numerous corrective programs. Let us now consider the practices that have developed in industrial settings in an attempt to overcome these difficulties.

Encouraging Interactional Involvement

Over the past five decades, there has been a succession of practices providing means by which the members of an organization may become better acquainted and devote more attention to one another, while at the same time possibly even improving their productive output. These practices include the famous Hawthorne experiments in the Western Electric Company, T (training) groups (Bradford et al. 1964), organizational development (Huse 1975), and the more recent emphasis on management by objectives (MBO) (Raia 1974). Often, the ostensible purpose may be directed toward a specific concern such as MBO, which focuses on objectives, or Sensitivity Training, which emphasizes self-awareness, but the implementation of all these programs necessarily results in the relevant persons becoming better acquainted. Similar in nature are a number of programs conceived to encourage subordinates to make specific suggestions for improving company performance and, if improved, to implement suitable innovations. Such examples include the much-copied Coordination-by-Committees practices by General Motors (Sloan 1964: chapter 7), the Multiple Management plan, or Junior Board of Directors (Craf 1958), first developed in the McCormick Spice Company, and the Scanlon Plan (Lesieur 1958), whereby workers actively participated in foreman and management discussions.

In addition to those programs focusing on some particular detail, there have been numerous generalized programs such as a series of changes in IBM's Endicott plant to bring about closer relationships between workers and foremen. There, foremen were urged to spend as much time as possible away from their desk, maintaining contact with and assisting rather than "bossing" their men as well as with all other plant personnel. To this end, foremen were provided with clerical assistants, and the number of workers reporting to each was greatly reduced (in one department from sixty-five to twenty-seven) despite a doubling in the size of the department (Richardson and Walker 1948:20–23).

Executive Courting

Some of these ancient and modern practices have involved more than a formal attempt to get better acquainted. Instead, the controlling executives require of their managers, administrators, or ruling lords, a major commitment to win subordinate loyalty. The IBM plan is a good case in point, as is the Multiple Management plan in which top executives court younger and lower-level managers, and the Scanlon plan in which managers, foremen, and workers regularly discuss production problems and where workers have a significant financial share in the enterprise. In some instances, company executives, in competition with labor leaders, have succeeded in winning over worker loyalty to such an extent that workers have no active desire to affiliate with labor unions.

Historically, taking the effort to court previous enemies and rivals is probably as ancient as civilization. A famous example is Alexander the Great, who took extraordinary means to win over the leaders of those he conquered, as did William the Conqueror to win over the English. George Washington demonstrated superior skill and tact in getting the colonial, and later the state, representatives to work together for a unified central government.

The expansion of organizations and their competitive survival requires that unfamiliar members acquire increasing understanding through closer acquaintance. It seems only natural, therefore, to infer a close connection, as did Homans (1950:110–117) between interaction, liking, and companionship. I would add cooperation also.

Strategy 4: An Ethological Approach: Comparative Human and Animal Behavior[2]

The truism that friends cooperate with each other more than with strangers and that the latter are often indifferent or hostile is apparently contradicted by the kindness that many exhibit to strangers, such as to the weak and the handicapped, or at the time of an accident or death. During dangerous situations, such as wars, fires, and

---

[2] See Richardson (1975) for fuller discussion of the material presented in this and the following section.

floods, persons sometimes even help rivals and enemies. On all such occasions, for those who proffer their help, there are others who harm, loot, and kill. The proposition is therefore presented that among friendly companions, cooperation is more automatically mutual or reciprocally programmed and, hence, less subject to chance or will. Among strangers, in contrast, cooperation and help depend more on conscious volition or on the personal needs, learned habits, and peculiarities of each individual.

That cooperation or reciprocal helping is far more reliable and usual among friendly companions than among strangers and enemies, slowly rose in my consciousness when I was repeatedly confronted by nearly identical intergroup difficulties. In one familiar work situation after another, I was forced to consider why problems and poor performance were commonplace among interdependent groups whose members were more or less segregated, who rarely intermingled, and who apparently often avoided each other.

Considerable experience in industrial firms, hospitals, and other organizations had led me to believe that conflict and cooperation were often attributable to imprecise causes. One of the examples that made this intuitive insight more precise was a carefully recorded situation which provided dramatic evidence concerning two rival and antagonistic cliques in a small department whose members remained exclusively segregated during the two daily ten-minute rest periods. One group, under the direction of management's designated leader, cooperated to withhold production, while the other group resented such behavior. A third group of workers within the same department formed a friendship group, as opposed to a clique, evidenced by the fact that during rest periods their members sometimes mixed with those of the two exclusive cliques and maintained satisfactory relations with members of each. Members had the greatest contact within their own closed clique where they were regularly friendly and exchanged favors with each other. They had a moderate degree of contact, greeting and conversing with members of the open friendship group, but with much less if any exchange of favors. Between rival clique members, contact was both hostile and limited.

The distinctions in intergroup contact were documented with considerable precision by quantitatively recording who was interacting with whom during rest periods. These data helped formulate an hypothesis that the greater the contact, the greater the exchange of favors; conversely, less contact is associated with less favoring and with greater potential for hostile exchange.

To test the hypothesis that gradations in contact and degrees of friendly to hostile exchange are closely related, a preliminary research was made of simple human societies, by perusing anthropological monographs. Three strongly supportive instances were found and no contradictory ones. However, most monographs neither contained the relevant information nor reported it in sufficient detail. Hence, this approach has not been further pursued. Strong corroboration, however, emerged unexpectedly from seemingly peripheral and unrelated evidence regarding other social mammals.

From numerous studies of bands of monkeys, apes, lions, wolves, prairie dogs, zebras, and others, it became evident that the close connection between gradations in contact and degrees of friendly to hostile exchange can be extended to apply widely to adult mammals living in child-rearing family groups (Richardson 1975:326–328). Commonly, if not universally, the adult members within a family group have considerable contact, are usually friendly together, and come to each other's assistance, whereas they are collectively indifferent or hostile toward nonmembers and strangers of their own species. Within a group or close community of members, the most regularly associating companions collaborate more closely for their mutual advantage than they do with other members (Van Lawick-Goodall 1971: note "friendship" and "alliances" in index; Eaton 1976). Morever, many of these families and genera of mammals emerged tens of millions of years ago and presumably evolved cooperative relationships automatically binding interacting individuals to one another long before the emergence of Man and his much enlarged outer brain.

Interactionally Pleasing
In contemplating this mutual assistance that characterizes cooperation, consider three other kinds of reciprocal behavior that companions commonly exhibit—and particularly human companions. One is imitation, each to a degree copying the other; and the second and third, both related to the first, are that companions are usually relaxed in each other's presence and, as judged by their facial expres-

sions, for example, they often indicate a mutual contentment, amusement, or pleasure. The proposition last mentioned is that the critical consideration is the contentment or pleasure they reciprocally induce in each other.

Consider the wealth of evidence that led to the so-called Learning Theory, and the recent applied programs in Behavior Modification, for which the critical consideration is that for both humans and other mammals a sensing of pleasure induced by a reward is an essential accompaniment to behavioral change. From this thesis it can be further assumed that to transform hostile subordinates into productive collaborators requires that such subordinates somehow derive pleasure therefrom. The more specific proposition is that the most successful leaders, in addition to material rewards, possess the interactional skill to induce more intangible ones.

It is recognized that effective leaders are often able to alter the moods of their subordinates in ways that spur them to greater effort. Sometimes the latter also derive greater satisfaction therefrom, which they in turn somehow reciprocally convey in ways their leaders also find pleasing. What are these intangible "rewards" that persons sense as mutually satisfying, and what are their inexplicit counterparts that alienate and annoy?

Touch, Warmth, Sound, and Distance

Four of the most basic means by which humans and all mammals induce emotion in one another are through touch, warmth, sound, and distance. In contrast to such hostile displays as striking, kicking, and biting, nonhuman mammals groom, nuzzle, and lick, while humans, for example, embrace and hold hands. When cold or chilled, individuals huddle, each warming the other.

Regarding sound, loud rasping noises frighten, displease, and agitate all humans and animals that hear them, while soft melodious tones generally calm and please. Moreover, as so clearly described by Hall (1966), the intervening distance that separates interacting individuals, whether human or animal, is critical in causing them to be agitated or at ease. To be too close or too distant are both commonly displeasing, whereas a satisfying distance lies somewhere in between. The specific distances involved vary from society to society, subgroup to subgroup, and from one kind of situation to another.

Rhythm

Less recognized than sound and distance as a means of inducing emotion between individuals is the importance of interactional rhythm. Consider first the daily or yearly periodicity of meeting, convening, and parting—the frequency and length of time that persons contact or avoid others. We all, for example, sense the annoyance or anger of those who are curt, who snub, or avoid, and that such behavior commonly induces displeasure in those toward whom it is directed. In contrast, a mix of short and long contacts, at an appropriate frequency, with initiative more evenly shared (referred to above as contact moderation) is usually indicative of cooperative persons and friendly companions. Not only do persons perform better work for those who achieve this contact moderation or golden mean (Richardson 1965:7, 11–14), but, judging by their facial expressions and manner, they also derive greater pleasure therefrom.

Consider next during a contact, the alternation of talking and silence or motions and nonmotions while, for example, two persons interact or converse. Such interchanges vary widely depending on the degree to which one individual yields to another, with both taking turns talking and listening, or whether both talk at once or remain simultaneously silent. Chapple (1970: 45–48, 73–76) has repeatedly pointed out that it is pleasurable for persons when the actions and sounds of one synchronously mesh with the inactions and silences of the other. The evidence for these claims becomes apparent once noted, yet, although most experienced persons may intuitively sense such interconnections, the human mind is apparently so constructed that such interactional, nonverbal insights do not reguarly rise to consciousness. As regards unpleasant sensations regularly induced by asynchronous conversing, Chapple (1970:76) writes:

Think how hard it is for a naturally "outgoing," "social," "friendly" person to try to keep from being exasperated by a stone-faced, unresponsive partner who appears to ignore each effort to strike up a conversation. Consider the bore who persists in telling you all the minutiae of his daily life until your every will to indicate attention by a smile or other signal becomes paralyzed to immobility.

In contrast to the above, the next time you see friends enjoying each other, observe them and note the scarcity and brevity of their interruptions and double silences. Kendon has apparently systematically established that synchronous interchange is far more frequent among close friends and compatible couples than among strangers interacting for the first time (Kendon 1963). Chapple and Lindemann (1941) have similarly demonstrated that with an interviewer, "normal" persons have a much higher frequency of synchronization than mental patients. These close interconnections between interaction and emotion are not merely limited to man but occur widely among animals and may even be universal for mammals. Thus, in fighting situations, two contestants simultaneously, and hence asynchronously, strike at each other, in contrast to the synchronously alternating give-and-take characteristics of courting, chasing, grooming, and many kinds of play.

Language, Humor, and Listening

In addition to the reciprocal impact that touch, warmth, sound, distance, and alternating rhythms of action–inaction have on emotions and feelings, humor is another and virtually unique human trait that instantaneously triggers changes in mood. Humor is distinctive in that it is tied closely to language whereas the nonverbal interactional traits are not. As Koestler (1967) has elaborated, incongruous contrasts provide the sparks that repeatedly ignite humor or laughter—not only incongruous behavior but also incongruity in verbal content. Hence, it is nearly always amusing to hear children seriously conversing in a grown-up manner, hilarious to listen to Charlie Chaplin scream and sputter while imitating Hitler, or Danny Kaye rapidly jabbering nonsense in imitation of foreigners talking.

Unlike sound, distance, body contact, and rhythm, all of which can reciprocally trigger among participants a wide gamut of negative to positive emotions—from anger to fear to fondness and love—most humor, by inducing pleasurable feelings, fosters the latter. In the form of ridicule, however, humor usually pleases some while belittling others, if not actually at times inducing hostile retaliation. However, humor usually fulfills a very special need to offset the innumerably annoying and sly ways humans use their much extolled languages and intelligence to gain personal advantage and discredit others without appearing to do so. Without humor to lighten their moods, the daily strain from unresponsive, overzealous, boring, and rude persons—not to mention their own failings—might be too great a burden for humans to bear.

In addition to humor, another means by which persons relieve emotional disturbance (although sometimes transferring it to others) is the practice of actively accusing and complaining to persons who obligingly and understandingly listen. In fact, a formal interviewing program, with professionals privately listening to workers' concerns and complaints, was for a long period of time once institutionalized in a large corporation (Dickson and Roethlisberger 1966).

When antagonistically relieving anger, frustration, or fear by destroying and harming, there is no place for humor or quiet attentive listening. Only for those who attain a degree of companionability does it become possible to listen and joke. Instead of intensifying belligerence, the various nonverbal, "intangible," peaceful means cited above interactionally serve to de-escalate conflict and have the potential to transform feuding into pleasing and productive collaboration.

The Evolution and Circumvention of Interactional Order

Cooperative Evolution

To continue surviving, the members of a species have been improving their cooperative strategies since the beginning of life by evolving increasingly complex practices that attract others of their own kind. Thus, countless eons ago, mating developed as a critical strategy for all but the simplest species; the feeding and care of the young became universal among mammals and birds perhaps 200 million years ago; and *lifelong* cooperation with group members, for example, excluding outsiders, evolved more recently among a small minority of mammals and birds. Such critical collaborative functions are too important to leave to chance, and hence means have evolved which strongly attract individuals to one another and induce in them a near automatic capability to perform the programmed collaboration required.

These functions of mating, rearing young, excluding outsiders, and the like are all similar in that individuals behaviorally attract one another in ways that induce in each a peaceful and apparently pleasurable internal sensation or mood as an essential prelude in the programming of the collaborative behavior. For the critical function of mating, as well as for social insects communally rearing their young, cooperation is usually more or less rigidly programmed through smell or biochemical emanations (pheromones), from one individual to numerous others or, as in social insects, from mouth to mouth interchange of an apparently communal fluid. In contrast, among mammals and birds, for the rearing of young and calming of adults, gentle touching and bodily warmth or tactile stimulation are widely characteristic. Among humans, in addition to the above, familiarity resulting from sufficient interaction, both visible and audible synchronous interchange, and contact moderation have apparently evolved to become the most common means by which adults mutually induce and maintain their companionship and collaboration.

In the evolution from amphibians to primitive lone-living mammals to man, there have been an increasing frequency and duration of interaction to the point that organizational leaders and managers, for example, devote from about one-half to nine-tenths of their working day interacting with others (Richardson 1965: 11; Burns 1954; Mintzburg 1973; Stewart 1967). Such interactional stimulation, and in particular pleasurable interchange, has reached the point that it has apparently become essential for human health and well-being. This has been repeatedly demonstrated by studies of neglected or lone-living versus gregarious persons.

One famous study demonstrated that infants, regularly fondled, handled, and played with, in addition to being dutifully fed, clothed, and cleaned, were much healthier than those who were given only formal health care (Spitz 1945, 1946). These latter infants were far more prone to illness, and some even died. It is well recognized, similarly, that following the death of one member of an old couple, the other often dies soon thereafter. Finally, suicide rates have frequently been closely associated with loneliness, as many studies of rooming house districts in large cities have shown in the recent past (Zorbaugh 1929; Sainsbury 1955) and studies of isolated young people are currently demonstrating. There is also the old revealing statistical study from France showing that suicide rates increased as family size declined (Halbwachs 1930).

Productive Cooperation

With regard to an increasing comprehension of human cooperation, particularly among superiors and subordinates, I suggest that the most significant discovery during the past few decades has been the identification of this unsuspected interactional-sensory and nonintellectual process. The following four-stage sequence is proposed as an approximate description:

First, moment-to-moment alternations of action-inaction and sound-silence sequences among interacting persons stimulate the lower brain which, second, triggers electrical signals that travel along the nerve network, rapidly permeating the entire body, and also hormonal secretions that move more slowly, activating usually a particular organ or a more restricted part of the body. This highly complex physiological process is internally sensed in ways that words imperfectly convey, but which can be impressionistically described as ranging between pleasure and displeasure or from high euphoria on one extreme to fear, anger, or violence on the other.

Third, in varying degrees, this internal physiological state in turn induces or inhibits work effort whereby "superiors" frequently stimulate their subordinates in ways the latter often find pleasing (although with some occasional fear and deference). Some such mix apparently tends to induce cooperative inclinations that often predispose members to work hard in contrast to a greater mix of displeasing ways that alienate and repel. This mix, in turn, predisposes members to withhold their productive effort, if not to engage in counterproductive or retaliatory exchanges that, fourth, determine the work output, productivity, or performance of an individual or group and, over time, their degree of well-being and health.

This alternating, interactional rhythm and pattern provide to participants a nonthinking automatic means of reciprocally regulating each other. As presented above, it is common among humans and other mammals that participants who induce in each other mutual feelings of pleasure become thereby automatically predisposed to cooperate. It was, in addition, proposed that for human beings the commonest behavioral means by which groups of individuals become mutually stimulated to cooperate include (1) familiarity or becoming acquainted through sufficient interaction, (2) synchronous interchange, and (3) contact moderation—in addition to some degree of deference and fear. It was further proposed that gradations of cooperation were more or less directly determined by the degree to which the interacting individuals pleasurably and reciprocally stimulated each other. Thus, for example, the less the acquaintance, synchrony, and moderation, the less pleasing to the participants, and the less their inclinations to cooperate.

The Interactional and Sensory Process of Reciprocal Control
Within a group or community of familiar individuals, relationships are not always peaceful, as members usually from time to time fight briefly, for example, over mates or simply who yields to whom. What, then, other than inhibitions from companionability, are the additional means by which members limit the intensity of such confrontations?

Among vertebrates, including humans, one common means is for the loser to defer, withdraw, or both, which usually more or less automatically causes the victor to desist (Lorenz 1966). When deferring, it is common also for the loser not only to avoid any appearance of threatening, by, for instance, lowering or cowering, but also by exposing a vulnerable part of the body as does a wolf by presenting his neck to the victor. Moreover, once having escalated a confrontation to a state of vicious hostility, two such rivals usually thereafter keep a safe distance (Lorenz 1966: 215).

In addition to these largely automatic reactions is the fact that rival members of the same species, age, and sex are usually closely matched in fighting ability and thus each is more or less equally capable of inflicting pain on the other. As a result, there exists within a group reciprocal means by which members interactionally limit their fighting in addition to the aforementioned interactional-sensory means of inducing greater or less cooperation.

This reciprocal, self-regulating, interactional-sensory process, moreover, is primarily controlled not by man's outer and newly developed thinking brain but by his inner and lower brain (Chapple 1970: 63–67), otherwise referred to as the old mammalian brain or limbic system which, when compared to that of apes and monkeys, has remained relatively unchanged (MacLean 1968). It is this ancient, inner, lower, and interactionally stimulated mammalian brain that primarily controls the emotions, as contrasted to man's newly developed outer brain or cerebral cortex that makes thinking, memory, and learning possible.

The fact that man's limbic system or old mammalian brain appears relatively unchanged, compared to that of apes and monkeys, strengthens the proposition that a similar self-regulating interactional process controls cooperation and hostility among human beings but obviously, because of the enormously developed outer, thinking brain, with less effectiveness than among other primates and mammals. It is proposed that the reason mankind's self-regulating process

functions less well is because the superior endowments that the
new outer brain makes possible—intelligence, technology, and
language—provide unique means for circumventing these automatically programed stimuli and controls (Richardson 1975:328–334).

In the first place, technology, when monopolized by a few, cir-
cumvents competitive equality or parity in power, especially when it
makes possible the killing or jailing of rivals, and hence eliminates
the confrontations by which members of approximately equal dominance reciprocally limit each other. Secondly, when dominant
members use their intelligence to subordinate more individuals than
they can ever know, the restraining influences of companionship are
also circumvented. Finally, as language makes possible indoctrination, conniving, and spying, and human memory prolongs hatreds,
superiors and subordinates often polarize into implacable feuding
classes and cliques, with the former refusing to desist and the latter
giving only the pretense of deference.

That interactional stimulation provides a means by which participants may reciprocally control cooperation and rivalry strongly
suggests that for humans, as well as for other family-dwelling mammals (and possibly birds also), this process results not from memory
and learning only but also from some inborn predisposition. To a
large extent, therefore, these cooperative, indifferent, and hostile
responses appear to be triggered by some inborn nonrational
process—some neuroglandular-sensory means more primeval and
programmed than thinking and learned.

Interacting and Talking While Simultaneously Feeling, Sensing, and Thinking[3]

Relationships among people, as they engage in discourse, can thus be
conceived as a highly complex behavioral-sensory and neuro-
physiological process. Communicatively, however, it can be conveniently conceived as a *dual* process: (1) interacting (the interplay of
actions or sounds vs. inactions and silences), and (2) talking (verbal
exchange). This duality is reinforced by the fact that not only humans
but all mammals (and to a degree, reptiles also) are controlled by two

---

[3] For a partially comparable presentation, see Johnson (1953).

vastly different but interdependent physiological or neuroglandular mental processes. One is intellectual and a late vertebrate development that makes possible the consideration of future actions in light of past experience. Among humans, this development is both intellectual and verbal. The other is a primordial, unthinking behavioral-sensory process concerned with immediate relationships with others. It is essential for health and well-being and a process upon which cooperation largely depends.

In our developed technological society, persons often tend to specialize in one or the other. Thus, thinking, scheming, and scholarly persons develop skill in the first-mentioned *intellectual-verbal* kind of intelligence, as evidenced by their IQ, articulating ability, or both; congenial, playful, polite, and considerate persons specialize in the second, or what might be called *behavioral* intelligence, as evidenced by their interactional manner. However, to be a successful leader of a competitive enterprise requires a *comprehensive* intelligence that specializes in neither but skillfully encompasses both. It is an unfortunate and worsening dilemma that, although leadership requires an all-inclusive, comprehensive intelligence—both behavioral and intellectual—our educational system focuses only on one.

5

DEVELOPING ANTHROPOLOGICAL KNOWLEDGE THROUGH APPLICATION

Jacquetta Hill-Burnett

The complexities of human organization and relationships in the institutions of contemporary societies require versatility not only on the part of managers and those they manage but also on the part of applied anthropologists. Jacquetta Hill-Burnett provides a perceptive glimpse into the theoretical and methodological versatility demanded of her as the director of a federally funded action research project which was designed to improve the intercultural educational processes of Puerto Rican youths in a midwestern urban school.

In this situation, the use of anthropological paradigms and knowledge continuously entailed the reformulation of the research design so that new knowledge could be developed and used in the school setting. The rigid hierarchical interaction of Puerto Rican students and their non-Hispanic teachers resulted in the intellectual comprehension of anthropologically based suggestions in ways that perpetuated stereotyped behavior between the two groups. Intergroup conflict inhibited the

Jacquetta Hill-Burnett (Ph.D., Columbia, Teachers College) is professor of intercultural education at the Bureau of Educational Research of the University of Illinois. She has done research in the United States, Puerto Rico, and Australia in the field of educational anthropology. She has been a consultant to the National Science Foundation, the National Institute of Education, UNESCO, the Peace Corps, and the United States Office of Education. She is a past president of the Council on Anthropology and Education.

Acknowledgments—The research reported here was supported by Research Grant No. RD 2926 G 69 from the Division of Research and Demonstration Grants, Social and Rehabilitation Services, Department of Health, Education and Welfare, Washington, D.C.

I wish to thank Delmos J. Jones for helpful criticisms and suggestions on revisions of an earlier draft of the paper.

novel behavioral learning experiences necessary for collaborative educational relationships.

While both teachers and pupils learned something about each other's behavior and the cognitive meanings associated with it, only a few individuals were able to adapt to the institutional setting. Those who did so displayed a behavioral intelligence which enabled them to decode the meanings of others' behavior and change their own behavior accordingly. This chapter illustrates not only the subtleties of turning institutionalized conflict relationships into productive ones, but also the "worsening dilemma" posed by the fact that our educational system fails to focus on behavioral intelligence. By combining an ecological approach with behavioral and cognitive approaches to her collection and analysis of data, Hill-Burnett demonstrates the ways in which the exclusive emphasis of formal schooling on intellectual intelligence perpetuates the present disadvantaged position of minority groups in our society.

THERE IS A common stereotype that applied anthropology consists of the application of already established anthropological principles to some problematic situation raised by a client, or communicating anthropological perspectives to a client who then makes practical use of the information. This concept is misleading because it implies that knowledge development is complete before the knowledge is used (Clifton 1970:xi). It projects the overly narrow view that client relationships with anthropologists primarily result from clients seeking out anthropologists to consult about a problem.

The use of knowledge entails its further development, not simply by adding to it but through transforming its assumptions, categories, and paradigms. Knowledge is *tested* in use; when found wanting, it must be further developed or clarified. In the social sciences, where experimental controls for testing knowledge are available to only a limited degree, applied anthropology should be the testing cauldron for the forward edge of anthropological knowledge.

This essay presents a story within a story. The documents, as well as the findings, of a federally funded project to study intercultural processes and problems experienced by Puerto Rican youths in a midwestern city are used as evidence for the proposition that the use of anthropological knowledge continuously involves its further development. The proposals and discussion papers of the project, when carefully examined in temporal order, lend evidence to, or, in the idiom of Glaser and Strauss (1967), "ground," the view that applying knowledge entails not only adding to it but transforming assumptions, manipulating categories, shifting paradigms, and coming to grips with the human consequences of using given conceptual schemata.[1]

Problem and Setting

The general objective of the EPIC (*Estudio de Problemas Interculturales*) project was to study the intercultural process and problems in migration, education, and occupations of Puerto Rican youths in a large midwest urban center, and, based on this knowledge, to design and implement educational procedures and programs that would improve their chances of obtaining better jobs. The project began with the proposition that cultural factors and differences were one major source of the educational problems experienced by Puerto Rican youths in United States schools. The educational questions were studied in the seventh and eighth grades of a grammar school in which over 75 percent of the children came from Spanish-language dominant homes, while their teachers came from a range of other, mostly second generation east and southern European, backgrounds. A second set of questions asked how educational problems and cultural factors affected occupational socialization and access to occupations for Puerto Rican youths in an urban setting in the United States.

The household of a Puerto Rican youth was regarded as the domain and conservator of a characteristic Puerto Rican culture. At the same time, the school was viewed as the domain and conservator of the professional educators' version of a dominant and characteristic North American culture. Peer relationships were a third domain, potentially of great relevance to acculturation of youth, but their cultural characteristics were unknown and had to be discovered.

We selected for study the pupils in a sample of thirty egocentric

---

[1] Space limitations do not allow complete documentation of the claims about conceptual statements and project decisions through quotations from the project papers. A fully documented account of the conceptual changes is available on request from the author. A report of research results is available in Burnett (1972, 1974b) and Hill-Burnett (1976).

networks which began with thirty egos who were chosen by stratified random samplings from the 1967–68 seventh grade of a large urban elementary school. By starting with seventh-graders, we could examine the effects of a difference in experience with school cultures. We included in the sample five girls and five boys who had attended Puerto Rican schools for at least five years of their school careers before coming to the city; five girls and five boys from Puerto Rican families who had spent all their school careers in this city's schools; and five non-Puerto Rican girls and five non-Puerto Rican boys. The last ten provided a "controlled" comparison for sorting out cultural factors from other factors that were endemic to the inner city: socioeconomic level, broken homes, and so on. It helped to keep us "honest" and self-critical about what might be attributed to poverty and urbanism rather than cultural difference (Burnett 1974b:24–32).

This methodological procedure allowed the identification of natural relational networks radiating out from the egos in relationship with three types of persons. We first established contact with a youth attending the school. We then established contact with that particular youth's parents so as to begin observations and interviews with them in their household about the course and conditions of their lives and their perceptions and interpretations of relations and events in the school. We next located the teacher or teachers who were in contact with each youth, and, through participant observers, described the course of school life. The researchers interviewed teachers and other professionals to learn their points of view on the problems, solutions, and irresolvable conditions that had bearing on the student's school life. Finally, we established contacts with the youth's friendship network and observed and interviewed his or her peers in nonschool as well as school contexts.

In the early project documents, the research problem was stated in ways that placed culture in a primary causal position. It was implied that doing something about culture difference would change educational circumstances for children. The methodological statements focused on behavior, action, and interaction (Burnett 1968a).[2] The cultural formulation of the school situation emphasized the idea of professional subcultures and defined the research setting as multicul-

[2] The theoretical and methodological concepts were based on the theoretical and empirical work of Chapple and Arensberg (1940), Arensberg (1951), Arensberg and Kimball (1965), Chapple and Sayles (1961), Barker (1963), and Harris (1964).

tural. The situation was conceptualized as probably imbued with misunderstanding and conflict inevitably arising out of the disparity between the culture of students and that of teachers. We suggested that Puerto Rican children, many of whom migrate back and forth from island to mainland, may often experience further complication because of their contact with the culture of Puerto Rican Schools as well as "mainland" United States schools.[3]

The opening statement of the project proposal expressed our concern that the burden of adaptation was being placed on students and not on adult professionals. This concern was the basis for including research questions that might lead to developing better intercultural teaching (Burnett 1968a). Despite my initial propensity to think of the teachers in terms of their ethnic background, rather than in terms of a professional culture or "code" for behavior to which they were socialized, certain facts about their backgrounds and observations in the school led me to believe the professional culture was more dominant than the ethnic culture. To my surprise, perhaps because most teachers were second-generation ethnic, they were adamant assimilationists and advocates of the necessity for cultural and linguistic replacement if the children were to find economic and occupational success within their lifetimes.

We were dealing with views, attitudes, beliefs, and guides to action that were acquired and developed while they were studying in the professional teacher training institutions of the city (where the great majority of them were trained) and through their early apprenticeship during the first years of teaching in city schools. Initially, we saw their reactions as coming out of middle-class cultural origins, but closer examination of the facts indicated that this view was too simple. It did not fit the facts of their ethnically mixed and largely lower income backgrounds. Their version of "Anglo" middle-class culture was not necessarily learned from households practicing "middle-class culture" but was the version or "register" learned in a higher educational setting that prepared them for the work place.

The methodological sections show the focus on behavioral stream and interaction as the data base for formulating recommendations to school people regarding changes in behavior. The theoretical position was that behavior is primarily a function of organization

---

[3] This is not an annual migration; its regularity is tied to the mainland economic cycle and thus is recurrent but not regularly periodic.

or structure in interactive relationships. For example, the first public report of the research presents a behavioral, interaction version of what later was to be described as "the joking relationship" and describes our methods for studying it in these terms:

. . . our next step is to follow the network of those Puerto Rican boys . . . to their households and to events in that household in order to see whether the pattern of interaction and the procedural aspect of activities directed toward sanctioning and toward inhibiting violations of behavior rules seem to follow the same procedures as those we've seen in school. . . . If there is sharp contrast then we can pursue the question through interviews with informants concerning how these behavioral procedures and their differences affect them and strike them in emotion and in value terms (Burnett 1968a:19).

It should be noted that the decision about similarity and contrast in the conduct of interactions was to be based on the researchers' own etic system (cognitive mapping) of distinctive features, not on the prior careful delineation of actors' categories and defining features. The data plan, in the early part of the research, was to locate contrast by using the researchers' cognitive mapping, and only then to turn to questions of affective and conceptual mapping by participants. In a subsequent project document, this behavioral emphasis was reflected in the claim that investigation of cultural conduct involved selecting a sample of events involving interacting persons rather than a sample of individuals (Burnett 1969:20, 1973).

Interviews were not precisely coordinated with the specific record of interaction (cf. Burnett 1969 with Burnett 1972). Deliberate attention to peoples' expression of perceptions and sentiment toward particular events was added as a result of a theoretical shift in the second year of the project. At that time, the idea of the "interview from a behavioral record" came with a later cognitive concern with "cultural mapping" (Burnett 1970).

As a result of our initial emphasis on interaction and behavior, we began the study with a strong bias which viewed intercultural teaching as more than curriculum materials, test performance, and grades. Rather, it had to do with regularities of behavior, initiation of action, and responses to actions. Moreover, we had a strong bias toward treating as mere rationalization the claims that lack of competence in English explained everything. Yet, in the process of neglecting the curriculum content, test performance and grades, and favoring instead the behavioral data, we found that our communication of results back to teachers had little meaning for them. While our observations of classrooms provided excellent opportunity to study the process of the structuring of patterns of social relations, the findings did not provide information that was useful in trying to respond to the cognitive, conceptual, and motivational kinds of questions teachers asked us to answer or to help them answer. Our data did not deal with the problems and failures that the school system defined as primary considerations. We were addressing issues and troubles that ranked low in the professional educator's hierarchy of things on which energy, time, and thought were to be expended. Because of this experience, we reexamined and reoriented our conceptual approach.

The Sociolinguistic Study

The teachers' explanations of intercultural problems became important to us in order to formulate specific hypotheses that could be tested, thus providing information relevant to teachers' belief and explanatory systems. The approach utilized the experience of full participants in the phenomenal context in which we were working, and subjected it, as well as our own explanations, to empirical test. It was our belief that by dealing with teachers' explanations, with the same regard and respect as we did our own, we would persuade them to consider other types of explanations should theirs not stand up well under empirical test. If they denied the adequacy of our empirical tests of their ideas, they might at least consider developmental plans based on other optional explanations, even if they did not entirely reject their own previous beliefs. Moreover, it would be easier to invent, create, or formulate an ameliorative plan that included measures which teachers themselves might act upon.

Since six of the seven eighth-grade teachers specified language, or Puerto Rican students' lack of ability to use the English language, as the main source of their problems (Burnett 1974b), we added a linguist to the staff. She addressed herself to the question of the role of language in the performance of students, and to some degree the judgments of those performances by teachers. She made a distinction between competence, the mastery of the rules underlying sentence construction (such as the passive rule) and language performance, the way in which the speaker uses the rules. She also studied what kind of English was spoken by whom, with whom, and where, in terms of linguistic distinction.

Loy, the linguist, reported that responses to her tests, along with evidence of fluency in interview situations, indicated that the Puerto Rican students participating in the study knew the underlying principles of English sentence formation. Students whom she interviewed were able to understand and produce novel sentences and to converse freely with her. She concluded:

The study of English capabilities and usage and attitude among Puerto Rican youth . . . indicates a strong trend exists toward native fluency and usage of English in nearly all domains. Although many Puerto Ricans speak standard English, many speak a dialect incorporating features of both the North American neighborhood dialect and Spanish. These findings suggest that educational problems encountered by Puerto Rican students cannot be assumed to be caused by lack of fluency in English, and that intensive or special programs to develop fluency in English as a second language, as distinguished from reading and writing skills, are not the sole answer to the students' problems (Loy 1974:324–325).

Having dealt with the linguistic explanation for school failure, we still had to examine the teachers' other favored explanation. Poor performance and lack of success were often attributed to the youths' lack of desire to learn or to parental lack of interest in their child's education. The language attitude questionnaire effectively contradicted any explanation based on negative attitudes toward English (Loy 1974:322–323). The results from interviews with families by the participant observer team also contradicted the teachers' view of the Puerto Rican families as uninterested and unmotivated. When compared with non-Puerto Ricans in the same neighborhood, our sample Puerto Rican families were characterized by higher positive evaluation of education and stronger desire for the success of their children in school (Burnett 1974b:116–133).

This finding was communicated back to the teachers. They were more skeptical of this information than they were of the results of the language survey, perhaps because they felt more expert in judgments of behavior than in technical judgments of language.

Culture Explanations and Stereotyping

Just as the teachers' favored explanation of culture difference between home and school ran into difficulty, so also did the researchers' explanation. We discovered the ironic fact that using culture at the level of generalized group norms to explain "puzzling"
student and parent behavior could support the stereotypes that feed
into an ideology rationalizing subordination and discrimination. Even
while the team focused on the interactive structure of social relations,
the behavior, in keeping with a long tradition in anthropology, was
still interpreted in customary terms. Knowledge of island cultural
norms of Puerto Ricans was used to interpret and explain behaviors in
the school. Since one member of the research team was a native of
the island, and the director of the team had lived and worked there,
this approach seemed legitimate.

While the behavioral data of the classroom were not interesting
to the teachers, some teachers were interested in the team members'
generalized cultural knowledge. Initially, the information seemed to
encourage more positive attitudes toward Puerto Rican students.
However, the use of generalized cultural knowledge about Puerto
Ricans led to stereotyping and overgeneralized explanations of their
behavior. Our knowledge input actually interfered with the process of
individualized diagnosis, explanation, and instruction of Puerto Rican
children in the classroom (cf. Leacock 1971, 1973).

Early in our work, we often presented the cultural point of view
to teachers by reinterpreting in cultural terms student conduct that
teachers described but interpreted as bizarre, strange, abnormal, or
deviant. To illustrate, one teacher described the "odd" behavior of
two Puerto Rican boys who fought in the shop class. It was not the
fighting but the incident which precipitated the fight that puzzled her.
Carlos was very attracted to Antonia, Mrs. Berger reported to me.
And Carlos had begun to pursue Antonia's attention with notable
ardor. In shop one day, as everyone was working on their lamp-
shades, Carlos, who was seated next to Antonia, engaged her in attentive, admiring conversation, when a messenger, Renaldo, Antonia's brother, walked in. As he started toward the teacher, he
suddenly turned aside and physically attacked Carlos. After the
teacher separated the combatants, Renaldo's only explanation for his
action was that Carlos was talking with Antonia, who had been told

by her parents not to talk with Carlos. In the eyes of the teachers, the physical attack was far too extreme for the explanation. We began to interpret the event in terms of Puerto Rican parental concern with the chaste reputation of their unmarried teenage daughters, and the role of brothers in guarding the reputation of the family. The family's reputation would be undermined should a daughter—like Antonia—compromise it by arousing suspicion about her proper conduct with a boy. Carlos was well known as a charming, sometimes ardent "ladies' man," but he was also a member of a street gang, the Latin Disciples. He was "danger" to a daughter's reputation.

Our good intentions were frustrated when the teachers fitted this perspective into the general stereotyped picture of amorous Latins and Don Juan exploits. It reinforced their notion that Puerto Rican parents cared only about their daughters' marital status rather than their schooling and future employment. This inference was not true; as we noted above, it was contradicted by our family interviews. It is an excellent example of how overgeneralization arises easily from knowledge *about* other peoples' culture, as contrasted with actual use of cultural knowledge in interaction.

Midstream in our work, we attempted to incorporate more refined cognitive data by adopting a more cognitively oriented theory of culture. This new framework guided us to a more situational view of culture and to an effort to collect cognitive as well as behavioral data on encounters and interactions.

We decided that the reason knowledge about culture was stereotyping was partially due to the overgeneralized way we had presented the descriptions. They did not include information on contingencies, variable conditions, and contextual constraints. Formulating descriptions at this more refined level would demand greater precision. We decided that preparation for intercultural teaching required teaching about culture more for use than for general familiarity. The decision to spell out relationships in such detail that one could probably teach them like a language would be taught, represented a second stage of our effort to persuade teachers to take culture into account when teaching children from culturally different backgrounds. We hoped to prepare teachers for intercultural teaching by persuading them to self-consciously learn "some culture."

We turned to the question of how to describe the culture of the Puerto Rican youth, or of adults in situations where Puerto Rican culture dominated, so that teachers could use those rules and guides, or culture code, at least to decode student behavior and hopefully to encode their own behavior in Puerto Rican terms when the situation demanded it. The techniques for doing this were most clearly offered in theories of cognitive culture, or culture as knowledge. Although we came to this decision late in the project, we still were able to gather some information, following Goodenough's ideas of rethinking role and status (Goodenough 1969). Culture was viewed as standards for deciding what is, what can be, what to do about it, and how to go about it (Goodenough 1963:258, 1971). The conceptual formulation, however, emphasized the event context as well as the symbolic rule guides:

When I use the notion of *reference culture,* I have in mind a concept of culture that includes not only the activity level . . . , but also . . . the "rule-guides" that summarize the activities in terms of ordered elements. There are then two fundamental aspects of culture—culture at the symbolic level consisting of rules and standards. The other basic aspect of culture is behavioral in the form of action, feeling, interaction, material items, all in time and space. The latter might be called the concrete level. From the point of view of scientific description, it is essential to distinguish these two levels. The operation of a rule-guide at the phenomenal level requires that it be referred to . . . the behavioral and situational context (Burnett 1970:5).

The data collection procedure, the interview from a behavioral record, was introduced to collect data in the required form (Burnett 1972; cf. Keesing (1970).

We tested the idea by singling out one relationship that had been associated with intraclassroom conflicts—the joking/teasing relationship between two identity "categories," Puerto Rican students and their teachers. Quite early in the project, the observational field data had reported frequent use of teasing and joking as a strategy used by teachers to relate with students in regularly occurring events: it was used in social control; it was used to reduce tension; and it was used as a way of being friendly and companionable with students. The occurrence of conflicts when the strategy was employed with Puerto Rican students suggested that it often was not interpreted in the same way by Puerto Ricans and teachers. My own knowledge of joking behavior in Puerto Rico suggested that the point at which teasing became malicious and baiting was different for Puerto Ricans than for American school teachers (Lauria 1964). Interviews with several Puerto Rican students about those episodes disclosed that they felt they were being "picked on."

To avoid stereotyping, we wanted to collect ideas on "rule guides" in such a way as to take into account human variability with respect to models or rules. The recurrent regular episodes, or events, of classroom and school had to be investigated both for standard models and for individual model variations. Not all students reported the same reaction to similar levels of joking on the part of the teacher. There was sufficient individual variation to survey the range of variability.

We decided to include the joking relationship in a questionnaire so as to collect data from a large population of students about who could joke with whom. We would try to discover the range of variation as well as central tendencies in youths' views of this domain of rule guides. Accordingly, we used questionnaires to ask eighth-grade students about the appropriateness or inappropriateness of joking and teasing between paired sets of social identities, such as male student and female teacher.

While the procedure was crude, it was a move in the direction of testing our notion of standard, and it offered an honest display of the differences among individuals that teachers might encounter. It could better reveal that cultural standards were subject to individual variation. We felt that individual variation might prove important to a teacher's plan of action in a given situation, thereby supporting an individualized approach in relating cultural experience to learning and teaching. In a sense, it was a step toward being realist, not academic and theoretical, about the nature of culture *in vivo*.

Briefly, the results suggested that the difference between island and mainland Puerto Rican standards for the joking relationship is a matter of a shift in referents of labels. To use North American coding, a Puerto Rican must change underlying principles of judging relationships as appropriate or inappropriate (Hill-Burnett 1976). Both the results of the questionnaires and our observations of the interactions of several Puerto Rican and other Latino boys in the top eighth-grade class suggested that some had learned to switch to North American coding of the meanings of the behaviors; other Puerto Rican boys in the same class had not developed code switching ability.

Yet, while the cognitive culture approach provided knowledge at a level which might be used more readily in interaction, the approach still placed the burden of changing institutional outcomes on those who suffered but had no means of redress. Even an improvement in the teachers' ability to encode and decode behavior in Puerto Rican terms would only relieve some of the symptoms of organizational impositions. *We had begun to recognize that not all cultural differences lead to conflict, and, further, that not all culturally based conflicts lead to educational problems for Puerto Rican youths.*

The Ecological Context of Interaction and Code

Our continuing collection of participant observations in the school as an organizational context for behavior gradually led us to another theoretical perspective which did not contradict the results we had obtained regarding culture, but rather questioned our basic assumption that culture was a primary determinant in what happened in the students' lives. Questions were first raised by our observation that some conflicts attributable to culture difference did not make any difference in what happened to students in the educational process whereas other conflicts did. In part, the significance of the effect of culture difference was not that of culture difference *per se* but of what the difference was, whom it was with, and its organizational consequences. For example, teachers spoke of the greater propensity of Puerto Rican pupils to touch them during communications. The teachers' withdrawal response resulted in a feeling on the part of students that teachers were "cold." The behavior bothered many teachers, but it did not lead to negative consequences in the youths' placement in the organization of the school. The same seemed true of the teachers' response to Puerto Rican students' propensity to inquire about matters that some teachers defined as personal and private.

Because the conflicts over joking often fell in the realm of social control, they appeared to be more serious. This was not due to the culture pattern *per se* but rather to the close association of the conflict with the patterns of authority in the organizational setting. Their importance is clear when one assesses the educational consequence of frequent conflicts in this area. Conflict with respect to joking rules led to the placement of students in social groupings that had access to fewer educational resources, and to a generally denigrated reputation among both teachers and other students (a judgment that was openly communicated to the students by teachers). The judgment of youths by teachers was one key to the consequences of culture differences. If conflicts led to behaviors that drew the attention of other teachers, other students, or the assistant principals, negative consequences were likely to result. Circumstances that had to do with noise control were particularly important in the development of negative consequences. Conflicts that led to the social adjustment office or to complaints that brought someone from that office to the classroom were the kinds of events that led to reconsideration of the student's placement. From an educational point of view, abundance of resources depended on the class to which one was assigned. Judgments on performance were key acts of power that had significant organizational consequences for students' differential access to the limited resources of the school.

For example, a rank ordering of the eighth-grade classes according to reading scores led to the clustering in one class of students who spoke little English. At the same time, some of the students whose conduct was "disruptive" of classroom routine were also placed in that room. A new, inexperienced noncertified temporary male teacher, who was monolingual in English, was assigned to the class. Thus, if events led to a pupil being assigned to that room, there were clear consequences in terms of the educational resources that were available to him or her. There was obviously less opportunity for those who did not know how to converse in English to learn to do so from peers, who are a major source of English language learning, according to our own and other studies. With a monolingual teacher, a second consequence was that those who spoke only Spanish were learning very little subject matter content or none at all. Inexperienced teachers seemed ingenious in devising ways of transmitting information, but they lacked the organizational skill to deal with problems of social control.

As I studied this set of conditions, I was struck not so much by the pupils' deficiencies but by the weight and extent of the school's deficiencies and those of the educational system itself. From an ecological perspective, the school was a disadvantaged one, unable to call on the knowledge and skill needed to deal in a professional manner with the population of students it was supposed to serve. From this point of view, the school was maladapted to its student body.

In part, the internal allocation of resources was poor. Thus, funds were going to a program of Teaching English as a Second Language (TESL) which was not an irrational allocation in view of the school board's perspective that children were in transition to English language speaking and to North American "core" culture. But money was allocated *first* to the TESL component of the program rather than to bilingual teaching staff, although many teachers favored a priority allocation of funds for the latter. Some expenditure for bilingual teachers would have provided Spanish language instruction in course content, allowing students to continue to learn other subject matter while at the same time learning English.

The school existed in an environment; it was not autonomous. Even had the principal decided that bilingual instructional staff should have priority, staff changes were partially controlled by the teachers' union, so that special staff had to be hired with special funds. The funds themselves were often earmarked. Expenditure for TESL was specified; its use for bilingual staff was circumscribed. In the follow-up year of our project, when our sample of students had either gone on to high school or dropped out of school, our contacts with teachers in the school brought news that the funds for the TESL activity would be withdrawn. Hence, funds and resources were uncertain, and the decisions regarding resources were made by the central board. External events that were unpredictable and nonrecurrent often forced the local school to cope with a state of disequilibrium on the basis of limited resources.

In summary, uncertainty overshadowed implementation of ameliorative plans. The lack of autonomy was evident in the frequency with which external events transformed conditions for the operation of school programs. Uncertainty about reliable resources seriously interfered with organizational adaptation to the special conditions of the population within the school.

This ecological approach led us back to a more materialistic theoretical framework for developing perspectives on the original problem. Competence in language and culture had to be expressed in performance. Educational effects from judgments on those performances depended upon the organizational consequences for particular students' placement with respect to resources that maximized their chances for success. Even those resources were marginal, however, and their allocation was so greatly affected by external agents that local programs were a tenuous illusion.

Conclusion

The research project described above clearly displayed the complementary nature of the interaction and cognitive approaches. Used in the same context, the strengths and weaknesses of both approaches showed up with great clarity. Each type of data—the behavioral and the cognitive—is conceptually distinct, and different methodologies are used to collect the two types of theoretically relevant data. Yet, viewed in synthetic perspective, each points up the limits of formulations based on the other type of data. "Minding" and "behaving" are interacting phenomena which should be embraced in the same theory as coordinated dimensions of culture, if the theory is to be used for understanding organizational behavior.

While our attention to interactive behavior and then cultural codes of knowledge allowed us to describe processes and procedural effects, the more primary causes in the system could not be delineated by these means. This is not to argue that the framework of power and material resources is contradictory with the other frameworks; it is as complementary to them as they are to each other. All three—behavioral, cognitive, and ecological—systemics are essential to a theory that purports to guide research to the point where policy decisions can be derived from it.

When anthropologists address themselves to problems raised by colleagues within the context of scientific inquiry, it is possible to constrict and simplify a theoretical framework and focus so that the conceptual postures detailed above might appear to be three different positions on theoretical issues. In practice, they are not three ways of approaching the same thing but three complementary and essential ways of approaching sets of data which, when synthesized, offer a more complex and powerful framework of ideas. It is a better framework from the point of view of action and policy decisions.

Applied problems arise from the conduct of social affairs, where either anthropologists or others may encounter them and engage in seeking solutions for them. Basic research problems arise from the problem posing and resolving activities of disciplinary colleagues. Both basic and applied problem-solving processes benefit from each other. A system that maintains an openness to both types of problem formulation and the free flow of information between them is more likely to be a vital center for the growth and development of substantive knowledge. The special contribution of applied anthropology to building theory arises from the demand that theory be sufficiently complex to address the realities of processes, as well as to distinguish symptoms from causes and primary from secondary causes in the social world.

6

ORGANIZATIONAL BEHAVIOR RESEARCH——
WHERE DO WE GO FROM HERE?

William Foote Whyte

The technological revolution of the modern world has been accompanied by the rise of organizational systems which are significantly different from those studied by applied anthropologists during the 1930s and 1940s. Today, organizations have considerably more specialized functions, and the task of coordinating their work so that people may receive products and services has become acute. The fact that human and social problems often present themselves in nonspecialized forms introduces the major problem of the fit between the generalized needs of people and the specific functions of the organizations that serve them.

William F. Whyte reviews the history of organizational behavior research and notes that the social-psychological questionnaire research of the 1950s has yielded little that is useful for the understanding of organizations as social systems which relate people to technology, to resources, and to each other. This latter type of knowledge is required if new organizational models are to emerge in response to human needs.

The understanding of organizations as social systems, which is historically rooted in social anthropology, means that anthropologists trained in this tradition have a unique contribution to make as diagnosticians of many of the organizational ills of our times. Echoing points made in passing by previous contributors in this section, and fore-

William F. Whyte (Ph.D., Chicago) is professor of industrial and labor relations and professor of sociology at Cornell University. He has carried out research on industrial social organization in the United States, Canada, Venezuela, Spain, and Peru. In recent years, he has concentrated his research on rural development in Peru and the problems of organizing for agricultural development. Dr. Whyte has served as a consultant and researcher for numerous business, educational, and scientific organizations in the United States and Latin America. He is a past president of the Society for Applied Anthropology.

shadowing a major point made by the contributions in the section which follows, Whyte warns of the adaptation required by academically trained anthropologists if their work is to be useful in applied settings. By undertaking research in diverse organizational settings and developing flexibility in the formulation of research methodologies, applied anthropologists enhance their contributions to organizational theory.

NOW THAT HALF a century has elapsed since the Western Electric research program was launched in 1927, we are in a good position to assess past trends and visualize future possibilities for a field of research increasingly called Organizational Behavior. While a beginning date for any field of study is necessarily arbitrary, it was the publication of the comprehensive report on the Western Electric program (Roethlisberger and Dickson 1939) which set off in the 1940s a rapid development of courses and research projects focusing upon the human problems of industry.

As reported in previous essays, anthropologists were a major force in the early development of this field. W. Lloyd Warner was a consultant to the Western Electric program and helped to shape the research methods used in the bank wiring room, a classic study of informal organization among workers. As part of the Yankee City study, Warner and Low (1947) published the first book examining a strike in social anthropological terms. In the first meeting of the Society for Applied Anthropology, Conrad M. Arensberg, Eliot D. Chapple, and F. L. W. Richardson Jr. reported (for publication in the first two numbers of *Applied Anthropology*) upon their research in industry (1941 and 1942). In 1945 Burleigh B. Gardner published the first textbook on *Human Relations in Industry*. After working on Warner's Yankee City study (along with Kimball, Chapple, Arensberg, and others), Gardner moved into research with Western Electric and subsequently joined with Warner in 1943 to set up the Committee on Human Relations in Industry at the University of Chicago. In 1946, Warner and Gardner organized Social Research Inc. as a means of applying their expertise to help business organizations solve their human problems (See essay 13).

This strong beginning justified hopes that organizational studies would become a major field for applied anthropologists, yet in succeeding years very few anthropologists joined these pioneers. Furthermore, we were swamped by other social scientists, particularly the social psychologists, who entered industry in large numbers and developed theories that for many years enjoyed great popularity in management circles.

Now the tide of social psychological studies seems to be receding, leaving little in the way of solid contributions to show for the innumerable dollars and man hours of talented people expended in this style of research. As disillusionment grows over the fruits of this research approach, the stage is set for reformulation of research strategies and a new forward movement.

This is a critical period for us, since the history of recent failures in social research points to the need for an anthropological orientation to research and for the skills of the applied anthropologist. This new forward movement demands people with the ability to conceptualize human behavior into systems of interpersonal, intergroup, and interorganizational relations, to relate the structure and functioning of the organization to the structure and functioning of the community, and, finally, to integrate economic and technological with social data.

How the point of view and the methods and diagnostic skills of the applied anthropologist can be applied to this emerging new style of social research, I will discuss later. First, let us consider past failures which have led to the present reassessment and reformulation of the field of organizational behavior.

Fixation on Democratic Leadership

Behavioral science activities in this field were partly a reaction against the authoritarian and mechanistic views of management represented by Frederick W. Taylor and his followers in the school of "scientific management." Taylor and his associates had placed their emphasis almost exclusively upon formal organization structure, technology, material rewards and the management methods required to operate a mechanistic system.

The Western Electric research led to the discovery of something which was then called "informal organization." Apparently, the behavior of workers did not correspond to the formal logics of management but instead, workers tended to develop their own subculture and their own group solidarity in opposition to management.

Since we could not regard workers as being motivated exclusively by material interests, it seemed important to study the attitudes and beliefs of workers regarding their work situation. For the investigation of the subjective life of organization members, the questionnaire or survey, developed and popularized particularly during World War II, proved an invaluable method. Use of this method permitted collection of a large body of quantitative data that, with the rapid development of computers in recent years, has made possible an enormous volume of data analysis on how workers think and feel about their organization.

While early researchers in the field were examining the limitations of formal authority, social psychologists sought to discover patterns of more "democratic leadership." Many hoped to discover that "democratic leadership," when skillfully practiced, was not only superior from a humanistic standpoint but also led to greater productivity. Early studies along this line, particularly at the University of Michigan's Survey Research Center, did indeed seem to show this pattern, but later research there and elsewhere brought out such discrepant findings as to discredit the comforting view that democratic leadership or "participation management," as it was also called, necessarily resulted in greater productivity than more traditional styles of leadership. This produced a period of confusion and frustration, while the researchers searched for new hypotheses and new strategies of research.

While "participation management" was for many years the most popular doctrine in management training programs, the studies designed to support this general orientation were subject to several serious weaknesses. In the first place, this work was based exclusively upon the survey, which is a valuable instrument for some purposes, especially when combined with other research methods. However, when used alone, it does not enable us to cope with the complexities of organizational behavior. While the social psychologists wrote about the relationship between participative leadership behavior and worker attitudes, their conclusions, in fact, were based upon a legitimated fraud. I use the word "legitimated" to indicate that the manner of reporting the presumed relationship was widely practiced by eminent social psychologists and sociologists, even though it clearly had no scientific foundation. In effect, the writers were relating worker attitudes toward the supervisor (as measured by responses to a number of attitude items) with the supervisor's behavior *as perceived by the workers* (in their responses to items describing various aspects of supervisory behavior). The survey researchers simply inferred from worker perceptions how supervisors were behaving and had no independent observations or interviews to provide more acceptable evidence on supervisory behavior.

This line of research also involved the study of interpersonal relations in a structural and technological vacuum. Writers provided some sort of orientation regarding the technology and organizational structure within which the study was carried out, but this was simply background information. It was not utilized for the establishment of typologies or variables related to organization structure and technology, which might have impacts upon individual behavior and interpersonal relations. To be sure, the survey researchers did eventually discover differences in leadership styles of more successful supervisors (as rated by their superiors) in a production organization compared with a maintenance organization, but this revelation did not lead—as it should have—to an effort to arrive at generalizations regarding interpersonal behavior related to structure and technology.

Furthermore, the social psychologists were almost exclusively concerned with only one aspect of organization structure, the vertical or authority relationship between a worker and his boss, the foreman and his general foreman, and so on. Most of the writers along this line have been completely oblivious to horizontal relations (those between individuals at the same hierarchical level in different organizational units) or diagonal relations (those between two individuals at different hierarchical levels in two different organizational units where neither one has authority over the other.) I do not mean to suggest that the work of all social psychologists is subject to these criticisms. I am simply describing the style of research most popular among social psychologists.

Re-Enter Structure and Technology

During the period of the popularity of "participation management", studies of human reactions to technology were not totally neglected. In fact, applied anthropologists Charles R. Walker, Robert Guest, and Arthur Turner (1952, 1956) carried out a series of studies of the impact of technology on worker attitudes and behavior. Nevertheless, these case studies of worker reactions to technology remained unrelated to research on managerial leadership—with one exception (Guest 1962). For leadership studies, the importance of structure and technology only came into focus later with the classic work of Joan Woodward (1965) in England. Seeking to check the relationship between types of technology and organization structure, she carried out an impressive examination of 100 firms. This enabled her to demonstrate that there were systematic differences in such aspects of structure as the span of control in different types of technology.

Woodward's work set off a burst of activity in which researchers concentrated attention on technology and formal organization structure and on the relations between these two factors. In a sense, the researchers were returning to the original field of interest of the scientific management school but with one basic difference. F. W. Taylor and his followers assumed there were principles of organizational structure that could and should be applied universally to any type of organization. Researchers now abandoned the search for the "one best way" to set up an organization and began examining the structural properties that tend to be related to particular types of technology.

The Woodward program also stimulated a number of macro-structural studies. Instead of concentrating on the analysis of a particular case, the researchers gathered comparative data on a large number of cases. While this has led to a discovery of some interesting quantitative relations among structural variables, the methodological problem of macro-organizational studies makes it impossible to glean data from a large number of organizations. Researchers must content themselves with items of information that can be readily picked up and that are reasonably objective in character. Then, while we may be encouraged to find correlations among a number of structural variables, generally the correlations are at such a low level that, however interesting they may be to theorists, they provide little guidance to the person of action. That is, a correlation of .30 may be statistically significant and of considerable interest to the theorist, and yet it accounts for less than 10 percent of the variance. This means that the consultant who uses these data can only report that if the organization is structured in line with the correlation found, there is a slightly better than 50-50 chance that the resulting structure will be more useful than competing models. Furthermore, while it is certainly of importance to learn more about the design of organization structures, the macrostructural approach leaves off at this problem, giving us little or no guidance on how to operate the structures that are indicated by the design.

Recent years have also seen a boom in interorganizational studies. We have come to recognize that civilizations advance through increasing division of labor and specialization, which means, among other things, the creation of a greater number of organizations to perform specialized functions. But human problems still tend to present themselves primarily in unspecialized form. Thus arises a lack of fit between human problems and the organizations created and developed to deal with those problems. If we are to deal more adequately with human problems in complex societies, we must provide new organizational forms and strategies that coordinate the specialized services and resources which people need. This means, particularly, studying the coordination and cooperation among organizations, or, more generally, interorganizational relations. While this is a field of rapidly growing activity, as yet we have developed no theoretical framework adequate to deal with the phenomena under study.

We are also coming to reevaluate the role of money and other material rewards in organizational behavior. The history of thought in our field seems to be marked by pendulum swings from one extreme to another. Thus, when the early human relations researchers discovered that the scientific management writers were wrong in treating money as the exclusive motivator of workers, we tended to swing to the other extreme, concentrating on other motivations and treating money as if it had little or no importance. We are now beginning to recognize that material rewards are indeed of great importance to organization members, but this recognition solves no theoretical or practical problems. It is important to know how decisions are made on the distribution of material rewards, how individuals and members of work groups feel their rewards compare with those of others doing work of comparable value, how grievances regarding inadequacies and inequities in the reward system are handled, and so on. In other words, economic rewards do not function by themselves but in the context of a social system, so that the impact of the particular reward can only be understood in its social context. (Whyte 1955; Lawler 1973).

Toward a New Theoretical Framework

While we still seem to be in the period of tearing down old theoretical frameworks and the dust has not yet settled sufficiently to reveal the building blocks that can be used for the development of a new and more useful theoretical framework, I shall try to take a first tentative step toward construction by outlining what seem to me some of the main elements of the new research strategy. I shall illustrate these ideas from my current studies of "Organizing for Agricultural Development" (1975).

We must think and act in terms of social systems consisting of horizontal and diagonal as well as vertical relations. The study of diagonal and horizontal relations, of course, takes us beyond the boundaries of a single organization into the exploration of interorganizational relations.

What aspects of these human relations do we study? While I continue to believe in focussing upon the observation and measurement of human interactions and activities, I now see these elements as embedded in a flow of resources within and among organizations. Though material resources are of obvious importance, I find it useful to concentrate upon the flow of *information,* which seems to me a resource of steadily growing importance as civilizations become more complex and specialized in their functions.

In the primitive tribe or small peasant community, the individual can acquire all of the information possessed by the adults of his or her community through growing up in the family, with perhaps the addition of a few years of schooling in the community. As civilizations advance, the individual finds that a steadily decreasing proportion of the information needed to orient him or her toward work and the world can be acquired in family and community and elementary school. As the bodies of information grow in volume and complexity, social and economic development comes to be largely a problem of acquiring, integrating and utilizing information.

Why speak of "information" rather than "knowledge?" Knowledge implies systematic bodies of validated data and relationships in particular disciplines. Information is a more inclusive term, covering not only formal knowledge but also where to go to find something out, who has done what and with what result, who has the money to support what project, and so on. By the use of the term, I do not mean to limit myself to *validated* information, and yet I find the common dichotomy between information and misinformation an oversimplification. The people who generate, transmit, or receive information develop ways of judging both the accuracy of the information and its relevance for their purposes. At some points information may be validated (or invalidated) through scientific tests; at other points it may be evaluated in terms of the reputation of the transmitter or in terms of the reactions of influential others in the social world of the receiver.

While the accuracy of information is important, we will concentrate here particularly upon the channels through which information flows—or should flow—for accelerated agricultural development. If the information does not reach the intended recipients, then, for their purposes, its quality is irrelevant. On the other hand, as we diagnose the gaps and blockages in information flows, we are necessarily dealing with factors creating distortions in transmission and misunderstandings in reception and indirectly focusing upon some of the influence affecting information quality.

If we begin where new scientific information is generated in research institutes and universities, we tend to visualize a one-way flow in research at these points and ending with the farmers. We need also to check on the flow in the reverse direction. Do farmers try to tell extension agents what they want and need? Do the agents respond? Do extension agents tell research people what kind of research projects and research reports would be especially useful to them? Do the researchers respond?

At the farmer end of the organizational system, it is a mistake—unfortunately quite a common one—to think in terms of the relations between the extension agent and individual farmers. The rural community has its own organization, with the relation of man to land providing the main structural elements. Rural areas differ greatly in degree of equality/inequality in land ownership, in the presence or absence of sharecroppers (and in the nature of their contractual relationship to the owners), in the degree of farm tenancy, in the use of full and part time farm labor, in the presence or absence of serfs who provide labor to large landowners in return for rights to cultivate their family plot, and so on. Intervention strategies must be adjusted to these structural conditions, and, under conditions of extreme inequality in landownership, land reform may be a necessary precondition to successful programs to improve the welfare of lower-class rural people.

Communities also differ in their structures of local government and in the capacity of local government to mobilize the citizens for improvement projects. The presence or absence of a farmers' cooperative also affects whether change agents should seek to work through an existing organization or whether the program they hope to develop will require building a new organization. The extension agent's success in promoting agricultural development will depend less upon skill in communicating with individual farmers than upon ability to comprehend the organizational structure of the community and to devise ways of linking the extension service effectively to that structure.

Reception of useful information is a necessary but not a sufficient condition for improving farmer productivity. At the local level, we need to examine the ways in which the flow of information is (or is not) coordinated with the flow of other resources (credit, fertilizer, insecticides, etc.) which poor farmers need. Similarly, for the organizations primarily concerned with the generation and transmission of information, those functions cannot be performed without the support of complementary human and physical resources which must be supplied by the administration of the organizations involved in these stages of the information flow process.

Diagnostic Research for Improvement of Organizational Systems

Crude as it is, the organizational systems framework presented here should enable the applied anthropologist to do in a short period of field work the kind of diagnostic research that is invaluable to the administrator or program planner. I use the term, "diagnostic research," to contrast with the stereotype of the traditional anthropological field study. We are accustomed to thinking of the social anthropologist as one who puts in a year or more doing a study of a primitive tribe or peasant community and then takes many months or years to write up his or her findings. If the objective of the anthropologist is to make an intensive and comprehensive study of the culture and social structure of tribe or community, then a year of field work is a short time indeed. But the administrator or program planner cannot afford to wait a year for the anthropologist to live with the organization before he or she reaches the point of saying anything useful about it.

If applied anthropologists have an organizational systems framework to guide them, they should not need the traditional long-term immersion before their analysis leads them to action implications. Consider, for example, the problem in agriculture of the relationship between the research and extension organizations and between extension and the farmers. There is no such thing as a good extension service without effective linkages to an agricultural research organization. A research organization may be rated good by tradition minded agricultural scientists if its scientists do "interesting work" and publish frequently in the best professional journals, but the farmers don't read the technical papers. Unless the research program is effectively linked with some sort of human service to bring the fruits of new knowledge to the farmers, and to bring the concerns of the farmers to the researchers, the organization's research output will serve only to enhance the professional standing of its scientists.

Given this necessary interdependency, it makes no sense for the researcher to undertake an intensive study of the research organization or of the extension organization. He or she can begin by asking: are the two organizations effectively linked together? If they are not (which is the case in at least nine out of ten developing countries), it should take only a few interviews with researchers, extension agents, and administrators to diagnose the general nature of the existing lack of coordination and absence of cooperative relations.

Of course, the preliminary diagnosis does not lead automatically to the solution to the problem. However, it does focus the researcher's attention upon a critical problem area and launches him or her on an exploration to discover the changes necessary to solve the problem.

From Diagnosis to Problem Solutions

In contrast to many other behavioral scientists, applied anthropologists do not look solely to changes in attitudes and styles of leadership for solutions to problems. They recognize that attitudes do not change in response to the consultant's recommendation but they do change, rather, in response to changes in organizational systems. They recognize that a leadership style should not be seen simply as the property of a leader but as a component in a total organizational system. Without denying the important roles played by individuals in key positions, they recognize that it is impractical to recommend a personality-changing program because adult personalities are exceedingly difficult to change, even under intensive psychotherapy. But they also recognize that individuals *behave* differently in response to changes in the organizational systems in which they participate. They therefore seek to discover the organizational changes required to bring about the desired behavioral changes.

Fortunately, the design of new organizational models need not depend solely upon the imagination of the applied anthropologist. Many government administrators and program planners in agriculture have recognized the deficiencies inherent in traditional organizational models and are striving to develop new and better models.

In recent field work in Mexico, Colombia, and Peru, I found that all three governments had been in the process of major reorganizations of their agriculture ministries and related programs. The reorganizations in Mexico and Colombia are designed in part to improve the working relations between researchers and extension agents and between extension agents and farmers. Peru has taken a more radical approach, eliminating extension agents altogether, but, at this writing, the nature of the emerging organizational system is not yet clear.

We may also be able to "learn from the thoughts of Chairman Mao" as we examine the Chinese system of research and development in agriculture. While our knowledge of mainland China since the revolution is still fragmentary, there is one point on which all outside observers agree: the Chinese have had extraordinary success in the production and distribution of food. No longer does China suffer through periods of famine or have millions of undernourished citizens even in nonfamine years. While a number of factors are undoubtedly at work here, let us focus upon the organizational aspects of research and development (Stavis, 1975; Science for the People, 1972).

In addition to its agricultural research institutes, China has established a large number of what are callled extension stations, but these function quite differently from extension services in other countries. While the basic research and the development of new high yielding varieties of seeds are the responsibilities of the institutes, the extension stations are actively engaged in applied research, as they test seed varieties for local conditions and make the necessary adaptations. In working with the communes, the professionals from the stations are thus linking the peasants directly with the research and development process.

To bring research and practice together in industry and in agriculture, the Chinese practice a three-in-one system. When the researchers at the experiment station have something that they want to try out among the farmers or when farmers in the commune have a problem on which they need scientific and technical help, commune and station get together to form a team: an old, experienced, and respected peasant, who has had little formal education; a young peasant with little practical experience as yet but with a relatively high level of education for the commune; and an agricultural researcher. (The team may consist of more than three, but always the principle of diversity in education, age, experience and position is respected.)

These people do not simply meet to have a discussion. The professional spends time in the commune, observing farm practices, studying the particular problem in question in the field, consulting with fellow team members and with peasants. The peasant team members accompany the professional to the station, where they inspect the facilities, learn about experiments in process, and meet the professional's colleagues, who are also available for further consultation. The team may then develop plans for new experiments to be carried out at the station, and they also generally extend the experimental process to the commune itself, as team members and peasants work together to carry out the experiment and to learn from it.

In this system, when a series of experiments leads to new knowledge, the extension station does not have to plan steps whereby this new knowledge may be introduced to farmers so that they may be persuaded to apply it. By the time the experiment is completed, the knowledge is already being utilized by the farmers in a particular commune. Furthermore, as representatives of various communes frequently meet together, along with the research specialists, the fruits of a successful experiment in one commune are rapidly transmitted to another. While traditional extension agents seek to set up demonstration projects under their control, within the peasant community, in China, the peasant commune which achieves particularly impressive results becomes in effect a demonstration commune to which many other peasants from many other communes come in search of knowledge and inspiration.

Conclusions

I have argued that the field of research which applied anthropologists helped so much to launch—but which they later largely abandoned—is now ripe for the theoretical and methodological reformulations that applied anthropologists are particularly qualified to contribute.

The research strategy I propose looks beyond attitudes and personalities in order to concentrate upon organizational systems. This means focusing not only upon vertical relations but also upon horizontal and diagonal relations, both within the organization and among organizations. I have suggested also that examining the flow of resources (with special emphasis upon information) provides an essential key to the understanding of the functioning of organizational systems.

In order to change the behavior of organization members, the applied anthropologist must devise means of changing the structuring of the sets of relations making up the organizational system. This requires an ability to conceptualize the essential features of the organizational model currently under study and to chart alternative change pathways, based upon an analysis of a variety of other organizational models which human beings have set up to accomplish the same general purposes.

In developing this argument, I have begun with industry and ended with agriculture. I have adopted this plan of exposition partly for reasons of convenience, for it conforms to the evolution of my own interests and activities, yet there is a broader justification. As applied anthropologists move from industry to agriculture, or *vice versa,* they find at first that they are confused by the terminology and technology of an unfamiliar field. However, once they have caught on to the principal features of the new terrain, they find they can use—with equal effect in both fields—the same organizational systems and resource flow framework. And, as they move from one area of human activity to another, but always focusing upon organizational relations and resource flows, researchers find that they can apply ideas developed through research in industry to their studies in agriculture, and *vice versa*. Furthermore, by adding to the variety of organizational systems they study, applied anthropologists reduce the danger of becoming prisoners of the beliefs and ways of thinking of the participants in one type of organization. Thus, they enhance their chances of making contributions to a general science of organizational behavior.

Part II

ROLES AND INSTITUTIONAL SETTINGS

The institutional settings in which applied anthropologists work are considerably more diverse than those of their academic colleagues. This diversity is increasing as growing numbers of applied anthropologists seek and find employment in college and university positions outside of anthropology and in foundations, governmental agencies, community organizations, consulting firms, and other places outside of academe. For some, nonacademic employment is episodic or temporary, as they alternate between nonacademic and academic positions. For others, it is a part-time role undertaken simultaneously and in conjunction with academic work. For a substantial number of others, nonacademic employment is a full-time and life-long career.

The contributors to this section illustrate these and other combinations of roles. Miller and Taylor, for example, are currently employed in institutions of higher education, but their work is largely outside of that usually associated with traditional anthropology departmental activities. Peterson and Medicine are currently full-time employees of anthropology departments, but their past and present experience includes work within quite different institutional contexts. For Neville, applied work is undertaken in conjunction with a full load of departmental teaching. Sayles, Gardner, and Dobyns are presently full-time employees of nonacademic institutions.

What are these nonacademic roles like? What types of demands are encountered in nonacademic situations that make work there different from the classroom and the academic department? How can anthropology be applied in the day-to-day professional activities of college administration, tribal organization, religious groups, hospitals, prisons, business consulting firms, or expert court testimony? What are the special opportunities and difficulties of working with one's "own" people? These are the questions which are addressed in this section.

Viewed as a whole, the essays which follow provide an extensive field report of nonacademic employment. Like all anthropological field reports, they are limited to the observations made by particular persons in specific career situations. Nevertheless, they tell us much about new and old fields of applied endeavor and reveal that anthropologists who work outside of academe must adapt to new and "strange" situations which require that they work as peers with other professionals who have not been trained in anthropology. Anthropological theory and assumptions are continually tested in these new situations as knowledge is put to use or further developed in the analysis of problems and the search for their solutions. In addition, anthropologists themselves are tested as they interact within social systems which they do not control or dominate. Thus, a higher premium is placed not only on theoretical contributions but also on behavioral ones. The personal reports of the contributors to Part II bring the subtleties of what is entailed into view.

7

ADMINISTRATIVE ORIENTATIONS FROM
ANTHROPOLOGY: THOUGHTS OF A
COLLEGE PRESIDENT

Paul A. Miller

Writing from the perspective of a long career as an administrator/anthropologist, Paul Miller describes the contribution of anthropology to his current responsibilities and duties as president of the Rochester Institute of Technology. Administrative actions and decisions require analysis of both the macrocosmic and microcosmic contexts of institutional relationships and the interplay between them. In examining the macrocosmic context of higher education today, Miller notes the historic tension between preserving and adding to knowledge and the function of channeling knowledge into use. The discipline of anthropology itself is confronted with this tension.

Miller exemplifies an anthropologist who has chosen to use anthropological training for the purpose of better understanding and coping with the daily demands of administrative work. Yet, he is not only a participant but also an observer of the social system of higher education. He reveals the need for administrative leaders to encompass both the intellectual and behavioral intelligence earlier described by Richardson. In addition, the essay is a testimony to the fact that the administrator/anthropologist can continue to make a contribution to the storehouse of knowledge. He tells us much about contemporary developments in higher education which need to be more fully understood by students, professors, and others who work within it.

Paul A. Miller (Ph.D., Michigan State) is president of the Rochester Institute of Technology. He has worked in such positions as county agricultural agent. professor of sociology and provost of Michigan State University, president of West Virginia University, Assistant Secretary of Education in the United States Department of Health, Education, and Welfare (1966–1968), and Distinguished Professor of Education and director of University Planning Studies at the University of North Carolina, Charlotte.

APPLIED ANTHROPOLOGY HELPS the college president to place a particular institution or class of institutions within the overall drama of historic context: how institutions are formed, how they adapt to social need and pressure, and how they fall into obsolescence. Anthropology, dealing as it does with the interwoven beliefs and values which give meaning to social activities, tries to understand the functions of social activities as they, patterned together, shape the lives of those who perform them. The anthropologist as educational administrator asks how the functions of education interweave and overlap with other institutions and organizations. This raises the further question of how the school or college in microcosm influences and is influenced by the beliefs and values of its members and the cultural forces which are linked to and patterned with it.

Anthropology helps the academic administrator to gain the perspective of the wide horizon. No other discipline can do this better if both understanding and the basis to act administratively are required. This larger view enables the administrator/anthropologist to understand how social need and pressure determine the nature of educational institutions, why new ones come into being, serve for a period as prototypes, then recede to a less illustrious place as other academic forms emerge.

In the United States, the anthropologist is drawn especially to the successive prototypes which have arisen to meet the evolving demands for education. At least three distinct American prototypes responded to such demands. Each adapted to change, yet other prototypes succeeded them. Responding to claims for suffrage and equal opportunity, the state universities were formed. A rebellious rural majority wanted something more,—a pressure that helped create the land-grant colleges in 1862, which mixed subjects in agriculture and engineering with those in philosophy and literature (Miller 1973). As the public school movement gained momentum, social demand created new offshoots, notably the normal school academies, which later became the teachers colleges. This overall public educational system grew for nearly a century, but it was unprepared for the upheaval in the meaning of higher education which emerged in the single generation which knew the Great Depression, the technology of World War II, and the Soviet sputnik.

From this more modern context sprang the community college, perhaps the major academic form thus far in the twentieth century.

The land-grant college made it fashionable to teach students how to work and live along with how to think. The community college emerged to do the same thing, but to do more of it—to serve more people, to meet the needs of the whole community, and to demonstrate the relationship of education to social and economic growth.

With such an historic succession as an example, applied anthropology helps the administrator to learn how prototypes adapt to new social needs, yet not so quickly that the force and haste of social pressure create new forms. For example, the land-grant college helped transform agricultural efficiency. But, as unneeded rural workers flee to urban centers, these colleges find it difficult to adjust to urban society, and voices are raised for the need of an "urban-grant" university (Johnson 1964; Watchman 1974:242–247). Teachers colleges helped to fashion staff, evaluate, and support the public schools. However, having weakened their local ties by emulating the more classic university, they have been unable to respond to the crisis of the urban school as a prime center of social disintegration in American life. Meanwhile, nontraditional education—the provision of external degrees, open universities, classrooms without walls, and the learning system which the electronic revolution has helped the whole community to become—creates doubt that community colleges will adapt rapidly enough to fulfill the aims for which they were invented. Perhaps a new prototype is now in the making!

As applied anthropology helps the administrator gain the perspective of the wide horizon, it also clarifies the college as a closely interwoven web of mutual and reciprocating relationships: in short, a natural community. The unity of such relationships becomes important to the administrator/anthropologist. It brings integrity to the institution and helps reveal how the various client groups—students, faculty, donors, employers, public officials—may influence each other. An interest in the college as a community, with its accompanying tendencies to localize and decentralize, will focus the fundamental concern of the administrator/anthropologist on the response to the growing tendency for external agencies to centralize the guidance of the university system.

For example, as democratization of higher education has sped forward in the United States, a new administrative class has arisen for guiding the larger and more complex institution by creating more and stronger measures of executive direction. The new academic managers have perfected formal managerial techniques. They specialize in the cultivation of clients and donors, invent interlocking links with state and federal governments, as well as with new planning agencies, become the customary and sometimes the only link between students, faculty, and trustees, influence the agenda of governance, and tend to strengthen vertical as against lateral channels of communication.

Another related example is the mushrooming of multi-institutional systems and consortia. The growth of federal financing of colleges and universities, which increased almost sixfold in the 1960s alone, ushered in a newly forged link to the federal government, together with a widespread orientation to research. It opened the way for a myriad of other formal arrangements, such as state systems of higher education, which have moved the location of planning and decision away from the inner life of the college as a community and toward the outer public life of society. The administrator/anthropologist is both concerned and curious about how such ties to the public world, and the manner of their management by the new administrative class, complicate the location of education as it is continuously absorbed into a bureaucratized society (Trow 1973, 1969:181–202).

The anthropologist's view is shaped by the basic concept of culture. While other disciplines may emphasize social conduct, belief, language, human artifact, and skill, the anthropologist focuses upon how such aspects of life are interwoven and patterned into a whole. Anthropology asserts that culture touches every part of human life— the visible, the invisible, the biological, the intellectual, the moral; that culture does not change nor can it be changed by addressing it part by part; that it is not possible to understand the life of mankind, nor any part of it, without a larger understanding of the culture in which that life, whether of a person or of society, is embedded (Hall 1976:22–35). In the instance of the school or college, the anthropologist's interest turns to the institution as a microcosm and how it links to and is influenced by the shape and direction of the more macrocosmic aspects of culture. The administrator/anthropologist seeks to know how the educational community links its efforts to the projects of the larger cultural and societal order.

This interest in the interplay of microcosmic and macrocosmic projects becomes the centerpiece of the academic administrator whose way of looking at higher education is anthropological in nature. These two aspects, under the cultural view, eventually fall together. As they do, the administrator finds in their relationships a way of viewing the academy in the holistic sense which is so characteristic of the anthropological method (Fallers 1974). Moreover, this method embodies interests which veer to lateral rather than vertical channels of communication, and to the ties between small and large systems. There is an emphasis upon working effectively within a given system of interpersonal relationships.

It may be possible to understand the macrocosmic (a cultural) context and the microcosmic (also a cultural) institution. But what does one do about it, as administrator or leader? The study of a particular field seems eventually to yield a cluster of values and techniques—a way of thinking that actually suggests a procedure for acting on the basis of it. In the realm of personal outlook and style of acting, one finds that applied anthropology offers much that is worthwhile.

The Macrocosmic Context of Higher Education

The specifics of administrative/anthropological actions within the microcosm of institution occur within the macrocosmic context of higher education today. Underlying the entire cultural context of higher education for more than seven hundred years is the fact that it institutionalizes and sustains two opposing ideas of Western thought and experience—the first, knowledge viewed as an end in itself, an intellectual challenge in its acquisition; and, second, knowledge seen as the solution to social problems. The academic center confronts, as do all of its component parts, including the discipline of anthropology itself, the tension between preserving and adding to knowledge and the function of channeling this knowledge into use, whether by teaching or in other acts of dissemination. Distinctive organizations within academic structures rise to sponsor these functions: in general, the disciplines for the first and the professional schools for the second. For example, the secondary position assigned by the early English university to the professions reenforced its faculties of arts to resist the inclusion of science in the curriculum. Likewise, the autonomy and prestige of the German professoriate placed the delights over the utilities of science. Conversely, part-time doctors, lawyers, and other professionals in Scotland facilitated an early interest in the practical applications of knowledge (Ashby 1959:6). This historic conflict in two basic intellectual functions sustains to this day a tension between general and specific studies and between the purely intellectual and the practical. Perhaps even more important is the historical suggestion of mankind's two different interests in the mode of observing the natural and human worlds—the one emphasizing intellectual adventure and enhancement of the person; the other, more active and short term, adding to social enhancement.

The slowness of change within the academic enterprise has been in one sense the basis of its durability. For it is therein able to tolerate two quite dissimilar functions—that which hoards knowledge and is personal in its use, and that which shares knowledge and is social (Ashby 1959:69–70). The university adapts slowly and imperfectly. The process invites and includes the creation of new institutions. Due in part to such durability, colleges and universities provide in their everyday activity a quite remarkable product. Through their academic channels, they send people to society who have been exposed to what is known about science, technology, the arts, and administration. Through their technical channels, they provide skills, ideas, and products which have come to bear fundamentally upon industry, agriculture, health, education, and communication. These channels function without much conscious design. But when "missions" are established, when limited projects are devised in response to special social needs and pressures, the accommodation tends to become more slow and incomplete (Moravcsik and Ziman 1975:699–724).

The traditional reverence of the United States for higher education's product has been strengthened by an ethic which saw higher learning as a chief avenue of personal advancement. The industrial revolution reenforced this belief and molded the culture to a concept of progress aimed at scientific–technological advance and material success. Educational institutions have managed to touch, influence, and be influenced by that culture in ways never before achieved. Yet disquieting cues forwarn that these points of contact are now blurred. Beset by swift change and new pressures of an interdependent world, both society and education are less sure of themselves today. Societal goals of technological and material advance are becoming more clouded, complex and filled with unexpected outcomes. Educational insti tutions are strained between the need to respond to new socioeconomic realities and their desire to be the embodiment of an active culture in a nation that many feel is floundering for lack of a cultural/ethical identity. During the very rise in size and prominence of higher education, the shared values which bind the social context have seemed to unravel and disintegrate (Blau 1974:615–635). Concern over the social costs of material progress is evident, but the search for new beliefs, legitimacies, and purposes seems sporadic and incoherent. Question after question arises. To what extent are the dissatisfactions with education related to broader failures to find new meanings and legitimacies? Has so much been expected of education that it is blamed for conditions quite beyond its control? Is education being asked to assume the roles of other social institutions and programs which have failed?

In the modern period, higher education has been characterized by a pronounced shift from the historic preparation of leaders from the elite classes to the training of great numbers of managers and technologists. From elitism to mass education to universal access has been the nature of an epochal transition (Trow 1973:6–7). While elite forms served to enhance the intellect and character of the few, the new mass forms respond to the many who demand access to educational opportunity. The rapid growth in higher education which resulted in the industrial countries has become the major element in the social context of higher education today.

This significant change shows how the cultural imperatives of the macrocosmic level of society may come to dominate projects at the microcosmic level. This influence changes the nature of institutions; it alters the very meaning of daily (the truly microcosmic) life and work and production. For example, early capitalism in America built upon an enormous resolve to achieve and produce, which drew upon the core values of self-discipline, objectivity, and rationality. These values were incorporated into the aims of mass education. In the later stages of secular capitalism, economic production grew more specialized in more complex work places (with attendant separations of production centers from family and community). The basis of employment shifted from a tie to austerity and achievement and toward the idea of work and production as a means to acquire goods, services, and possessions: in short, to achieve affluence and to consume. A heightened devotion to pleasure, to hedonism, was introduced (Etzioni 1972:2–11). These shifts were accompanied by growing interests for acquiring the knowledge, skill, and status necessary, initially, to produce, and then to produce in order to consume. Education swung inexorably to honoring these qualities, and academic institutions assumed the major task of sorting and credentialling human talent so that it could be more rapidly and efficiently allocated.

This evolution sped onward and apace with the democratization of culture. Human skill and economics became inextricably linked. Then the experience of World War II ignited the unprecedented move to technologize society and to democratize education. Pressured by such social need, higher education exploded along a sharply rising curve of growth. The institutions themselves became bureaucratized. As the doors opened to the mass desire to share in culture and technology, and as knowledge was demanded for direct use in community and society, the obligations of the academy multiplied. Nearly all the historic functions have seemed useful and have been carried forward to the new day—professional training from Bologna, the nurturing of gentlemen from Oxford, the conduct of research from Berlin, the grooming of technologists from Zurich (Ashby 1959:68).

Along this way, curriculum became more flexible and varied. Teaching of skill and application grew more rapidly than the teaching of theory and concept. Old differences between secondary schooling and college receded, so that attending the latter became more of a continuation of experience already in process. Educational standards became more varied as they responded to differing interests and capabilities of students. Standards also differed in response to the ranking and other characteristics of fields of study. Consensus over standards weakened as the mass approach grew. The old idea that the professoriate is the very heart of the college was seriously eroded.

These shifts indicate that mass education has now arrived at a watershed of academic history of no less enormity than those of earlier times. Comment about this watershed has dominated the discussion and planning of higher education for nearly a decade. Some have come to hold the ". . . view that the Golden Age of higher education lies more in the past than in the future" (Carnegie Commission 1973:7). The monumental studies of the Carnegie Commission on Higher Education have examined, analyzed, and measured higher education. They describe new problems of politicization, the unwillingness of the public to transfer income from other sectors to higher education, the lagging productivity of academic people, and the almost certain decrease in numbers of conventional students in the next twenty years. These features of the "crisis of confidence" which now envelops the academic world suggest that the hypotheses which seemed implicit in earlier watersheds—the overriding power of the social context, the split in basic educative functions, and the slowness of prototype forms to respond—will be much in evidence for the balance of this century.

The administrator/anthropologist searches behind these profiles for new shifts in values and beliefs about higher education. The search leads back to the cultural context that surrounds the work, production, and achievement that went far in underwriting the transition from elite to mass education: first, the shift from production in relation to personal austerity and, second, achievement in relation to consumption and possession. Now it is possible to detect a third era, one that would justify work and production as a prime source of personal enjoyment (Bell 1976:37). This new era, defined not alone, as supposed, by young people, subscribes to work and production but does not view the success that comes from them as the primary measure of life. These new values rise to challenge clusters of values which have shaped both American society and its institutions of higher education.

First, there is the stronger hold that personal pleasure has taken upon life in general, and the hedonistic element contained within the new demand that success in life is measured by enjoyment and self-understanding rather than by work for individual achievement, and production (Yankelovich 1974; Gottlieb 1974:541). Second, research and observations indicate that younger people fear economic disaster less than their elders. They may worry over the lack of personal fulfillment, but worry less about economic catastrophe. Third, there is what some term the new psychology of entitlement: that society has achieved such a level of technology and material means that each person has earned the right to a job that gives satisfaction, to participate in the decisions that affect that job, to a secure old age, and to have major health care provided. Moreover, this view holds that it is natural for people, once they have food, shelter, and safety, to pursue self-development. Fourth, the challenge made of the impersonal by the personal also questions the rationality upon which modern efficiency and science are founded. Whether in the distrust of management (as when some educators find efficiency and learning antagonistic, for example), in the views of the counterculture or occasionally within the environmental movement, efficiency is here and there alleged to be exploitative and inimical to future society (Etzioni 1972:5).

As an overview, one may say that the first third of the present century gave rapid rise to modernism in the arts, literature, and science. The middle third employed mass education to democratize the fruits of this modernism by disseminating it into the common culture. The final third of the century looms as a period of confusion, tension, and uncertain reform of colleges and universities; for they confront the conflict between the rational use of knowledge and a resistance to the modernism which such use has been dispersed to achieve. One must wonder what new prototypes may now be conceived to answer the question: having moved from cultivating character to training and certifying the uses of technique, where will the liberated autonomous person be educated (Lasch 1975)?

The Microcosmic Context of Higher Education

What values and skills evolve from anthropology to guide the administrator within complex organizations? What values and skills help one to achieve consensus about goals and objectives? How does the administrator/anthropologist think of and comprehend the academic institution as a whole?

Anthroplogy encourages the administrator to seek the boundaries of the institution, whether ecological or functional. Of similar interest will be the zones of tension, how well personal and institutional goals mesh, and where incentives reside and how they function. The administrator/anthropologist is motivated to think of the institution as a whole. Applying anthropology helps the administrator to face three ways at once: to groups which provide resources and support; to the institution itself; and to those for whom its product is intended. Anthropology becomes directly useful when one must deal with connections and with relationships and the values and symbols which sustain them.

How these questions and principles assist the administrator will doubtlessly vary from person to person; however, they tend to instill the following values about how one conducts overall administrative tasks in the university, especially those of the university president. They do not stand alone nor do they represent all that is possible from the study of anthropology. Further, they doubtlessly spring also from the trial and error and the successes and defeats which characterize any administrative career and outlook.

One such value encourages the administrator/anthropologist to improve the unity among the several disciplines which compose the college or university. This value is fed by a concern for the gulf between the issues of society, which grow more interdependent, and the nature of knowledge, which grows more specialized. Thus, the disintegration of shared values in the larger world, and the evident despair of matching specialized solutions with generalized problems, both relate to the academic manner of separating rather than fusing the many categories of knowledge. Moreover, the old historic tension—knowledge for its own sake or for use—is everywhere evident. The academic form continues to be absorbed into technological society, as it has come to depend upon the linkages of its mission to state and federal governments and as the shift continues from cultivating citizens to training technologists. Accordingly, academics have been led to perhaps overstated premises of certainty and precision. They tend also to isolation, suspicion, and distrust between the disciplines, especially when enrollment growth and resources are jeopardized. They have been only partially capable of responding usefully to those grievous issues of the modern world—e.g., food, energy, pollution, population, human settlements—which persist at the intersections of the boundaries among disciplines.

Anthropology helps an administrator to look below the surface of the college or university in order to see how its missions and the location of knowledge may be brought into harmony. Related ways of planning must be found, as well as the manner of allocating resources, securing personnel, and adapting organization. The anthropologist will search for integrative ideas and will help them rise alongside of the customary compartments. Such themes may respond to real problems, as when the agricultural colleges once placed departments geared to segments of industry next to disciplinary departments in order to focus both the natural and social sciences upon actual problems of farm production and marketing. Themes dealing with communications and environment, or with technology and values may arise in such professional schools as engineering and architecture, in order to attempt fusions of scientific and humanistic values. Or more general and linking disciplines may emerge, as happened in biophysics and biochemistry, as well as in the *bauhaus* conception of building a bridge between art and technology.

A second value that emerges from the theory of culture into the guidance of institutions is that which strengthens the administrator's desire to seek outcomes from interpersonal relationships rather than from formal rules of organization. To be sure, such values and skills will conflict from time to time with the seeming necessity of position and authority. But an anthropological accent remains upon those shared beliefs and symbols which reflect the self-consciousness of the institution as a community, to include those usages and ways of thinking and doing which are reflective of culture. This interest calls on one to know how people feel about their part in the institution, to be concerned for their personal growth, to know why they may become alienated. This valuing of interpersonal meanings will lead to interests in informal and lateral communications, their special good sense and durability, over those formal and vertical channels which carry the official messages of guidance and response (Gouldner 1959).

Two examples serve this concern for the meaning of interpersonal relations. Both illustrate that one of the great influences which anthropology brings to the administrator is that it reminds over and over again that compiling a useful ethnography of the campus results from direct involvement rather than from the reconstruction of official memoranda and interpretation. The first refers to how the administrator/anthropologist will be concerned with the incompleteness of the formal environment for schooling. Applying anthropological insights turns such a person to the "third world" of the campus—the informal experiences along human developmental lines—and how they link up with classroom and residential activities (Panel on Youth 1974). For example, anthropological interests will point out the need for more and continuous studies of incoming new students, about varied human developmental stages and potentials, and further reviews as students proceed with and depart from college careers. Such interests are not without strain, for they challenge the conventional meaning of the educative process. They call also for alternative learning environments, an activity which tradition insists is solely the province of the faculty. But anthropology leads the administrator to ask: "Is there a campus culture, and what is its meaning for student growth?"

The second example refers to the embarrassing lack of academic interest in adult development. This is especially the case when faculty growth itself is held back by the failure to relate learning to adult growth and development. Informed research on adult development of faculty is rare. An anthropological view will detect the anomaly between what appears as a natural web of intellectual relationships amongst faculty and the presence of frequent isolated and narrowed life cycles and styles among many of them. The isolation of the classroom model, the privacy of much research and scholarship, disciplinary loyalties which run to specialties rather than within institutions, success defined by peers—all combine with the decay of mentoring roles (as among departmental chairmen and deans) to yield an incomplete climate for potential growth, especially for those at mid-career (Hodgkinson 1974: 263–274). Anthropology helps one to examine and improve the mentoring function (who are the helpmate/advisors?) and to devise projects and personnel policies to increase variety and change. Since lines of status and power tend to confine the administrator to the center, the field orientation of the anthropologist nevertheless insists that attempts must be made to overcome it. Anthropology suggests that one may do so by interacting informally in the faculty precinct, by gaining firsthand information about campus events and personalities, and by working at the grassroots, and in person to reconcile policy and rumors of policy.

The third administrative value which emerges from the study of anthropology suggests a preference for a course of studies to be learner-centered rather than dominated by the authority of teacher and subject matter. This value points to another incompleteness of higher education: the reluctance of most colleges and universities to devise inventive ways to conduct the educative process, as they are more apt to do in scholarship. At the national or other macrocosmic levels, higher education has engaged in projects that were truly transforming, but the mode of transmitting knowledge to students has changed very little. The university has not seriously studied its own educational role; its abdication to the professional schools of education merely weakened the overall concern with innovative research and development on the subject of human learning itself. A basic challenge results therefrom for the administrator/anthropologist—overcoming the inherent limitations to fostering independence of students whose college participation should help them make a mature transition to adulthood.

Anthropology gives to administrators a view about transmissions of ideas between cultures and cross-cultural influences, whether in small or large societies. Anthropology reveals how important out-of-school instruction is, especially the informal learning that occurs in family and other intimate groups. The administrator/anthropologist will try, therefore, to lead in ways that reduce the tendency of the academic form to narrow to (and sometimes trivialize) the classroom model. Such leadership will introduce concepts and practices about how people learn from the tension between the isolated and sometimes exclusive assumptions of the single institution and those stimulants and media of culture which condition not only the learners but the institutions themselves. Surely anthropology, perhaps more than other fields of study, reminds the administrator that a single institution is but a fractional and humble part of the total educative process in the society.

The fourth value which emerges from the influence of anthropology gives the administrator a concern for strengthening the "natural-system" model of organization in contrast to a more "rational-legal" model (Gouldner 1959:404–405). That anthropology would influence one in this manner roots somehow in a basic tenet of the field—to study the manner of life of people—and the humanism which emerges from the responsibilities of such study. It is a short distance from there to a sympathetic and even ethical concern that the lives of people properly change indigenously rather than by the direct intervention of others (Thompson 1970; Hymes 1969). To be sure, the administrator must strive to reconcile the natural and rational models, for both are present. But the underlying interest which draws the anthropologist to observe the meaning of group life creates a desire to see that such a community is sustained and strengthened. When choices have to be made, they tend to be made on that side. Genuine role conflicts and personal ambiguities will result from these actions to balance the natural and rational systems as one acts on the basis of formal authority on the one hand and tries to sustain informal community on the other hand (James 1971:223–228). There is no better example of how these choices occur than by what happens to an administrative posture in issues of academic governance.

Complex, slow to change, and generally imitative of a widespread model, overall academic governance—who joins in the definition of goals, the allocation of resources, and the creation of policies—is perhaps the most complicated and elusive problem to test the application of anthropology in the administration of a larger college and university. Great pressures to reform academic governance have followed the rise of an academic managerial class and the shift from elite to mass higher education. Academic constituencies feel, on the whole, that they have lost power. Hopes that greater participation might generate more power have been disappointed. Meanwhile, institutions continue to juggle three different, sometimes contradictory, forms: the ancient idea of the "collegial" or self-governing community; the corporate model of formal and hierarchical levels of decision-making; the organization of the university as a companion to the professional systems of society, e.g., engineering, medicine, business, law, education, social work, and agriculture. It is characteristic of American academic institutions that they accommodate to all three forms: it is better done than many expect or believe.

At the heart of institutional governance rests the critical question of who, and by what terms, takes part in the process of allocating resources. Governance remains but an exercise until the question arises over who has knowledge of and access to the process of making a budget. It is here that both the "rational-legal" and the "natural" systems come into play and not infrequently into conflict. The key decision involved here, both for the present and for its precedence for the future, involves how much financial knowledge should be shared broadside with the institutional community as a whole. The administrator, an agent of the fiduciary body, will reserve final determination; but this is the "rational-legal" claim at work and will not normally satisfy the "natural" community's desire to be aware and involved. This example brings to view the manner in which anthropology induces loyalty to the natural community. One may expect the administrator/anthropologist to move on the side of open disclosure of financial knowledge. For here, there is in test the question of what is the most durable component of the leader's authority: competence as perceived by the community or power as defined by statute.

Thus, the administrator/anthropologist will likely respond to such problems by an interest in the *process* of governance in contrast to its *structure*. Anthropological exposure creates a posture that advocates administrative decentralization, task-oriented coalitions, and problem-solving styles. However, strengthening the natural system may increase the institution's resilience and endurance but weaken its capacity for sensitive adjustment and invention. Indeed, perhaps the chief problem of the applied anthropological view for the administrator is the conflict between helping to sustain a decentralized community with its own natural ecology within a formal bureaucratic medium which demands, under its sponsors and charters, that accountability for institutional results be defined and accepted.

Summary

The manner in which anthropology influences and sharpens certain basic values for the administrator cultivates distinctive styles and outlooks for the conduct of administration in the corporate society.

Such an administrator is likely to exhibit a mood of detachment from the administrative process. The related tasks will in all likelihood be viewed as necessary and important to organizational life, objects of professional study in their own right rather than objects of power and status. Such a practitioner will want to understand prestige and its symbols; hence they will likely offer no unreal inducements. This mood fosters an interest in being intellectually and physically mobile in the institution. It provides a positive regard for all the specialized talents of higher education which, in the end, must be integrated.

A related aspect of style will be a mood of dispensability, a view of administration that defines each task as the choosing of courses within shifting purposes. This mood requires one to be able to understand and restrain personal identities, tensions, and private expectations. Certainly the holistic character of anthropology, its overall interest in the activities, patterns, and symbols in human groups, will soon reveal that administration can be at best but a means of dealing with conflict and consensus, and that only continuous compromises for the common good will attain the goal. Each administrative choice, in the face of the always uneasy tension between rational and nonrational forces, can be the final one; hence, a steadfast mood of dispensability.

Another aspect of style is an accent on consultation. Academic people of exceedingly specialized talents function with a mix of both manifest and latent identities, as is illustrated in the conventional suspicion of faculty for elective and representative forms of governance. To move from conflict through consultation to consensus requires more than casual skill with helping members of the institution to free themselves from the outlooks of their own compartments and to assume both the role and the outlooks which others have. However, the administrator/anthropologist does after all practice administration, and sometimes even the most mundane of its functions cannot be avoided. Real skill is required in knowing when and where consultation must cease and a sequence of actions begin. Organizational ends tend to break down into an often elaborate means–ends scheme, with each step at once an end and a means to still another. Deciding what this sequence will be like, who will and should be involved, how much time the sequence should take, and what groups in and out of the institution may help or retard its flow, are all questions for which administrators must find answers. They cannot be answered with assurance unless the executive mind is able to systematically comprehend the institution as a whole and the general terms of who gives and who receives from its presence (its "support-recipient" situation).

But nobody can sort very clearly those forces which together shape both personal outlook and style. Family and social origins, the nature of schooling, the kind of organization, even the not-so-subtle differences between line and staff duty—all these and more are ingested into the strain which the corporate society asks all administrators to pay. One does little better in trying to note those uses of anthropology which seem to alter administrative behavior. But when the measure is taken of complex corporate life, and what administrators can and are expected to do is placed against that measure, the influence of anthropology will likely stand on the side of the following elements.

Anthropology leads one to grasp the wholeness of a situation, to get at the kinds and diversities of human patterns as well as the values which sustain them and the symbols which communicate them. This is a competence for sensing first and knowing later that less is happening than is possible. Certainly in a time when the specialization of technological society obscures the ties between people, acts, and events, the uses of anthropology point to administration which is reasonably at home with social complexity.

Anthropology further leads its student into expanding awareness of the interdependence among groups. For example, the connection between the myriad of projects at the working and living level of society and those projects of larger societal systems (as in the relation of a university to Washington, to the international community, or to a state planning agency) sharpens understanding of invention, change, stability, transmission, and reaction. Such an administrator veers unhesitantly to the study of social change, how it evolves and from where, and who is implicated in its impact and resolution. All administration in the corporate society works to diffuse and utilize knowledge and skill, a core value indeed. Thus, the uses of anthropology help the administrator to identify, understand, and practice at the crucial interfaces of this flow in technological civilization.

Anthropology strives to discover the core values of groups—families, communities, universities, corporations, societies. It is a search for how the group perceives its own world—all those intimately possessed values and concepts about social order, of the proper way by which people of different classes may function together, of the meaning of personal identity, of the self and how it is defined, and of how best to organize space, direction, and time. The anthropologist learns how people in groups come to grips with all the ambiguities of their own perceptions, thus giving a glimpse of how universal the condition and the study of humans are. Is it surprising that an administrator prepared in this way would have sympathy for those whom he or she has come partially to know, and understand that their chance to build new forms beyond where they are belongs to them and not to those who would intervene? We may safely say that we need more not less of those administrators who hold affection for people in whose service they have been called to administer.

8

THE CHANGING ROLE OF AN APPLIED ANTHROPOLOGIST

John H. Peterson, Jr.

The process of becoming an applied anthropologist is a continuous one. Each new situation presents unique learning opportunities and possibilities for expanding one's repertoire of interactional and analytical skills. The complexities of human organization and interorganizational relationships are understood in new ways when one learns about them not from the textbook but from personally experiencing the consequences of erroneous assumptions about human behavior.

For several years, John H. Peterson has worked with and for the Mississippi Choctaws. During this period, these working relationships have significantly changed in response to alterations in the role of native Americans in tribal government and Peterson's own professional development. Peterson articulates the uncertainties felt by many who accept opportunities for nonacademic employment and fear that such work will jeopardize their professional careers as anthropologists. When he decided to become a tribal employee, he did not know that the Choctaws would continue the work of educating him as an applied anthropologist and that he had much to learn. He describes his learning experiences and illustrates the contributions that nonacademic work situations make to the professional development of the anthropologist.

John H. Peterson, Jr. (Ph.D., Georgia) is chairperson and associate professor of anthropology at Mississippi State University. His fieldwork has been among the Mississippi Choctaw. He has done applied work as chief planner for the Choctaw Tribal Government, project director for water resource development and information dissemination in northeast Mississippi, and in bilingual education among the Choctaw. He has been a consultant to the National Science Foundation, the Brookings Institution, the United States Army Corps of Engineers, the Mississippi Band of Choctaw Indians, and several educational institutions. He is currently a Congressional fellow of the American Anthropological Association.

THIS ESSAY DESCRIBES the changing relationship between one anthropologist and one client group, the Mississippi Choctaws.[1] During the past eight years, my role as an anthropologist changed from that of a neophyte fieldworker to a middle-aged department head at a nearby university. My positions with the client group included working as an externally funded fieldworker, unpaid friend, paid consultant, full-time tribal employee, and subcontractor on tribal programs. The client group also changed from an Indian tribe just beginning to question the complete authority of the almost totally white-staffed Choctaw Agency, a branch of the Bureau of Indian Affairs (BIA) to an aggressively emerging tribal government and an Indian-directed Choctaw Agency. Under the circumstances, my role as anthropologist shifted in accordance with my own knowledge and capabilities, the needs of the Choctaws with whom I was working, and their knowledge and capabilities for utilizing my anthropological skills and talents.

The approximately 4,000 Mississippi Choctaws live in seven small reservation communities scattered across a seven county area centered in east central Mississippi.[2] They are the descendants of those who resisted both the general Indian removal from the Southeast in the early 1800s and a later removal effort in 1903. These Choctaws were not legally recognized as an Indian tribe until 1918 when the Choctaw Agency was established. The Agency bought land in the areas of existing population concentration, thereby creating the seven separate reservation communities of today. Although medical and educational services were provided from the very beginning, the Choctaw Agency has been underfunded throughout its history. As a result, the educational level remained extremely low until the past decade. There was little out-migration, and the population remained primarily Choctaw-speaking. A tribal council was not established until 1945, and most issues on the reservation continued to be determined by the Choctaw Agency.

I first visited the Mississippi Choctaw reservation in 1967 when preparing to undertake fieldwork for my dissertation. I was accompanied by Professor Wilfrid C. Bailey, who had previously assisted

---

[1] The basis for this chapter can be found in a series of papers: Peterson (1973a; 1973b; 1974a; 1974b) which describe my changing role with the Choctaw Tribe.

[2] Detailed descriptions of the Mississippi Choctaws can be found in Peterson (1970a; 1970b; 1972); Peterson, Spencer and Kim (1974); and Thompson and Peterson (1975).

the Choctaw Agency in carrying out a total tribal survey in 1962. I originally intended to focus my research on the Choctaw schools. I had hoped to enter the field supported by the GI bill and a small research grant from the University of Georgia.

The Agency superintendent strongly discouraged me from attempting a school study because a major new program in the schools had recently caused some disruption. He felt that another outsider would only exacerbate the situation and increase the confusion. Instead, he proposed a new tribal survey along the lines previously carried out by Professor Bailey. If I were willing to complete a questionnaire, train and direct interviewers, and analyze and prepare a final report, the Choctaw Agency would supply ten people to undertake the survey. Under the circumstances, this seemed to be a good alternative to my original plan. So I returned to the University of Georgia to complete my academic work there, and to draft a questionnaire. I returned to the reservation at the end of the spring term, 1968.

Anthropological Field Worker

Arrangements were made for me to share office space in the Branch of Social Services of the BIA in Philadelphia, Mississippi, which is located seven to fifteen miles from the three reservations in the county and much further from the remaining reservations located in nearby counties. The location was ideal for the purposes of working with agency interviewers, checking interview forms for accuracy, and comparing interview data with other available data. Further, since interviewers were selected from many different branches of the Agency, including social services, home economics, employment assistance, credit, and education, I had an excellent opportunity to rapidly gain an impression of the Choctaw people and the Agency programs for them. As a result, I soon developed a degree of insight into the various BIA programs as well as into individual employees.

Through daily interaction with BIA employees within their own offices, I observed the vast range of attitudes toward the Choctaws associated with different programs, and between individuals on the same program. Within the BIA structure, there was a general dichotomy between those who perceived themselves as working for the

Choctaws and those who perceived themselves as working for the BIA. Although the local distinction was never made in these terms, the "hard-liners" took a literal letter-of-the-regulation attitude and described others as "soft on Indians." In contrast, those who perceived their jobs as working on behalf of the Choctaws viewed the "hard-liners" as legalistic bureaucrats.

As the months passed, I began to feel that I was buried under a mound of questionnaires. Nevertheless, I took pride in the fact that I was avoiding the conflict between the "hard-liners" and the "soft-liners." I felt I was carrying out the ideal role of the applied anthropologist by finding a balance point between my own research interests, the interests of the client group, the Choctaws, and the interests of the service agency, the BIA.

Because I worked with the personnel and in the offices of the Choctaw Agency, I was often perceived by others as an Agency employee. Even those who knew differently classified me as working with the Agency rather than as an independent researcher, since the task of supervising the survey occupied most of my time during Agency working hours. This was no great disadvantage in terms of meeting the Choctaw people, however, since most community activities took place at night in the form of intercommunity ball games in the summer, school related activities during the winter, and church activities throughout the year. As the year passed, I came to know many of the Choctaw people personally; nevertheless most Choctaws continued to perceive me as an Agency employee.

There was little reason for the Choctaws to assume that I was not an Agency employee. With the exception of two candidates for master's degrees who had undertaken brief periods of summer research, there had been no major anthropological field research among the Choctaws for almost thirty years. Indeed, one of my aims was to create a role of anthropological researcher working on behalf of the Choctaw people. For this reason, I periodically reported on the progress of the survey to the tribal chairman, as well as to the superintendent of the Choctaw Agency. The tribal chairman, Mr. Emmett York, was supportive of my work. Thus, although the majority of the Choctaw people did not know of my work, I believed the role of independent researcher was being accepted by the Indian leaders with whom I had direct contact.

Unanticipated Conflict over Research Data

In the closing days of my fieldwork, this illusion was rudely shattered. Robert Benn, the housing officer of the Choctaw Agency, was preparing a proposal for a federal housing program and was able to use the questionnaires to determine the number of potentially eligible families. I was pleased with this development; it underscored my assumption that the survey results would be of benefit to the Choctaw people. Shortly thereafter, a private company, under contract to the BIA, for relocation training, also requested use of the raw data and offered secretarial assistance for cross-checking the validity of questionnaire information. The head of the Choctaw Community Action Agency also offered secretarial help for this purpose. Both organizations were interested in using the raw data for the preparation of refunding or supplementary funding proposals for their respective programs. It seemed like a good idea to me. It would save time, make the data available sooner, and hopefully result in expanded programs for the Choctaw people.

My positive feelings about the above requests were not shared by the leaders of the Choctaw Agency. They informed me that data collected by personnel of the Choctaw Agency belonged to the Agency, and that I should not have entered into such discussions without their prior approval. Suddenly, satisfaction about my role as an applied anthropologist who worked in the interests of both the Choctaw people and the agencies serving them fell apart. I was forced to recognize that only my previous insignificance, in terms of the forces operating on the Choctaw reservation, had protected me from the conflict which now engulfed me. The potential importance of my work did not become evident until the questionnaires were used to support the Choctaw Agency's housing effort. It was after this event that other organizations on the reservation expressed interest in the survey and the analysis of the data for their own purposes.

I had been keenly aware of the conflicting attitudes toward the Choctaws and their needs among the different branches of the Choctaw Agency. I belatedly understood the existence of potential conflict among all agencies working on the Choctaw reservation. I was informed that since the bulk of the effort behind the tribal survey had been furnished by the Choctaw Agency, the decision for the release of the data must be made by the Agency. At this point, I feared that nine months of work would go down the drain. However, an agreement was reached that no data would be released to any individual or group prior to completion of a published report. This compromise insured that the data would become public property, thus safeguarding my need for use of the data as well as the needs of other organizations working on the Choctaw reservation.

From hindsight, I realize that part of the dispute over the data was due to my naïveté and failure to make detailed written agreements concerning the project prior to undertaking the task of directing the survey. At the same time, the direct experience with this problem of ownership of research data provided me with a more graphic education about the problems of applied anthropology than I would have otherwise obtained.

Ironically, I had been trying for many months to disassociate myself in the minds of tribal officials from employees of the Choctaw Agency. When they came to understand that I was an independent researcher. I found that in fact I was not. My only choice was to return to the private firm and the Choctaw Community Action Program and explain why I could not accept the offer of help on the survey, and to promise that I would get the material into print as rapidly as possible so that it would be available to everyone. Although this decision was accepted with relatively good grace, I felt that I had let the tribe down. This situation was to affect my choice of a job in the year following the completion of my fieldwork.

Academic Anthropologist

With my fieldwork drawing to a close, I began looking for an academic position. While I was being interviewed by several universities outside the state, I was asked if I would be interested in a potential position with the Choctaw Agency. I was told that I could be assigned to complete the survey. The salary was higher than that which had been offered by universities and, given my financial situation, I was tempted to accept the offer. But the tribal chairman, with whom I discussed the matter, stated bluntly that if I accepted the position, I would be on the other side of the fence, and we could no longer be friends. Moreover, my major professor emphasized the importance of completing the dissertation and beginning publication if I wished to be an anthropologist.

Since I had just spent several years studying to be an anthropologist and felt obligated to the Choctaw Tribe, I decided to take a university position. Because I had over 500 household surveys to analyze, support for data analysis was a primary consideration. Only nearby Mississippi State University could provide both released time and funds for code clerks and data analysis; so in July 1969, I accepted my first academic appointment there as a full-time researcher with the Social Science Research Center.

When I began my work at Mississippi State, I believed that the conflict I had experienced could be resolved by getting my data into print quickly so that it would be equally accessible to all parties, and my obligations as an objective scholar would be fulfilled. Within a year, I completed both a research report and my dissertation. I was gratified to find that my published data were found useful by both the Choctaw Tribe and the Bureau of Indian Affairs. I was almost convinced that my earlier questioning of the role of the applied anthropologist was premature and resulted largely from my inexperience.

Technical Assistance to the Tribe

Upon the completion of the research report, I began to receive requests for assistance from the Choctaw Agency, the Choctaw Tribe, and the Choctaw Community Action Agency, headed by Phillip Martin, a Mississippi Choctaw. At first, these requests were primarily for specific socioeconomic or historical data needed for program planning or funding requests. In giving this technical assistance, there was never any question of consultant fees or research potential. I was not working as an outside consultant; rather I was simply helping my neighbors and friends. For example, I was asked by the Branch of Employment Assistance of the Choctaw Agency to reanalyze the Choctaw population and employment data to fit the data categories required by the BIA semiannual manpower report. At the request of the tribal chairman, I worked with HUD planners to provide data to meet the needs of the Choctaw Planning Commission.

A broader range of requests came from the Choctaw Community Action Program, and I gradually became involved in considerable technical writing which went beyond simple data analysis. This expanded role was not a new development. Even during my initial fieldwork, I had prepared a critique of a proposed Indian village development proposal at the request of the tribal chairman and the Choctaw Agency. The difference now was primarily in terms of increasing frequency and scope of these later requests.

The technical assistance I provided was quite different from my earlier role as an independent researcher who hopefully was contributing to both the Choctaw Agency and Choctaw Tribe. The new role was essentially one of technical assistance in the preparation of what might be called background briefs such as proposals, position papers, and correspondence supporting a Choctaw position. The word "advocate" has sometimes been used to describe this role, but the term is misleading in that the tribal leaders were completely capable of personally presenting their own cases and in outlining the scope and content of the written material they wished me to prepare. My task was to translate their ideas into a written form acceptable to agency officials and elected representatives, and to provide detailed supporting data. One of the primary factors in the increasing number of requests for my help was my willingness to offer such support without formal recognition that I had given it.

As time passed, I became involved in projects which went beyond the socioeconomic or historical data I had under my control. Hence, I was dependent upon being furnished information which would not normally have been available to me but was now provided. My access to information was given with the understanding that I would use it to document the case in hand. I made no attempt to keep notes on either the data or the discussions of the direction which the draft material should take. I believed it would be unethical to utilize information, given to me in confidence for a specific task, as data for possible future academic publications.

With the election of Phillip Martin as tribal chairman in 1971, my involvement rapidly increased. Under Martin's direction, the tribal government was restricted by the 1971 Tribal Council (Mississippi Band of Choctaw Indians: 1972–1973). Community Action programs and tribal programs were consolidated, and the Tribal Council adopted the goal of an expanded effort in self-development and self-determination. Unlike the previous tribal administration, the 1971–1973 tribal administration established a Tribal Planning Center. As a result, rather than working alone, I found myself working on assignments with other consultants or members of the tribal planning staff. In most of these efforts, the fact that I was an anthropologist was not as important as whether I could provide the needed technical assistance. Rather than preparing initial drafts of documents for tribal leaders which were then reviewed by others, I myself reviewed documents prepared by full-time tribal employees and suggested revision. Thus my role had changed from that of technical writer to a technical adviser. As a technical writer, I had worked on specific issues, proposals, or documents. With the consolidation of tribal programs, these individual efforts became less important than the contribution they made to the overriding cause of Choctaw self-development. I began to understand the importance of every action becoming part of an expanded effort at tribal self-government under the direction of the Tribal Council.

Unanticipated Conflict over Time Commitment

As my activities increased, I began to experience some conflict with my position in the university. From the beginning, my university appointment had been predominantly in research, with only one-fourth to one-half of my time spent in teaching. In my academic role, I was continuing typical work as an applied anthropologist. In simple terms, my salary at the university partially depended on my ability to secure funds for applied research projects. But, the more I assisted the tribe, the less time I had to invest in securing funds for my own university-based work. As I assisted both the tribe and other branches of the university in developing programs for the Choctaws, senior faculty members within my own department began to ask questions about the potential benefit of my activities for the department. As a junior nontenured faculty member, these questions were a cause of concern to me. Fortunately by the spring of 1972, funds were secured for a joint university–tribal effort in the field of education, which allowed me to work with the Tribe under a subcontract, in ways which more nearly approximated my other efforts in applied anthropology.

Full-Time Tribal Employee

Before the above program became operational, the tribal chairman requested that I take a leave of absence from the university to become chief of the Choctaw Planning Center. This request caused me to seriously consider my role as an applied anthropologist. By means of the subcontract, I had hoped to reduce the pressure on me by becoming a university based researcher working on a funded research project with the Tribe. Yet, now I was being asked to become a full-time tribal employee for a year. I worried about my status within the profession. As a young anthropologist, how would a year of nonproductivity, in an academic sense, affect my career? A future factor in my consideration was the growing conflict between the Choctaw Agency and the Tribal Council as the latter continued to press for expanded self-government on the reservation. Members of the Council were actively advocating the replacement of the Agency superintendent. I was still agonizing over my decision when I was warned by Choctaw Agency personnel who were unfavorable to the tribal government, that a petition was being prepared for recall of the tribal chairman. Even if this move was unsuccessful, it was doubtful that there would be sufficient funds to permit the tribe to employ me. At this point, my position in anthropology seemed to be less important than my willingness to respond to a request to support Choctaw efforts and to trust the tribal government to provide the financial assistance to enable me to do so.

I have elsewhere described some of the general orientations and skills which were required in my position as chief of the Tribal Planning Center. (Peterson, 1974b) It is more difficult to describe the change that this position brought about in my relationship with the tribe. The title of chief of the Planning Center created humor, especially among Choctaw friends who would remark, "Now we have a white man chief." A solution to this problem occurred when an older Choctaw brought me a newspaper clipping which described my appointment. The headline stated "Anthropologist Appointed Tribal Aide." I was told, "John, now I know what you are doing."

Titles such as chief of the Planning Center or chief planner indicated someone in authority who was responsible for telling others what to do. On the other hand, several positions on the reservation utilized people as "aides" such as teacher aides, nurses' aides, and social service aides. I used this description of "tribal aide," as a mental orientation to my job. This approach was also taken by the tribal chairman when he introduced me and other new employees at a series of community meetings. He simply stated that he had asked me to leave the university for a year and come down and "help out."

The difficulty in undertaking my new assignment was the identification of exactly whom I was to help out. When based at the university, I undertook efforts which I believed were helpful to the tribe generally. When I had been previously requested to carry out a specific assignment, I worked on a single program or with a specific group. But as a full-time employee of the tribe, I had to fit into the structure of an existing tribal government. Although I understood the need for the overall goal of increasing tribal self-government, there were multiple relationships to be established with many individuals and groups.

The Planning Center was organized to provide technical assistance to the Tribal Council as the governing body of the Tribe. The Council was composed of sixteen members representing seven distinct reservation communities. The chairman of the Council was employed as the full-time top administrative officer of the Tribe and charged with implementing the decisions of the full Council. As a result, the Planning Center worked directly under the tribal chairman. The work of the Center was intended to assist the chairman in the implementation of policy decisions decided upon by the Tribal Council as a whole.

It would be simplistic to state that members of the Planning Center could assist the entire Tribe by carrying out the direct instructions of the tribal chairman. Any active tribal chairman is far too busy to be able to give detailed daily instructions to his staff. In the case of Choctaw tribal chairman, Phillip Martin, this involved some twenty-two separate program directors. He also served as the official spokesman of the Tribe in negotiations and program coordination with state agencies, various federal agencies, and related agencies on the reservations, such as the Choctaw Agency and the Public Health Service. This resulted in extensive travel on behalf of the specific tribe and of Indians in general. Finally, a tribal chairman is an elected official whose door must be open to all tribal members.

In summary, members of the Planning Center worked under the broad direction of the tribal chairman to implement the policy decisions of the Tribal Council. They were forced to learn to anticipate the desired means for carrying out these broad instructions and were subject to the approval of the tribal chairman and Council. One consequence of this situation was that the Planning Center was potentially subject to the same diversity of interests as those to which the chairman had to respond. In discussing my potential employment with the Tribal Planning Center, the tribal chairman made clear that one of my specific responsibilities was to maintain a balance between these diverse pressures.

At the time of my employment, there were two polar viewpoints expressed by individuals within the Planning Center. The first of these viewed the Center as accountable solely to the tribal chairman. When carried to an extreme, this perspective led to a lack of communication with other Council members, the Choctaw population, and representatives of other agencies. The negative aspect of this position was that it tended to result in a definition of the Center as an elitist group of non-Choctaws who planned actions for the Choctaw reservation without sufficient input from the Choctaw people. More positively, this position clearly removed planners from policy or political decisions and reserved these for the Tribal Council.

In contrast to those who held the above position, others believed that true implementation of increased self-government on the reservation demanded close interaction between reservation planners, all Council members, and a broad base of community members. The positive aspect of this view was a broader understanding of policy alternatives by both Choctaw officials and planners. The negative aspect was that planners became involved in policy decisions which were the legal responsibility of the Tribal Council. My charge was to insure that the Planning Center achieved a degree of balance between these two alternatives. I was employed not so much because my judgment in this context was superior to that of other planners, but because I had the necessary background and knowledge to understand the various alternatives.

The second charge I received at the time of my appointment was to effect liaison with the BIA and other agencies. Other planners within the Planning Center were young men committed to the common cause of Indian self-government, but with divergent views about the best ways of implementing this goal. Because of their youth and enthusiasm, they tended to take a combative attitude toward the Bureau of Indian Affairs. The tribal chairman made it clear that, despite the political and policy conflicts between the Tribal Council and officials of the Choctaw Agency, it was my responsibility to establish amicable working relationships between tribal and Agency personnel at the program level so that effective delivery and coordination of services could be maintained while political and policy issues were being resolved. This was easier for me than for other tribal planners since I had been working with many Choctaw Agency employees for several years.

My new position had an important effect on my relationship with the Tribe. I was now a tribal employee, answerable directly to the tribal government, and working daily with many members of the Tribe, but especially with tribal program personnel and elected tribal officials. Some of these were older people whom I had met in the past, while others were younger individuals whom I had first met when they were college students. Whereas my doctoral field work had located me in the offices of the Choctaw Agency and labeled me as working for the Agency, I was now labeled as working for the Tribe. Even today, when I meet Choctaws, I am asked, "Didn't you once work for the Tribe?" It is a quite different relationship from that of student field worker or part-time technical assistant, and one that I cherish.

At the end of my leave of absence, I returned to Mississippi State University on sabbatical leave. I had hoped to devote much of my time to writing about my recent experience on the reservation, but this was not to be the case. First, I had to devote considerable time to technical assistance as other people began to take up the work I had left uncompleted on the reservation. Second, a new relationship had developed between Mississippi State University and the Choctaw Tribe during my leave of absence.

Previously, since entrance examinations at the university had blocked admission of more than one or two Choctaw students, the remainder usually went to college in other states. During my year on the reservation, meetings between tribal and university officials resulted in entrance requirements for Choctaws, which recognized their problems with the English language. This increased degree of cooperation enabled the Choctaw Tribe to secure funding for an Indian teacher training project which they subcontracted to Mississippi State University. Through this project and a related one, eighteen Choctaw students enrolled in a university which had formerly not recognized their existence. (Martin, Peterson and Peterson 1975:1–9). Some of these students had been fellow employees the preceding year, and considerable time was required in assisting them to adjust to the university. It was also necessary to help faculty become accustomed to having Choctaw students. The success in this first year led to an expansion of cooperative university-tribal efforts which included, in addition to the Indian teacher training program, a bilingual program, an educational evaluation project, and a manpower survey to replicate my earlier survey. I was the principal investigator for the university phase of most of these programs and was looking forward to a second attempt to establish my role as an applied anthropologist, this time under contract from the Tribe. Unfortunately, the scope of my activities was limited, this time by a request from the university rather than the Tribe.

University Administrator and Program Coordinator

Anthropology was scheduled to become a separate department during the same year that the above subcontracts were to be carried out. The coordinator of anthropology, who had laid the groundwork for establishing the department, resigned to accept another position. At the request of university officials, I assumed the headship of the new department in addition to my research commitments. Thus, I had to hire other people to carry out the research I had intended to do myself. Although I continued to be involved with these projects, my role was that of research supervisor and administrator rather than researcher.

I was now once removed from the actual research, but even worse was the conflict between my position as subcontractor to the Tribe and my responsibility as a university administrator. In the past, I had been somewhat critical of the university's response to tribal needs. Now, I experienced firsthand the problems created by the limitations of funds and personnel in an academic department and the need to insure that work carried out for the Tribe did not exhaust available resources. My discussions with tribal officials seemed to be limited to contracts, finances, and personnel.

The conflict between my role as director of some of the Indian programs and as head of an academic department quickly became apparent. Moreover, the time involved in both roles was far beyond that available to me. This conflict was particularly acute because of the administrative problems of a new department, staffed largely by young faculty who were just beginning their own experience in funded research. From hindsight, it is obvious that I attempted to undertake too much. I gave insufficient time to the department, and was also unable to provide any technical assistance to the Tribe beyond contractual work.

Academic Anthropologist Again

In preparing for academic year 1975–1976, both the university and tribal administrations agreed that Indian programs in the university should be carried out by people with a full-time commitment to them. Thus, in some ways, my relationship with the Tribe completed a full circle. The major difference, in terms of the university, is that formerly I was the only person working with the Choctaws; today there are now four university personnel working full-time with the Tribe. Whereas there were almost no Choctaw students formerly, there is now a significant group of Indian students, a Native Heritage Club, and an Indian Program Office located in the same building as the Department of Anthropology.

At the same time, my relationship with the Tribe has been altered. The tribal chairman under whom I worked was defeated in the election of 1975, and the new chief tribal official is a man whom I have known well for some time, but for whom I have never worked directly. Yet, the new Tribal Council contains many people with whom I have worked, and some of the Choctaw students with whom I worked at the university.

The tribal government itself has changed significantly over the past seven years also. At the end of my first period of field work, the tribal chairman, Emmett York, indicated that he wished he could offer me a job, but the Tribe lacked the necessary resources. Under Phillip Martin, I was the first academic professional to be hired under the expanded tribal programs. Now, however, three Ph.D.s and three individuals who have completed Ph.D. course work are on the tribal payroll. In short, the Tribe's level of in-house technical expertise has increased to the point that the type of assistance I gave in the past is less needed.

Furthermore, there has been a significant change in the relationship between the Choctaw Tribe and the field of anthropology. In 1960, Pamela Coe could accurately title her master's thesis on the Choctaws, *Lost in the Hills of Home*. During the first several years of work with the Choctaws, the ethnohistorian, Bob Ferguson, was the only individual I met on the reservation with an anthropological orientation. Yet, during the summer of 1974, a total of eight anthropologists were present for the Choctaw fair, including four of us who had worked directly for the Tribe. It is particularly gratifying to see the growth of research which will benefit the Tribe. Moreover, the contribution of the Choctaws themselves to published material on the Tribe is expanding (*Nanih Waiya Magazine* 1974).

In addition to changes within the university and the Tribe, there have been personal changes as a result of the natural aging process. When I first went to the Choctaw reservation, I was still learning to be an anthropologist; now I am a department head. At that time, also, some of my closest friends were Choctaw college students and Choctaws who had low level appointments in the Bureau of Indian Affairs and the Indian Health Service. The Choctaw housing officer was the only Mississippi Choctaw in these organizations in a professional position. Today, however, Mississippi Choctaws occupy positions as superintendent of the Choctaw Agency, head of Choctaw schools, three principalships, and director of the Choctaw hospital, in addition to the expanded number of tribal positions.

In summary, most of us have become "established." We are no longer on the outside saying, "Why doesn't the university, or the Tribe, or the Agency do something about this?" We are now experiencing the limitations of the bureaucracies in which we work. We spend more time on budgets, personnel actions and committees than on discussions of what we really believe should be done.

There has been improvement in employment and housing on the Choctaw reservation, but much more needs to be accomplished. Instruction in the Choctaw schools and in the university has improved, but it is still not what it should be. I would hope that I and my colleagues on the reservation have learned more about improving these conditions than we knew seven years ago, and that we are putting up with immediate problems while we work on long range goals. Yet, there is an attractiveness in my past role of full-time tribal employee. There was great freedom in the lack of organizational responsibility which enabled me to work with the full energy and dedication of youth attempting to understand and change social systems without preoccupation with either bureaucratic or ivory tower concerns.

I carried out my first field work with no financial security and very limited funds, because I believed it would benefit both me and the Tribe. I was willing to risk unemployment to work for the Tribe a second time. I wonder if I would run such risks and commit so much time and energy now that I am a tenured faculty member, own my own home, and have a son half-way to college!

I owe more than I can ever express to the members of the Choctaw tribe, who have accepted me and helped to sharpen my skills in a diversity of applied settings. My knowledge of the limitations and potential uses of applied anthropology has been both deepened and broadened, and my personal and professional orientation has been greatly shaped by my Choctaw experience. My hope is that the Tribe has benefited equally and that the expansion of tribal governments will permit other anthropologists to establish mutually beneficial relationships with them and with other Indian tribes.

9

LEARNING TO BE AN ANTHROPOLOGIST
AND REMAINING "NATIVE"

Beatrice Medicine

Both Miller and Peterson have reported that the role of the applied anthropologist entails working amidst institutional restraints and groups with conflicting interests and goals. For native Americans and other minorities, these restraints and divergent demands are experienced in a highly personal way. Beatrice Medicine vividly describes her experiences of learning to be an anthropologist while still remaining a native American.

Medicine's identity as a Sioux creates problems of professional identity as an anthropologist when colleagues persist in using her as an informant. Her identity as an anthropologist opens the door to similar exploitation by the Sioux, who view her as a counselor and a liaison to agencies outside the reservation community. As an advocate of Sioux interests, Medicine is especially concerned with this latter role.

While Medicine is not a tribal employee, as was Peterson, her professional status results in demands for her specialized knowledge and skills. These demands are often emotionally stressful. Her advocate role requires commitment to her people as a whole in the face of segments and factions which press for diverse and special interests. The hierar-

Beatrice Medicine (M.A., Michigan State) has done fieldwork among numerous Indian groups of the United States and Canada. She has worked as a teacher for the Haskell Institute of the Bureau of Indian Affairs, the United Pueblos Agency of Albuquerque, and in Indian schools in South Dakota. She has taught anthropology at the University of British Columbia, University of Montana, University of South Dakota, San Francisco State University, Dartmouth College, and most recently at Stanford University. Professor Medicine serves as a consultant to public and private agencies concerned with American Indians, and was recently appointed to the National Advisory Council on Ethnic Heritage Studies of the United States Department of Health, Education, and Welfare.

chical relationships between governmental and other service agencies and the human communities which receive the policies and programs designed by the dominant society create formidable tasks for her role as a culture broker.

I AM A part of the people of my concern and research interests. Sometimes they teasingly sing Floyd Westerman's (1969) song "Here Comes the Anthro" when I attend Indian conferences. The ambiguities inherent in these two roles of being an "Anthro" while at the same time remaining a "Native" need amplification. They speak to the very heart of "being" and "doing" in anthropology. My desire to be an anthropologist has been my undoing and my rebirth in a very personal way, but this topic is outside the scope of this contribution.

Recently, many students—particularly native Americans—have been dazzled by Vine Deloria Jr.'s scathing attack on "Anthros," as we are called by most native Americans. His article, which first appeared in *Playboy* (August 1969), has since been reprinted in many anthropological works. Besides serving as a "sweat bath" to purge anthropologists of their guilt feelings, it has become a rallying cry for Indian militants and tribal peoples alike. Many native peoples have articulated their discontent with the exploitative adventures of "Anthros" in the American Indian field. (See, for example, a symposium entitled *Anthropology and the American Indian,* held in San Diego at the 1970 annual meeting of the American Anthropological Association, and published by the Indian Historian Press, 1973.) However, native readers seemingly do not go beyond page 100 of Deloria's manifesto entitled *Custer Died For Your Sins.* Later, he states: "This book has been the hardest on those people in whom I place the greatest amount of hope for the future—Congress, the anthropologists, and the churches" (1969:275). Since the churches and Congress have eroded my faith in the institutions of the dominant society, I shall focus on anthropology. It is, after all, the source of my livelihood.

"Anthropologist" as a role designation has been traditionally meaningful to American Indians or, as we have recently been glossed, "Native Americans." In the early days of American anthropology, we were seen as "vanishing Americans." Thus, students of Boas collected data on Plains Indian reservations and Northwest Coast villages in order to recapture "memory cultures" which reflected the "golden days" of natives whose aboriginal culture was denigrated and whose future was seen as oblivion or civilization. Many feel that American anthropology was built upon the backs of natives (DeLaguna, 1960:792), but the contributions of American Indians to the discipline has never been fully assessed. (Recently, Panday (1972) has detailed the interactions of "Anthros" and natives at Zuni pueblo.)

Initially, it was Franz Boas' interest in folklore, linguistics, and other aspects of culture which led him to seek and train indigenous persons who seemed especially responsive to viewing their own cultures. Among the tribes of the American Midwest, there were persons such as Francis LaFlesche, an Omaha, and William Jones, a Mesquakie (Fox), who worked in the discipline. The latter died on a field trip to the Philippines while working among the Ilongots.

Nevertheless, the role of informant as anthropological reporter creates qualms among natives who contemplate becoming anthropologists, and it is not surprising that early contributions by Native Americans were primarily in texts on the native languages and in folklore and mythology. A pertinent observation is made by a black anthropologist:

In the same spirit that Boas encouraged natives to become anthropologists, he also encouraged women because they could collect information on female behavior more easily than a male anthropologist. This attitude strongly implied that native and female anthropologists are seen as potential "tools" to be used to provide important information to the "real" white male anthropologist (Jones 1970:252).

The late Ed Dozier, Pueblo anthropologist, once commented that many native Americans "went into anthropology as a means of helping their people." This suggests strong interest in the application of anthropological knowledge and is tied to the native idea of education, no matter in what field, as a means of alleviating problems and providing self-help among native groups. It may also reflect the dominant white society's designation of "the Indian Problem." Moreover, anthropologists are the educated persons with whom most Indians are familiar, and they justify their data collection to us on the basis that "we want to write down your history and culture so that your grandchildren will know something about it."

The "personal communication" aspect of anthropological reporting upset me when I began reading interpretations and analyses of us (Lakota/Dakota: Sioux), based upon E. Deloria's "field notes," "personal communications," and "personal conversations," in such works as Mirsky (1937) and Goldfrank (1943). Later, I realized that these and similar excellent studies based on others' field notes were common and acceptable in the discipline. Nevertheless, native populations are wary of others' interpretations of their behavior, even when they are dealing with "one of their own." An added native concern is that areas of living will be presented which they do not want revealed.

In all anthropological investigations, mutual trust and understanding must be built carefully and sensitively. As with any human relationship, reciprocity, responsiveness, and responsibility are essential. I myself learned this lesson early during an intensive year I spent in a southwestern pueblo noted for its conservatism. There I learned to eat hot, spicy foods and to leave the pueblo along with the non-native teachers on special ceremonial occasions. I learned, too, that I would never write about this pueblo.

The pueblo experience affirmed the importance of segmentation for survival. An elder of the sacred and secret realm always spoke to me in his native language, as he held my hand and put a turquoise ring on my finger during each visit to his home. Later, I saw him in his trader role in the southwestern city and heard him converse in excellent English. I rushed home to tell my son's father, "Mr. Z speaks English!" Little did I realize that I was being tested. Was I native or white-oriented? Was I informer or friend?

While resident in the pueblo, my research interest in child-training methods was fulfilled. I established strong ties with the people and maintained visiting patterns and exchanges of gifts. However, my input into the village was minimal, consisting mainly of writing letters, purchasing materials, doing odd chores, and interpreting educational policies. With respect to the last activity, this was my first experience in a Bureau of Indian Affairs "day school." It was my unhappy chore to explain to Pueblo parents why their kindergarten children could recite "Dick and Jane" stories by rote, even though they did not understand a simple question in English. Theories of social change and social organization made my year tolerable as far as the school structure was concerned. Hopefully, I was a means of explaining the rigid educational system to the pueblo people, who knew precisely what skills they wanted their children to have—mathematics and "enough English to get by." Their belief system, however, was a secret never to be divulged; I still heed this directive when a pueblo student asks me not to discuss pueblo religion in my classes.

Being a native female delineated areas of investigation which were closed to me. This was aggravated by my prolonged infertility. Conversation or gossip about such matters as deviant sexual practices, abortions, and pregnancy taboos was immediately terminated when I appeared at female gatherings. It was only after ten years of marriage and producing a male child (!) that I was included in "womanly" spheres. Until then, I was referred to as "Little Bea." The cultural constrictions of working within my own group caused me to reexamine value configurations, sex roles, Indian–white relationships, and socialization practices by spending most of my time with the children. Some persons in my *tiospaya* (extended kin group) said I "spoiled" (i.e., "catered to") children. But by treating children as people, I was only acting in the way I myself had been socialized.

In the contemporary era, the concepts of acculturation or culture change, cultural transmission, role-modeling, bicultural and bilingual education, cultural brokerage, and others are highlighted in anthropological research. For me, these concepts have become personal and concrete during years of learning to be an anthropologist while remaining a native. My learning began in childhood and continues in the present.

Early Learning

Of significance to many of us Lakota people was Ella Deloria, a daughter of a Santee Dakota Episcopal missionary who worked among the Hunkpapa and Sihasapa (Blackfeet) bands of the Teton (Western) Sioux who were placed on Standing Rock reservation. She and other native Americans and Canadians came within the orbit of Boas with whom she coauthored a book on Dakota grammar (Boas and Deloria 1941). Her other work included further linguistic, folk-lore, and kinship studies (Deloria 1944).

As a child, I observed Aunt Ella asking questions, taking notes and photographs and, according to my mother, "finding out how the Indians lived." Even in those days, the divisions of intragroup polarities of "mixed-blood" and "full-blood" were operative. Because my father was a "full-blood," he was a good source of linguistic and other information. Very often, questions were transferred through my mother. The division of Lakota souls into various Christian denominations, though arbitrarily assigned, could not obviate kin loyalties and expectancies. I am certain that Aunt Ella forgave "poor Anna" (my mother) for marrying a "full-blood" and a "Catholic."

Aunt Ella's participation in a world far removed from Standing Rock reservation where she lectured "about Lakota" presented a model which I found attractive. Much later, I attended a lecture by a physical anthropologist (now deceased) who asked, "Will all the persons in the room who have shovel-shaped incisors please indicate?" This experience and being used as an informant (together with a Swedish student) in a "Personality and Culture" course raised many questions in my mind about becoming an anthropologist. Would it be possible to retain dignity as a native while operating in roles other than informant? Would anthropological training alienate me from my people? Would it affect marriage? Aunt Ella had never married. Lakota ideals for women included marriage and children. I knew my father did not believe in what he later termed "cross-cultural" marriages.

In retrospect, I am pleased that my father was sufficiently far-sighted to enroll his children as full-bloods. It has made my life and acceptance on reservations and reserves easier. I am also appreciative that my father took me to tribal council meetings when I was young. It was in this context that I was remembered and asked to translate for a Lakota male elder who was a non-English speaker in the Wounded Knee Trials of 1974. Such was socialization for modes of Lakota adaptation and persistence and the demanding and expected behavior of a native ("Anthro"—and female, at that!).

During my early life, I was cognizant of living in a society which was different from the one in which I would eventually interact. Many natives have to learn to assess cross-cultural cues and circumstances as techniques for accommodations and adaptations. Although we were trained for adaptation in the superordinate society, the ideals of expected behavior or responsibility and commitment of the native society were constantly held before us. Being Lakota was seen as the most essential aspect of living. It was from this cultural base that strong individual autonomy was fostered and an equally strong orientation to the group's welfare and interest was instilled.

Early in my college experience, I was asked to read treaties, Bureau of Indian Affairs (BIA) policy directives, and write letters involving pony claims for elderly people on my reservation. Later, while doing fieldwork on Pine Ridge reservation, I was asked to edit an elder Oglala male's collection of Lakota folktales which began with "And a Hearty *Hou Kola* (Hello, friend) to you all!" He was collecting these for a well-known female "Anthro." As I congratulated him on his excellent collection, he said, "I got them from a book put out by the Bureau of American Ethnology and changed them here and there." This raised issues of ethical consideration which were unimportant at that time, but it also indicated that many native societies had access to previously published data.

At the time, I was not too concerned with his approach. I had already seen anthropologists offering old clothes to natives in exchange for art objects, and I had witnessed courting behavior on the part of male anthropologists with young Indian women. On the other hand, I had seen the equally horrendous scene of a large, aggressive Lakota woman forcing a thin, young, intimidated archeologist to dance with her and buy beer in a border-town tavern.

My brother felt sorry for the archeologist and allowed his crew to camp in our "front yard." In the Northern Plains, rapport between archeologists and the local Indian group has been generally good. Many archeologists have maintained contacts with the tribes. Their domain of investigation differs from that of ethnographers and social anthropologists, and they were more aware of my place in the social system and did not use me as a source of information. They also heeded the advice of my father (then a tribal council chairman) who, after feeding them buffalo steaks, said, "All we want from you guys is a good report." (It is the lack of good reporting back to the tribes under investigation which has evoked the ire and discontent of so many.)

The same young archeologist witnessed border-town "justice" when one of my kinsmen was beaten by the police while in jail for intoxication. His attempt to intervene in the city court was negated as he was threatened with contempt of court. This need for intervention frequently presents itself to anthropologists. Working with powerless people has its heartaches and times of despair. For me, these relatively common "advocate" involvements with police made later appearances in court in support of native women (one arrested for shooting her child's molester) somewhat less emotional. With increased articulation and age, by the time I testified in the case upholding our 1868 Sioux Treaty, I was classified as an "expert witness" (Jacobs 1975). I thought I was upholding family tradition and honor. My great grandfather, Sitting Crow, was a signer for the Sihasapa (Blackfeet) band of the Teton. He had signed in good faith. My father had been involved in treaty rights and other government obligations, and tribal attempts to enforce them. Nonetheless, the Wounded Knee Legal Defense and Offense Committee, which was concerned with the dismissal of the occupiers of Wounded Knee hamlet, apparently expressed some hesitation in my court appearance. I was not seen as an overt supporter of the American Indian Movement (AIM).

Looking like a "native" has been advantageous in my work. Although I have what Nancy Lurie (personal conversation 1973) has described as a "universal field face," which has often led me to be classified as northern Chinese, Japanese, and Filipino, my main research has been with the natives of North America.

The Teacher Role

Early in my career, I was assigned the teacher role by the majority of tribal peoples. Not having attended a Bureau of Indian Affairs or a parochial boarding school, my decision was to teach in one. I went with a baccalaureate degree to Haskell Institute, which Ed Dozier has referred to as "the Harvard of the Indian Service." There I encountered bureaucracy more concentrated than on reservations and the complete institutionalization of native students. To be fair, there is tremendous *esprit de corps* among graduates of this former business college, now a junior college. "Haskell Clubs" are common throughout the country. Many graduates feel sorry for those of us who never attended its hallowed halls.

At Haskell I first encountered differential evaluation. "For after all," I was told, "you did not spend ten years at an isolated school on some reservation but came here right from graduation." This merited me a rating of "good" rather than "excellent" teacher. I resigned. However, the teacher image still predominates, for the "professor" role is currently in the forefront of my activities.

Parents and others assume that I have information regarding aspects of career opportunities for students. They are continually reassured that educational activity on a post-high-school level is not necessarily alienating when they see me participating in "pow-wows" and "give-aways" on Standing Rock and other reservations. My current role also involves advisement and support to native and other minority students enrolled in colleges and universities.

A major request made of me is the distribution of anthropological sources to various tribes or native organizations for specific, usually legal, cases. This is a continuing process, as is the dissemination of knowledge about private and governmental sources of funding which can be utilized by these groups. The monitoring of proposals, without jeopardizing one's position as a reader of them, entails a constant weighing of benefits to both tribal groups and educational agencies. Extremely delicate situations are created when cousins and other relatives call for special considerations. Reliance on "old Lakota values" such as integrity is a healthy and understandable resolution for all concerned.

There are other requests of a general nature. These include native persons seeking genealogical information, and non-native students writing at the request of their anthropology professors. Two examples from letters in my files are as follows: "What we need is a list of Sitting Bull's nine wives and a list of his many sons and daughters. . . ." "I want to work on an Indian reservation—preferably for money—this summer. Can you give me information?" There are constant requests for information about the treatment of foster or adopted Indian children, e.g., "This child was fine until he went home to the reservation when he was thirteen. Now we can't do anything with him. Do you think his family gave him drugs—peyote—or something?" I am certain that requests of the kind described here are the lot of many natives, not only in anthropology but in other professions as well. Fortunately, having worked as a psychiatric social worker with Metis and native persons in Canada, I am able to use my training in psychological anthropology in meeting them.

Work among natives, however, is difficult when they view anthropological reports about their tribes as unreliable. Susie Yellow Tail (Crow) defines ethnographies as "Indian joke books." There is no noticeable reliance or reference to many of the earlier ethnographic sources, especially linguistic and ethnohistorical studies. Many tribes are writing their own tribal histories in an attempt to present their experiences from their own unique point of view. Native Americans often believe that most anthropologists enter an indigenous social system with a theoretical framework and collect and report data in support of this prior formulation.

I have attempted a concerted effort to let people know the focus of my own investigations. Among the Lakota on Standing Rock, it is customary for "pow-wow committees" from various communities to ask visiting returnees to the reservations to address such gatherings of people. I have found this an ideal way to present interpretations of research in an acceptable manner. There is response and reaction to the speech-maker and members of my *tiospaya* (extended family). It is also an accepted means of conforming to tribal expectations. Many of us have been criticized by persons in governmental agencies, such as the United States Public Health Service and Bureau of Indian Affairs, who see our statements as ego-centered accounts of our activities in the "outside world." They fail to understand that this modern form of "coup-counting" is viewed by most community members as a means of modeling and enhancing Lakota values and conforming to expected behavior in contemporary reservation culture. It is a valuable outlet for letting the people know what will be written and for obtaining their assessment of it.

Many native enclaves today are aware of the large amounts of money poured into the funding of research on such topics as Indian education. Statements such as the following:

The Indian teachers, then, seem to be characterized as a group with close contacts to the Indian communities and firm Anglo orientations for themselves and in their view on the role of the school (Fuchs and Havighurst 1972:197).

cause Indian education committees of tribal and community councils to request that this and other studies (e.g., *An Even Chance*) be presented in terms which they can more readily understand. Native enclaves are aware of the large amounts of money poured into the funding of such research. In their minds, natives involved as token researchers and validators tend to confirm their negative views of anthropological researchers. To explain without being patronizing is a skill to be learned, as is the need to be charmingly combative in certain anthropological arenas.

The translation of research terminology into an English vernacular which native parents and students can comprehend is a formidable task which "target populations" take for granted. This is not to disparage the intellect of tribal peoples, but rather to acknowledge their estimate of anthropological research and indicate their preoccupation with the many daily tasks of reservation life. It speaks to the need for less jargon in anthropological reporting. The increasing number of native college graduates who return to reservations or urban Indian centers and survival schools seldom utilize these studies at all. Their concern is the development of curricular materials which are more pertinent to their own and their students' needs.

One of the most successful educational endeavors in which I have worked was with the Sarcee tribe living on the outskirts of Calgary. I had already become involved in the social aspects—"powwow" and "give-away" events—before I began working there as a teacher-counselor. The aim of the Indian Affairs Branch of Canada was to enroll and keep Sarcee students in the public and parochial schools of Calgary, for there was the usual high dropout rate.

I visited every home on the reserve and became acquainted with the parents and grandparents. Fortunately for me, the chief was married to a Dakota female from Manitoba, and a pseudo-kin relationship was initiated by them. My goal was to enroll students in a kindergarten in the city and to hire a local native man to drive students into the city. This was accomplished, and the man now has a fleet of school buses which transport all Sarcee students to city schools. Although he says, "I am still driving buses," he is also Band chief. Today a Sarcee college graduate is also working in native education, and many of the young people are involved in tribal affairs.

During this time, some of my white Canadian friends and I worked to establish an Urban Indian Center in Calgary. Some of these white friends have continued their work with urban groups and one has received a degree in athropology. Many of these individuals, who are both native and Canadian, are involved in national Indian educational associations in the United States. A truly binational interest in native education and native issues (National Indian Education Association, North American Bilingual Education Association, and, more recently, the North American Indian Women's Association) seems to be emerging. Much of this involvement is attributable to the growing self-determination and articulation of native peoples in North America. The thrust of commitment has gone beyond the mere networks of "pow-wow circuits" and kinship ties.

One aspect of concern and meaningful education for native students has proven counterproductive to my own professional development. Additionally, I cannot seem to cast off the indispensable mother role. (I once overheard my son telling his friend, "You've heard of Jewish mothers; Sioux-ish mothers are worse.") Native pressure to take fellowships and jobs to ensure continued occupancy by native peoples is great. Although I have, since 1969, spent two years in "my own area" of Montana and South Dakota, I have frequently moved to areas where Indian students have expressed interest or initiated action in hiring me. A common accusation, especially in California, is, "Why aren't you working with your own people?" This is an indication, it seems to me, of a growing tribalism with its incipient and, in some cases, strong ethnocentrism. As far as moving so often is concerned, I jokingly refer to the former nomadism of my people. More recently, I have utilized a Pan-Indian joke: "Sioux are just like empty beer cans, you find them everywhere."

Increasingly, native students who have been in my classes are fulfilling my expectations. Many have entered into occupations with tribal groups and educational endeavors. They are, hopefully, negating my fears of untrained Indian educators replacing uncaring and, in some cases, badly trained white educators. A number of these students, who have absorbed anthropological theories and research methods, are working in areas of concern to our peoples. An interesting dilemma exists. Many tribal councils often "resolve" a problem with a statement: "We need a study on this." Yet, it is in the areas of research and writing that the lack of skills is most evident in the training of native college graduates. White "ghost writers" are too prevalent!

Affirmative action policies in institutions of higher learning raise other problems. Administrators are seeking names of native Americans to fill these slots. An onerous aspect of this recruitment is the validation of self-ascribed natives, whom I have termed "woodwork" Indians, who emerge to fill the slots of the momentarily "in" people ("Indians" and other minorities). This poses critical questions. How does one deal with a person who claims to be one-sixteenth or one-thirty second Indian ancestry (usually Cherokee)? What is a cultural native versus a native of convenience? We know that there are many blacks who, either through intermarriage or miscegenation, fit into a similar category. A more recent anomaly is the use of the gloss "Native American" by Samoans and Hawaiians in the quest for federal funds. These and related issues create real problems for the native anthropologist. Does one set up a registry for "Red-bloods"?

Even more challenging dilemmas result from requests which native intellectuals make upon anthropologists. One example came from an Oglala (Sioux) law graduate who requested that I present evidence that the Native Americans originated in the New World. (What temptation for a native American Piltdown "plant"!) Concerns of this nature have even greater future repercussions because of the current rejection of the "Bering Straits Migration theory" advocated by some tribal leaders. Many tribal peoples are as committed to their origin and creation statements as any other people. "What do you think of the story told by the anthropologists that we all came across the Bering Straits?" was the question asked of me by a Navajo teenager in 1960.

Issues based on Indians' tribal sovereignty, water, and treaty rights, will make the future interface of anthropologists and natives a vital concern for those of us committed to a changing profession. This is especially evident in the use of the latter in the "contrived cultures" of native militants.

"Traditionality" is often seen today as a selective mechanism which includes persons whose rhetorical "right-on-ness" negates tribal heritage, oratorical wisdom, and concerted action which have sustained the nativeness of the group. "Identity-questing" assumes a new perspective and reflects generations of superimposed policies of change. It is tragic to view some individuals who do not know their own unique tribal heritage amid the vast cultural heritages of native North America. Thus, respect for elders is eroded in the exploitation of native medicine men and translation of native prayers into slogans.

However, a common denominator is that we native Americans are varied hues in a bronzed and battered native world and present uneven views of tribal traditions. More importantly, our sheer survival has hinged upon a flexible ability to segment, synthesize, and act in changing situations. While this should be understood and respected by anthropologists and others, a lack of sensitivity and perception has been a main tragedy of comprehending native life. There is often a unidimensional aspect of power. The indigenous society is seen as a target population for manipulation and change with little or no attempt to understand the textured and realigning configurations of persons and ideas, through time, which have allowed for native persistence. For me, the categories of constituency are meaningless because my identity rests as a constituent of a viable native group. Advocacy is constant and resides with the powerless peoples. Involvement is ongoing, demanding, and debilitating emotionally, economically, and educationally.

To me, the most important aspect of applied work is the delineation of social forces which impinge upon indigenous societies and the ways that these affect each distinctive group. Social change and how it is understood and acted upon by native Americans is the crux of anthropological understanding. It is through the role of cultural broker that the lack of insight and understanding of a more powerful social order may be mediated. The fact of living in social situations of administered human relations, where decisions affecting the present and future of native Amerians are controlled by external power components, is understandable and workable with anthropological concepts. In educational aspects especially, it has been imperative to reinterpret and to flesh out the parameters of methods and techniques of change in terms which are meaningful to native aggregates. Moreover, it is important that persons on both the receiving and applying levels understand the nature of factions in these societies. For native societies, the labels "Progressive" and "Traditionalist" have many different meanings.

The "full blood"/"breed" constellations have been correlated with both "traditionalists" and "progressives" in some Lakota reservations. This division of allegiances to old values and affinity toward "feathering one's own nest" at the expense of the other group are basic to understanding factions on contemporary reservations. Recently, the "progressives" or "featherers" have begun to harken back to "traditionality" which is operationally part of the reservation political arena.

The politics of social capital and power are elements which are forever present in native social systems. They have served as vehicles for differential adjustment to the dominant culture. To the anthropologist from the native enclave, kin affiliation is often within both spheres of social structure, necessitating a constant reassessment of power and emotional alliances. Surges of disaffection and disenchantment have to be isolated and put in proper perspective as a prelude to action.

There are events with simple and fulfilling moments, such as sitting around a campfire visiting with friends and kin "waiting for the coffee to boil" or watching Lakota children "playing cowboy" in the bright moonlight. On other occasions, listening to the Sioux National Anthem and then "dancing the drum out" in the cold dawn of a Northern Plains summer have become memories which sustain me in university settings, governmental "advisory" boards, or anthropological "tribal rites" (annual meetings) where we hear new interpretations and speculations about our native life-styles. Being home and doing fieldwork recall Al Ortiz' significant statement: ". . . I initially went into anthropology because it was one field in which I could read about and deal with Indians all of the time and still make a living" (in *Anthropology and the American Indian* 1973:86).

I know I went into anthrophology to try to make living more fulfilling for Indians and to deal with "others" in attempts of anthropological application meaningful to Indians and "others."

10

MARGINAL COMMUNICANT: THE ANTHROPOL-
OGIST IN RELIGIOUS GROUPS AND AGENCIES

Gwen Kennedy Neville

Professional training as an anthropologist and the prevailing social organization of anthropology departments have traditionally expressed a
value system which rewards research undertaken in other societies, but
penalizes those who seek to undertake research in our own society. Yet,
as Goodenough has reminded us, multiculturalism is found in varying
degrees in all societies but especially in complex ones. Within American
society, anthropologists have long recognized this by supporting those
who studied native Americans. Nevertheless, their failure to encompass
other American groups as legitimate fields of anthropological inquiry is
only now beginning to be questioned.

Gwen K. Neville forcefully questions the rigidities of past anthropological practice and attitudes toward American society. Like Medicine, Neville is learning to be an anthropologist while working among
her own people. While her situation is distinctly different from that of
Medicine, she too experiences emotional stress and involvement of a
personal kind as she encounters distrust of her activities on the part of
professional colleagues and members of the religious groups with whom
she works. In this situation, she describes her role as that of a marginal
communicant. She underscores a theme which is expressed elsewhere in
this volume, namely, that the role of the applied anthropologist is partially defined by other groups in our society. Her distinct contribution to

Gwen Kennedy Neville (Ph.D., Florida) is associate professor of anthropology at Emory
University. Her research has been concerned with the processes of cultural continuity
in the ceremonial life of complex societies, and she has undertaken research on this
topic in the American South and the Scottish Borders. Her activities in applied anthropology have included consultantships with business and church-related institutions
on religion and culture and the role of women in American society and culture.

this theme is her analysis of the way in which the discipline of anthropology itself has failed to fully incorporate Americans and applied anthropology as valuable areas of professional endeavor.

ANTHROPOLOGISTS WHO WORK in their own society are constantly poised between two worlds. They must maintain a degree of analytical objectivity while at the same time making use of the insights and knowledge to which they have access only by growing up in a particular culture. Native anthropologists who focus their study on belief systems, religious communal life, or on the structure and process of religious organizations face an even more difficult challenge. There exists a tension between the desire to understand one's former religion from the anthropological vantage point and the intuitive awareness of the meanings and values held by those who continue to be true believers. As a native white Anglo-Saxon Protestant in the American South, I have spent the past ten years studying my own people. In the process, I have become interested in the problems associated with cultural marginality. The hazards of this marginal position and the fear of them have kept anthropologists away from their own society, and especially from studies of American religious life. In this essay I explore the problems and possibilities of doing research as a "marginal communicant" in American Protestantism.[1]

I have participated in three basic types of anthropological inquiry and application which I consider possible areas of involvement for anthropologists interested in religious life and activities. The first is basic ethnographic research on religious communities and congregations. The second is the application of anthropological knowledge and skills to the teaching of religion and the teaching of anthropology in professional theological schools. Finally, applied anthropologists have much to offer as consultants and advisers in denominational policy formulation at the board or agency level. These areas are discussed here as I have experienced them. However, as a

[1] The term "marginal native" was used by Morris Freilich (1970) for the anthropologist in the field who successfully plays the ethnographer's role of participant observer. I have coined the phrase "marginal communicant" to refer to the ethnographer of a religious community of a denominational group. I have also drawn on the concept of "liminality" described and explored by Victor Turner (1958).

background for this discussion, it is important to consider first the concept of marginality as it has emerged in anthropological fieldwork and to give special attention to the pertinence of marginality for the anthropological study or lack of study of American religious groups.

The Formation of Marginal Communicants

All of the social science disciplines can be said to be filled with socially marginal people, but several elements in the professionalization of anthropologists give them a special niche among their fellow students of society. One of the trademarks of anthropology is "cultural relativism," a posture that ideally prevents anthropologists from taking religious, political, or other value-laden positions. Instead, the anthropologist should be able to examine all sides of a question with equal consideration. Although anthropologists debate about whether or not this is a tenable, possible, or even a moral position, the traditional process of turning undergraduates into professional anthropologists includes the attempt to break them out of their enthnocentrism and to open their eyes to the beauties of *scientism*.

Anthropology students report a form of conversion experience during their training. This conversion is one in which the belief system of the discipline itself replaces their former faith, whatever that may have included. During this process, the religious beliefs of one's culture of orientation are replaced by the dogmas of functionalism, evolution, relativism, structuralism, cognitive anthropology, cultural materialism, and so on.

The graduate training of anthropologists, especially the final phase of initiation in fieldwork, is designed to replace systematically any vestiges of religious explanations with appropriate cultural explanations for human experience and social organization. Objective fieldworkers are created by clearing away old values or preconceptions that may interfere with data gathering and analysis. This necessity is partly due to the techniques used by fieldworkers, which are primarily based on participant observation and ethnographic methods. If one is to be submerged in a new culture as a lone observer and recorder of human behavior, it is essential to be as nonsubjective as possible. The usefulness of ethnographic data is constantly being questioned by colleagues in other disciplines whose methods and procedures rely more heavily on sterile statistical techniques. To avoid having all their ethnographic babies thrown out with the bathwater of individual bias, anthropologists have concentrated their efforts on producing fieldworkers who have been properly inducted into the new religion of scientific objectivity.

Master fieldworkers and teachers admit that, as human beings, ethnographers retain a degree of subjectivity. The ideal student-ethnographer, however, has a minimum of conflict with her or his own world view and eventually is able to transcend cultural biases. Graduate courses in field methods communicate these disciplinary norms. Students are taught ways of entering the new society, becoming a part of its everyday life, getting "inside the heads" of the people so as to understand their views, and then withdrawing from the field to return to the culture of academe. This process of entry, participation, and withdrawal must be accomplished without falling into the trap of "going native," or becoming a *bona fide* member of the culture under examination.

Those who successfully complete the transformation from student to anthropologist find themselves in one of the subcultures of academe, the belief community of anthropology, complete with its own meanings, values, and rituals. As with any culture, there is a pattern of social relationships and social support groups. Those who fit most neatly into the traditional role structure of the anthropological world are those whose research is clearly in accord with one of the traditional subject areas. There is a particularly well-defined social support system for those whose work is done in other cultures—the "Latin Americanists," the "Africanists," et al. Those who choose to work in contemporary American society are often accidentally or purposefully mistaken for sociologists, and white Protestants who concentrate on their own subculture of orientation are frequently left with little or no group support at all. As a consequence, these latter researchers are limited in number. The majority of graduate students direct their specialties into areas of anthropology which are congruent with traditional emphases on foreign study, nonindustrial societies, or social change in developing countries.

There is a glaring absence of ethnographers in the study of American Protestantism. This is partly due to the dynamics of professionalization described above. In the process of being turned into objective scientists, anthropologists are taught that their own culture and society is less prestigious for study than other, more exotic cultures and societies. The study of one's own religious subculture is deemed to be not only less prestigious but impossible because of a belief that one cannot retain the degree of distance necessary to produce a scientific appraisal through the methods of ethnographic fieldwork.

Other social scientists who rely on statistical measures have approached American denominationalism with questionnaires and attitude scales. Their analyses have filled journals devoted to the sociology and social psychology of religion. These types of measures insure researcher perspective and distance; meanwhile, the practice of ethnography is like trying to go away to college and then to return home again, seeing all the old patterns with new eyes. Can one, in fact, go home again? This is the question that plagues the ethnographer of religion.

A number of anthropologists have demonstrated that it is possible to do research in their communities of origin after returning from formal training in anthropology. Edward Dozier, for instance, returned to his home village in Arizona to study and write about his people, the Tewa (Dozier 1966). John Hostetler, who was brought up in an Amish community, returned as a researcher to describe and analyze the Amish people (Hostetler 1968, Hostetler and Huntington 1971). Black researchers have successfully studied black neighborhoods; Mexican-Americans are working in projects directed toward understanding the dynamics of the Chicano community. Thus, precedents exist for Americans to return to their own communities of origin for anthropological study. It is theoretically possible, therefore, for those who have left the fold of religious belief and denominational life to return as marginal natives for the study of their former groups in order to develop an understanding of communal life among white Protestant Americans.

The Marginal Communicant at Work

My own experience of studying, describing, teaching, and advising in Protestant denominations began when, as a doctoral candidate in anthropology, I selected a Presbyterian summer conference center for dissertation research. My theoretical questions concerned the processes of cultural continuity and transmission in urban society. I had defined myself as an "urban anthropologist" and had concentrated in the subfields of community and culture, anthropology and education, and applied anthropology with special attention to urban studies. In order to explain the mosaic of urban communities, I became interested in the internal processes of community life and the social and cultural means of maintaining and transmitting the heritage of communities to the next generation.

During my final graduate year, I read W. Lloyd Warner's *Black Civilization,* which describes a widely scattered hunting and gathering population who meet annually for an elaborate ceremonial period in which all the central values and meanings of their culture are restated symbolically through the use of time, space, and social relationshps. This regathering enabled a dispersed people to maintain itself as a social and cultural entity and to pass on to their young all the sacred meanings associated with that particular way of life. Suddenly, other ceremonials of this type rushed into my consciousness—the Sun Dance of the Cheyenne, the *gumsaba* of the Washo, the pig festival of the New Guinea tribespeople. In juxtaposition to these ceremonial assemblages was the annual summer conference season at each of the southern denominational conference centers.

Each summer, urban and town residents from throughout the South attend the American equivalent of the annual ceremonial assemblage of peoples previously described by anthropologists. The summer community with denominational homogeneity in the North Carolina mountains, the assemblage of participants over the generations at the same campmeeting grounds in East Tennessee or North Georgia, the recurrent regathering of kinfolk for family reunions, the congregation of birth returning to a rural graveyard and church for the annual homecoming and graveyard association day,—all these events began to fall into place for me as powerful cultural expressions in a society which on the surface may appear to be homogenous.

As ethnographer and marginal native, I set out to study one of these assemblages, a Presbyterian summer community and conference center at Montreat. Here, in the mountains of western North Carolina, the modern version of the Celtic sacred grove, I found Scottish and Scotch-Irish Presbyterians annually reestablishing a cultural pattern and community form that gave full expression to the worldview and beliefs of their Reformed Tradition ancestors and to the cultural style of traditional Lowland Scotland. Residents, who in the winter participated fully in the expected behaviors and beliefs of the industrial modern society of their home cities, were entering a world of separate cultural identity during the summer (Neville 1971, 1975).

During subsequent years and later research efforts, I have followed urbanites into other religiously based events in order to fill in the picture that is emerging of Protestant ceremonialism in the American South. It is a picture of a multiplicity of sects, denominations, and churches, uniting culturally similar peoples into continuous belief communities and setting them against the forces of assimilation and disruption that they face in their daily urban routines. The segmentation of southern society is not social so much as it is cultural, and it is reinforced and preserved by ritual participation. Families, it is becoming clear, are not isolated and nuclear except in their suburban daily living. In the overall yearly cycles of family life, southern families are kin-based, extended, and reinforced by religious coparticipation. By focusing on ritual and on ceremonial cycles, my co-workers and I have identified, to some extent, a set of cultural subsegments within all strata of southern society, an especially surprising fact among elites, who otherwise might be expected to give up their religio-ethnic identity in favor of identification with their socioeconomic group.[2]

The collection of ethnographic data on the ritual life of Presbyterians, Baptists, Methodists, and others is no easy task. To be a native is of immeasurable help in gaining access to many events that are central to cultural understanding. In order to attend a family reunion, for example, one must be kin or be married to a member of the kin group. Teenagers and unmarried young adults may bring a friend of the same sex. Friends of the opposite sex are considered to be candidates for marriage, who are being "looked over" by the family. On several occasions, one of my students has invited me to her or his reunion and then later withdrawn the invitation after having checked it out with grandmother. Grandmothers are not fond of being studied by anthropologists, nor are they fond of having their reunion invaded by an outsider with the motive of "studying" it.

The same suspicion of being "studied" is found among some ministers and religious specialists. However, this can almost always

---

[2] For further information on this work, see Neville (1971, 1975).

be allayed by a full explanation of the research—that it is directed toward an understanding of the history, culture, and the kinship system of the American South and that the church is a central aspect of southern culture. After my initial publications on Montreat and Presbyterians appeared, there was general acceptance of my work by several churches, denominational communities, and seminaries. My information began to be viewed as valuable in gaining a deeper understanding of the cultural roots of denominational communal life.

Religious groups began to request talks on southern culture and copies of my writings. A Baptist Sunday School class, for example, became interested in the research and its underlying hypotheses about urban life. The participants were bright young college graduates and readers of popular social commentaries, and they wanted to understand how these gatherings served to preserve tradition. The class became a lively source of information, and later they invited me to return with the findings of the project and to talk about the implications of the research. In this and other groups, I find that people are fascinated with their own traditions and gain a renewed appreciation of the continuance of customs they had formerly scoffed at as simply "old fashioned" or "country."

As a participant observer, I have attended and recorded information on church services, baptisms, weddings, and funerals. I have studied family dinners and reunions, church homecomings, campmeetings, conferences, and the unfolding calendar of gatherings of particular families and congregations over the annual cycle. My students in cultural anthropology classes have observed and described their own life crisis rituals and those of their congregations, thereby extending my own ethnographic arm.

After only a few years of delving into the ritual life of southern Protestants, it became clear that there were deep cultural roots in English and Scottish community life that must be understood if cultural persistence was to be properly traced. At that point, I took my inquiries to the Scottish Lowlands and began to ask the same questions there about family, church, and town ceremonies that I had been asking in the American South. It is only now, after six years of painstaking excavation of cultural materials from human interaction and symbolic expression, that important patterns of continuity are beginning to emerge. At the same time, I am seeking to understand more fully the explicit dynamics of cultural transmission from one generation to another, and I am beginning to identify the connections between community and culture in mobile populations.

Thus far, my treatment of the marginal communicant at work has primarily considered the collection of basic ethnographic data and the formulation of models for the study of Protestant communalism as an aspect of urban life. As a parallel to the collection and analysis of data, I have participated in the ongoing dissemination of this information to denominational groups themselves. This has happened through teaching southern Protestant students about their own cultures and consulting with policy-making agencies and church boards. Teaching is seldom considered as an aspect of applied anthropology. Yet it can be an important vehicle for implementing social change when one is teaching students to look at their own backgrounds and to invent constructive changes for the benefit of the society of which they are a part.

I consider my teaching to be a form of applied anthropology. For the past five years, I have taught liberal arts undergraduates in a private university. During the same period, I have intermittently taught classes of graduate students in sociology/anthropology of religion and theology students working toward a professional degree in church ministry. All three categories of students present challenges in bringing cross-cultural understandings and new analytical skill to their own society.

In the liberal arts colleges, a traditional goal of education is to lead the student out of a narrow into a broad understanding of the world. As future decision makers in the South, liberal arts graduates can become important agents of change in medicine, law, education, or business. Anthropology is a crucial ingredient in the broadening of the backgrounds of these future leaders. Too frequently, this aspect of anthropology becomes subservient to the goals of producing trainees for anthropology graduate departments or for the job market.

Teaching anthropology creatively—especially teaching the anthropology of religion or the anthropology of American life—can indeed be a radical activity. In presenting data on ritual analysis, lecturing on cognitive encoding, mythology, or symbolic behavior, the teacher is given the opportunity of cutting through deep cultural grooves and allowing the student a new and fresh look at formerly implicit presuppositions.

In teaching undergraduates, the understandings of religion and society within America can be made concrete by assigning student observations of church social organization, religious services, customs of dress, use of space, and sequences of activity. My own classes have encompassed field projects on every aspect of American religious life, including the ceremonies of Catholic and Jewish groups in addition to Protestant ones. Students have done event analyses on holiday dinners, bar mitzvahs, christening parties, and a host of other gatherings. As they chart interaction in time and space, as they observe and record modes of dress, food, behavior, and ritual observances, they often develop an awareness of human communities and of species that had never soaked through in formal lectures.

In addition to bringing creative insights and appreciation for culture, the teaching of anthropology brings the understanding of social organization that is essential for change agents. Practical fieldwork and ethnographic training are particularly valuable assets to students in professional theology schools. Ministers in the South have historically been among the important agents of change. As in other areas of applied anthropology, change agents must be familiar with cultural arrangements and regularized patterns of human interaction if they expect to make innovations that will be accepted by those they serve. In the past, ministers as change agents have not taken these principles seriously. They assume that if a program is worthwhile, and if they themselves are effective, new programs will be adopted by their congregations. A knowledge of the tenacity of human interaction patterns and the imbeddedness of traditional ways of structuring behavior is an asset in planning new programs and in their implementation. The teaching of principles of human groupings to theology students becomes a significant activity in the constructive use of the knowledge and skill of applied anthropology.

My own teaching by means of the classroom lecture method has been augmented by writing as an important means of teaching the wider audience of the educated public. In the case of writing about and for religious groups, one's audience may include colleagues in the chemistry department or in the office of the president of the university. When an anthropologist teaches by describing the ceremonial life of southern Presbyterians or the church homecomings of Methodists in North Georgia, natives and academics blur into one population. It is at this point that writing joins teaching as truly a radical activity (see Westerhoff and Neville 1974).

The protocol of anthropology and the assignment of prestige in the field again rears its head. The established informal norms place the writer for a general audience in a marginal position. This is especially true of the person who writes for the educated church public or for theology schools and their students. Through teaching and writing, however, the information of anthropology becomes known and hopefully begins to take effect in creating an accepted and institutionalized role for the anthropologist as adviser to policy-making church boards and agencies.

The area of advising and consulting is the last of the three areas I wish to discuss. It is a natural outgrowth of the first two, those of basic research and of teaching/writing. Applied anthropologists have previously made their expertise available to agencies of the United States government, to the United Nations, and locally to school systems, hospitals, and industry. In a few instances, anthropologists have attempted to make their information available to church agencies. These instances can be vastly expanded if both churches and applied anthropologists extend their willingness to accept one another's presence.

One of the best opportunities for this type of consulting is in the implementation of programs designed by national church boards to be carried out in local congregations. There is a parallel in the implementation of programs designed by the Department of Agriculture in the 1930s or the Bureau of Indian Affairs. These programs were not always wise and they did not always benefit the populations they were created to serve. Anthropologists have learned a great deal from their advising of government agencies in the past, which is useful in working for church boards. Surveys of community patterns and ongoing traditional structures can potentially inform church boards about what is needed in the way of programs and what is possible in the way of local acceptance.

The applied anthropologist can play an interpretive role between the Great Tradition of denominational dogmatism and ecclesiastical bureaucracy and the Little Tradition of folk religion and its accompanying cultural practices. Seminaries, boards, and agencies tend to deprecate as "empty ritual" or "cultural trappings" some of the recurrent ceremonies that bind together the local life of a group of people. The onslaught of the Great Tradition can have a disastrous effect on the cohesion of a local community or, on the other hand, it may result in an even tighter retention of older, more satisfying cultural ways. The anthropologist, as interpreter, is in a position to read the text of culture and clarify its meaning to the architects and planners of programs for education and change. It is a role of educator, of culture broker, and of entrepreneur of ideas.

My own work as adviser/interpreter has included consulting with a national board on its program design, serving as a resource person in consultations of the World Council of Churches, leading workshops for church educators through a continuing education organization, and giving lectures as a guest at theological seminaries. In each of these encounters, I became increasingly aware that many of the goals of these organizations are the same ones held by the traditional agencies with which anthropologists have worked. The goals of humanizing education, recognizing cultural integrity, providing food for world hunger, and supporting justice for the oppressed are not the exclusive property of any one altruistic organization.

The clinical, or applied, aspects of working in religious groups are somewhat more problematic than the academic ones. Even if one can overcome the barriers of resistance by academe, the church, and the individual personality, only the braver person will venture into this formidable border territory between "the Church" and "the World." The marginality created by this particular limbo is unusually stressful. The most hardy churchfolk will silently accuse the applied anthropologist of being a nonbeliever and a skeptic; academic colleagues will suspect her or him of having "sold out," being converted, or, at the very least, of being "soft."

Applied Anthropology and Religion—
Future Directions

There is a vacuum of anthropological research in contemporary religious communities within the mainstream of American denominational life. These communities of belief and behavior need to be identified and their dynamics understood if we are to gain a unified picture of the complexities of urban society and community. In order to fill this gap, anthropologists interested in the formal study of religion will have to be willing to undergo the resistance of their colleagues, the churches, and their own personal socialization. Perhaps the practitioners can apply anthropology to themselves and their departments in order to tap the heretofore unstudied territory of American Protestantism.

As research is done and new community studies reveal the social and cultural processes of denominational community, there should gradually be greater demand for anthropologists to utilize this knowledge in implementing programs directed toward educational and humanitarian goals. In view of the fact that an increasing number of individuals venture into the never-never land of consulting for church agencies and other religious-affiliated organizations, the practice of accepting money from religious people should become more acceptable.

In the event that a new anthropology of religion does emerge, complete with applied aspects, those who study and practice the new craft will gradually discover some colleagues who are perched on the edge of other belief systems. The precarious position of marginal communicant will be made safer and more comfortable. It is even possible to anticipate a marginal community composed of all those anthropologists who did go home again, survived the experience, and have unabashedly assumed their places in the subculture of academic anthropology as full-fledged citizens.

11

BEHIND LOCKED DOORS

Myrna Sayles

There is a common stereotype that bureaucracies are huge people- and paper-processing machines, and that those who work within them have little emotional commitment to their work. One of the discoveries of applied anthropologists, reported earlier by Arensberg, Richardson, and Whyte, is that this image is a false one. Here, Myrna Sayles reports her personal learnings about the human and emotional involvement of staff and inmates in the daily work and activities of a large bureaucratically administered prison.

As she describes her work in the prison, Sayles candidly relates her failures and successes and her own emotional reactions to the several situations she encountered. She quickly learned the need for flexibility on the job and the difference between talking about change in the classroom and having to implement change in the prison setting. The ways in which she gained entry into the prison and her gradual acceptance as one who could be trusted required both intellectual and behavioral intelligence. Her own emotional commitments were publically and privately tested by all groups, and she was unable to make any contribution until she acceptably passed the test period. She makes a unique contribution to our understanding of the emotional aspects of work in nonacademic settings.

Myrna Sayles (M.A., Florida) is administrative assistant to the director of Social Services in Alachua County, Fla. After receiving training in anthropology, she worked for three years as a research assistant for the Division of Corrections of the State of Florida. She also has worked as a researcher for the North Central Florida Health Planning Council and as primary investigator in a study designed to identify and evaluate county sponsored or funded health care programs and make recommendations to the County Commission on unmet needs.

BUREAUCRACIES ARE USUALLY viewed as barriers to change, filled with faceless men and women merely "doing a job" with little sense of personal and emotional commitment to either the institutions they serve or their fellows in the bureaucratic ranks. Having little commitment, bureaucrats also are alleged to be uninterested in meeting new challenges with imaginative responses. In 1971, I was hired as a researcher in a state correctional agency designed to plan and introduce changes in prison programs. I soon learned the limitations of this stereotype of bureaucracy.

Doing anthropological research in a prison offers a look into the problems of large bureaucratic structures. It allows an analysis of situational factors and the impact of emotional relationships on the operation of the penal system. This essay describes a sequence of events that began with an unsuccessful attempt to gain access to the prison system and culminated in another approach that worked. The latter approach entailed the development of a role that permitted me to work effectively at a women's prison for three years from 1971 to 1974.

The express purpose of the state correctional agency for which I worked was to plan an experimental institution for the treatment of mentally disordered sex offenders. Each staff member assumed additional tasks in order to become acquainted with institutional living. I spent most of my time at the state's only women's prison. The diversity of personal and professional experience within the correctional setting demanded flexibility.

Prisons are like other closed institutions; they are characterized by emotional interpersonal relationships among staff and inmates. The personal lives of both groups are intricately involved in the operation of the prison system. For the anthropologist, personality differences and diverse cultural values demand an openness that is often more difficult to achieve in one's own culture than in another. Rural and regional values, racial distrust, manipulation, homosexuality, and the other subcultural values of prison life may be offensive and threaten to distort one's perception of what is actually occurring.

I will begin with a description of the ways in which my position within the prison became secure. Attention will be directed to the problems faced in gaining entry to the system, developing an approach that was both practical and flexible, and establishing rapport, trust, and credibility among staff and inmates alike. The focus then turns to the integral workings of the prison. How are groups formed? What groups are most important and why? What is the impact of the "human" element on the prison environment? The answers to these questions will reveal that manipulation of emotional feelings plays an important part in the life of the institution. The anthropologist's task is to carefully balance personal feelings with other, often conflicting, individual and group interests within the prison regime.

The Setting and Problems of Entry

In the early 1970s, corrections work gave major emphasis to the extensive counseling of prisoners. This concern was one aspect of wider public interest in the rehabilitation of prisoners. In 1971, there was little formalized counseling in the women's prison; most opportunities for counseling occurred informally between trusted staff members and inmates.

My initial task was to introduce counseling as an important activity that deserved equal priority with other activities of institutional living. Through the director of my agency and the superintendent of the 400-bed capacity women's prison, arrangements were made to meet with the counseling coordinator of the prison. Another staff member was assigned to assist me. Together we went to our meeting with the counseling coordinator.

The First Entry
As the meeting began, my assistant explained that we were there to make certain that counseling was occurring in the prison. If it was absent, our purpose was to insure that a counseling program was initiated. I was astounded by this statement. I tried to restate the purpose of our visit, but to no avail. The resulting hostility was overwhelming. We were told that all the counseling necessary already existed, and that there was nothing we could offer the coordinator that she had not already thought of herself. Needless to say, our stay was short.

After an explanation to my supervisor of what had happened and an intermission of a week or so, I returned alone in an effort to repair the damage that had been done and start anew. The more apologetic I appeared, the more opportunity the offended counseling coordinator saw to put me in my place.

As counseling coordinator, she viewed our presence as a challenge to her competency, although her title had little to do with her everyday tasks. In reality, she functioned as an administrative aide to the head of the prison's education department. Nevertheless, she felt threatened by the suggestion that she work with others to establish formal counseling. She explained that she had devised a system to randomly connect inmates with staff she thought would make good counselors. If they needed someone to talk with, inmates could contact one of these "counselors," who would then report that this interaction had occurred and the nature of the talk. No trust existed, no confidentiality was tolerated, and no personal choices were considered. Fortunately for all, it never happened.

During the following weeks, my initial attempt to gain entry into the system reached a total impasse. We were reported to the superintendent as irresponsible college kids who were threatening to the institution. My own feelings at that time obscured what I learned about the system. Instead of recognizing what I had discovered, I felt abused and misrepresented. I had failed. How could the superintendent believe someone whom I perceived to be incapable and untrustworthy? The explanation given to me was that the counseling coordinator was a loyal member of long standing in the corrections field. I had to accept the fact that the superintendent had only contempt for me. (Many months later, the superintendent and I would laugh uproariously at this disastrous beginning and her disgust at me.) This was my first lesson in the overwhelming sense of suspicion and job insecurity that existed among nearly all the staff. I was to have others as time passed.

The Second Entry
The next attempt at entry involved a more structured plan to introduce counseling. The psychologist on our staff would supervise (with help) two communication labs (low-key encounter groups) that would include a mixture of black and white, male and female, staff and inmates.[1] The intent was the development of communication skills between conflicting groups and individuals. Though this plan interested the superintendent, she insisted upon two stipulations: first, that she and her staff determine those who would participate in the program; and second, that there be a way to evaluate the program.

[1] Male inmates were transported from a small minimum security camp across the road, located there to help with construction and maintenance at the women's prison.

As the psychologist tried to explain that the experimental project was directed towards personal growth which was unmeasurable, I presented an idea that would benefit both groups and allow me entry into the institution. I suggested that I evaluate the effect of the program on the institution as a whole. I explained that such an evaluation could help determine how well a program of this kind worked and the responses of staff members to it. Intrigued by the idea, the superintendent agreed to take a chance. She also asked me to participate and observe one of the groups, since they were thought to be more instructional than encounter sessions. In this way, I finally got my foot in the door.

The series of events associated with my entry into the prison system served me well. I gained an appreciation for the need to dispense with theoretical explanations to justify my work and to concentrate on explaining in concrete terms the practical value of my work for the institution. In this and similar situations, it is a mistake to try to explain anthropology as a discipline. Besides the inability to understand an academic approach, there is resentment among many in closed institutions towards university trained "experts" tampering with what are often long-standing operational policies. Rather, the first question asked by prison authorities is: What can you do for me and how? I was soon to learn the next logical step of implementation.

If you can suggest what, and know how—then start doing it. I became aware that if I suggested an idea I must be prepared to carry it through. The realization that one does not just talk about change, as in the classroom, but actually effects it can be a jolt to the novice in the field, where pressures to reduce change become real.

The Role of Stranger as Confidante
I cannot emphasize enough the importance of my participation in the communication lab experience. We met for two-hour sessions twice a week for a total of thirteen weeks. The persons chosen for participation were "cream of the crop" among both staff and inmates. The idea was to insure a success. Most participants were open to the idea of exchanging views. The group in which I participated became more emotionally intense as time went on, but this was a constructive development.

My presence was conspicuous but not as unusual as it may seem. We were all equal as novices in this learning experience. Yet,

I was aware of being an outsider and did not pretend otherwise. I was straightforward about my feelings in the group experience because both staff and inmates were quick to spot a phony. Through this experience, I slowly became trusted and respected among this group of key individuals who represented all major factions within the institution. Later, these persons were crucial in the establishment of my acceptability among a diversity of groups.

During this time, the approach that was to be extremely productive for me began to take form. A natural outcome of my participant-observer approach was the role of outsider-insider. Georg Simmel, a sociologist in the early 1900s, explains this phenomenon as the "stranger-closed group" relationship in which the outsider offers the members of the closed group an opportunity to share views and information with one who has knowledge of the situation but is not personally identified with it (Wolff 1950:76). Hence, the frustration that results from the inherent frictions within any large scale organization or system is directed toward one who has an understanding of what it is to participate in the group, but who cannot endanger group security because he or she is an outsider.[2] A natural outcome of this approach is the stranger in the role of confidante. Trust is paramount, and the use of information is extremely delicate.

In my work within large scale organizations, one of my most vivid impressions has been how "locked-in," lost and unappreciated people on the staff feel. Contrary to those who state that individuals caught up in the bureaucracy feel nothing, I contend that, at least in total institutions, staff are highly emotional and increasingly meld their personal lives and feelings into their jobs.

As stranger in the role of confidante, I offered an outlet for feelings while receiving important, practical information about the prison system. The group sessions permitted me to establish this role. The things discussed there could not have been more pertinent to my understanding of the system. Inmates talked of the pressures of institutional life and their feelings as a group towards the staff and *vice versa*. I was privy to those contradictions and inconsistences about roles and expectations that were confusing and destructive to both inmates and staff.

In many ways, my role seemed too easy, but new problems soon

[2] A synthesis of being both near and far is what Simmel calls a "unique sense of objectivity."

dispelled this impression. I had no idea then how much I had yet to learn. How I longed to retreat with pad and pencil in hand to write it all down! Practice in recalling entire conversations became a must.

Evaluation of an Innovation

In order to evaluate effects of the communication lab experiment, I had to understand how the system worked in general. How was I to see all areas of the entire institution without causing alarm? I relied on a method I had used before: a spatial study. I had done studies on space and human behavior as part of my graduate work, and I knew the kinds of information these studies could offer. What places are restricted for what groups and why? How are they marked? How do different groups use space? Where are groups of people located and why? What areas are neutral to everyone? How do people feel about the space they occupy? How do groups distinguish themselves spatially? What channels of communication are reflected in space? Who goes where and why?

I explained my proposed study to the superintendent as an attempt to gain the knowledge needed for an assessment of the counseling program. Mainly out of her disbelief and curiosity, I was permitted to enter all areas of the prison to undertake the study. I can think of no other circumstances in which this would have been allowed at that time.

The physical structure of the prison is divided into two main sections. The first is located near the entry point of the institution and includes the departments of business, administration, custody, and classification. The other part of the institution is called "over the hill," an expression of literal translation which refers to all residential quarters, the dining facilities, the education department, and some custody personnel. Among the four major departments, business and custody (or security) are primarily maintenance functions, while education and classification work together on program ideas. Most conflicts center around the custody, classification, and education departments. The decisions of each of these departments immediately affect the others.

I began my survey by going from department to department. Traveling through the different sections of the institution provided opportunities for others to question me. In total institutions especially, there is a network of information about outsiders. Inmates and staff alike watch the outsider's behavior. What is she doing? Why? Can she be trusted? Trust and credibility are desperate issues in a closed society.

I began by asking nonthreatening questions about the needs for physical space to perform tasks. As initial suspicions were allayed, these conversations led to information on a range of other topics. I usually commented on the amount of work required of the particular individual with whom I was speaking. This simple recognition was appreciated, eased the tension surrounding my presence, and allowed confidential relationships to develop over time. These relationships eventually provided me with a cross section of opinions within the institution.

While I was becoming acquainted with staff, learning their biases and how the institution functioned, many inmates began to ask me what I was doing. I later learned that only the general population of inmates inquired; higher status inmates found out through their informational networks. Once identified with the experimental counseling project, no additional explanations seemed necessary. I took the time allowed inside the prison to chat informally with those female inmates I had known in the group project. These talks, in turn, encouraged talk with other inmates. These early relationships proved extremely important later on.

My study resulted in an array of data pertaining to the physical use of space, the departmental conflicts expressed by space and perceptions about the effect of the group counseling experience for the participants and the rest of the institution. In trying to absorb the flood of information, feelings, and perceptions, I sometimes experienced a sense of helplessness—wanting to shout, "Not so fast, I have to get all this in my head." I felt many of the inadequacies that others do in traditional field work. What are the signals? What's going on that I do not see? What cues indicate what thoughts and feelings? How am I to know when I have done something wrong? What questions or topics are particularly sensitive? Yet, I was eventually able to prepare a report which was useful to the superintendent.

First, I described the institution in terms of the physical relationship of buildings to each other, departments to departments, and the arrangements of offices. The conflicts between formal staff groups were similar to those in other large scale organizations where job descriptions and departmental functions overlap. Business was antagonistic to administration; each department made decisions which the other departments felt were their perogative. Classification and custody represented the more security conscious elements of the institution, but their functions were sufficiently different that they often supported one another. The education department was considered by others to be comprised of liberals who always took the side of the inmate. Each department believed that its function and insight were most important and that its members saw the inmate at times when she showed her "true colors."

The business department believed that the budget controlled the institution. Those in administration saw themselves as the most important decision-makers. Custody personnel felt that the primary reason for the prison was security. Those in classification who assigned inmates to a job or school, followed their progress, and made recommendations for parole defined their work as the *sine qua non* of the inmate's life. Similarly, the educational staff felt that, without their program ideas and personal concern and advocacy for inmates, the plight of the prisoner would be left unattended.

As simplistic as my analysis was, the superintendent gained insight into some of the reasons for constant bickering and antagonism between departments. The daily aggravations were put in perspective in terms of the functional scheme of the institution. Hostility between factions was more easily understood in terms of overlapping roles, confusion of institutional priorities, and personality differences. I had several examples of how the institution functioned informally—i.e., how decisions were really made, what networks of information existed between staff and inmates, and how groups, even though hostile to one another, were dependent on each other for their contribution to the information pool. All these factors were discussed separately and in relation to the counseling experience.

Working to Promote Change

My report was well received, and I was asked to stay on to evaluate other programs and help plan new ones. For the next two years, I became more involved in the daily prison routine. I came to understand

and work within the informal social networks and subgroups that were so important in the institution. These social networks existed among staff, among inmates, and between the two groups. The points of contact between the two groups were barometers which reflected human relations in the rest of the institution.

I was accepted by many inmates because of the communication lab experience and the trust I had established with others. Since it is impossible to relate to four hundred prisoners, I established contact with key individuals representing different factions of the inmate population. As I learned more about the nature of these groups, one fact became clear. The emotional impact of the setting itself breeds confusions and ambivalent emotions among both staff and inmates. Yet, a premium is placed on keeping a level head and "being cool." The release of emotion is often channeled in strange ways, sometimes constructive, sometimes destructive.

I found myself becoming attached and entangled with staff and inmates. The situation required involvement coupled with enough distance for objectivity—a delicate synthesis of Simmel's "near and far." For example, one evening, I stayed late working out a problem with particular staff and inmates. Both groups were emotional and illogical, causing frustration in everyone. Here were staff members who should have been home cooking dinner for their husbands but were too emotionally involved to give up the issue at hand. As I walked out of the institution, I saw the superintendent's office light still on. I walked in and exclaimed, "This place is sick! Doesn't anybody go home around here? There's an attraction and repulsion to this place that screws people up emotionally." She smiled at me and said, "So what are *you* doing here? Nobody pays you overtime." I knew then that I was hooked.

As I became involved in the daily activity of the institution, several difficulties arose. Once I had established trust and credibility, inmates and staff latched on to me. There was tremendous need to confide in someone outside the system who was aware of what went on. I became so entrenched with personal conversations, that I could not get other work done. I was swamped with sad stories. I felt obligated to listen to people who needed this release.

Occasionally, I would stay away so as to regain my own composure and perspective. I was so emotionally drained from listening to hard luck stories that I had to fight off depression myself. There were days when I arrived at the institution and turned right around to return to my office; I could not take the tension and depression that sometimes engulfed the entire place. Nevertheless, the knowledge I was gaining was to enable me to begin to work for changes within the institution.

Working With the Staff

One of the first problems that concerned me was the communication between the superintendent and her staff. As my relationship with the administration grew stronger, many people thought they could use me to get to the superintendent; others distrusted me for this association. For the most part, my role was nonthreatening enough so that I could talk easily with all staff groups through key contacts who became friends in the process. What were these relationships all about?

The most important cleavage between informal groups among staff at that time was the division between those supporting the superintendent and those who did not. Other alliances were often based on long or short term political expediency. Diverse attitudes about prisons distinguished still other boundaries between groups.

The superintendent had worked her way up through the system, demonstrating her administrative capabilities. Many staff members found her fair and straightforward. Others hired locally from around the small, southern rural town had difficulty accepting a woman as superintendent. Theirs was a more conservative view of the proper role of women. Moreover, the institution was frequently called upon to try innovative programs and projects. This put additional pressure on staff and often rankled the more conservative groups. As the superintendent tried to move the institution toward new programs (many of which were born in the state division headquarters), the antagonism of some staff grew.

Poor relationships were also fostered by those in the higher echelon in state headquarters who advised the superintendent to sever previous friendships at the lower levels in order to maintain administrative integrity. Many former friends did not understand the burden this placed on her and became bitter about her aloofness. There seemed to be an undeclared plot by some to hurt her for the lack of attention shown to them. Others saw her confidence and progressive programs as arrogant. Many did much to discredit her. Emotions ran high, and some staff behavior was getting out of hand. She had become a parent figure for some who desperately needed her approval and viewed her need for privacy in the job as a personal slap in the face. A few sought to discredit her by revealing facts about her past personal relationships.

The superintendent was unaware of what was going on, and no one could risk telling her that some of her trusted colleagues were against her. Finally, I was asked to do so by a close friend of hers. Although some told me that nobody could talk to the superintendent about her private business and that she would throw me out, I decided to try. That was the first major important decision I was to make in the institution. My approach helped me work out some of the more subtle implications of my role. As a stranger or outsider friend, I could take chances that others could not. If anger was directed toward me, the unity of the group would still be preserved, at least superficially. I was in the best position to tell her with the least amount of threat. I was beginning to learn that this is the real stuff of applied anthropology.

Applied anthropology is not like watching some strange ritual from some objective level high above the arena. It is getting to the very heart of other peoples' ways of life, knowing how important their values are to them, no matter how different from your own, and finding yourself in a situation that affects their personal lives. The staff personnel I describe are human beings whose personal lives are intermingled emotionally and contain all the ingredients of a soap opera—the terminally ill dying young, homosexual experiences, pregnancy, heterosexual affairs, and more. But in the prison, all of these things are for real and have an effect on the day-to-day decisions within the institution. Thus the staff are not aloof personnel running a closed system with little emotional feeling. Instead, they are emotionally tied to the system, with their personal lives often indistinguishable from their work lives.

When I asked to speak to the superintendent alone and out of the institution, she knew something was up and responded to the solemn tone of the conversation. We went to a restaurant and talked over coffee about what I knew. Much of it was intra-institutional politics, but there were personal implications. She was shocked and hurt; but as we talked and she cried, I knew that I had made the right decision. She knew that she was one of the very few who were willing to take risks in hopes for something better for that institution. It became apparent that only a handful of people really appreciated what she tried to do. It was a difficult session for both of us. She recognized the risk I took and saw it for the supportive concern that it was.

We tried to work out ways to make some staff members feel more involved with decisions and to bring her closer to her staff, but it was almost too late. Some ideas worked to ease tension and establish better understanding between friends. Other ideas did not work at all. Her work load was enough to keep three people busy. If she allowed everyone to talk to her when they wished, nothing would get done. Many staff seemed to need her direct attention and approval. It was a never-ending conflict. Over the next few months, the situation improved; but in the long run it deteriorated due to lack of unity throughout the institution, fragmented relationships and irresponsibility on the part of staff and inmates. A year after I left, the superintendent had outlived her effectiveness there and was promoted to a state-level position in Corrections.

Working With Inmates
The inmates, of course, are at the heart of the institution. In the formal organization, they are categorized by the kind of security assigned to them and their place of residency. There is maximum security (meaning little mobility "inside"), medium and minimum security, all color coded by dress. The movement of an inmate from one residence to another is progressive. All start at the reception and orientation center for one month's institutional adjustment. Then on to the general population where, with a good attitude, one can progress from the open-bay dormitory beds to one of the few private two-bed rooms. There are degrees of prestige attached to different residency halls. If progression occurs, one finally reaches the honor dorm where there is little supervision and more privileges. This graded tier system is supposedly based on good conduct, participation in extracurricular activities, and good job performance.

All inmates work either in school (G.E.D. program and Junior College) or in jobs that range from the laundry sweat room (considered the worst) to a clerical position (considered the best). There are activities after hours for those who are not exhausted. Choir participation is sometimes popular because the men across the road participate as well. Also, the chaplain's approval can be important for advancement in the system or as an informal sponsor for parole.

What kinds of informal social groups occur and what are the ear-marks of prestige among the inmate population? The only time the entire group is unified is when it is under threat. In times of crisis, inmates have different ideas about what to do, but they back each other with emotional support. Common fears pull inmates together during a crisis. Inmates have their own power, to be sure; but when staff feel threatened enough to call support (i.e., national guard), the inmates know their collective backs are up against the wall.

I was there during one such major crisis, precipitated by the death of an inmate whose night-long screams and pleading with the nurse to call the doctor went unattended. Whether inmates knew the dead girl or not was beside the point. They became anxious and emotional. I talked to a friend who was a lifer. She explained the fear shared by all inmates that they would die inside the prison, without seeing the outside world again. This incident reaffirmed to them that others control their destiny. Their lives are not their own.

Unfortunately, as in most crisis situations of this sort, the two opposing sides pulled back and retreated to their own distinct groups for safety, thereby creating further distance and misunderstanding. Unity and support were more important under threat. The tension was prolonged, and the national guard was on alert nearby. The situation finally cooled down, and an investigation took place over several days. The nurse was cited for poor judgment but was not removed.

During normal times, inmates formed small groups based on sleeping quarters, job assignments, and personal, intimate relationships. Clusters were based on a system of receiving and giving information. There were all kinds of different groups of diverse size and significance. In broader terms, there were those in reception and orientation who were novices and had little control outside their own group until they moved into low levels of the general population where they were indoctrinated in "how to play the game." The general population differed in status according to their length of time in the institution. Many in this group were young and loud. They constantly voiced opinions, cut up like junior high school kids, and were thought to be "uncool" by their peers.

Many inmates were short-timers (short sentences) and had little effect on the internal structure of the inmate group. The young blacks who came in were proving to be a disruptive force, finding themselves to be in the majority for the first time. Old-timers and lifers, both white and black, had settled their differences and were dismayed at the young black militants.

There were three prestigious groups among inmates. One of these comprised those who were housed in the honor dorm. Although other inmates had contempt for them, these persons had privileges and responsibilities that others lacked. These included going into the nearby town to the movies or to dinner with a staff member of their own choosing. No one could deny their status. The method of choosing these individuals was ambiguous, but it was usually through favoritism and a display of "good attitude." In many ways, this group was like a sorority who got along better with some staff than other inmate groups and was, therefore, suspect among the rest of the inmate population.

A second type of prestigious group was formed around individuals who occupied key jobs in the prison, especially those who worked for important staff members. The exchange of information is the most important commodity in prison, and the prestige of these groups was based on their access to information pertinent to the inmate population.

Finally, the third and most prestigious group was comprised of lifers. Those with life sentences were the most settled group in the prison. They knew the ins and outs of the system, and all the necessary information about the private lives of staff members. I spent most of my time with lifers because the short-timers were difficult to know; they were edgy about doing their time and getting out.

Lifers were important to other inmates for their understanding of the system and the support they provided. The core of the group was a few aggressive, homosexual women who enjoyed being in control and often held key jobs or positions in the system. These women, in many cases, were the backbone of the inmate internal structure and did most of the hard work. Many staff had only contempt for them but did not show it, in deference to their power and status. Within this group, there was an exchange of emotional needs. Many insecure inmates attached themselves to these women for both personal security and as protection against other inmates. Some of these relationshps were sexual; many were not. The homosexual leaders got the prestige they never had in the "free world."

Their role was intensified by the overwhelming, negative response to homosexuality by the staff. No "known homosexual" (butch-looking) could participate in any honor program. This was a means of staff harassment veiled in rules and regulations. Ironically, most of these women had never been disciplined for homosexual practices. They were far more discreet about their activities than many other women who came into the institution and played around with the idea of homosexuality by kissing and hugging with some sexual activity. These were mainly situational homosexual activities, if sexual at all, and were thought "uncool" by the long-standing homosexuals.

After awhile, I became comfortable with most of the lifers and homosexual leaders. Trying to catch people off guard is part of their game. I got used to the sexual propositions given mostly in jest. My ability to handle this kind of pressure, with joking relationships to ease the tension, won respect and trust. Many of these women were sociopathic charmers who were perceptive about people and used the knowledge to their own advantage.

The Points of Contact

How, then, do the informal inmate and staff groups connect? There are different points of contact. Occasionally, trusted staff who give moral support (and some services or gifts) are linked together in giving and receiving information in the hope of changing things for the better. Most often, staff and inmates were linked for political expediency. Staff individuals depended on inmates to give them information about what was going on "inside." These staff then used the information either for their own benefit to be recognized as someone-in-the-know to the administration or for departmental use to further their position on a given issue.

Inmates were often caught in the middle, but many times they were as manipulative as the staff. If an inmate gave information, there was promise of better treatment and more privileges. If she did not, harassment or avoidance might result. Many brash inmates knew which staff were corrupt and made small bargains about mutual exchange of information or services.

Unfortunately, there was not much consistency. Some inmates and staff gave only worthless information that looked good at the time. Other inmates cared nothing for their peers and would do anything for a promise of something better. Some female inmates resorted to pay or sexual favors to bribe guards for drugs or liquor. Periodically, the division cleaned house to sweep out the more blatant incidents of this practice.

Little unity existed among any large sector of the inmate population. Only small clusters of people remained loyal to one another. Distrust was as rampant among inmates as it was toward staff. The process of manipulation was self-perpetuating in the system. Often, there was not an honest exchange of goods and services between people, but only one done with contempt for the other person. The process was a destructive one.

The major formal and informal group leaders worked on planning and implementing programs. Often, I acted as mediator between groups to show how each could benefit from change. Increased opportunities were sought to give women more responsibility, autonomy, and self-respect. There were times of great breakthroughs, and there were times of total failure.

Specifically, I tried to institute an inmate government. My reasons were twofold. Many honor dorm residents had privileges with little responsibility. I contended that most females inmates would like more responsibility in their daily routine to promote self-reliance instead of an adolescent doling out of privileges by the parent institution. In addition, my hope was to decrease the privileges gained by telling tales and other destructive modes. However, I learned that, while many women were able to govern themselves in their own living area, they were reluctant to voice opinions as a group and to confront staff. I was strongly supported by the administration to hold meetings in which women could organize themselves, govern themselves in their living quarters, and present ideas to redirect goals. The attempt was sabotaged by lower echelon dorm staff, who intimidated inmates and made them their mouthpieces.

The women were not equipped to start making major decisions after so long a period of having been taught subservience by the base line staff. The strongest and most viable inmates often got what they wanted through the informal structure of the institution and distrusted any open display of trust with the staff.

To cut through this never-ending cycle of "don't trust a staff member no matter what they promise," I started a program that did work, at least while the administration at that time was there to lend support to it. Instead of constantly using valuable staff time to orient new inmates, I suggested that honor-dorm women come in, without the presence of a staff member, and tell the newcomers how to "make it" in the system in a constructive way. This short-cut the normal indoctrination through the general inmate population, where real distrust builds rapidly, and sarcasm and suspicion often lead to trouble. The honor women welcomed the opportunity to do something for fellow inmates, while at the same time receiving responsibility and prestige. Very few abused the privilege. The initiates appreciated hearing from those who had "made it" through the system.

One goal that did not materialize was an attempt to allow homosexuals in the honor programs. I gained the support of the administration and some key staff personnel by explaining that to exclude the main supportive group within the inmate ranks was to make a farce of the honor program. Many of the stronger women would have provided some needed structure in what was a rather suspect group. However, the woman in charge of the honor program threatened to resign if any homosexual was allowed to participate. Since she had been there for nearly fifteen years, the administration supported her authority in the manner.

The elite homosexual group would have been an asset to the honor programs because it was an integral force in preserving order among inmates. Instead, the members of this group were kept outside many programs and privileges, and were forced to gain respect and attention from staff in ways that were less constructive. The honor programs were doomed to eventual failure due to lack of consistency in promoting people and lack of integrity for what they were supposed to represent. These two elite groups were forced to be in conflict, when they should have been able to pool resources and offer stability to an otherwise superficial honor program.

With the new public awareness of the early 1970s, many citizen groups wanted to inspect the prison. The demands were overwhelming in terms of staff time. I encouraged the administration to trust honor dorm residents to show the institution to outsiders. I felt that no inmate would risk her stay in the prison by abusing the role. At first, a member of the staff accompanied the two or three women, but at times she felt comfortable enough to let the inmates go with visitors alone. This gave significant status to the inmates and helped staff use their own time more constructively. The administration was amazed and pleased to learn that they could trust the inmates.

The above are a few programs, representative of small changes, that occurred while I worked in the prison. The big changes I was able to direct were often more in attitude than in kind: to allow a more relaxed relationship between staff and inmates, to ease the harassment of ''known homosexuals'' who were discreet, to end the harassment of females and males who wanted to talk together between classes or in a regular work situation, to discourage the put-down hostility toward blacks or simple displays of affection between women, and so on. This relaxed attitude did much to insure a less emotionally volatile situation inside the prison.

In summary, my experience in finding an appropriate role in terms of prison values was crucial to gaining entry into a closed and suspicious society. With concrete, practical explanations of what I could accomplish for them, I set the tone to gradually build a viable ''stranger-closed group relationship'' that allowed me access to important information on which to base judgments about the internal workings of the institution.

What I found was considerably different from the usual stereotype of bureaucratic indifference. Bureaucracy can, indeed, become a rigid and unchanging hierarchy into which people feel they are locked. Staff and inmates alike are unwilling to take risks if they cannot perceive or predict the outcome. But the reason lies not in their lack of commitment, nor their dispassionate involvement with each other on their tasks. Emotional attachment to both persons and positions and highly personal interaction among people characterize the women's prison. The anthropologist who would work effectively for change within such an institution ignores the important role of emotional involvement to his or her peril. Success lies in harnessing these human energies, not in denying their significance.

12

ANTHROPOLOGIST-IN-RESIDENCE

Carol Taylor

In an earlier essay, Whyte notes the potential contribution of working in a variety of organizational settings to the reduction of organizational ethnocentrism and the enhancement of organizational theory. Carol Taylor is an anthropologist whose experience is an example of the type of research career pattern proposed by Whyte. As an "anthropologist-in-residence," she has undertaken applied research in factories, government agencies, international organizations, and health delivery systems. Here she reports some of her changing roles as an applied anthropologist in these diverse settings and the ways in which her understandings of bureaucratic structures have been modified over a lifelong career of studying organizational behavior.

Taylor's account discloses the many occasions anthropologists have to create job opportunities and to define specialized roles for themselves within bureaucratic structures. Success in doing so requires the ability to provide a variety of services which organizational members define as useful. Trustworthiness in human relationships, analytical skills, the inclusion of others in one's research efforts, and the willingness to undertake mundane tasks which help others are among the several key talents demanded of the anthropologist in nonacademic work. While these skills are also needed in academic field work in general, a major difference in being an employee outside of the traditional anthropology department is that one has to become skilled in understanding and working with modern "tribes" whose language, customs, and world views are quite different from those in the academic mainstream of anthropology.

Carol Taylor (D.Sci., Birmingham) is research associate at the J. Hillis Miller Health Center in Gainesville, Fla., and teaches in the Department of Anthropology at the University of Florida. In recent years she has been especially interested in health care and delivery systems. She has conducted research in England and the United States on industrial social structure, complex social organization, and bureaucratic systems.

WHEN WORLD WAR II was about to break out, I decided that it would be interesting and productive to become a participant observer in a mass-production factory. Charlie Chaplin's performance in *Modern Times* had drawn the submachine role of the factory worker to my attention, and I was interested in discovering how humans are organized into work situations which deprive them of the right to make decisions and the sense of working cooperatively with each other. I wanted to take an anthropological look at the various ways in which Industrial Man organized the immediate world in which he lived. *Modern Times* was not only my introduction to factories, however. It also marked the beginning of a long career as an anthropologist-in-residence within differently purposed large scale organizations which, over the years, have included government departments, international organizations and health delivery systems.

The role portrayed by Charlie Chaplin in *Modern Times* was that of a worker in a totally rationalized production system. All tasks which could be done by existing machines were allocated to them, and the necessary work for which machines had yet to be invented was separated into repetitious tasks which would eventually be better done by machines. Until competent machines were invented, humans were offered a living wage to do the work of tomorrow's machines.

Max Weber, the German sociologist who initiated the systematic study of bureaucracies, took a mathematician's delight in the efficiency of the rational bureaucratic approach to the accomplishment of large scale tasks, but he recognized the price which must be paid by people living and working in a completely rationalized world.[1] He asked whether it would be possible "to keep a portion of mankind free from the parceling-out of the soul, from this supreme mastery of the bureaucratic way of life." (Quoted in Coser 1963:177) Charlie Chaplin's portrayal of the submachine role made Weber's reservations about the "mastery of the bureaucratic way of life" visible and explicit.

[1] The German sociologist Max Weber initiated the systematic examination of Western bureaucracies, and his book *The Theory of Social and Economic Organization* (1964) is valuable as a guide during the exploration of large-scale organizations. Chester I. Barnard, another major contributor to bureaucratic theory, provides an equally valuable guide in his book *The Functions of the Executive* (1938). My own book *In Horizontal Orbit: Hospitals and the Cult of Efficiency* (1970) focuses on the various ways in which people abort bureaucratic attempts to behave in a rational fashion. In his book *Sociology Through Literature,* Lewis A. Coser places the theory about bureaucracies in perspective (1963:176–78).

In this film Chaplin is one of many workers servicing a conveyor belt. The belt carries engine blocks, and the workers tighten nuts on them with large wrenches. The second time I saw *Modern Times* I used a stop watch. According to my calculations, the conveyor belt was forcing the workers to tighten 450 nuts an hour. Assuming full employment for a working life of forty years, allowing for six statutory holidays and a two-week vacation, and multiplying these totals by the 55-hour workweek characteristic of that period, Charlie Chaplin portrayed the role of a man who's life work would be 38,610,000 nut tightenings!

When the film opens, the audience suspects that what Weber refers to as "the parceling-out of the soul" has become a threat to Chaplin's sanity. He falters at the conveyor belt, is reprimanded by his supervisors, and makes heroic efforts not to let the conveyor belt and his fellow workers down. As the workday progresses, his plight goes from bad to worse, and audience suspense is focused on the question: Will he make it?

In this rationalized production system, the midday meal break has been eliminated, and mechanical arms descend from the ceiling to feed the workers. On the particular workday depicted in the film, corn-on-the-cob was part of the menu. The corn, glistening with butter and salt, looked delicious. Mechanical hands rotated and moved the cobs along each worker's teeth at a calculated average bite, chew, and swallowing speed. The workers continued to tighten 450 nuts an hour while they were fed a balanced diet served at a speed which permitted them to chew each mouthful the forty times recommended by nutritionists.

When Chaplin's turn came, the mechanical feeding hands went beserk; the cob they presented to him rotated and moved from side to side so rapidly that popcorn bounced off his teeth. From that moment of mechanical mishap to the end of the day, it seemed as if the system was out to get Chaplin. His efforts to keep up with the conveyor belt became increasingly bizarre, and his supervisor, a remote control face, appeared with increasing frequency and ferocity on the supervisory television screen. Meanwhile, audience responses became increasingly verbal; some viewers appealed to God; others offered our poor hero advice.

The workday's end was announced by a siren, and the conveyor belt ceased to move. The workers downed tools and moved to the clock-out machines as Charlie Chaplin stood beside the immobile conveyor belt. A large door to the outside world begins to open, and Chaplin, with his work wrench in hand, moves toward the door. At this point audiences express premature relief—He's made it! Then a young woman, wearing a coat-dress buttoned from neck to hem appears in the doorway. The buttons are the same size as the 4,500 nuts Charlie Chaplin has just tightened. Responding to the buttons as unfinished business, rather than to the woman as a desirable female, he raises his wrench, tightens the buttons and strips them from the dress.

I found it difficult to believe that real people could be induced to subject themselves to work life depicted by *Modern Times,* and I decided to find out what the true situation was within a factory. Having decided on the "tribe" I intended to study, my next task was to discover how I might become a participant observer in this type of setting.

My first notion was to approach the manager of a mass-production factory and ask if I could examine it as if it were a small society. I was sure that I would discover something of use, and I offered to provide this sort of information in exchange for the opportunity to study the factory system. During my first interview, I realized that the only way I could gain entry was to permit the factory to pay me for what I wanted to do. If I were to sign on as a factory hand or seek a position in one of the offices, I would not be free to wander about the factory at will and to talk with and listen to persons at all levels in the hierarchy. My need for this freedom meant that I had to design a job which required access to persons throughout the factory, whether in supervisory positions or not.

I selected three industries which I knew would expand if and when war broke out, and I thought about the problems each might encounter. An obvious problem was a decrease in the male working force, the training of women to replace the men who were called up, and an expansion of the work force which would entail hiring mostly women, many of whom would be without working experience. Next, I sought out the managing director of each of the target industries and proposed that, in return for a salary, I would explore this potential problem and search for possible solutions.

All three managing directors refused my offer on the grounds that I was exaggerating the manpower problem they would face. Several weeks later, however, war was declared, and I was hired by a woman member of parliament to look at the displacement of female labor in the center of London, a task which took three months to complete. Shortly before the displacement study was finished, the managing director of one of my original target industries asked me to undertake the study I had originally proposed.

Because there was no precedent to follow, I gave thought to my role as participant observer and my relationships with factory employees. It seemed logical to model my role and its relationships on that of anthropologists in the classical fieldwork situation. Those fieldworkers were strangers who somehow managed to become, for a time at least, an integral part of the social system being studied although they did not become members of the tribe. I pieced together, as best I could, how and why anthropologists were tolerated by the small societies they studied.

The work of experienced field workers suggested that anthropologists might be tolerated, and even valued, because they provided something their tribes needed or wanted but could not provide for themselves. For example, Malinowski never went into the field without a pocketful of tobacco and during one seminar he suggested that training in first-aid and a plentiful supply of bandages and aspirin would be useful in the field. Joseph Rock was valued by Tibetans, in part at least, because of his skill in devising traps for man-eating tigers. After he had established this reputation, it was not unusual for emissaries from distant villages to seek him out and ask him to come and stay with him.

I also knew that the participant observer relationship must be built on something less romantic than rapport. In the 1930s, anthropological mythology held that one entered the field, established rapport with one's tribe, became enamoured with its way of life, and wanted to become a member of the tribe. The neophyte was expected to establish rapport but at the same time was warned against retreating from his or her own culture into that of his or her "people." There also were accounts of anthropologists who were valued by their "people" but found many of their customs revolting and prolonged immersion in an alien culture difficult to tolerate. With these meager clues to guide me, I became a participant observer in a mass-production factory.

Before leaving the ivory tower environment in which I had spent major portions of my professional life, I talked with Karl Mannheim, who suggested that I take two theoretical props with me: Weber's notions about bureaucracy, and Simmel's analysis of the trader role. His advice was invaluable. Weber was my guide and interpreter as I explored alien territory; Simmel provided a role model of sociological stranger which enabled me to avoid many pitfalls and to understand those I fell into.

Both Simmel's sociological stranger and my role as anthropologist-in-residence have characteristics which violate bureaucratic custom and correct bureaucratic behaviour. The "company" expects employees to demonstrate loyalty by defending it to outsiders, covering up the mistakes it makes to both insiders and outsiders; and by reporting to the proper authorities deviant behaviour of other insiders.

I explained to the managing director and to those in key positions in the factory's hierarchy that my ability to analyze their social system and identify its problems would be jeopardized if I could not guarantee the confidentiality of the information I received and if I were to cultivate the habit of whitewashing the system. I offered confidentiality instead of company loyalty, and I asked key members in the company's hierarchy to think of me as "physician" to the system. In that role, I would be able to maintain objectivity by remaining an outsider who would not skew diagnoses of the system in such a way as to encourage decisions I considered suitable. I specifically requested to have my attention drawn to any behavior in which I began to identify myself as one of the factory's decision makers by saying such things as "We should do this or that." Associating myself with decisions would be a symptom that I had unwittingly decreased social distance and become an insider rather than an outside-insider.

Initially, I did not describe the second social distance identified by Simmel, that of extreme closeness. I was not confident that this distance would emerge in the fragile commuter society I was attempting to examine, and I left discussion of this characteristic in abeyance until it emerged. In due course, I began to receive the sort of confidential information which Simmel claims indicates extreme closeness. When I established the reputation that I could not be tempted into bruiting about confided information, individuals, particularly those in key management positions, began to use me as a sounding board. This practice put me behind the scenes when decisions were being made and provided me with intimate information about the company's decision making patterns.

As noted earlier, in order to become intimately acquainted with a bureaucracy, the field worker must have access to persons at all levels in the hierarchy. This means that the first task is to interview those holding key positions in the system and find out from them what they are responsible for and how their part of the organization fits into the task the entire bureaucracy has been organized to accomplish. After key persons have been interviewed, arrangements are made to spend time exploring the domain of these persons. During these interviews and explorations, the field worker is questioned, scrutinized, and tested.

I was not surprised when this happened in my first mass-production factory; at that time an anthropologist in a factory was unusual. And I was not surprised that during the 1940s, subsequent explorations of other large scale organizations elicited this same response. But it has surprised me that thirty-odd years later, this sort of testing continues to occur despite the fact that behavioral scientists are often found studying various segments of our society. This response suggests that until the analysts of bureaucracies and other social systems prove themselves to be trustworthy persons, they will be offered innocuous information and smoke screens of misinformation. However, this circumstance is useful, because those who hold key positions in the formal system use their informal networks to test for trustworthiness. Consequently, the field worker being tested can use the series of tests to which he or she is subjected to diagram the bureaucracy's informal system.

As a technique, discovering the informal system in this fashion resembles injecting dye into a vein and plotting its passage through the body. In a bureaucracy, the tester, a person occupying a key position in the formal system, inserts a tempting morsel of information, either innocuous or erroneous, into the conversation at initial interviews. A few key persons not yet interviewed will be informed of this ploy. During interviews with them, they will create opportunities for the field worker to pass on the information inserted, like dye, into previous conversations. If the field worker avoids the trap, the person being interviewed will increase his or her attempts to trigger a breach of confidentiality. The field worker must figure out what information is being fished for and link the person who provided that information with the one fishing for it in order to diagram the informal organization of the system. The resulting diagram can be validated by the field worker if he or she inserts information back into the system and waits for it to resurface.

The informal system can also be observed as segments of it cluster during coffee and meal breaks, and it can be overheard as one member of it communicates with other members over the telephone. When the bureaucracy under scrutiny has become comfortable with its ethnographer, members of the informal organization will discuss their relationships openly and in considerable detail with the anthropologist-in-residence. Usually, the informal system consists of persons in middle management, supervisors, and the personal secretaries of those in top positions in the bureaucratic hierarchy.

According to Simmel, the sociological stranger becomes an integral part of the group without being a member of it because he or she provides something the group needs but cannot produce for itself. Malinowski's pockets full of tobacco and Rock's cunning in constructing man-eating tiger traps had alerted me to the trade aspect of my role as anthropologist-in-residence. By having arranged to provide something my first mass-production factory needed and was not producing for itself—a decrease in the turnover of employee rate—I did not initially give further thought to the trading aspect of my role as sociological stranger. But as time passed, I began to discover that this aspect was more complex than I had realized.

The factory was paying me to analyze a problem and to develop remedies for it. In order to do so, it was necessary to intrude into the territories of many different people. Some of them either would not benefit from the trade I had arranged or did not believe that I could deliver what I had promised. This state of affairs raised the question: What, if anything, are each of these people receiving from me that they need but cannot produce for themselves? Those I dealt with and into whose territories I intruded, were generally cooperative and seemed hospitable. The fact that I had been hired by the managing director made open rejection of my intrusions unlikely, but at the same time I noticed an increasing tendency to seek me out, even by some of those who had attempted to discourage my intrusions into their territories in the first place.

For example, one of the ways in which I sought information about what kinds of people would be best suited to specific jobs, was to learn how to do a number of these jobs myself. The shop manager in charge of the floor on which I first proposed to collect information in this fashion, did not consider it politic to refuse entry, but he did attempt to discourage me. As we were about to leave his office for the machine with which I was about to begin work, he said, "Let me look at your hands." He held my hands, turning them about, and examined them for a minute or more. I was delighted, assuming that one could tell by looking at hands the jobs they would be most capable of. When I asked him to tell me what clues he was looking for, he said, "I'm just looking to see your hands whole for the last time. You're not used to factories, and it will be a miracle if you don't lose a few fingers."

About a year later, some of the innovations I had suggested began to produce a decrease in the turnover rate, and this shop manager began to seek me out when he needed to talk about innovations he was thinking of introducing. One day he said, "My Missus can't understand what I'm talking about, and until I'm ready to move, it wouldn't be wise to talk to the other chaps about it. As far as I'm concerned, you're a safe ear and you've got a good head on your shoulders."

Since that time, I have found it fascinating to identify the trade items I use. Acting as a sounding board is frequently in demand. In addition to being a trade item, the fact that persons in key positions in bureaucracies usually do not have safe and knowledgeable sounding boards readily available to them makes this role one way in which valuable and intimate information about the decisions being made in the organization can be collected. At lower levels in a bureaucracy's hierarchy, treating people like human beings rather than sub-machines frequently becomes a trade item. Another trade item is the involvement of others in one's research. In our scientifically oriented society, research seems glamorous to neophytes and, in addition, many jobs in bureaucracies are so routinized as to be positively boring. This combination of circumstances makes collecting information for a research project seem exciting to many workers.

The fieldworker's idiosyncratic characteristics also have a tendency to become useful as trade items. In my own case, ghost writing a speech or a report has from time to time resulted in an informant releasing more intimate information to me than he or she was prepared to volunteer before this sort of service was offered. It is as if, by demonstrating an area of superiority, one had become worthier of receiving secret information, including trade and professional secrets. I first encountered this particular phenomenon when I wrote a speech, which was to be published, for a physician who was an excellent speaker but experienced difficulty articulating his thoughts on paper. This doctor had been an excellent informant, and I had not realized that he was withholding information which physicians do not offer to lay people until he began volunteering this sort of information after I had written his speech.

When I began to examine a complex of interrelated bureaucracies—a teaching hospital and the three colleges using that hospital for its students—I encountered a new problem. Hospital directors most frequently climb their success ladders by moving from hospital to hospital. In the complex I was examining, hospital directors changed, on an average of every two years. This meant that I had to discover a way to rapidly establish my usefulness as anthropologist-in-residence. If I was unable to do so, part of the complex of bureaucracies I was observing—the hospital—could become forbidden territory to me. In each case, I had met and talked with the new incumbent before he took office. In addition, each new incumbent had been informed about my function and role in the institution, and was assured that I would prove to be invaluable to him. Most hospital directors are proper bureaucrats; they believe in the bureaucratic way of doing business, and a person like myself who is free to go directly to anyone at any level in the hierarchy must inevitably appear threatening to them. The unbureaucratic pattern of behavior on the part of an anthropologist-in-residence violates correct channels of communication and in doing so, invades the decision making territories of every management person in the system. I devised the following method of dealing with the particular problem of the turnover of hospital directors.

For the first month or six weeks after the newcomer had taken office, I avoided him and spent time in the cafeteria watching for changes in clustering patterns. I also read the in-house paper circulating through the hospital and from it to the colleges the hospital serves. I did not seek information directly from those who worked in the teaching hospital, but on the other hand, I did not refuse volunteered information either. When I felt that I had some notions about the functional style of the new incumbent, I made an appointment to see him. I began this encounter by saying that I had been trying to discover what his functional style was like by observing changes of behavior in hospital personnel and reading the paper circulating in the hospital and between the hospital and the colleges. Then I would present my analysis, asking the new director to correct any errors. This approach created an opportunity to demonstrate my own functional style and make visible the way in which an anthropological look at a bureaucracy might throw new light on dysfunctional aspects of the system.

One characteristic problem in a bureaucracy is that the flow of information from functional levels to top management levels is inadequate. A free floating observer is in an ideal position to supplement the information flowing up the system. Since discovering this technique, I have used it not only on new hospital directors, but also in situations where it is necessary to establish a functional relationship with anyone not accustomed to utilizing the kinds of services which an anthropologist-in-residence can provide.

If we are to become useful to the host bureaucracy, we must translate observations and findings into the tribal language of those who work within the bureaucracy. The fieldworker begins to learn how to do so by learning the world view and the jargon used by each category of specialist in the system. Jargon from the social sciencies should be avoided. It is best to use simple everyday language, and understanding seems to increase when some of the jargon used by specialists in the host bureaucracy is borrowed. For example, in health related tribes (the two major tribes are nursing and medicine), I call the way in which America segregates its senior citizens into retirement communities and nursing homes, *the living cemetery syndrome*. Physicians and nurses are accustomed to thinking of a complex of symptoms as a syndrome, and labeling complex social situations as this or that syndrome increases understanding and makes it easier for physicians, nurses, and other health related specialists to remember complex social concepts.

Another aspect of the anthropologist-in-residence role which is sometimes difficult is deciding what should be done with and how to best handle one's findings. In my opinion, social scientists should assume some degree of responsibility for the way in which the information they produce is used. In practice, this means that the anthropologist-in-residence should take the best interest of the system into account, as well as protecting sources of information, when reporting to the system's decision makers. In addition to deciding what information should be reported or withheld, decisions about whom to inform and how the information should be transmitted also must be made. Who needs the information and how should it be presented in order to avoid distortion? The following examples suggest the nature of the problem.

While looking at death and dying, American style, I became aware of problems which the staff on the medical unit in a teaching hospital had attempted to have corrected through channels. Because the staff lacked access to a part of the informal system which could bypass the formal structure in order to draw the hospital director's attention to these problems, I was asked to help. It would have been appropriate for me to take the problems directly to the hospital director, but I decided to teach the staff new ways to handle their difficulties.

Most of the problems I used as teaching opportunities had nothing whatever to do with my examination of dying, American style. In this case, I was "trading" an understanding of and help with chronic ward problems for the staff's hospitality towards my death study. Eventually, the study itself provided trade items, but initially my interest in death was considered morbid, and there was some hostility towards it and me. My interest in and help with staff problems balanced out initial resistance to my research.

Some of the problems seemed trivial: Sterile Supply refused to stock bedpan covers; the unit was infested with palmetto bugs; and the hospital's wheelchairs were in bad repair. These chronic problems had been repeatedly reported to higher authority but nothing had been done about them. Upon investigation, I found that they had been dismissed as symptoms of low morale. As one assistant director said, "When morale is low, workers complain about trifles, and it is management's job to ignore what is complained about and concentrate on morale." It was obvious that problems dismissed for this reason would not be solved until they were recognized as genuine bones of contention. Thus, I set about teaching the staff how to make them visible to management. We drew attention to the need for bedpan covers with a humorous poem entitled "Ode to a Bedpan." The report of one dramatic death in the palmetto bug population enabled top management to realize that members of this species were present in their hospital and had become a problem. Maintenance began to repair wheelchairs the afternoon of the day on which the director of the hospital was pushed around the hospital in a wheelchair.

Most chronic hospital problems cannot be approached in the lighthearted fashion suggested above. Physicians, nurses, and other hospital specialists sometimes put excessive pressure on patients and their families without realizing that they are doing so. Such cases are extremely difficult to handle. One is tempted to intervene and draw attention to what must be treated delicately and under propitious circumstances. In some cases, intervention of any sort causes the situation to deteriorate, a circumstance I find extremely difficult to tolerate. I will use kidney transplants to illustrate problems of this sort.

Our society expects its members to want to live and that its members will help others to live, particularly those close to them. Consequently, many physicians assume that family members really want to donate a kidney when called upon to do so. When the selected donor seems reluctant, the physician assumes fear and, having assured the donor that he or she should do well with one kidney, may attempt to shame the person with a matching kidney into donating it. One reluctant donor said, "All of us volunteered, but I am unlucky enough to be the only match." After recovering from donating his kidney, he said, "That's one decision I won't be called upon to make a second time."

Sometimes potential donors refuse. The most moving refusal I encountered was made by the mother of nine children. One of the children needed a kidney transplant. The mother and the father volunteered to be donors, but their kidneys did not match. The physician suggested that one of the eight siblings might make a suitable donor. The mother said, "They are under age and should not be burdened with this decision. Each one of them would give a kidney if asked to do so, but it is too much to ask." The nurses who looked after the patient when he came in for dialysis condemned the mother, and one of them said, "It's inhumane, forcing him to wait around for a kidney from a cadaver when he is almost certain of a match with eight brothers and sisters." In situations of this nature, interventions must be handled with great care lest they become disastrous.

In some cases, staff put excessive pressure on themselves as well as on patients and the families of patients. I will use institutional death to illustrate this sort of chronic hospital problem. At the turn of the present century, death in our society began to move out of the home into institutions. Today, most Americans die either in hospitals or in nursing homes, and this change in locale has altered our grieving patterns. When death was a family affair, family and friends remained close to the dying person until death had occurred; the task of caring for the person was a family responsibility. Institutional death places the primary responsibility of caring for the dying person on nurses and their assistants, who are often strangers to the individuals involved. The family's access to the patient is restricted.

Because those previously closest to the patient are excluded when death is imminent, they begin to grieve in anticipation of death. If sufficient time has elapsed, the bereaved family and friends have partly completed the grieving process. Thus, when death is announced, they do not appear to grieve. Nurses, who do not realize that the bereaved frequently are well advanced in their grieving, may accuse the dead patient's family and friends of failing to grieve appropriately. Moreover, it is not unusual for these same nurses to grieve for the deceased patient as if they themselves had been suddenly bereaved. Whereas family and friends have moved into a less intense phase of the grieving process, nurses, having worked intensively with the patient for a short period of time, have bonded with the deceased person and are, in fact, newly bereaved. Some nurses consider this sense of bereavement, and the deep grief accompanying it, unprofessional and inappropriate. In most cases, hospitals and nursing homes do not provide their bereaved staff with opportunities to work through their grief.

Partly because both the nursing staff and the patient's family and friends grieve for the same dead, this sort of hospital problem can be readily solved as soon as it is understood. Nurses who know that those close to their dead patient may be well along in their grieving do not treat them as if they are unfeeling and unloving. When they are aware of the various ways in which institutions isolate patients from those closest to them, nurses use their authority over the situation to allow patients and those close to them to be together whenever possible. Most nurses are relieved to discover why they grieve for some of their dead patients as if they themselves were bereaved. This understanding removes the guilt nurses experience when they think they are grieving inappropriately. After understanding why they grieve as if bereaved, nurses have shown considerable ingenuity in inventing rituals to assist in handling the grief that institutional death has thrust upon them. For example, in one hospital the staff mounts a wake from time to time. The nurses provide a potluck meal. The physicians spike the punch. During the sharing of food, grief is shared and dissipated. In this particular hospital, the wake is announced over the loudspeaker system as a medical round—"Liver rounds in the conference room."

Despite its difficulties, the role of anthropologist-in-residence has a number of advantages. Anthropologists-in-residence, like colored telephones, are status symbols. The bureaucracies which hire behavioral scientists to monitor their social systems know how to use colored telephones, but they usually do not know what they should expect from an anthropologist-in-residence. As a consequence, the job can often be designed to suit the interests of the incumbent. This approach ultimately seems reasonable to the host bureaucracy, because anything an applied anthropologist might decide to do usually yields useful insights. Bureaucracies are not as efficient as the theory about them suggests, and an anthropological look at any part of one invariably yields valued explanations and provocative suggestions.

It is also an excellent position from which to test emerging theories. During the past twenty years, large scale organizations have toyed with notions about decentralizing, developing collegiate or corporate forms of organization, and eradicating the submachine role which initially horrified me into a systematic examination of bureaucracies. During the period when bureaucracies have been hospitable to explorations of this sort, I have had numerous opportunities to experiment with organizational innovations and modifications. These opportunities have sharpened my understanding of existing theory and permitted me to add to it. This aspect of the job of anthropologist-in-residence is especially rewarding to me.

Having taken Weber as my guide when I entered the alien world of rational large scale organization, I expected to find absolute efficiency and to feel free from "the parceling-out of the soul" which Weber saw as the price mankind must be prepared to pay for maximum productivity. These expectations were not met, and I was surprised to find that bureaucracies were inefficient and that the workers in them could, and did, cooperate with each other to counter what they considered to be the inequities the system was trying to impose. Discovering the numerous ways individuals cooperate with each other in efforts to retain a sense of self-determination increased my respect for my own species.

In the past decade, I have added a third pleasure to the rewards of being an anthropologist-in-residence in a large scale organization. When acupuncture, as wedded to scientific medicine, first began to emerge from mainland China during the early 1970s, I was examining the American health delivery system and was in an excellent position to observe an interesting phenomenon. An ancient therapy which worked but could not be satisfactorily explained was being absorbed into the practice of scientific medicine. This exercise in opportunistic rationality alerted me to the fact that Industrial Man was not as rational as his scientific posture suggested. This fact becomes vivid when nineteenth-century science is compared to twentieth-century assumptions. For example, during the 1830s, science had proved that masturbation caused criminality and insanity and was so widespread as to threaten the safety of the nation. Today, masturbation is viewed as normal in children and a therapeutic modality for sexually malfunctioning adults. An examination of this and other nineteenth-century researches suggests that Industrial Man rationalizes his mythologies into logical postures, an observation confirmed by the emerging science of acupuncture.

My own experiences as an applied anthropologist in a number of differently purposed large-scale organizations encourage me to suggest that anthropologists and other behavioral scientists who value the freedom of designing their own jobs will find the role described in this paper rewarding. For those who can tolerate the idiosyncracies of Industrial Man's Commuting Tribes—his bureaucracies—the role of anthropologist-in-residence is challenging because it must be reinvented not only when one moves from one organization to another but also when one seeks answers for new questions. It provides opportunities which permit one to put theory to the test and to develop theories which will not be confounded by reality when they are taken out of the ivory tower into the real world.

13

DOING BUSINESS WITH MANAGEMENT

Burleigh B. Gardner

Although many anthropologists are consultants from time to time to government and community agencies, foundations, international organizations, and other groups, only a few have become full-time employees of private consulting agencies. In 1946, Burleigh Gardner and W. Lloyd Warner organized Social Research, Inc., in the city of Chicago as a means of providing help to business organizations in the solution of human problems.

Gardner describes the work of this consulting firm which still exists today. Unlike most firms of this kind, Social Research, Inc., utilizes social anthropological perspectives and field techniques in combination with other methods of data collection and perspectives derived from both psychology and sociology. Contractual relationships with clients necessitate an emphasis upon prespecified services and products. Persons are hired as employees in the firm because of their abilities to contribute to the various kinds of research and reports required in this type of contractual work. Broad interdisciplinary training and methodological versatility are a prerequisite for effective work performance. Gardner repeats some of the points made by Whyte in his emphasis on the need for research methods that can gather pertinent data quickly and provide the basis for reports that are useful to managers and administrators alike.

Burleigh B. Gardner (Ph.D., Harvard) is president of Social Research, Inc. Dr. Gardner was a participant in the now famous "Yankee City" and "Deep South" studies before serving as a founder and executive director of the Committee on Human Relations in Industry of the University of Chicago. In 1946, he founded Social Research, Inc., of Chicago. As head of Social Research, Inc., he has been nationally influential in gaining business acceptance of the value of social sciences and their application in the field of motivation research.

THE WORK DESCRIBED here began in 1946 when W. Lloyd Warner and I organized Social Research, Inc. as a means of applying our expertise as social anthropologists to help business organizations solve their human problems. We were accompanied in this venture by Dr. William E. Henry of the Committee on Human Development at the University of Chicago, who was trained as a clinical psychologist and also worked with Warner on studies of Navaho personality. We soon added sociologists and others with interdisciplinary degrees in Human Development. It was on this base that we built the organization and have had opportunity to study a wide range of business problems.

Every business organization is a social organization which must function within the society of which it is a part and survive within the boundaries of law and custom set by that society. Each business organization also has its own internal social system with its own set of rules and customs affecting and limiting the behavior of people within the organization. The task of management is to maintain effective relationships, both externally and internally, so that organizational problems may be solved in the areas of customer relations, relations with the community and the broader society, and the internal aspects of work organization and human relations. Throughout the past thirty years, the consulting work of Social Research, Inc. has been primarily concerned with these three major types of human problems. Before presenting specific examples of some of the types of work in which we are engaged, I will describe briefly the range of our activities in each of the three areas listed above.

Since every business organization provides products or services which must be sold to customers if the business is to survive, business executives are concerned with a range of problems involving what is sold by their firms, the price of these products or services, how they are sold, and the ways in which the firm communicates to the public about the products, the services, and itself. Our consulting work related to these and other problems of customer relations ranges over a wide field and includes such things as the roles and symbolic meanings of products, customer reaction to new products or product variations, customer motivaton for buying, and communications to the public through advertising, packaging and publicity. Though they are somewhat different in nature, we have worked on media studies investigating audience reactions to television or radio programs and to the format and content of magazines and newspapers. In the case of media, the product is communication, and it is necessary for the media to attract an adequate audience in order to survive.

The external relations of business firms are not solely a matter of relating to customers. Business organizations must also adjust to laws, community expectations, the demands of special interest groups, and so on. The recent and growing concern about "corporate social responsibility" reflects the needed adjustment between the company and the larger society within which it functions. Our work in this area entails the general field of public relations and social responsibility and includes studies of corporate images, public reactions to corporate programs and reactions to corporate advertising.

Closely related to studies of the external relations of business are studies of social change and their significance for business, government, education and other institutions. For example, the rapid and dramatic changes in our society and its value systems during recent years have been accompanied by the emergence of such issues as integration, women's liberation and consumerism. These issues have been of such deep concern that they have become political and legal issues. They have had strong impact on business, both as a result of laws and because executives reflect general public sentiments. Executives are part of our social system and respond to changes in values.

One element in the public image of any large business or other organization is how it is seen as serving the community, its employees and its customers. In studies of the public image of "big business," we found that through the 1950s the image was that of a benign power concerned with the quality and value of products, with serving the community and fairness to employees. In the mid-1960s that image began to slip as people viewed "big business" as self-serving and indifferent to people and the community. These negative attitudes have increased over the last decade.

Another area of social change was among working-class women. We studied these women for McFadden Publications over a period of twenty-five years. In the late 1960s, we saw a sharp change as women emerged from the narrow confines of husband, children, and home and became more active in the community, more alert to the broader world, and changed their concept of the woman's role. We saw how women were reacting to the women's liberation movement, but with acceptance of many of the goals of equal opportunity for education and jobs and equal pay.[1]

Finally, the third major focus of work at Social Research, Inc., has been related to problems of internal organization within business. Internally, a business must be concerned with a variety of human relations and organizational problems. These range from problems of the formal or technical organization necessary to accomplish tasks, to problems of employee morale, union organization, personality conflicts, interdepartmental frictions and other human relations concerns. We have worked on many types of problems related to the internal social structure of business, including the relationship of individual personality to functioning in specific roles.

Case Examples

The activities of Social Research, Inc., can best be understood through specific examples of some of the work we have undertaken in response to requests for our services. Historically, our initial work was on internal organization problems, and our first major client was Sears Roebuck & Company.[2] One of our assignments there was to develop a system of employee attitude surveys which could be used company-wide as a regular management information system. In the late 1930s, Sears had used an outside consultant to conduct an employee attitude survey, but due to the chaotic conditions during World War II they had done nothing since that time.

In our first work with Sears, we studied a number of specific problem situations using personal interviews and observations as the methods of data collection. However, we believed that the general organizational climate was such that it would be possible to develop a survey system using questionnaires instead of the more cumbersome (and expensive) personal interviews. In developing this system, our criteria were that the system should show the patterns of interpersonal

[1] This study was distributed under the title "Working Class Women in a Changing World."

[2] We were working primarily with James C. Worthy, Assistant to the Director of Personnel and Clarence Caldwell, Director of Personnel. Mr. Worthy is now Professor of Management at the new Sangamon State University, Springfield, Ill.

relations and employee attitudes clearly enough to identify problem situations. The new system also should be simple to administer and analyze, should provide quantitative measures sensitive enough to show differences between groups and changes over time, and should be able to be handled by the corporate personnel department without dependence on outside specialists. These criteria were important if the employee attitude (or morale) surveys were to be widely used in a company where cost was an ever-present concern.

The tasks involved in the development of the survey system began with the design of an experimental questionnaire. In this step, we explored the employees' perceptions of areas and relationships which are matters of concern in most work situations. Since we knew a great deal about a wide variety of organizations and were experienced with the organizational and people problems of Sears, we were able to select a small number of important areas to explore. These were: identification with the company, supervisory-subordinate relations, interdepartmental relations, relations with fellow employees, pay, benefits and opportunities for advancement. Each of these areas was explored by a series of statements for which the respondent marked on a scale the extent to which he agreed or disagreed. To reduce bias, we developed for each area, five statements, some phrased negatively and some positively.

The experimental questionnaire was tested in selected situations. We selected stores or departments where there was reason to believe morale was poor and some where it was good. The questionnaire was then administered to all employees in group meetings where the purpose was explained and their cooperation requested. After tabulating the responses, we prepared profiles showing the areas of concern or subgroups with high or low morale. We then personally interviewed a sample of employees from each location in order to test the accuracy of questionnaire results. In this way, if employees complained about their supervisor, we were able to verify it in the questionnaire profiles. After these tests, the questionnaire was redesigned to make it more efficient. The redesigned questionnaire was then used on other organization units, some of considerable size, such as a mail-order plant. Follow-up interviewing was then used, but only where the questionnaires showed a trouble spot.

Our final task was to train a group from Sears's personnel department to handle the surveys, including the administration of questionnaires, analysis of data, interviewing in trouble spots, preparation and presentation of reports to management, and feedback to employees. Once the system was functioning, there was no longer a need for our services. Sears is still using employee morale surveys as a regular tool and has established one department which devotes itself solely to this work. The questionnaire and the methods have been revised and improved during the years since we first started to work with Sears, but the basic structure still remains.

The initial work with Sears has been followed by many other opportunities to work on the internal organizational problems of business. For example, a company operating a chain of drug stores was having problems with its pharmacists; there was much evidence of poor morale among them. We were asked to study the nature of the discontent and what management could do to correct the situation. We designed a survey with several sources of data. These included interviews with management to get their views on the situation, interviews with a dozen pharmacists and a mail questionnaire to all pharmacists employed by the company. The latter consisted of a few major questions, and the pharmacists were asked to write their views in detail. We received lengthy responses to the questionnaires, often several typewritten pages, in which the pharmacists explained their views and complaints.

We soon learned that the pharmacy departments were only a modest portion of the total store operations, and rarely were there more than three pharmacists per store. The store management group was small: a manager, first assistant manager, and sometimes a second assistant. The pharmacists were not considered a part of store management and often reported to the first assistant manager, though they had full responsibility for all prescription and over-the-counter drugs.

One of the sensitive issues for the pharmacists (though seldom expressed directly) was based on their identification as professionals. With a college education and professional training, they were placed in positions subordinate to assistant managers, who often had less education and experience and knew nothing about pharmacy. Although they were responsible for the department essential to being a "drug store," and with responsibility to service physicians and their patients, they were not considered part of store management. This issue of status and recognition was behind much of their discontent and often hostile reaction to the company and its policies. Attention by top management to this problem improved morale and laid the basis for improved cooperation within the store.

In another case, the administrator of a large hospital requested a training and development program for his department heads. He complained that they could not make even simple decisions, they had no leadership skills in dealing with subordinates, and there was constant friction between departments. The administrator was overworked because he had to constantly intervene in problems which his subordinates should have been able to handle. With such requests, we try to remain objective until we can diagnose the problem ourselves, We insisted, therefore, that we had to have our own view of the situation.

One of my associates spent about a week observing the administrator at work and interviewing his staff. A particularly striking observation my associate made was that the administrator spent his time with an endless stream of people coming to him for decisions. Sometimes department heads would be lined up waiting to see him. It was obvious that many of the decisions should be made by the department heads, and many matters of interdepartmental conflict could be resolved at lower levels. A major problem was the administrator's behavior: he provided answers, made decisions and generally acted as a crutch to his subordinates. He had created a set of expectations in which it was easier (and safer from criticism) for his employees to seek his judgment rather than to make decisions themselves.

Once we saw this pattern, we were able to get him to change his behavior. Instead of making decisions, he insisted that his subordinates use their own good judgment or at least come to him with a proposed course of action. (This oversimplifies the matter but was the crucial change.) While he was altering his own behavior, we continued to observe him and to interview key people to help them through the process of change. The changes took place, and a formal training program was never needed. In fact, after two years, the hospital was running so smoothly that the administrator became bored and subsequently went to a larger and more complex hospital where he was faced with fresh administrative challenges.

Our studies in the area of customer relations cover a wide range of products and services. Studies of various media and specific elements have from the beginning been important types of projects. In studies of newspapers, we have explored basic questions such as the following: What place does the newspaper have in the daily lives of its readers? What needs does the newspaper fill? What satisfactions do the different types of content provide? What kinds of people (in terms of social and psychological typologies) are attracted to different content? Why do people choose one paper over another?

With any paper or magazine, one of the crucial and often most difficult questions to answer is why a person reads it at all. This is a question for which the reader can give conventional or superficial explanations, but the actual reasons are usually quite subjective and must be deduced by the researcher. That is why the ordinary pollsters rarely get at the dynamics of behavior. Their methods provide only a quantitative portrait of behavior and of the rational explanations. This counting of readers is very important to a paper or any media, since advertising rates are based primarily on audience size. However, it is not very useful to the editorial department, which is concerned with the content appropriate both to current readers and to others whom they wish to attract in order to expand their audience. This latter need is the basis of most of our studies of newspapers.

The Anthropologist as Business Consultant

Thus far, I have summarized the general types of business problems which have concerned us at Social Research, Inc., and given a few examples of specific jobs we have undertaken. Now, however, I want to turn to a discussion of anthropological perspectives which have guided my work for many years and some of the major adaptations required of the anthropologist who enters the business field.

All research in the social sciences is concerned with perceiving the structure of the universe of people's behavior. The assumption of any science is that there is structure in the universe, and the task is to discover it. We cannot assume a universe of myriad idiosyncratic entities—whether people or molecules—behaving in a random manner that has no pattern. Unless there is a pattern or structure, there can be no continuity of either the physical or the human universe. Because of this structure and its continuity, we wake up each morning the same person with the same body and mind as the night before, and we usually find ourselves in a familiar place which is perceived to be the same as it was before.

The role of science and research is to discover and describe the structure and to pass this knowledge on to others. Each of us does not have to repeat the experiments of Newton to know the force of gravity, nor do we have to sail around the world to convince ourselves it is round. In the same way, social scientists bring to bear on problems of human behavior a large body of knowledge drawn from researchers who worked and studied before us.

We cannot discuss here the whole problem of the nature and structure of this human world. Rather, the focus is on those views which have been found useful in dealing with behavior in business organizations. These views have been widely studied in both academic and applied research, and there has been considerable experience with them as useful tools. In the research undertaken at Social Research, Inc., we generally deal with individuals as entities who fit into some pattern or group structure. We assume that knowing the position of individuals in these social settings tells us something about their probable behavior or the forces acting on them. Thus, if we know an individual is a male worker on an auto assembly line, we can predict a lot about his daily work situation—what is expected of him, what his role is, and so on. If the individual is a teen-aged black girl in a ghetto high school, we can predict a great deal about her daily life.

To state this another way is to say that there are social systems—i.e., community, factory, university, family, kinship and other groups—whose members have a place and behavior, beliefs, reactions, etc., appropriate to their place. In very stable societies, the individual may deviate only slightly from the behaviors appropriate to his or her position. In changing societies such as ours, the range of deviation is great, and even the structure may be changing. The rapidly changing nature of contemporary societies creates a need for consulting anthropologists in business and other institutions that does not exist within stable traditional systems where deviations are well established and conflicts are resolved in traditional ways.

There is no need here to elaborate on this basic view of man and society, but it is useful to keep it in mind when considering the role of the social anthropologist as consultant. Basic to this systems view of social organization is the assumption of interaction and interrelationship between different types of behavior. Thus, the behavior of people as consumers, clients, employees, or corporation managers is related to their roles in particular social systems. Their religious behavior, their relations with family members, their personal dreams of glory, their treatment of subordinates or their reactions to superiors—are all somehow linked together.

Among corporation executives, for example, each position carries a point of view which, when imposed on the organization, can create problems. The president projects his own motivations on workers; the production vice-president thinks in terms of output; the sales manager focuses on sales. Top executives often project their own attitudes and motivations in decisions about employees or customers. There is an assumption that other people are "just like me." Thus, advertising executives who are upper middle class and live in upper middle-class suburbs may prepare advertisements with people like themselves in mind and "talk to themselves" rather than to the large lower middle-and working-class market. Or an executive may refuse to sponsor a television program because his "wife doesn't like it." These types of difficulties are well illustrated by the case of *True Confessions* magazine, which had problems for many years because executives asserted that women who read that type of magazine could not be taken seriously as potential customers.

In our work at Social Research, Inc., we are constantly alert to the distortions that result from the assumption that others are "just like me" and the failure to recognize the importance of social systems in shaping human behavior, attitudes and values. This is true not only in the research we undertake but especially in helping management solve problems. We often must convince advertisers that they should not be talking to themselves, or presidents that they do not really understand how their workers feel. To do this requires a relationship where there is confidence in the consultant and a personal rapport.

In the business world, as elsewhere, the role of the anthropologist is to discern the interrelationships between different types of behavior and to understand how they will be affected by changes undergone by individuals and the social systems of which they are members.

Furthermore, the anthropological view does not accept jurisdictional bounds within the social sciences. The problem is to understand people and how they function. Social systems are a product of their interactions, and even though they may deify their particular social order or theory of it, their society is still a product of their behavior. A corporation, a legal system, capitalism, or communism are all products of human behavior and beliefs. They are not something imposed by some nonhuman force although they may be shaped by it. This must be kept in mind, since all too often the executive, the politician, or the average citizen is prone to think that the human world as *he* or *she* sees it is somehow the "real" world for everyone. (Remember all the efforts to explain slavery as a part of an ordained "natural order?")

To help clarify the significance of the anthropological viewpoint, I want to make some comparisons between Social Research, Inc., and the majority of pollsters or market research firms. When we started in 1946, we were emphasizing the understanding of the social system and social class as a useful way of classifying people instead of only the standard demographics such as sex, age, and income which were used in most polling or market research. In the same studies, we also classified families by stages in the family life cycle. These gave useful ways of examining groups of people and projecting results of studies to larger populations.

In the early days, our work aroused considerable interest on the part of executives, business, advertising, and media. However, other researchers continued to be committed to using simplistic data and quantitative methods. In fact, one leading pollster in about 1955 asserted that social class was nonsense; he had been studying public opinion for over twenty years and had never seen any evidence of social class. To him, all people in a certain income or age bracket looked the same in the computer output.

While we found that social class provided a useful way of classifying people, it was not meaningful for all problems. We were constantly examining other characteristics which could help with specific problems. For example, in studies of advertising themes with products such as Alka-Seltzer, we found that people could be classified as "head-achers" or "stomach-achers" and that advertising needed to reach both types. These types did not seem to be related to social class. A conventional study of these products would have identified samples of users and nonusers, and would have used a structured questionnaire to collect and tabulate questions of age, sex, income, frequency of use, brand preferences, etc. The result inevitably would be a huge volume of statistical tables, but no fresh insight into the psychodynamics of use.

I have long believed that the basic difference between our firm and most others is that we came from a background of trying to understand the dynamics of behavior and attitude and then, if appropriate, quantify them. Most other market researchers came from a background that assumes they already understand and only need quantification as the goal of the research. This difference is important in our age of computers. It is easy to be entranced by the beauties of statistical differences and masses of quantitative output and to lose sight of the need to understand what is going on. This is seen in the interest of many researchers in "psychographics" and "life style," which are ways of setting up new classifications of people and showing complex relationships but often with no understanding of how people function.

I do not mean to dismiss the value of computers and statistical analysis. We have used multivariate analysis as a regular tool for many years. In fact, for any large study we combine quantitative data, including specially designed rating scales and semantic differentials, with a great deal of qualitative material in the form of open-ended or discussion questions and projective techniques. We rarely try to reduce the open-ended material to statistics, but instead we use the statistical data to classify people and then examine how they respond to the open-ended or projective questions. Our reports are discursive, telling what we have learned; statistical material is only an appendix for those who want it.

When considering the whole field of consumer research, we can draw an analogy from anthropology. In the early days, anthropologists were ethnologists who collected the artifacts of a culture or described the behaviors. Then came others, such as Malinowski, Radcliffe-Brown, Margaret Mead, and Lloyd Warner, who tried to understand and describe the way a society functions and the role and meanings of artifacts and activities. Today, most market researchers are ethnologists enumerating activities, characteristics, or expressions of attitude. In fact, some of the largest of the research firms do nothing else.

At Social Research, Inc., we are more than cultural anthropologists looking for the functional meanings and trying to tell our clients how the social system—or some detail of it—works. We are trying to use our interpretive skills to help them solve their problems. For us, competent applied anthropologists must be social scientists in a broad sense. They must have assimilated knowledge and concepts from all the disciplines and must use them to help think about concrete problems. The concern is not with being an anthropologist, sociologist, psychologist, but only with understanding the behavior relevant to a specific problem. The applied anthropologist is thus a generalist in social science and not a circumscribed specialist.

The anthropologist or any other social scientist working with business must keep in mind that the client wants his or her services to help solve problems and that these do not reflect disciplinary boundaries. It is the rare company that will support the pursuit of knowledge for its own sake. Knowledge must lead to action, or its pursuit cannot be justified. Thus, the social scientist finds that the business executive believes that basic research which produces only papers that may be contributions to knowledge should be left to the universities. As a consequence, the consulting anthropologist does not approach an assignment as does his or her academic counterpart with a research grant. Instead of planning a study to produce a publication which will enhance one's professional standing, it is necessary to plan a study designed to solve a practical problem quickly and to enhance one's reputation with satisfied clients.

Moreover, the applied anthropologist cannot expect to approach his or her assignment at a leisurely pace with time to review the literature in a scholarly fashion, develop elaborate theories or methods, and then have ample time for digesting the data and writing and rewriting a report. Time and budget do not allow such luxuries, but rather require restraint in deciding how much data and what data are needed in any study. A study of the structure and interpersonal relations within the management group in a corporation may require that the anthropologist personally interview the members of the group and observe them in action. A study of employee reactions to the company benefit plan may require only a questionnaire sent to their homes. However, since the data are usually limited and there is no time to return to check up on other information, it is important to design the questionnaires or conduct the interviews in such a way that respondents can express their ideas and feelings and not merely respond to the questions posed. It is important that new ideas not anticipated in the original conceptualization be allowed to appear in the data.

Since time is always limited, the consultant must be prepared to analyze the data and report promptly. Thus, for most of our consumer studies, we have a report ready for the client within two to six weeks of completion of the field interviewing. If a study requires 200 interviews with open-ended questions, this means that the researcher must read all of the material, examine the computer output on the quantitative data, draw conclusions, and prepare a report within a short period. The work is done under pressure with little time to write and rewrite a report. Unfortunately, there is no training method where the social scientist in training can work with real problems of the business world. As a consequence, the adjustment to the business work setting is often a difficult one and will continue so until we develop a system similar to that of medicine where the new graduate works as an intern alongside the experienced doctor in the real world of sick patients.

Working as a consultant to business also requires other adaptations on the part of the applied anthropologist. In dealing with the problems of any organization, it must be kept in mind that the organization's authority system is important to any changes. Each organization has its hierarchy and its key management group at the top. The belief of these key people about how to manage the efforts of those below them sets the tone of the organization. Much work has been done on authoritarian versus democratic management, or people-centered management, or other forms. Often the theories have been well learned by management people coming from business schools, but sometimes there is dissonance between expressed belief and actual behavior. Frequently, presidents and vice presidents talk about need for concern for employees, yet in their daily actions on the job, it is clear that they are basically autocratic, intent on imposing their ways upon subordinates. The consultant has to work with the realities of the situation, and, when change is needed, must find ways to influence the top level.

There is also the problem of people in all levels of authority who differ in their capacity to accept and utilize fresh ideas or approaches. This is especially difficult when individuals need to change behaviors and attitudes which they unconsciously feel have contributed to their success in the past. The ambitious man or woman who has achieved status and recognition often finds it hard to reexamine ways of dealing with people and especially subordinates. There is a tendency to see suggestions for other ways of dealing with people or solving problems as a threat which must be resisted.

Social scientists working with people problems in an organization must face these difficulties in making things change. If they are part of the organization, their ability to effect change is limited by their position. Usually they are brought in as part of the personnel organization, which is generally felt to be out of the mainstream of the organization's purpose. In a factory, production is the goal; in a department store, it is sales. Personnel is a staff function, there to serve the others, not to interfere. In such a position, the anthropologist must gain influence, though he lacks the power base to command it.

If the anthropologist is an outside consultant, he or she is usually brought in by someone in authority, often a vice-president or president. If good working relationships are developed at that level, access to others employees may be gained and thus the chance to aid and influence the organization. However, as an outsider, the anthropologist is dispensable, and, with changes in the business climate or changes in people at the top, his or her services may become unwanted. This is a common fate of many outside consultants. One reason is that there is no area in which the expertise of anthropologists and other social scientists gives them a monopoly. In our society, any executive, engineer or business major feels that he or she understands people and human motivation. As human beings, they (we) all tend to believe that they (we) understand other human beings, what makes them tick, and how they will react in given situations. These have been proven to be faulty assumptions, and especially faulty because we are a society undergoing rapid change in which experience is an inadequate teacher for helping us to cope with the changing situations of contemporary life.

In looking back over our experiences at Social Research, Inc., in applying social sciences to the practical problems of business, I feel that training as a social anthropologist provides a valuable basic orientation. The emphasis on social structure and on the interrelations of all activities and cultural artifacts into a social system provides the conceptual basis for examining the wide range of people problems with which business must deal. Within this conceptual system, the special knowledge and skills of the psychologist, the sociologist, the political scientist, and all the other disciplines can be brought together into effective tools for problem solving.

During the last decades, we have seen the steady introduction of knowledge from the social sciences into the training of executives. The business schools have given increasing emphasis to social sciences in their curriculae; companies sponsor seminars on understanding people, and management trainees are being recruited from psychology, sociology and other social sciences. We can expect to see more anthropologists finding careers within business as well as providing business with their research and consulting skills. It has been my purpose here to suggest some of the opportunities that exist and some of the perspectives that are needed if anthropologists are to fully develop and use their talents in the business and industrial field.

14

TAKING THE WITNESS STAND

Henry F. Dobyns

In complex societies, conflicts between groups or individuals are increasingly resolved through formal litigation procedures. Contemporary American society is especially litigious. The courts and quasi-legal bodies are playing a greatly expanded role in settling the claims of citizens who feel that they have been victims of injustice, malpractice, fraud, or other actions which impinge upon their civil rights. One result of this development has been a growing demand for expert witnesses who can testify for one side or the other on the basis of specialized professional knowledge.

Henry F. Dobyns describes this role as he and others have experienced it in native American claims cases. Although the role is episodic, it is extremely demanding in terms of the time, energy, and resources required to prepare for a case. There is little in the training of anthropologists to prepare them for such work, which typically entails the confrontation of anthropologists with each other on opposite sides of the issues involved. Other difficulties arise due to the expectations of clients and the important implications for future relationships with plaintiffs or

Henry F. Dobyns (Ph.D., Cornell) is scientific editor of the *Indian Tribal Series*. He has directed and carried out research in Peru, Ecuador, Bolivia, and Mexico in Latin America, and among the Northeastern Pai, Northern Piman, Apache, and Kaibab Paiute Indians, Spanish-Americans, and Anglo-Americans in the United States. Dr. Dobyns has taught anthropology at Cornell, the University of Kentucky, Prescott College, the University of Wisconsin, Parkside and the University of Florida. He has worked as a consultant to UNESCO, the Peace Corps, and the Organization of American States. He has testified twice as an expert witness before the United States Indian Claims Commission.

Acknowledgment. Numerous expert witnesses contributed to this analysis by evaluating earlier drafts and sharing their experiences. They included R. C. Euler, P. H. Ezell, C. H. Fairbanks, B. L. Fontana, W. R. Jacobs, T. F. King, N. O. Lurie, M. E. Opler, O. C. Stewart, H. H. Tanner and W. H. Unrau, plus attorney A. S. Cox.

defendants as a result of court testimony. In litigation of this type, the macroculture and the microculture come together in a unique manner, and the expert witness role offers unusual opportunities to affect the way in which problems are defined and solved in the interplay between them.

DAMAGE AWARDS RUNNING into millions of dollars have stemmed in part from anthropologists and historians testifying as experts before the United States Indian Claims Commission. Native Americans have been kept out of prison when state courts accepted expert anthropological testimony about the Native American Church. Testifying, therefore, meets Lantis' (1945:20; Lurie 1955:357) criterion of true applied social science: the practical application of research findings on behalf of a group of people. Because more social scientists are likely to become expert witnesses in the future, this essay undertakes some analysis of this role.

Numerous anthropologists and historians have already taken the stand as experts before various federal and state courts as well as the Indian Claims Commission. Their experiences provide useful guidance for future anthropological expert witnesses in these and other types of litigation.

That more social scientists will play the expert witness role is certain. Federal and state legislation now requires that environmental, social and cultural impacts of proposed governmental projects be assessed beforehand. Consequently, archeologists and other anthropologists are at present busy writing environmental impact statements, predicting how highways and other projects will affect existing resources. Litigation is already occurring over environmental impact issues. Such litigation will involve many professionals of various disciplines, who prepare the necessary statements and also serve as expert witnesses in court proceedings. In fact, one archeologist has already paved the way for future litigation by testifying in a case in which he himself was one of the plaintiffs.

As long as the nation pursues a policy that recognizes the value of cultural diversity, anthropologists and historians will be responsible, because of their specific expertise, for becoming involved in litigation generated by conflicts between culturally diverse groups. Anthropologists are also testifying as experts in cases involving native American treaty rights that have been violated by state game and fish managers or by corporate leaseholders. And in view of the increasing public awareness of these problems, tribes will need expert testimony as they litigate to compel faithful observance of treaties. One reason for analyzing the expert witness role is its relative periodicity. Foster (1969:49) considered all applied anthropology to occur as part-time activity by persons otherwise engaged during most of their careers. Taking the witness stand certainly is episodic. Testimony can become necessary over a period of many years. For example, I appeared as a witness for the Gila River Indian Community in a 1974 water right hearing seventeen years after testifying for the Hualapai Tribe in a 1957 land loss hearing. Social scientists appearing as expert witnesses seem to average two such assignments during their career. Only about 14 percent of those who have been expert witnesses spent five or more years on research leading to testimony, with 3 percent spending ten years or more.

Such periodicity of role performance means that an expert witness can train for the role to only a limited extent. One may gain some experience testiying before legislative committees or regulatory commissions. Whether these bodies allow cross-examination of witnesses or not, the expert who is testifying inevitably learns formal testimony procedures and at least some role constraints.[1] Nevertheless, most of the socialization for the expert witness role must perforce be anticipatory. Thus, this essay is designed to guide the future expert witness.

Recruitment

The nature of topics upon which social anthropologists can testify as experts tends to channel the process of expert recruitment. Omer C. Stewart's (1961a:18; 1970:4) frequent testimony as an expert on the Native American Church is an excellent example of this. His expertise stems from both participant observation in peyote ceremonies—good ethnography—and careful tracing of the diffusion of this denomination among tribesmen—good ethnohistory. In other words, an expert witness must in fact be expert on some aspect of the subject of litigation. For, "the good faith, scholarly conventionality, and academic correctness" of anyone offered as an expert is likely to be

---

[1] Archeologist Thomas F. King (Wilke, King, and Hammond 1975) found such less formal testimony before other public bodies helpful preparation for expert testimony in federal court.

challenged (Lurie 1957:68). This means that a nonacademic person with firsthand knowledge gained from several years of research with a particular group may be better qualified to testify about that group than would an ethnologist who has made only a brief survey of the population (Lurie 1955:358).

Because anthropologists and historians conduct research with people, the recruitment process at times incorporates a measure of ideological sorting. Historian Wilbur R. Jacobs and anthropologist Bea Medicine testified in 1974 in United States District Court in Nebraska concerning what Sioux chiefs meant when they signed the 1968 Treaty of Laramie with the United States. They appeared as expert witnesses for the defense in cases arising out of native American occupation of Wounded Knee, South Dakota, in 1973. Jacobs' (1950, 1954, 1972, 1974) published works establish him as expert on native American government relations, particularly Indian treaties. Yet, these same works also identify him as a revisionist historian who has used extensive interdisciplinary and comparative data to challenge Anglo-American elitist interpretations and stereotypes. That general scholarly status and his concern for the welfare of contemporary Indians "preselected" him, by creating defense attorney expectation that his expert opinions would fit into a defense theory of a particular case. Jacobs clarified his views to defense attorneys before testifying, pointing out that he would willingly testify on historical evidence and interpretations, but that he did not agree with many of the actions of native American defendants or some of the policies of the American Indian Movement (AIM). Jacobs has indicated that the prosecuting attorneys followed the same practice in obtaining sympathetic witnesses.

Medicine's expertise on Sioux oral tradition stems in part from her ascribed status as a Pine Ridge Sioux and in part from her achieved status as anthropologist. That unique combination also "preselected" her as a suitable defense witness.

During the past twenty-five years that the Indian Claims Commission has been in existence, such sorting has been clearly perceptible. Attorneys representing Indian plaintiffs have often recruited anthropologists and historians convinced of the merit of native American claims before research on specific cases began.[2] Attorneys

---

[2] One demographer has accused all anthropologists of pro-Indian bias (Petersen 1975). "Preselection" clearly occurred in Indian Claims Commission litigation (Lurie 1956:261).

employed by the U.S. Department of Justice to defend the government have been able to recruit experts from the same disciplines who opposed Indian recovery of damages.

Basic motivations of the latter individuals are understandably difficult to determine. Nonetheless, the moccasin telegraph (Witt 1968:71; Rachlin 1968:107) has compiled and and disseminated information culled from public pronouncements and private utterances. Those who listen to the moccasin telegraph hear that some experts opposed the Indian Claims Commission Act and its goal of recompensing Indian groups for unjust and unconscionable loss of resources. So they enthusiastically testified for the defendant. On the other hand, the moccasin telegraph also says that others took the witness stand for the defendant from professional motives, insuring that defendant's expert testimony was scientifically unbiased. Their premise was that testifying would serve the goals of both science and justice. Much less ideologically, some experts take the stand simply as an opportunity to earn money.

The specificity of anthropological and historical research significantly influences recruitment of experts. The research activity of the social scientist with any given group of people rather narrowly defines his or her expertise. In other words, the researcher's personal and professional relationships with the people whom he or she studies are often crucial to his or her recruitment. Thus, the chairman of the Papago Tribal Council initially recommended the author to attorneys representing his tribe before the Indian Claims Commission. Typically, recruitment rests partly upon one's professional stature. Toward the end of his long career, the late A. L. Kroeber tremendously impressed attorneys with cases before the Indian Claims Commission. In other words, recruitment also rests upon litigant and attorney perception of qualifications. Thus, Thayer Scudder testified in Hopi–Navajo litigation as an expert on forced relocation rather than as an expert on either ethnic group.

Expert–Expert Confrontation

Once an expert witness is recruited, he or she faces a set of role demands that are often quite outside previous professional experience. Anthropologists prefer to perceive themselves as working within a *gemeinschaft* discipline. They are, therefore, typically startled by the adversary proceedings of litigation, a *gesselschaft* situation. Both sides can and very often do retain experts to testify on the same issues. The Indian Claims Commission Act of 1946 authorized the Commission to establish a research division (Lurie 1955:360; 1957:59; 1970:5), but the attorneys appointed to it did not elect to do so. Commissioner John T. Vance (1969:335–336) proposed activating the research unit to expedite decisions, but his colleagues continued to rely on traditional adversary suits instead.

Adversary proceedings are actually scientifically positive, because they generate checks on the quality of each expert's research product. The direct hearing room confrontation has proved even more effective than has customary ''scrutiny'' of findings by scholarly colleagues with no personal practical responsibility. Certainly, such confrontation between social scientists testifying for opposing sides generates greater methodological sophistication in the interpretation of many kinds of evidence than anthropologists customarily employed prior to the appearances of many of them before the Indian Claims Commission.

The courtroom confrontation sometimes contains elements of the same kind of drama as that depicted by fictional television programs. The circumstances produce more than face-to-face confrontation between two social scientists. Adversary proceedings pit a team of attorneys, historians, or other experts who supply attorneys with questions to ask during cross-examination against each expert, a tactic that frequently is most effective in revealing ''inaccuracies and/or slipshod research methods,'' as one who knows phrased it.[3]

Cross-examination constitutes the core of adversary proceedings. In fact, the Indian Claims Commission has in recent years insisted that expert direct testimony be offered in written form. During cross-examination, attorneys put questions, but these are typically suggested by experts. Since the attorney usually lacks comparable acquaintance with the expert's scientific field, it is the expert who, in all likelihood, will recognize any inaccuracies, omissions or distortions in the report or testimony of another expert in the same field. Thus, an expert witness may provide indispensable material to the lawyer who is cross-examining an opposing expert witness. This

---

[3] Stewart (1961b) cites numerous instances of ''works listed in bibliography not cited in report''; reference to works not describing Southern Paiutes, the litigants; secondary works by popular writers; and unevaluated scholarly works.

phase of expert-witness/attorney cooperation can and has mercilessly exposed unscientific research. The expert suggesting questions to the cross-examining attorney is limited only by his own knowledge and skill in data storage and retrieval under time constraints. Inevitably, the very merciless quality of cross-examination makes it unpalatable to many potential expert witnesses.

One dynamic of the involvement of anthropologists as expert witnesses before the Indian Claims Commission has been the reluctance of commission members to accept at face value the testimony of native Americans belonging to plaintiff groups. The commissioners preferred to have Indian testimony evaluated by experts accustomed to analyzing such statements before admitting it as legal evidence (Lurie 1955:359; 1957:59–60). Consequently, the Commission even considered archeological evidence of aboriginal land use and occupancy (Dobyns 1974).

Since the passage of the National Environmental Protection Act, prehistoric remains have also become a resource at issue in litigation. Because of the passage of so many years since the United States seizure of Indian resources, and because of memory loss and destruction of physical evidence, the quality of available data often parallels that in industrial product liability litigation. The process, therefore, occasionally becomes "a sophisticated guessing game" because of the imperfect nature of evidence (Piehler *et al* 1974:1092). Nevertheless, the adversary procedure and standards of proof observed by courts tend to demand from social scientists an unusual quality of data collection and its analysis. The prospect of involvement in litigation as the pawn of a federal agency and its attorneys has been known to frighten an archeologist away from a research contract he would happily sign under other, more propitious circumstances.

The role strain generated in many anthropologists who testified before the Indian Claims Commission led some of them to conclude that adversary proceedings are "patently unpleasant to most of the experts" (Manners 1974:18).

Attorney/Expert Relations

Actually, adversary proceedings are not in and of themselves necessarily unpleasant for an expert witness. Some social scientists consistently enjoy serving in that role. Personality differences affect one's emotional response to stress during a hearing. Verbal and well-prepared experts welcome the challenge of turning cross-examination into an opportunity for creative testimony.

Intensity of commitment to an abstract goal of scientific truth also affects one's witness-stand reactions. Those with a strong commitment to such truth can exult in cross-examination which exposes inadequate preparation or conceptualization on the part of presumed experts. The social scientist considering this applied role should, in a word, keep in mind the Harry Truman dictum: Those who can't stand the heat should stay out of this particular kitchen.

Yet personality and goals of the expert provide only partial keys to successful performance of the witness role. Technical and legal researchers have analyzed the conduct of litigation over corporate liability for manufactured product malfunction (Piehler et al. 1974:1091). They have concluded that attorney/expert relations really determine whether an expert carries out his testimonial role with enjoyment or degradation. This is also true of social scientists as expert witnesses.

A complicating factor is that people as well as artifacts provide social scientists with data. The influence of counsel upon clients such as Indian tribal council members compounds the role of a social scientist expert witness, compared to that of a technician dealing only with artifacts. Manufactured goods pose problems such as the preservation of crucial physical evidence until it can be studied. Attorney influence over clients upon whom the social scientist depends for data adds complications for the latter far beyond those of destruction of physical evidence or natural memory loss in any human group. What some anthropologists find unpleasant in adversary proceedings stems from attorney/client/expert relationships which depend on how lawyers define their own roles, and how they influence their clients.

Informant Bias

This component of role strain for the expert witness was quickly and explicitly recognized by some anthropologists employed to testify before the Indian Claims Commission. Desirous of continuing research among specific peoples, they anticipated being unable to convince informants that the latter should provide them with future data (Lurie 1956:262–263). Manners (1974:132) relates his role strain when Havasupai individuals did not wish him to interview them.

Manners (1974:140–143) also inveighed against "New Yorkerish" behavior of attorneys because a Paiute informant handed him the business card of an attorney whom the Paiute reported had told him not to talk to anyone without consulting said lawyer first.

Because litigation is an adversary proceeding, the expert witness role often throws this specific kind of role strain upon the anthropologist. Cases docketed by the Indian Claims Commission or involving treaty provisions frequently require experts for both an Indian plaintiff and a government defendant to interview native Americans. Generally the latter show a firm grasp of the necessity for adversary proceedings, and they cooperate with social scientists retained by the governmental agency as well as those retained by their own counsel. Nonetheless, at least some anthropologists retained by the Department of Justice have felt impelled to present to potential informants a somewhat stronger statement of benefits to be gained from cooperating with the government's expert than was really true. Some experts whose personal value structure led them to object to the entire concept of awarding damages to surviving Indians for historic unfair and unconscionable dealings with their ancestors by representatives of the United States government, became especially odious to Indians for their self-serving claims of this nature.

This pattern of conduct, plus the involvement of such social scientists in litigation upon which millions of dollars depend, accounts in part for Indian skepticism about anthropologists expressed in recent years. Vine Deloria Jr. (1969) has eloquently phrased the view that anthropologists are powerful and exploit Indians. Admittedly, some anthropologists have wielded, albeit indirectly, considerable power as expert witnesses. Some of them have even exploited that temporary role in order to facilitate their own data collection.

Being experienced and wise in the ways of Anglo-Americans, most Indians do not overgeneralize in the Deloria style. Nonetheless, many of them recognize the inconsistency of the social scientist's role in eliciting statements in order to testify as an expert on behalf of the adversary of their own group. Consequently, such Indians tend to identify social scientists who testify as experts for plaintiffs before the Indian Claims Commission or courts as ethical. They also tend to stereotype those testifying as experts for defendants in litigation initiated by Indians, after obtaining Indian cooperation in collecting data, as unethical.

Whether or not Indians formally cooperate with the social scientist they consider unethical, their perception of such behavior cannot help but affect their enthusiasm in collaborating with such a person. This throws significant role strain on the social scientist. Litigation which necessitates taking a firm stand appears to be on the increase. Historian William E. Unrau already has testified in 1974 in a U.S. District Court as an expert on Kaw history, in litigation over which faction constituted the legal government of the group. Ethnohistorians, specializing as have Jacobs, Unrau, and Medicine, may well find themselves called upon to play the expert witness role in similar litigation. Under such circumstances, whenever both sides introduce expert testimony, those taking the stand on either side must anticipate lessened access to informants with vested interests on the opposite side. That implies diminished expertise both as witness and as researcher. Such applied social science will, in other words, redefine the research role.

If attorneys influence their clients' behavior toward expert witnesses who must elicit statements from them, those attorneys even more directly structure expert witness roles. Lurie (1956:265–266) hinted at role differences between attorneys when she noted that the lawyer who propounds the questions asked of an expert witness governs the "selectivity of data." I maintain that courtroom confrontations do not strike experts as unpleasant because these are adversary proceedings. Instead, rewarding or punishing confrontations are defined long before an actual hearing by attorney/expert relations. I perceive attorneys who utilize expert witnesses as falling into at least two distinct types.[4]

Litigation Directors and Team-Leaders

One type of attorney has been clearly identified in other litigation. Lawyers representing either plaintiff or defendant in product liability litigation typically view themselves as the main "directors of the litigation" (Piehler et al. 1974:1091). As a result, the attorney tends to relegate an expert to a "service position." In other words, the attorney may not even explore the subject of the litigation with an expert,

[4] The following discussion assumes attorneys to be technically competent. Green (1975:1, 4) reports increasing concern among judges whether many attorneys admitted to the bar are in fact competent.

and clearly develops his or her own theory of the case. This kind of lawyer expects the expert to fill in evidentiary gaps in the attorney's theory. It is my belief that many attorneys in Indian Claims Commission hearings or in similar cases in federal courts closely resemble those in product liability litigation.

Possessing the power to impose their own definition of the role-set (Merton 1957:372), such attorneys do so without being aware of counterproductive consequences. These attorneys typically do not realize how ill-trained they are in gathering and analyzing oral and written evidence pertinent to issues litigated by special groups such as Indians. In one extreme instance, an attorney neglected to inform an expert what another expert testifying for the same client was preparing until the day the hearing began. Consequently, the error-filled report of the second witness "nearly threw me for a total loss" reports the witness who was taken by surprise.

The litigation-director attorney rarely educates an expert witness as to the legal criteria involved in a case before channeling the expert witness into a subordinate role. The witness therefore, may take the stand unaware of how the lawyer might employ legal discovery procedures to facilitate arriving at the truth. The expert may not know how the attorney could at least try to redefine by motions the court-established parameters of the litigation.

A minority of attorneys recognize some of the pitfalls involved in playing a litigation director role, and play more of a team-leader role. In Mertonian (1957:374–376) terms, these lawyers strive to make their activities visible to the expert instead of insulating themselves from observation. Such an attorney spends much time deliberately consulting experts in order to find out what theories the experts can contribute to a case under active litigation. Lurie (1957:69; 1970:6–7) noted that some anthropologists persuaded attorneys to amend the very petitions upon which cases were based. Stewart and Morris E. Opler report, in personal communications, uniform success in persuading attorneys to alter dates-of-taking, exclusive use-and-occupancy areas, etc.

During hearings, team-leader attorneys frame questions that enable an expert to present his or her opinion clearly and fully during direct testimony. This tactic helps the experts avoid the strain of having to try to cram their expertise and data into a framework artificially restricted by a lawyer's theory of a case developed without adequate input from the expert. Such a witness finds an astute attorney of this type most rewarding to work with.

Because a hearing is an adversary proceeding, opposing counsel's function is to impute testimony by witnesses for the other side, if he can possibly do so. The attorney who has experts testify for a client also relies upon these experts to suggest cross-examination questions that will expose any serious defect in opposing expert testimony. Two specific traits of litigation director style attorneys compound the role strain inevitably induced in social scientists by the basic adversary proceeding to which they are subjected.

The litigation director forces experts to try to fit their opinion and information into an attorney-framed case theory which has been formulated without adequate consultation. This often exposes the expert to brutal cross-examination by opposing counsel which is "personally degrading" as well as extremely frustrating. The litigation director also displays the role attribute of seeking an expert opinion stated with the highest possible degree of certainty (Piehler et al. 1974:1092). The litigation director who succeeds too well in persuading an expert to disregard those limitations inherent in his or her formulation of an opinion exposes that expert to the embarrassment of cross-examination which backs him or her steadily away from "absolutism."

The team-leader attorney, in contrast, elicits from an expert only direct testimony which can be absolutely defended on cross-examination. The team-leader lawyer does so, first of all, by framing a case-theory that adequately takes into account the expert's theory and data. Next, the team-leader recognizes, from prior disposition or consultation with the expert, the inherent limitations in the expert's opinion. The lawyer then presses the expert for an expression of certitude commensurate with the data and no more. This enables the expert to answer cross-examination without having to maintain inflated claims—other than those of his own making. Indeed, the team-leader attorney lays a basis for the expert to strengthen his or her opinion during cross-examination.

Research Time

One serious constraint sometimes built into the expert witness role is preparation time too brief to allow for adequate research into the litigated issues. For example, even I have suffered from severe role strain generated by having less time to investigate a question than I thought necessary. I have also watched the agony of a witness being cross-examined upon testimony that revealed totally inadequate preparation time. Again, this aspect of the expert witness's role frequently appears in product liability litigation, when a technical expert enters a case too late to allow adequate investigation (Piehler et al. 1974:1091).

A team-leader style attorney endeavors to avoid placing an expert witness under this handicap. Yet, even the best intentioned lawyer may not understand the complexity of the research operations required in a given case. Nor will the attorney always be able to predict correctly when a given case may come to trial. For the social scientist working part-time as an expert witness while teaching at an academic institution or otherwise engaged, full preparation for testimony may prove difficult.

A social scientist's problem in preparing for testimony often stems from inadequate compensation rather than from a true lack of time. The social scientist may have two to four years to prepare for a specific hearing, yet he or she may not be able to do so adequately because he or she cannot devote full time to the project. Lacking adequate case-preparation funds, or not realizing the inordinate amount of time required for thorough research, or being downright unethical (Shipek 1974:2), the party to the litigation pays the expert too little, with the result that the expert witness lacks funds to pay for time taken from his other duties. Academicians employed by public institutions which expect them to render public or community service, more than occasionally find themselves in the time/money bind when conducting such research unless they receive released time from other duties.

Social scientists and technologists suffer from two handicapping expert witness role stereotypes among attorneys when compensation is settled. One role perception derives from physicians and similar experts whose "research" can be carried out in a few hours or days, instead of months or even years. Attorneys in large legal firms which devoted years to preparing cases before the Indian Claims Commission have earned fees running into hundreds of thousands of dollars. Yet, they regard social scientists as "instant" experts, not recognizing that truly competent testimony also requires great expenditures. A second role perception of social scientists views them as partisans willing to donate their expertise to a cause. "Patsys" seems a more accurate label.

Conclusions

A few morals drawn from this consideration of attorney relations vis-à-vis experts and clients may aid future social scientist expert witnesses. First, the social scientist needs sufficient sophistication in terms of hearing procedure to know that the burden of proof falls upon a plaintiff. A defendant has only to raise doubts and pose questions, and often strives to confuse and obscure issues (Lurie 1956:271). Within that framework, an expert must anticipate greater role strain working for a litigation director type attorney than cooperating with a team-leader style lawyer. In other words, expert and attorney present the most effective case when both recognize the utility of a high degree of interaction between attorneys and experts at all stages of the litigation (Piehler et al. 1974:1090).

Social scientists could well emulate land assessors, medical doctors, mathematicians, and technologists who testify in a professional capacity for plaintiff in one case to become defendant's expert in another (Lurie 1956:267). Those whose pursuit of truth is firmly embedded in their social personalities can enjoy the confrontations of experts during litigation. It can expose shortcomings of method, failures to consider all of the accumulated data, inaccuracies of execution, and faults of all kinds. Those whose ideological commitment to scientific truth is less than their commitment to a litigant can suffer personal degradation and severe role strain and feel that they have aged a decade during a single hearing. So can those whose methods or procedures are at fault—and perhaps even those who simply lacked sufficient time and money to prepare to testify.

Part III

ANTHROPOLOGY AND PUBLIC POLICY

The dialogue between anthropological theory and application, and the roles and institutional settings in which applied anthropologists work, bring them into direct contact with major issues in the field of public policy. Yet, even applied anthropologists have seldom thought of themselves as policy scientists, and the influence of anthropologists on public policy has been extremely limited. There are three reasons for this situation: the nature of policy formulation and implementation as a continually changing political process with which anthropologists have little familiarity; the fact that mainstream anthropology has largely ignored contemporary social problems; and the limited use of empirical data of any type in many policy decisions.

The essays in Part III explore some of the key issues which confront America today and the potential contribution of anthropology to them. Viewed as a whole, they constitute a preliminary statement about potential new frontiers of engagement between anthropologists and our society. More than this, they explain the complexities entailed if a meaningful dialogue between anthropologists and policy makers is to emerge.

The introductory essay by Kimball sets forth the essential conditions for the development of anthropology as a policy science. Following this, Hicks and Handler review the historical interplay between anthropology and public policy as it has affected native Americans, immigrants, and black Americans in our society. Next, Eddy discusses the gap between anthropological studies and current educational policies and practices in American public schooling. Partridge's essay reveals a similar gap in the field of drug abuse but shows that in this field other types of empirical data are ignored as well. Makielski examines the work of anthropologists in the area of population studies, indicates the limitations of past work in terms of

American society, and the possibilities for anthropologists to utilize their talents in realizing better solutions for population problems in the United States. Finally, Heighton and Heighton examine the field of social planning and the ways in which anthropological theory and methods can be used in applied policy situations.

15

ANTHROPOLOGY AS A POLICY SCIENCE

Solon T. Kimball

The development of anthropology as a policy science will not be easy. It will require a greatly expanded research emphasis on contemporary complex societies and a vigorous development of applied anthropology so that data may be provided for the better understanding of the consequences of strategies used to achieve programmatic goals and to test theories of change. Research methodologies which produce only ethnographic description must yield to methodologies rooted in the natural sciences which allow a systemic analysis of communities, organizations, and processes within them.

Solon T. Kimball develops the above themes and describes the difference between policy recommendations based on empirical analysis and those based solely on one's own moral judgments. Pronouncements about policy issues do not necessarily constitute policy analysis. Unless such pronouncements are based on scientific methods of investigation, the policy statements of anthropologists are similar to those of any other citizen with an opinion.

THE USE OF social science as an instrument of public policy and programs is not new. Spokesmen from political science and eco-

Solon T. Kimball (Ph.D., Harvard) is graduate research professor of anthropology at the University of Florida. He has contributed widely to the fields of educational anthropology, theory and method, and applied anthropology. His fieldwork has been in rural and urban Ireland and in United States communities. Dr. Kimball has been a fellow of the Social Science Research Council and a Guggenheim Fellow. He has served as consultant to the United States Departments of Agriculture and Interior, UNESCO, the Brazilian Center for Educational Research, the Peru Educational Development Project, and the Brazilian Fulbright Binational Commission. He is a past president of the American Ethnological Society and the Society for Applied Anthropology.

nomics, in particular, and to a lesser extent from sociology and psychology, have become involved during recent years in the discussion about the direction of our national life. The listing of such notables as Charles Beard, Charles Merriam, Adolph Berle, Jr., Harold Lasswell, Karl Menninger, John Galbraith, Milton Friedman, and Daniel Patrick Moynihan reminds us of their connection with public issues. That intervention by scholars is part of our Western heritage is attested to by such other illustrious names as Montesquieu, Auguste Comte, Jeremy Bentham, and John Stuart Mill. The efforts of these and others to influence the course of events is testimony to the application of systematic thought for public purposes.

The conspicuous absence of anthropologists from comparable involvement merits examination. The absence of applicable research interests may be judged partly responsible. Whereas major segments of political science and economics are directly linked with contemporary problems, the subject-matter interests of most anthropologists, in contrast, are with remote peoples or in the past. The trash heaps of ancient civilizations, the bones of ancestral primates, or the social-climbing feasts of isolated tribes may conceivably yield some cosmic truths, but they contribute little to explaining the price of beans. In truth, the expectation that such research findings might have some practical value has hardly been a consideration. Even so, some limited use has been made of anthropological findings during pre-World War II days in Dutch and British colonial rule. A few American anthropologists became involved with farm programs and Indian affairs during the New Deal and later in wartime activities and the administration of Trust Territories in the Pacific after World War II. In these and other instances, the anthropological contribution was nearly always of a technical sort.

Even so, a participation which only touched a small portion of the non-Western world and involved a bare handful of anthropologists aroused misgivings in the breasts of most anthropologists. Their aversion to engage actively in the world around them can be linked to deeply embedded views about the objectives of their discipline. Even during World War II, two spokesmen for the ivory tower tradition, Evans-Pritchard (1946:92–98) and Sol Tax (1945:21–23) argued cogently to retain the purity of scientific spirit and to reject involvement in practical problems.

A commitment to the search for "truth" as the overriding objective of anthropology has had certain consequences. First, there has been a willingness to accept the accumulation of knowledge as an intrinsic end in itself. Whenever some Babbitt queried the usefulness of a supposedly arcane fact, the response was likely to be a rejection of both the question and the Philistine world of the questioner. Second, most anthropologists confined their search for "truth" to non-literate and peasant peoples and rejected outright the legitimacy of contemporary society as a field of study. This narrow focus provided no substantive base from which to comment on current issues, although that did not always deter such action. Third, the traditional scientific procedure of lengthy and often arduous field studies seemed to exacerbate in anthropologists the monastic tendency found among many scientists whose work is exclusively undertaken within the halls of academe. Lastly, it is not often that anthropologists have been invited to become involved in practical affairs. Those who are the managers of our society have habitually turned to soothsayers who carry the labels of economist, political scientist, sociologist, or psychologist.

Within anthropology, however, there are a few who have set a course counter to the traditional current. They have conducted research in contemporary society and have taken the lead in developing an applied science. The history of their activities and the specifics of their point-of-view and accomplishments are described in preceding essays. My purpose here is to explore the policy science potentials of anthropology—a topic which will be more fully elaborated in the essays to follow.

Anthropology and Public Policy

The growing maturity of social sciences in recent years has increased their value in the formulation and implementation of public policy. For example, the Roosevelt New Deal was the first national administration to extensively incorporate academics into the circle of policy makers and program planners. Receptivity to this professional wisdom has fluctuated under subsequent administrations, but has never been extinguished. The real issue, however, is not the source of policy, be it professors, politicians, or businessmen, but its conceptual origin. Harold Lasswell, the most consistent advocate of a social science contribution to policy makes the distinction between decisions based on theological, metaphysical, or other explanatory grounds and those derived from scientific evidence. He states that "the policy sciences study the process of deciding or choosing and evaluate the relevance of available knowledge for the solution of particular problems" (Lasswell 1968:181).

Any scientific discipline whose findings are directly applicable to the clarification of issues which determine a course of action may be deemed to be a policy science. This definition excludes physics, chemistry, and biology. Although the research findings on nuclear fission, insecticides, or the genetic code may have incredible implications for the future welfare, even survival, of mankind, these scientific disciplines cannot be counted as among the policy sciences. This does not prevent the practitioners of these sciences from becoming alarmed about the consequences of their discoveries and urging the adoption of policies that would control their uses, as indeed they have. Their statements, however, are based upon moral considerations rather than those of their objective findings, and this is the crucial factor which makes the difference.

The capability of the social sciences to make policy statements does not differ too markedly from the physical sciences with one important exception. Within anthropology, for example, most research is stimulated by academically posed questions. The result is all too often a flat, descriptive account topically organized around standard categories. If those who conduct such research were pressed to justify their activities, they would probably do so on the grounds that they add to the store of human knowledge and represent the scientific search for truth. Many would either deny or disavow any intent to solve practical problems since such a posture might contaminate their scientific neutrality.

Some anthropological research, however, lends itself to policy formulation. To mark the distinction between that which does and that which does not is more than a matter of either intent or use. More explicitly, the difference is a function of the theoretical perspective which guides the collection of data and their analysis. An ethnographic inventory of customs and groups is not enough. The researcher must have made observations of individuals engaged in events in the variety of situations characteristic of that group. From these data can be derived the detail of the systemic arrangements by which a specific group meets its problems. It is this type of knowledge which contains the answers for those who would seek to formulate policy.

Substantive knowledge derived from appropriate procedures for gathering data, theory based on natural systems analysis, and a concern for understanding the processes of change are all necessary ingredients of policy science. Practitioners in many professional fields are building programs based on implicit or explicit policy goals which run into difficulties because one or more of these aspects are inadequately incorporated. The deficiency is usually in the failure to see the problems in systemic terms or in understanding the processes of change. These two aspects are linked. For example, attempts by nutritionists to modify food habits have often foundered on inadequate data and theory. They do not reckon with the strong linkage between values, social context, and food patterning. The vitamin-packed menus they recommend may be esthetically, socially, and religiously objectionable. There has been a failure to identify the variables and to see their interconnections. This is in addition to the absence of the culture specifics on food behavior. Furthermore, innovative style must conform to cultural practice. The Madison Avenue technique that reaches the flotsam of the city streets may produce only bewilderment in the back country. Modifications of superficial practices should be left to the hucksters anyway since the important thing to know is whether or not it is possible to wring from the data powerful explanatory concepts such as Darwin's natural selection. Such principles provide the ultimate understandings of a natural universe.

But before anthropologists become too deeply enmeshed in the arena of policy science, it is essential that they make explicit to themselves any ideological commitment or operating assumptions they may hold. This problem is quite separate from the methodological one of data bias induced by the presence of the fieldworker in the social context being examined. Nor is it a question of the capability to attain an absolute neutrality or objectivity. It is primarily a problem of the basic premises of the discipline of anthropology, especially as they may be shaped by inherent cultural perspectives.

In recent years, discussion about scientific objectivity has led to a recognition that attainment of such purity is limited by the cultural tools of thought and language. This conclusion has been as salutary for science as the acceptance of organic evolution was for Western thought. Within these limitations then, and they are modest enough, there is nothing in the methodological stance of anthropology which should inhibit statements of the kind which specify that "under these conditions we may expect these consequences." Such an accomplishment is the *sine qua non* of an applied science.

Unfortunately, such a capability does not fully deliver us from the confusion of the intellectual forest. There are some premises of anthropology, derivative of scientific findings which, when combined with a humanistic perspective, inevitably limit some of the courses of action. Although these limitations do not subsume allegiance to any specific religious, political, social, cultural, or technological system, they do recognize that some conditions limit, if not prevent, the achievement of the human potential. No anthropologist could ethically subscribe to any policy which led to such a result.

It may be useful to restate the principles which govern here. The genetic programming of individual and species in the context of surrounding conditions includes the potential and sets the limits of the life-cycle of individual or group. Every known society carries a culture which brings its young into the full humanity of symbol-using social adults. Although the style and complexity of cultural details vary widely from society to society, there is no society which lacks the essential ingredients of cosmic explanations, stabilized social groupings, and technological devices. But not all societies extend in equal measure full access to the humanizing process. The deficiencies are a consequence either of traditional social arrangements (such as slavery) or the inadequacy of knowledge or resources. As example, endemic starvation or disease that misshapes the minds and bodies of its victims, or social practices that limit the capabilities or spirit of its members, may be judged as conditions harmful to the achievement of the human potential.

If we assign to this potential the stature of a natural right, then we cannot design or approve any course which inhibits its realization. As a basic humanistic principle, it becomes embedded in the perspective of anthropology. Such a commitment, however, does not link anthropology to any particular form of political organization, religious expression, or technological system. Only the naïve believe that a problem-free utopia is either achievable or desirable.

Perspectives within Anthropology

An uncritical acceptance of anthropological data as suitable for policy formulation would be unwise. Certain anthropological perspectives automatically orient research focus and findings because of the premises which they include. In order to identify implicit biases, it is necessary to identify the assumptions which influence the ordering and interpretation of data. For example, anthropologists whose activities are shaped by an ideological bias based on race, religion, or some form of political utopianism have already made commitments which may or may not have anything to do with the facts. As advocates, they exploit data to prove their position, rather than to acquire enlightenment. A number of avowed activists expressing political, racial, or sexist causes have surfaced during the past decade. However meritorious their intentions, their commitment brings into question their judiciousness in matters of policy science.

Presumably, mainstream anthropology should be free of such biases. However, close examination often reveals a shaping of the data due to both inadvertent and unconscious factors. For example, it is fully recognized that much of the detail of ''female'' culture is not available to the male ethnographer. In addition, many areas of behavior, such as child training, were once almost uniformly ignored until a belated awareness of their significance appeared. The recognition and gradual correction of deficiencies of this type are part of the growth of any science. Of greater concern, however, is the influence which a deeply held intellectual commitment will have on the direction of inquiry and uses of data. The effect of such a linkage is clearly illustrated in the career of Franz Boas who comingled the idealism of socialist democracy with late nineteenth-century scientific absolutism.

Boas took strong and often outrageous stands on public issues. Furthermore, he encouraged research in areas that were relevant to these issues, such as the condition of minorities. Notwithstanding his deep concern for achieving justice for the individual in contemporary society, he never became an applied anthropologist as we understand that term today. This step was neither necessary nor possible since he had already synthesized his science and his ideology. Thus his scientific findings confirmed his moral perspective about humans and humanity. These aspects of Boas' career are so illuminating of both the relatively unfavorable intellectual climate for applied anthropology under such conditions and the problem of public policy based on data rather than on personal views that some further examination of the details is merited.

There is no necessary connection between an American political party and anthropology. The late Fay Cooper-Cole, distinguished chairman of the department at the University of Chicago, was a stalwart Republican. Yet no one could ever say that he mixed his political views and his anthropology. But when an individual is commited to a political ideology, as was Boas, it may be difficult to disentangle the extent to which the scientific posture is influenced by political morality and *vice versa*. Some of his students see them as entwined.

Ruth Bunzel, in her introduction to the reissue of Boas' *Anthropology and Modern Life,* reports that:

Boas was educated in the tradition of liberal romanticism that produced Carl Schurz and the philosophical anarchists of the nineteenth century. He was the essential protestant; he valued autonomy above all things and respected the unique potentialities of each individual. He believed that man was a rational animal and could, with persistent effort, emancipate himself from superstition and irrationality and lead a sane and reasonable life in a good society . . . (1962:6)

William S. Willis, Jr. added to the picture when he wrote: "Boas' political commitments can be traced to his German Jewish background and his family's response to the Revolution of 1848. Life in the United States intensified Boas' commitments, making them more explicit as he moved into the Socialist Party and finally toward the communist movement" (1975:309–310). Alexander Lesser also confirmed this activism when he wrote:

. . . and Boas spoke out boldly throughout his life against racism and race prejudice, against narrow nationalism and war, and for an internationalism based on the common interests of humanity. Boas believed that truth, widely shared through publications and education, can serve to liberate the mind from traditional confusion, error and prejudice (1968:107).

For Boas, the subject areas and concepts of anthropology furnished the source of the ammunition for his battle on behalf of liberal ideas. Willis, (1975:309) who suggested "that the clash between politics and professionalism is the main key to Boas as a person and as a scientist,'' calls attention to the remarkable congruency between Boas' liberal ideas and anthropological interests. For example, Boas was committed to the concept of the psychic unity of mankind, a view which contradicts the assertions of the racists. His focus on linguistics and folklore was also connected to his political views. The former ''revealed the complexity of all languages and the existence of identical processes of abstraction.'' The latter ''as tradition provided an alternative to racist explanations for many real and alleged deficiencies of contemporary colored peoples'' (Willis 1975:311).

Other dimensions of Boasian thought and political activity also connect with these aspects. The growth of culture through diffusion, for example, confirms that all people contribute to the growth of culture. Hence the attention given to historical reconstruction. Further substantiation in support of his views was provided by the conclusions he reached about mental processes. He saw cultures as the ''beneficial environments in which human thought and feeling are structured and operate'' (Lesser 1968:102).

Boas' views of the individual were summarized in *The Mind of Primitive Man* (1911). He believed that behavior is an expression of habits, not instincts. The human environment, not the biological inheritance, explains variation in behavior, hence culture, not race, is paramount. For Boas, ethnology became the study of the mental life of man and dealt with characteristic forms of thought (Willis 1975:310). An infusion of moral purpose looms large in his concern with folklore, language, and behavior, and the prevailing prejudice and superstition which rationality will dissipate through the spread of truth which liberates the mind (and implicitly changes behavior) from ''traditional confusion, error and prejudice'' (Lesser 1968:107). This intricate intermingling of a political-moral philosophy with a congruent scientific approach, helps to explain the quick defense by Boasians to criticism of him or to competing approaches such as that of functional social anthropology. The challenge was more than just a threat to the adequacy of a scientific approach; it was an assault upon an implicit but deeply entrenched utopian view of the universe.

It seems unnecessary and perhaps unproductive to attempt to determine whether Boas' public pronouncements should be counted as primarily reflecting his political views or his anthropological findings. They did both. More serious is the question of the extent to which his political views encased his anthropological ones. For example, he suffered no reluctance in making sweeping generalizations about cultural variability, human growth, and learning when he was attacking racial or other kinds of ethnocentric prejudice, yet he consistently cautioned against attempting to prematurely establish scientific laws. His crusade against prejudice (a mind-set), echoes openly in his emphasis on the mentalistic aspects of behavior to the near exclusion of the social. Boas found support within anthropological studies for his view of the direction which mankind should go. He was not concerned with nor did he leave as a legacy the use of anthropology as a policy science.

There is no intended condemnation in this examination of an avowedly great man. But there is need to make blade-edge sharp the distinction between advocacy and data based policy. Speaking out on public issues does not a policy scientist make.

Further Considerations

The essential conditions for the development of a policy science within anthropology have now been established. Briefly restated, the primary requirements are:

1. That natural systems analysis, rather than the prevalent flat ethnographic description, be utilized in describing and interpreting communities, organizations, and processes.

2. That research on contemporary societies be greatly expanded.

3. That a vigorous development of applied or non-academic anthropology continue in order to provide empirical data about the consequences of strategies in achieving program goals and to test theories of change.

4. That caution be exercised to prevent the ideological contamination of anthropological evidence and to recognize that pronouncements on public issues do not constitute public policy analysis.

Further discussion of the characteristics of a policy statement are still necessary, however. In the early phase of developing anthropology as a policy science, we cannot be too cautious in our attempts to define the problem. For example, the condemnation or approval of some situation or condition may carry policy implications but is not in itself a policy position. A resolution deploring hunger, disease, crime, or the unequal status of some sex or race cannot be considered as policy. It should be viewed as the public affirmation of a *position*.

From this perspective, a position paper should be viewed as the formal statement of belief or program emanating from some ethical, political, or economic consideration. In a strict sense, these are policy statements only if they are based on evidence drawn from systems analysis. I shall sharpen this point in a moment.

We must also be wary of slogans. These ringing phrases are bait for the innocent and may appear to be either truths or basic policy but are in reality verbal traps. Such ringing phrases as "educate the whole child," "families that pray together stay together," or "make the world safe for democracy" have all the appeal of a siren's call but eventually turn out to be only temporary rallying cries. However, slogans may be connected with programs and policies as is true of those cited above.

Indication of specific areas where anthropological data are of significance will perhaps assist in further clarification. For example, local authorities are sometimes faced with the necessity of responding to changed conditions in their communities. Important areas often include the social services, education, health, and welfare; land use; traffic management; public safety; and recreation. Programs which emerge from consideration of these problems may be viewed as reflecting the diverse interests of a community. The national government faces many of the same problems on a much larger scale, but there are also some which are distinctively national such as policies about food, resource use, population, technological developments, defense, and international relations.

Anthropologists have seldom been invited nor have they shown much interest in participating in the activities which determine policies at either local or national levels. Where participation has occurred, their contribution has largely been as applied technicians. They report cultural practices of social groups that are expected to influence reception of a program. I maintain that the anthropological contribution can be much broader than heretofore accepted. Its contextual emphasis adds meaning to data beyond that supplied by other disciplines. Furthermore, from applied anthropology we learn about the procedures through which policy and program are formulated.

Even a brief examination of some specific topic such as food reveals both the complexity of the problem and the powerful contribution of anthropology. We can also learn how remote, perhaps even harmful, are such slogans as "Feed the World's Hungry." I select food as my example both because of its importance and because it has been an area of concern to me (Kimball 1974a).

The economic policy of the Department of Agriculture of the United States Government has for some years been derived from the theory that the "natural" economic laws of the marketplace determine type, quantity, and price of agricultural product. The logic argues that if the price of a commodity is high due to demand, the causative limited supply will encourage greater production since farmers are motivated by the principle of self-interest to make money. The resulting increased production brings a decline in prices. Thus, the self-interest of the producer serves the self-interest of the consumer. The dynamics of the marketplace, to which many agricultural economists subscribe, assumes a universal motive of self-interest which, combined with a postulated law of supply and demand, regulates price and production and results in profit or loss. These concepts provide the perspective which has shaped the recent policy and program of the American government toward food production. Would the justifying concepts have been changed if the policy had been one of using food for world domination? Or let us suppose that policy was based on principles of reciprocity and status as exemplified in distribution of the meat of newly killed animals among the Bushmen; the exchange of ceremonial bracelets and necklaces in the Kula ring of the Trobriand Islands, or the giveaway Potlach feasts of the Kwakiutl. It is obvious that principles other than those of the marketplace govern the exchange of goods in these situations. Furthermore, these illustrations clearly demonstrate the connection between perspective and policy.

The important principle to be remembered is that basic conceptualization guides the selection, organization, and analysis of data, and shapes policy and programs. The simple conceptualizations of traditional ethnographic descriptions provide inventories of cultural items but are inadequate for policy purposes. Instead, it is the systemic approach of the natural history method that proves productive. For example, if we focus on the behavior surrounding food, we search out the specifics and connections among the variables of macro-system including environment, technology, organization, customs, beliefs, and population. From the analysis emerges three contrasting food-chains or cycles of food production and consumption associated with foraging, agrarian, and corporate cultures. Food data, thus conceptualized, provides the basis for both policy and program (Kimball 1974b).

The comparative approach of anthropology readily establishes its superiority for this type of problem. Each one of the three major types of food cycles is connected with a distinctive organizational and valuational system. "Foragers" live in camps as members of band-type communities. "Agrarianists" live in households in open or closed sedentary communities. The "corporate" system of organizational linkages characterizes our own and other contemporary societies.

Migratory hunter-gatherers link all members of the band, in all phases of the production-consumption cycle. In agrarian societies, the production-consumption cycle is sex differentiated and centers in household and field. Activities are sequenced but with usually regular involvement of kinsmen and neighbors at such times as harvest and festivities. In corporate society, institutions and households are centers of consumption. The food chain becomes greatly extended and organizationally complex, and there is a sharp demarcation of personnel involved in the multiple steps of production and consumption. There is no necessary connection between the food producer and the consumer.

From this conceptually structured base, it is now possible to extend the systemic detail for any specified situation in order to describe how groups organize in cooperative tasks; enumerate the cultural practices which surround the uses of food; adduce the symbols, values, and sanctions associated with a worldview; and provide examples of the process by which modifications occur. Through such knowledge, we can identify the situations where a land tenure system drains off increased production instead of expanding the diet of the poor as the intervenors anticipated; or how a status system regulates production; or how cosmologies may inhibit innovation. More significantly, the systemic approach identifies the basic process (the food chain) and its system variations (foragers, agrarianists, corporate) which organize essential knowledge for both policy and program. By definition, policy which is systemically based is contingent, provides for alternatives, and includes self-correcting mechanisms to incorporate new data or changes in conditions. Its formulation must also involve those who are affected by programs which emanate from policy.

Food policy utilizing this approach, reflects the connection between behavior and its conceptual setting in precisely the same way that current agricultural policy reflects the concepts of classical economics in the United States or that a socialist bias in anthropology expresses the views of its progenitors.

Unfortunately, most policy fails to take into account the social context within which programs will be carried out. This lack of consideration includes both knowledge of and sensitivity to the people involved. This vital flow may arise from the absence of a sense of community. Anthropologists should correct this myopic deficiency. They know that the effects of decisions surface at the community level. The activities associated with promoting economic well-being, health, or education must inevitably reach the institutional arrangements of community where these are incorporated. Although administrators sometimes take the dimension of community into account, more often than not the specialists are blind to such considerations. Recent federal programs in the areas of urban renewal, crime, school desegregation, poverty, and highway construction furnish examples of the prevalent tunnel vision. And where production decisions are linked with profit, as food policy has been so linked with the philosophy of the marketplace, we have permitted an ideological instrumentality to obliterate other variables. In contrast, it is the human community which should receive first consideration as the ultimate social context.

Conclusion

This broad overview should help us to understand the ramifications of the uses of anthropology for influencing the course of human affairs. If the distinctions which separate the roles of anthropologist as citizen, as applied technician, and as policy scientist are kept clear, there should be no difficulty in understanding the operations associated with each. The anthropologist as citizen can take sides on such crucial issues as world peace, energy conservation, environmental protection, women's liberation, abortion, or dozens of other matters which evoke diverse sentiments. Nor does there seem to be any special talent needed by those who declare for honesty, responsibility, and decency.

Although no special certification is required to take sides on public issues, there are situations where specific anthropological skills are needed. Possession of factual knowledge is a requirement for one who testifies in an Indian Land Claims case. Applied anthropologists require a broad range of competency. They use theory, as well as fact, and utilize their principles of process to develop sequential courses of action. Competencies essential for the anthropologist as policy scientist are even more rigorous and extensive. Those qualities already listed include freedom from ideological bias, a research interest in contemporary society, the empirical experience of applied anthropology, and natural systems analysis. The ultimate distinction, however, is a function of the analytical process. The policy scientist, unlike others, derives his formulations by asking questions which subsume knowledge of the dynamics of systems; the resulting propositions are consequences of the interplay between organized data and the method of analysis. They are statements of contingencies, not probabilities, about potential courses of action. The discussion of food policy exemplifies the point.

The time is ripe for qualified members of the profession to become involved in policy formulation. With the continued growth of competence in organizational dynamics and in professional and topical fields such as education and health, those anthropologists who have been concerned with contemporary society hold relevant knowledge of immense value for projecting future goals and programs. Our knwledge of the ongoing processes of community should also have prepared us to recognize that policy making must also be an ongoing and adapting process. Future prospects do indeed seem bright for anthropologists to become engaged as scientists with conceptual and research tools which can illuminate many of the problems which vex policy makers today. The way is already being paved by those who have begun to rethink anthropology in terms of the modern world and our society. A sampling of current efforts as they relate to policy issues in the areas of United States population, ethnic relations, drug use, education, and urban planning may be found in those essays which immediately follow. These reveal not only the need for the anthropological contribution but also some of the barriers which must be overcome if that branch of anthropology known as applied or development anthropology is to fully emerge as a policy science.

16

ETHNICITY, PUBLIC POLICY, AND ANTHROPOLOGISTS

George L. Hicks and Mark J. Handler

The orientation of Americans toward the present and the future often results in each generation confronting contemporary social problems as if they were appearing for the first time. What is true of Americans generally is also true of American anthropologists in particular. This ahistoricism means that we are often unaware of the lessons of the past and assume that there are no past guideposts for present actions.

George L. Hicks and Mark J. Handler present an historical review of the relationships between anthropologists and public policies with respect to ethnicity. Using the case studies of native Americans, immigrants, and black Americans as examples, they demonstrate the failure and success of anthropologists in influencing the major policies which have affected these groups. Present issues and concerns about ethnicity are then discussed within the context of historical developments of ideas in the discipline of anthropology and the meaning of ethnicity in American life.

From Hicks and Handler, we learn a great deal about the complexities entailed in studying our own society and the problems of separating our roles as researchers from our roles as well-intentioned citizens.

George L. Hicks (Ph.D., Illinois) is chairperson and associate professor of anthropology at Brown University. He has specialized in the study of American Indians, utopian communities, Southern Appalachian communities, and the Azore Islands from the perspective of interethnic relations. Mark J. Handler is a Ph.D. candidate at Brown University, who has done fieldwork in interethnic relations in rural Saskatchewan and the Azore Islands.

ANTHROPOLOGY, WE ARE told, is besieged by crisis on several fronts. As a child of imperialism, it is guilty of the sins of the fathers. Our principal areas of research, the Third World, no longer welcome us. Acknowledging the weaknesses of traditional functionalism, we are bereft of theoretical paradigms. Whatever problems the discipline faces, the sense of crisis is largely nourished by inattention to history. The ahistoricism that we share with fellow Americans leads us to experience the events and ideas of our society and discipline as unique. Thus, we have recently *discovered* ethnic populations in our midst and declared the "melting pot" a misleading fable, therby demonstrating a lapse of memory about the debates over immigration restriction in the 1920s that involved debunking that same melting pot. Our response has been similar to the issues of relevant research, academic freedom, ethics, and espionage. It is not that we deny a parallel between the Thailand controversy and Boas' public attack on the espionage activities of anthropologists in World War I. It is simply that we know little of these events and, in a world so rapidly changing, assume that the past offers few guideposts for the present. It is not that anthropology has no problems but that those we have appear as crises which not only overwhelm us, but keep returning because we forever face them for the first time. As a corrective to this ahistoricism, this essay begins with the past.

Of all the social problems subjected to public policy concern and social scientific investigation in twentieth-century America, none received more attention than those of the Indian, the immigrant, and the Negro. These three cases provide ample opportunity for examining the interplay of anthropology and public policy in dealing with ethnicity. While each has its own unique history in America, in some ways they are different facets of a single phenomenon. Each presented similar difficulties from the policy makers' perspective: poverty, mortality, deviance, crime, the potential of revolt or rebellion. Beyond their definition as social problems, Indians, immigrants, and Negroes share experiences that reflect fundamental contradictions in American society: between pluralism and homogeneity, between equality and individualism.

The role of social science has been twofold. At the level of social problems, findings of social scientists justified attempts and refusals to design and implement amelioration programs. On the ideological level, social science theories of human nature, treatments of race and culture, and descriptions of Indians, immigrants, and Negroes, have explained and challenged explanations of the contradiction between the situation of these groups and the claims of American ideology. Ralph Ellison's (1966:292) observation on the place of Negro studies in the 1870s applies to the cases considered here: "Here was a science whose role . . . was to reconcile the practical morality of American capitalism with the ideal morality of the American Creed." As objects of exploitation and as prime examples of the killing power of social fictions, "niggers," "redskins," "wops," and so on, have always confronted anthropology with the issue of interrelations between power and symbolism. But these issues are only now beginning to draw our attention (for an interesting example, see Cohen 1974).

These themes are taken up here. Following the historical review, we discuss the political strategy of cultural nationalism and the development of public policy that supports ethnic pluralism.

Case 1: American Indians

An embarrassment of riches faces the student of anthropology and public policy in the case of American Indians. No other ethnic category has been subject to such elaborate and shifting policy, and the discipline of anthropology in the United States has been largely shaped by its involvement with North American Indians. In no other case have anthropologists had equivalent opportunities to influence policy decisions.

After an initial period, from 1754 to 1871, of public policy culminating in large-scale efforts to concentrate the Indian population in the lands west of the Mississippi River, federal policy fluctuated between trying to retrain and incorporate them into the body politic and attempts to preserve them in isolation.

In the last half of the nineteenth century, educated Indians and sympathetic whites concluded that the "reservation system *per se,* . . . [was] responsible for impeding Indians in their course toward 'civilization' " (Lurie 1968:70–71). The General Allotment Act of 1887 (Dawes Act), authorizing a system of individual tracts for Indian householders and sale of surplus land to non-Indian interests, was promoted as a reform measure (Haas 1957:13). Forty-five years after the Act, two-thirds of Indian lands belonged to non-Indians, leaving 90,000 Indians without land ownership (Haas 1957:15). Enforcement of the Act was marked by "forced acculturation," with a major effort launched by the Bureau of Indian Affairs (BIA) to destroy the last vestiges of distinctive Indian cultural traditions.

Significant new policies towards American Indians did not emerge until after the inauguration of President Roosevelt in 1933, when there was a radical change of direction in federal policy (Tyler 1964:51–60). John Collier, commissioner of Indian Affairs from 1933 to 1945, administered the new policies, particularly the Indian Reorganization Act (IRA) of 1934, that sought to promote cultural diversity and tribal self-government, while at the same time retaining federal supervision. Within a few years, Collier was in difficulty with Congress, which apparently had not anticipated so far-ranging an implementation of its various acts. But Collier's interpretation could hardly have had a more favorable political climate than the Great Depression: encouraging Indians to stay on the reservations reduced their potential strain on state and local government in a period of severe economic distress (Tyler 1964:62).

Although there is a great deal of statistical evidence that Collier's programs were successful in reducing high mortality rates, landlessness, and extreme poverty among American Indians, basic antagonism to special Indian status and concern for the future of Indian resources led to repeated attacks from Congress and others, and as a result, Collier resigned in 1945. Within a few years, his policies were dismantled.

With the end of World War II, during which 65,000 Indians left their reservations for military service and defense work, public opinion opposed special status and work projects. The emphasis of policy was to relocate Indians to urban centers and terminate their reservations and federal supervision. The Senate's *Survey of Conditions of the Indians of the United States*, begun in 1928 and ending with over 23,000 pages in its final report in 1944, called for the "liquidation of the Indian Bureau" (Tyler 1964:91–92). The House of Representatives' Mundt Report of 1947 called for off-reservation boarding schools, voluntary relocation programs, and individual ownership of independent, family-sized farms—a return to the policy of the Dawes Act of 1887. The Indian Claims Commission Act of 1946 established a means for settlement of claims as a necessary step toward breaking down Indian dependence on the federal government and terminating reservations.

Criticism of the postwar termination policy began even before its enactment. The effect of wholesale termination would be, as Collier said in 1943, to "create a permanently dispossessed and impoverished group that either would live on the dole or would become one more sore spot in the body politic" (quoted in Tyler 1964:109). The practicality of the policy was not debated. Rather, the issues were ideological: civil rights, democratic ideals, equality. Although the statement of congressional demand for termination was not repudiated, the movement lost its momentum in the 1950s. Soon thereafter, Indians were affected by the new programs of the 1960s aimed at the poor in general.

Anthropology and Indian Affairs

Founded in 1878 originally as part of the Smithsonian Institution, the Bureau of American Ethnology (BAE) was, until 1910, the major sponsor of ethnographic research in the United States. A major argument for the founding of the bureau was that it would provide scientific information for the administration of Indian affairs. The first head of the bureau, J. W. Powell, set out the bureau's policy orientation in his first Annual Report in 1881 as an effort "to produce results that would be of practical value in the administration of Indian affairs" (quoted in Barnett 1956:3). It is striking that the two areas for special research attention, emphasized by Powell—Indian progress and the causes and remedies of culture conflict—are precisely those in which anthropologists had little to say when, fifty years later, they were called upon to advise the Collier administration.

During the 1930s, anthropologists were drawn into federal research on Indian problems requiring administrative decisions. The IRA called for tribal constitutions and modifications of economic and social conditions on those reservations choosing to reorganize under its provisions. To provide information for these programs, anthropologists were hired by the BIA. In other developments, the BIA education division contracted with anthropologists to provide bilingual texts and other materials for use in Indian education. These were needed for Collier's new program of fostering Indian identity and cultural distinctiveness. Other anthropologists engaged in making surveys and conducting problem-oriented research for the Human Development Unit of the Technical Cooperation group of the Soil Conservation Service. Seventy-five to eighty studies were made between 1936 and 1946 for use in making administrative decisions (Nash 1973:26).

With few exceptions (Nash 1973:26), anthropologists knowledgeable about the BIA (e.g., Steward 1969; Nash 1973) conclude that anthropological activity had little impact on policy. For example, the massive interdisciplinary Indian Personality and Administration project directed by Laura Thompson was explicitly established to provide policy recommendations, yet Kluckhohn and Hackenberg found that "six years after the termination of the Thompson project, the Indian Service has apparently taken no action on recommendations it contains" (1954:33). Even more telling, twenty years later Nash could still detect no impact of the Thompson studies (1973:27).

Several factors limited the impact of research on policy. Statutory deadlines for tribal adoption of self-government sometimes forced action before research was completed (Barnett 1956:37). Anthropologists' inexperience in dealing with administrators played a part (*Anthropology and the American Indian* 1973:32). More importantly, anthropologists in the 1930s were "unequipped with relevant knowledge" (Steward 1969:3). Finally, Collier was guided by his own ideas about Indians and administration. "Even if anthropology had a body of theory about modernization it would not have been permitted to use it; for the utopian dream of preserving 'Indianhood' was unassailable" (Steward 1969:15).

At times, anthropologists have had more than an advisory or research role in Indian policy. In the late 1940s, a professional anthropologist, John Provinse, was assistant commissioner, and from 1962 to 1965 two others headed the Bureau of Indian Affairs: Phileo Nash as commissioner and James Officer as assistant commissioner. From his experience as commissioner, Nash suggests that research was not "very action-related" in the BIA "because the fundamental decisions that affect the lives of the people touched by the Bureau . . . are not made by free agents . . . because every one of these decisions is made while looking simultaneously in two directions . . . to look to the tribal leaders on one side and to the appropriating committees of Congress on the other" (Nash 1973:28–29).

Within Congress, anthropological work was often opposed. For example, Steward (1969:4) reports that the federal government, prior to the Collier administration, "had impeded ethnographic research, which had been directed toward recording aboriginal cultures which Federal policy was attempting to eliminate." Even Collier's support did not quell opposition. Research went on "in spite of a growing hostility in Congress toward anthropological investigations; indeed, in spite of Congress' attempted prohibition of them" (Thompson 1956:521; see, for details, *Anthropology and the American Indian* 1973:32–33). Complementing Congressional displeasure was opposition from within the discipline itself. Kroeber doubted that anthropologists could retain their independence in research when they were employed by a government agency. Indeed, the results were few (Beals 1969:52).

Anthropological Directions and Indian Policy
Until World War II, American anthropology's research interests, methods, and theories were primarily developed in its relation with North American Indians. The major approach of the first generation of academically trained American anthropologists was the use of key informants in an effort to reconstruct "aboriginal" Indian culture. Operating with the ideals of "the tribal isolate," "the primitive," and the melting pot assumption that minorities were due for inevitable acculturation, anthropologists were professionally blind to contemporary conditions among American Indians. By implicitly suggesting that Indians had no culture worth maintaining, this orientation supported a policy of forced acculturation. Nevertheless, government officials objected to ethnographic recording of cultures they were trying to eliminate.

New research interests, particularly culture and personality and acculturation, emerged in the 1930s. Acculturation studies tied directly to American Indians shifted the focus of research to ethnographically "contaminated" and nonisolated Indians who had previously been ignored. Anthropologists now sought to delimit the processes of change and adaptation subsequent to European contact; acculturation as an appropriate subject was formally recognized with the 1936 *Memorandum* by Redfield, Linton, and Herskovits. While the shift in anthropological perspective appears to have coincided with the New Deal, Margaret Mead's pioneering *The Changing Culture of an Indian Tribe* (1966) marked anthropology's first venture into "reservation sociology."

Both anthropology and policy apparently responded to common influences, such as the social circumstances of the Great Depression, and policy affected anthropology through the funding of research. Yet, the study of acculturation was only partly consistent with the goals of the Indian New Deal. The focus of acculturation studies on present conditions of American Indians was congruent with Collier's ideas. Just as the Boasians recorded the past at a time when the BIA tried to destroy Indian traditions, students of acculturation emphasized culture change while the BIA tried to minimize it.

Indian Policy and "American" Values

No consistent development marks federal policy toward American Indians (Zimmerman 1957:39). A common element in all policies, however, has been the belief that the Indian problem was environmental and cultural rather than genetic and racial; this, as we shall see, was not the case with Negroes or immigrants.

Shifts in Indian policy reflect fundamental contradictions and alternatives in American ideology, particularly those conveniently labeled as *individualism, free enterprise, equality,* and *freedom.* Individualism and free enterprise support assimilation of Indians as individuals and oppose the BIA (because it is restrictive of individual freedom), federal trusteeship (because it restricts free enterprise), and tribal organization (because it appears contrary to individualism).

Equality is often equated with uniformity, and in Indian policy it stands in opposition to special status and distinctive culture. Yet the American concept of freedom supports individual and local community autonomy and toleration of difference. In the history of Indian policy, these latter values have been invoked less often than the others. Equality of opportunity as part of the national ideal justifies federal supervision and special services as a means of balancing the accumulated disadvantages of Indians. These basic contradictions in American ideology are increasingly evident in current federal policy for minority groups in general.

Although there is some broad correspondence between the selection of one or another of these alternatives and changes in national socioeconomic conditions—termination and allotment during prosperous times, cultural distinctiveness in the Depression—simple economic determinism fails as a satisfactory argument. Changes in anthropological perspectives and research interests have coincided with policy changes, partly due to government influence in research funding and partly because both policy makers and anthropologists hold some common assumptions and are subject to similar social conditions. One might have expected, given anthropologists' expertise about American Indians, a great deal of influence to flow from anthropology to national policy. It is nevertheless an inescapable conclusion that anthropology has had little effect.

Case 2: Immigrants to the United States

For the first time in American history, immigration policy was fundamentally altered with legislation passed between 1921 and 1929. Open immigration was radically restricted by sharply discriminatory nationality quotas that reflect racist doctrines of Nordic superiority by favoring northern Europeans over people from southern and eastern Europe. (In the first quarter of this century, what are now referred to as nationalities were also classified as races. In addition, Europeans were subdivided into Nordic, Alpine, or Mediterranean races.)

During most of the nineteenth century, immigration to America was actively encouraged by the federal government. Strong sentiment for restriction appeared with the racist nativism of the late 1880s. At that time, the volume of immigration was less troubling than the ethnic composition of the immigrants. Both concerns were satisfied by legislation of the 1920s: total immigration was reduced by 76 percent, with a disproportionate ratio affecting those from southern and eastern Europe. Italian immigrants fell by 87 percent, Russians by 99.9 percent, but Germans declined by only 58 percent.

With the Immigration Act of 1965, national origins and other discriminatory bases for quotas were eliminated, and the door was opened for a new immigration drastically changed in ethnic composition. From 1965 to 1975, the number of immigrants averaged 380,000 per year. Once again, the countries of southern and eastern Europe are the leading donor nations, along with Asia: in 1974, the first three European countries sending immigrants were Italy, Portugal, and Greece. In recent years, there has been a shift to non-European donors: from 1881 to 1920, Europeans constituted 88 percent of the immigrants, while between 1966 and 1977 they accounted for only 28 percent!

Immigration Policy and Legislation

Immigration involves several policy issues. Some concern the status of aliens: grounds for deportation, economic rights (for example, head taxes, occupational restrictions), and naturalization requirements. But the fundamental issue is open versus restricted immigration and the basis of restriction.

American immigration legislation is largely a series of successive steps in a tightening pattern of restriction. In 1882, convicts, lunatics, idiots, and those likely to become public charges were barred. An attempt to curtail the importation of contract labor (previously *supported* by federal law in the 1860s) was passed in 1885. The Immigration Act of 1891 brought immigration, for the first time, wholly under federal control.

The first general restriction law was passed in 1917. It required that all immigrants (with a few exceptions) be able to read some language. First proposed in 1887, the literacy test was the focus of the restrictionist campaign and was from the beginning intended as a respectable way to discriminate against newcomers from southern and eastern Europe, where illiteracy rates were highest. Presidents Cleveland, Taft, and Wilson vetoed literacy bills in 1895, 1913, and 1915, but Wilson's veto of the 1917 version was overridden. This act also excluded "persons of constitutional psychopathic inferiority" (a eugenics concept), vagrants, chronic alcoholics, alien radicals, and Hindus and East Indians.

In the post-World War I period, the literacy test proved ineffective in checking immigration, and temporary nationality quotas were established by law in 1921. The Johnson–Read (National Origins) Act established permanent policy in 1924 by setting quotas at 150,000. Each country's quota was to equal the proportion of people from that country (by birth or descent) in the total United States population in 1920. After two postponements, the national origins quota system took effect in 1929.

Opposition to Immigration

Business and labor are the most readily identifiable interest groups whose efforts affected immigration policy in this period. During the 1860s and 1870s, business groups actively promoted immigration, arguing that it provided positive benefits by increasing the number of workers and consumers in an expanding economy. By the late 1880s, after such highly publicized anarchist incidents as that in Haymarket Square, business leaders turned against immigrants and identified them as the source of radicalism and labor unrest. With the economic depression of 1893–97, this negative attitude hardened. But the economic boom of the early 1900s brought new demands for unskilled immigrant labor to tend the new semi-automatic machines. From about 1905, big business opposed literacy tests and quota restrictions while supporting Americanization programs.

Labor opposed immigration more consistently. Industrial labor, in direct competition with immigrants, was involved in all the anti-immigration moves in the nineteenth century. Although they earlier distinguished between voluntary immigration and that induced by contract labor supporting the former, organized labor had by 1906 abandoned the distinction and called for restriction of immigration. Immigrants were used to break strikes and undercut wage demands, and labor's support of restriction culminated in 1918 with the American Federation of Labor's demand for a two-year suspension of immigration.

Labor and business do not exhaust the list of pressure groups involved. The Immigration Restriction League, for example, was founded by "practical-minded intellectuals from well-to-do, long-established families steeped in Boston ways and Boston ideas" (Higham 1974:102). Their opposition to the influx of new immigrants was founded in *nativism*—"intense opposition to an internal minority on the ground of its foreign (e.g., 'un-American') connections . . . a zeal to destroy the enemies of a distinctively American way of life" (Higham 1974:4). Although nativism has been present in all periods of our history, it apparently erupted with special strength during times of national crisis. In these crises, Higham contends that "confidence in the homogeneity of American culture broke down. In desperate efforts to rebuild national unity, men rallied against symbols of foreignness that were appropriate to their predicament" (Higham 1974: preface).

Of the three recurrent themes in American nativism—anti-Catholic, antiradical, and racial nativism—it was racial nativism, phrased in anthropological terms, that underlay the restriction of immigration from 1910 to 1924. The influence of racial nativism began with the identification of the national genius as Anglo-Saxon, a notion imported from England and achieving wide currency in the 1840s.

As the different immigrants of the late nineteenth century— Italians, Slavs, Jews, and others from eastern and southern Europe— captured attention, only their lack of an Anglo-Saxon identity appeared as a common trait. To define the special threat of these immigrants, a system of racial classification distinguished clear-cut racial types among Europeans, and established an affinity between the old Americans, presumed to be Anglo-Saxon in descent, and northern Europeans.

Two currents of European thought reached America at the turn of the century and were combined into a scientific racism that found ready use in the arguments for restriction of immigration. Based in the new science of heredity, the eugenics movement gained great popularity after 1910 and appealed to both nativists and progressives. Eugenics was a scientific challenge to the regnant environmentalism: an individual's most important traits derived from heredity and were not subject to environmental modification. Hence, immigration restriction was necessary to protect the American population. Although the eugenicists' hereditary determinism called for screening defectives, it was silent on racial categories.

The second European contribution to American racial nativism came from physical anthropology.

In the end the race-thinkers had to look to anthropology to round out a naturalistic nativism. Anthropology alone could classify the peoples of Europe into hereditary types that would distinguish the new immigration from older Americans; it alone might arrange these races in a hierarchy of merit and thereby prove the irremediable inferiority of the newcomers; and anthropology would have to collaborate with genetics to show wherein a mixture of races physically weakens the stronger (Higham 1974:153).

This kind of physical anthropology, nonexistent in America, was imported from Europe, where it had become well developed by the late 1800s. The assumptions and findings of this new science were developed in America by nonanthropologists. Although William Ripley, an economist (originally trained in anthropology at Harvard), in his 1899 *The Races of Europe* adopted the anthropometrically based European racial classification—Teutonic, Alpine, and Mediterranean—it was the dilletante naturalist, Madison Grant, who provided the classic formulation of racial nativism. Blending racial classification, biological determinism, and rabid nativism, his *The Passing of the Great Race* first appeared in 1916 and was to have its real impact in the 1920s.

The scale of immigration in the decades after 1890 was too great for anyone to maintain the faith in the natural assimilative power of American institutions that had marked earlier nineteenth-century attitudes. For nativist and reformer, the twentieth century alternative to restriction was directed assimilation—in short, Americanization.

Americanization as an ideology and program was born in the 1890s from the efforts of two very different groups: the settlement house programs of social integration and the hereditary patriotic organizations. The former aimed to Americanize immigrants only in the most general way, by attempts at what we might today call "Community development." The patriotic societies, however, had specific notions that adult immigrants should be taught loyalty to their new nation. After 1915, the goal of Americanization was, for liberals and progressives, no longer immigrant welfare but the breaking of Old World ties and speedy, thorough naturalization. The major Americanization organization of the political progressives, the Committee for Immigrants in America, changed its slogan "Many Peoples, But One Nation" to "America First."

With the end of World War I, fear of the foreign-born continued, with "Bolshevism" replacing Germany as the national enemy. Political radicalism and labor turmoil were, as in the 1880s, attributed to the foreign-born; Americanization became the means to fight this foreign menace. With the end of the Red Scare in 1920, the Americanization movement collapsed. It did not, however, carry nativism into oblivion.

Moves Toward Restriction

With tolerance for ethnic minorities exhausted and Americanization in disrepute, restriction seemed the only solution to a problem of growing dimensions. Scientific racism gained its widest acceptance at this time. The Ku Klux Klan, reborn in 1915, spread to the north in 1921, Tom Watson won a Senate seat with an anti-Catholic campaign, and Henry Ford emerged as a leader of anti-Semitism. In this xenophobic climate, Madison Grant's *The Passing of the Great Race* achieved the popularity it had failed to receive at the time of its publication in 1916. Grant's vision left no room for Americanization: the science of eugenics had destroyed the "pathetic and fatuous belief in the efficacy of American institutions and environment to reverse or obliterate immemorial hereditary tendencies" (quoted in Baltzell 1964:97–98). Madison Grant "taught the American people to . . . identify themselves as Nordics, and to regard any mixture with [Mediterraneans or Alpines] . . . as a destructive process of 'mongrelization' " (Higham 1974:271–272).

Franz Boas and the Immigrant Question

Racial nativists' claims couched the restriction debate in anthropological terms, and the leading anthropologist of the period, Franz Boas, responded. As mentioned in essays 1 and 15, Boas was a strong advocate of rigorous empirical standards. His research was nonetheless deeply committed. His humanistic values influenced his choice of research topic, and he sought to make the political implications of his findings explicit. Boas' perspective—combining liberal ideas about "equality of opportunity, education, political and intellectual liberty, the rejection of dogma, and the search for scientific truth" (Stocking 1968:149)—was a fusion of scientific and political elements. In America, he was not only an egalitarian socialist; he was an immigrant and a Jew. While he worked actively in the cause of Negro civil rights, most of Boas' research on race was concerned with European immigrants.

Boas never denied the operation of biological processes, including heredity, but insisted that they were subject to environmental modification, and that culture, not biology, accounted for observed patterns of human behavior. Summarizing Boas' contribution, Stocking (1968:264) writes: "The whole thrust of his thought was in fact to distinguish the concepts of race and culture, to separate biological and cultural heredity, to focus attention on cultural process, to free the concept of culture from its heritage of evolutionary and racial assumption."

All of Boas' thinking on race was relevant to the immigration question, but he made one direct contribution to the debate. His report *Changes in Bodily Form of Descendants of Immigrants* appeared in 1910 as one of the forty-two volumes issued by the United States Immigration Commission, an agency established as a result of the 1907 Immigration Act, to investigate the effects of immigration. From 1908 to 1910, Boas obtained body measurements of 18,000 persons: East European Jews, Bohemians, Neapolitans, and Sicilians, all living in New York City at the time. He made direct comparisons between children and their parents and between the American data and available European measurements.

While consistent with his earlier research in showing environmental influences on rates of growth, the immigrant study yielded unexpected results. With other anthropologists of the time, Boas considered cephalic index as a stable, hereditary trait and expected "that the headform of the [children of] immigrants would remain the same." Instead, he discovered "far-reaching change in type" of each immigrant group which varied directly with the "time elapsed between the arrival of the mother and the birth of the child." He concluded that this change could "only be explained as due directly to the influence of environment" and that "all the evidence is now in favor of a great plasticity of human types" (quoted in Stocking 1968:178). Given that the changes in headform tended toward a common intermediate form, Boas provided a reasonable conclusion in respect to the restriction of immigration: "all fear of an unfavorable influence of South European immigrants upon the body of our people should be dismissed" (quoted in Stocking 1968:180).

Boas' study had no discernible effect on the Commission's recommendations, which were restrictionist in favoring a literacy test, but it gave the environmentalist position the kind of scientific authority that eugenics provided for the racial nativists.

Immigration and the Other Anthropology

Anthropologists carried out few studies of American ethnic groups until long after immigration had been restricted by law. Searching the literature, Spiro (1955:1241) found only two anthropologists who called for immigration research in the early 1920s: "Wissler (1920) and Jenks (1921) perceived the immigrants of their day as threats to American culture . . . and urged that anthropology take a 'paramount' role in their 'Americanization.' " The positions of Jenks and Wissler illustrate the non-Boasian anthropological response to immigration. Wissler declared immigrants "a menace to our own culture and national existence . . ." (1920:9–10).

Albert Ernest Jenks was professor of anthropology and director of the Americanization Training Course at the University of Minnesota. The Americanization program, established in 1919, was directed to "the training of Americanization leaders to hasten the assimilation of the various peoples in America toward the highest common standards and ideas of America practicable for each generation" (Jenks 1921:241). Leaders from the course served in local governments, civic organizations, churches, and schools. As the following passage makes clear, Jenks's anthropology was distinctly not Boasian: "It is commonly supposed to be true that their differences are only 'skin deep,' but biologists know that ethnic groups differ beneath the skin . . . there is scientific reason to speak of different 'breeds' of people whose differing physical characteristics are today due to the factors of heredity resident in the reproductive germ cells . . ." (Jenks 1921:242).

There is no doubt that Boas' refutation of racism reached an ever wider audience after the publication of his book, *The Mind of Primitive Man* in 1911. Simultaneously, however, Jenks was training teachers, and he exemplifies an anthropological viewpoint consistent with the assumptions of the eugenicists and restrictionists. His position blended theoretical genetic determinism and practical environmentalism. Education, he proposed, is the means to Americanize the different "breeds" with their innate dispositions. When the Americanization movement crumbled, such viewpoints provided the scientific rationale for discriminatory restriction.

Unlike the long-forgotten Albert Jenks, Clark Wissler is an important figure in the history of American anthropology, and he had considerable influence in government circles at the time of the debate over restriction. The non-Boasian position on race and immigration cannot be dismissed as an idiosyncratic aberration of marginal anthropologists. Its central location is well illustrated in the relation between cultural anthropology and the National Research Council from 1916 through the 1920s. The following account is drawn from Stocking (1968).

Organized in 1916 as part of the national preparedness campaign, the National Research Council created a committee on anthropology in an effort to apply science to the war effort. The committee's major concern was physical anthropology. There were few professional physical anthropologists in the United States, and Boas, despite his qualifications, was excluded from the committee because of his outspoken opposition to the war and his personal enmity with key figures in government science. The Council's director appointed Charles Davenport, the eugenics leader, and Madison Grant to the committee. Davenport took control, and those involved in the committee included "other anthropological writers who argued the existence of hierarchical racial differences" (Stocking 1968:288).

During this period, biologists and other scientists resisted the claim of cultural anthropology to being a science. A close link between this resistance and the nativists of the eugenics movement was significant for immigration policy. A major opponent of anthropology's claim was the Galton Society, a group organized in 1918 by Davenport for the study of "racial anthropology." Its membership included prominent foundation heads and government scientists. Another member of the Galton Society was Clark Wissler.

A postwar reorganization of the National Research Council included the creation of a Division of Anthropology and Psychology. Initial efforts to exclude Boas from the new Division resulted in a compromise agreement by which representatives were chosen by the American Anthropological Association. Wissler, nominated by Boas, was elected president of the Association in 1918 and in the 1920s served as chairman of the Council's new anthropology and psychology division.

Conflict between Boasians and the "Washington School" heightened, and at the December 1919 meeting of the American Anthropological Association, Boas was censured, stripped of his office in the organization, and pressured into resigning from the National Research Council. Ostensibly, this action was taken because of a letter he had written to *The Nation,* attacking four unnamed anthropologists for "prostituting science by using it as a cover for their activities as spies."

By late 1923, Boas had regained his power in the Association and towards the end of the decade was able to influence Research Council policy. Yet the key years in immigration restriction were precisely those when Boas was ostracized. Through sympathetic congressional committee chairmen, Madison Grant and the eugenicists influenced the framing of legislation. In May 1921, the first quota system became law, and three years later the National Origins bill was enacted. Thus, it was the anthropology of Madison Grant, not Franz Boas, that underlay immigration legislation.

If, in the early 1920s, cultural anthropology had little influence on racism, the reverse was not the case. Stocking suggests that the postwar reaction against cultural anthropology, with its demand for broadening anthropological interest beyond American Indians and for emphasizing biological factors, "was related to the national outburst of nativism" and "mediated in part by the institutional channels established under the peacetime Research Council; this externally conditioned reaction had a definite impact on the research orientations and to some extent on the theoretical assumptions of important cultural anthropologists" (Stocking 1968:297).

Boasian anthropology, together with liberal and progressive thought in general, suffered a setback in the 1920s. Most of the darker manifestations of this era (the Palmer Raids, the rise of the Ku Klux Klan) faded and disappeared by the end of the decade, but restrictive and discriminatory immigration laws remained in force until 1965. An entire generation would pass, unique in American history, when immigrants would not be a significant factor in American life. For cultural anthropology, the adversity was only temporary. By the mid-1930s, the culture concept (and the concomitant rejection of genetic determinism) was accepted in all the social sciences.

Case 3: Black Americans

Although the immigrant and Indian problems had a moral component and definitions and solutions were set largely by prevailing ideological assumptions, they were seen as pragmatic problems requiring concrete programs and policies. But the Negro problem was preeminently moral (Myrdal 1944). For most of this century, national policy toward Black Americans has been a policy of neglect, of maintaining the *status quo*. That *status quo*—pervasive inequality of conditions and opportunity of blacks in America—called into question the nation's egalitarian ideals.

After the Compromise of 1877, marking the withdrawal of active Northern interest in the Negro, the federal government's stance was noninterference in the development of the Jim Crow system (Woodward 1957). Large-scale black migration to northern cities, from 1914 until the Great Depression set in, once again brought the Negro problem to national attention. Policy, however, changed little.

There were some ameliorative measures taken by presidential orders: Roosevelt barred discrimination in much of the federal government and in industries with government contracts; Truman abolished segregation in the armed forces. The Supreme Court, beginning with decisions in 1946 and culminating in the school desegregation orders of 1954 and 1955, reversed its 1896 approval of the Jim Crow system. Until the congressional acts and "affirmative action" programs of the 1960s and 1970s, however, there was no positive policy towards blacks.

During the first quarter of this century, anthropology's relevance for the Negro problem lay in its attack on scientific racism. After the mid-1920s, scientific racism had been discredited; the culture concept was dominant in anthropology and spreading to the other social sciences. We shall now therefore consider the elaboration of the culture concept as it related to blacks.

Boas and the Negro Problem

As citizen and anthropologist, Boas was actively involved in the cause of Negro rights. Closely associated with W. E. B. DuBois, he was a founder in 1910 of the NAACP. In public lectures, newspapers, and magazines, he argued for Negro equality. It was at this time that his widely read refutation of racism, *The Mind of Primitive Man,* was published.

Boas' discussion of the Negro problem came from two directions. First, as he had in the case of immigrants, he distinguished race and culture. He statistically demonstrated that variation within the "races" was greater than that between them, and argued that an individual's racial identity, therefore, could not predict his cultural capacity. This was his contribution from physical anthropology. From ethnographic evidence, he marked another path. Pointing to the complexity of African cultures, he argued that these African achievements demonstrated Negro cultural competence. This provided the theme for his 1906 Commencement Address at Atlanta University:

. . . to those who stoutly maintain a material inferiority of the Negro race and who would dampen your ardor by their claims, you must confidently reply that the burden of proof rests with them, that the past history of your race does not sustain their statement, but rather gives you encouragement. . . . say that you have set out to recover for the colored people the strength that was their own before they set foot on the shores of this continent (quoted in Herskovits 1953:111).

Anthropological Approaches to Black America

Three approaches can be distinguished. The first two, diametrically opposed on the question of distinctive Afro-American culture, are developments of Boas' thought. The third, community studies in the South, is independent of Boas. Only the denial of distinctive culture received general acceptance in the discipline; it was this view of blacks that precluded ethnographic research.

1. *Cultural stripping and Negro acculturation.* While his explanation of Negro traits was unequivocally environmental rather than genetic, Boas did not completely extend the assumptions of cultural relativity to his treatment of these traits. Contending that American Negro traits can be explained by history and social status, he wrote:

The tearing-away from the African soil and the consequent complete loss of the old standards of life, which were replaced by the dependency of slavery and by all it entailed, followed by a period of disorganization and by a severe economic struggle against heavy odds, are sufficient to explain the inferiority of the status of the race, without falling back upon the theory of hereditary inferiority (1911:240).

The total loss of African traditions is a notion repeated in the writings of Boas' students, such as Benedict (1947:86–87) and the early Herskovits. Boas and his students, however, did not view American blacks as "decultured" but as fully acculturated: their culture was American, identical to (or a variant of) the culture of white Americans. As Szwed notes, "the overlapping statistics of the physical features of the two races together with overlapping scores on intelligence tests may have led Boas to infer that blacks as a group simply 'overlapped' white American culture, if only imperfectly" (1972:157).

2. *Study of Negro folklore and Afro-American culture.* Willis (1975) has documented a less well-known aspect of Boas' involvement with black Americans, his support for the study of black folklore. His efforts ranged from an early (1903) unsuccessful attempt to have Negroes included in the scope of the Bureau of American Eth-

nology, through a partial success in arousing interest in Negro folk-lore on the part of the American Folklore Society, to supervising the principal students of black folklore. Quoting from Boas' letters and articles, Willis indicates that the motivation behind these efforts was to undermine the notion of white supremacy by documenting black achievements (1975:313).

Elsie Clews Parsons was the first of Boas' students to work in this area and became his principal colleague in the study of black folklore. Other students of Afro-America, trained by Boas, include Arthur Fauset, Zora Neale Hurston, Martha Beckwith, and Melville Herskovits (Willis 1975; Whitten and Szwed 1970). Among these, Herskovits did most to develop the study of Afro-American culture. He systematically elaborated Boas' suggestion of African survivals in American Negro culture, doing so on the basis of extensive fieldwork and communicating to a wide audience.

Herskovits' thought closely reflects that of his mentor, but what were unresolved oppositions in Boas appear as successive developments in Herskovits. His early work was anthropometric; his position on race was identical to Boas and he at first shared the Boas–Benedict assumption of complete Negro acculturation. Beginning after his re-search in Surinam (1928–29) and developing during years of field-work in Haiti, Trinidad, Brazil, and West Africa, Herskovits rejected this early view and argued that persisting Africanisms were the basis of distinctive Afro-American cultures. To counter racist use of these findings, he stressed the validity of such cultural differences and somewhat mischievously noted "that American whites had unknow-ingly absorbed a great deal of African culture" (Szwed 1972:165). His mature position appeared in 1941 with the publication of *The Myth of the Negro Past*. His purpose in this book was to make avail-able "a foundation of scientific fact concerning the ancestral cultures of Africa and the survivals of Africanisms in the New World" that would promote confidence among Negroes by providing "an appreci-ation" of their past. The dissemination of "such a body of fact, solidly grounded," would perhaps change attitudes about Negro ca-pabilities "and thus contribute to a lessening of interracial tensions" (1941:32). Boas had set forth the same goals thirty years earlier.

3. *Community studies and the southern "caste" system.* The third anthropological approach can be represented by Powdermaker's

After Freedom (1939) and Davis, Gardner, and Gardner's *Deep South* (1941). These and similar studies focused on social structure and social control, analyzing black–white relations as a caste system supported by an ideology of race.

Many studies conducted in the 1930s and 1940s by social scientists fall under this heading. While the study of American Negroes was for many years dominated by the influence of Robert E. Park and the "Chicago school" of American sociology, W. Lloyd Warner, an anthropologist, was also a prime mover. The results of research range from *Black Metropolis* (Drake and Cayton 1945), a study of Negroes in Chicago, to the project at the University of North Carolina, directed by anthropologist John Gillin, entitled "Field Studies in the Modern Culture of the South" (Lewis 1955, Morland 1958, and Rubin 1951).

Cooperative effort in the funding, direction, and execution of a number of studies is evident. Lewis' study, one of several in the project directed by Gillin, was submitted as a dissertation at the University of Chicago (Lewis 1955:xi). When Powdermaker began planning her fieldwork in Mississippi, she was a researcher at Yale University's Institute of Human Relations, the same institutional base used by John Dollard, a social psychologist, for his research in Mississippi (Dollard 1937). Later, Dollard collaborated with Allison Davis, a co-author of *Deep South,* in writing *Children of Bondage* (Davis and Dollard 1940). Financial support for many of the studies was provided by the federal Works Progress Administration and the private Julius Rosenwald Fund (see Drake and Cayton 1945:vii; Davis, Gardner and Gardner 1941:xii; Morland 1958:xi). Taken together, these studies provided a massive documentation of inequality and the disadvantaged position of the Negro in American life. Nevertheless, their impact on policy-making came only in the Supreme Court decision of 1954 when some of them were used as supporting evidence for the Court's opinion.

The New Orthodoxy
While most anthropologists continued to concentrate their research on American Indians and, to a lesser extent, upon nonliterate peoples in other countries, few of them followed the leads of Davis, Gillin, Warner, and Powdermaker in research on American communities and black Americans. The assumption of Negro acculturation dominated

anthropology, and, without a distinctive culture, blacks held little professional interest for those who defined anthropology as the study of non-Western peoples. A concern for the political implications of the two Boas-derived positions on African survivals or full acculturation must have been a factor in this lack of interest. Most anthropologists probably shared the liberal opinion that the solution to the Negro problem lay in integration. Ethnographic research revealing distinctive Afro-American culture could be used by the two anti-integrationist forces: white supremacists could argue that Negroes were nonassimilable, and black separatists (like Marcus Garvey) could bolster their nationalistic claims.

Other reasons for this tendency of anthropology to ignore black Americans have been suggested (see, for example, Mintz 1970; Willis 1970, 1975). John Szwed summarizes various explanations:

The "impure," "acculturated" nature of American blacks made them poor subjects for a cultural anthropology originally bent on reconstructing the ethnographic past of isolated societies. . . . Afro-Americans were geographically too close and of too low status for professional prestige in American society . . . field work among lower-class Afro-Americans lacks the exoticism that so appeals to anthropologists (1972:155).

On the first point, Willis has objected that no American Indian tribe was truly unacculturated when studied and thus "anthropologists had the option of ignoring white cultural influence on Negroes as they did with Indians" (1970:35–36). It may be that most anthropologists at the time *believed* there were still Indian "memory cultures" to be recorded but that those of blacks had long disappeared. The fact remains that when, in the 1930s, there was a turn from ethnographic salvage to studies of acculturation, when cultural purity ceased to be a fieldwork requisite, the "acculturated" Negro was still largely ignored.

Defending anthropology's sharpening boundaries and avoiding competition with other disciplines also played a part in leaving the Negro to sociology and history. Powdermaker indicates as much in describing the reaction of Robert Lowie when he heard of her plans to go into the Deep South. Lowie, she says, "wrote me that although a study in Mississippi might be interesting, I should not go too far in the direction of modern communities. After all, anthropologists were then supposed to limit their studies to primitive peoples" (Powdermaker 1966:133).

Enter the Sociologists

With the northward migration and new black protest after World War I, what had been a "Southern problem" since the Compromise of 1877 became once more a national problem. Sociology responded, with the cooperation of a few anthropologists.

From the end of the war through the 1930s, the Chicago sociologists were preeminent in the study of American Negroes and race relations. Their abiding interest was urban social problems, and Chicago served as a natural laboratory for the investigation of social pathology. Park and his students—principally E. Franklin Frazier—studied the Negro largely as a social problem. Their approach included the use of statistical surveys to demonstrate personal and social disorganization, an emphasis on pathology aptly labeled the "pejorative tradition" (Valentine 1968).

Park and Frazier developed their approach when scientific racism had been discredited, and the culture concept was supreme in their work. In explaining pathology, they did not invoke innate racial factors, as had a previous generation of sociologists, but, instead, they enlarged on the lead offered by Boas to shape a cultural explanation. If in previous hands American Negroes had been racially inadequate, they were now painted as culturally inadequate (Frazier 1939). The Park–Frazier approach was sympathetic to the plight of blacks: they were portrayed as victims suffering from deculturation or a pathological culture, the result of slavery and its aftermath.

What are some of the implications of this viewpoint? Both anthropological and sociological approaches rejected genetic factors. By identifying environmental causes for the Negro problem, the Park–Frazier view held out the possibility of change. There are, however, differences between the anthropological and sociological positions. Boas was a militant integrationist, associated with DuBois and the NAACP. He argued that there was neither racial nor cultural differences between blacks and whites in the United States. Park, on the other hand, was a moderate, supporting Booker T. Washington's accommodationism. Park's model of race relations postulated the *status quo* as a natural stage in a developmental cycle: race prejudice would eventually disappear.

Only in the 1960s, when the federal government began to act in regard to blacks, did the policy implications of these positions become manifest (in, for example, Moynihan's recommendation of "benign neglect"). Until then, these ideas served to justify the *status quo* and encouraged, if they were noticed at all, a policy of inaction.

In the immigrant case, the absence of a developed American physical anthropology enabled nonanthropologists to distort the concept of race into doctrines of Nordic superiority. In parallel fashion, anthropologists with few exceptions abandoned the study of Afro-Americans to nonanthropologists, and the result was a distortion of the culture concept. "Witness the wide popularity of the notion of 'cultural deprivation' among politicians, educators, and social workers by which . . . material poverty is grossly confused with ideological poverty, culture now being given a remarkably restricted definition" (Szwed 1972:162). On the interpretation of low test scores by Negroes as cultural deprivation rather than as the result of low incentive, Murray says:

By ignoring the most fundamental definitions of anthropology . . . the contemporary American social science technician substitutes academic subject matter for culture. He then misrepresents deficiencies in formal technical training as cultural deprivation . . . (1973:110).

Overview: Indians, Immigrants, and Blacks

It should now be clear that similar policy alternatives were present in each of the three cases. A choice between homogeneity and pluralism appears in the case of American Indians (forced acculturation versus quasi-autonomy under the Indian Reorganization Act), immigrants (Americanization versus cultural diversity), and blacks (special educational programs versus cultural nationalism). These similarities express the possibilities inherent in American national ideology.

A comparison of these cases uncovers differences as well. For example, the late nineteenth century and post-World War II periods saw changes in policies toward Indians and blacks. In the 1950s, Indian "termination" and court decisions reversing the "separate but equal" doctrine, both aimed at ending special status and drawing blacks and Indians out of isolation. In contrast, the Compromise of 1877 "got the government out of the Negro business" just as Allotment aimed to get it out of the Indian business. Allotment, however, looked to integration of Indians, while the Compromise, confirmed by the *Plessy v. Ferguson* decision (1896), abandoned blacks to Jim Crow segregation (Woodward, 1957). Thus, a policy intending to end Indian special status occurred at a time when blacks were subjected to a special, inferior status.[1]

Anthropology, however limited its immediate impact on policy decisions, has been influential by establishing a *cultural* rather than a *racial* view in ethnic affairs. The policy interpretation of this environmentalist victory has promoted education as the solution to minority problems, cultural homogeneity as an attainable possibility, and, contrary to the intentions of the theorists, has blamed ethnic minorities for the inequities they suffer.

We have seen a strong tendency toward the conformance of anthropological views with the dominant ideology and policy in American society, at least in portraying "vanishing" Indians, "melting" immigrants (or, in the 1920s, racially inferior ones), and "deculturated" Negroes. Anthropology has also passively served the *status quo* by ignoring the political situation of the groups it studied.

Understanding the relationships of American anthropology and American society requires careful historical research, for which Stocking's work provides an excellent start. It is too simple to shrug off anthropology's relationships with public policy as an exercise in *post hoc* rationalization or a reflection of popular ideas. Efforts like those of Wolf (1972), while provocative as programmatic statements for studying the history of American anthropology, surely overstate the ease and directness with which anthropology has responded to changes in American life. Anthropology's connection with public policy might be understood better by a comparison with the relationships of British and French colonial policies to the anthropology of those countries. This kind of comparison is necessary if the putative relationship of imperialism and anthropology is to be more than empty polemics (see Kaplan 1974:835).

---

[1] (Editors Note) The "special status" of native Americans is a legal status stemming from treaty rights to land, water, timber, mineral and other resources and protected by the wardship of the Federal government. The end result of termination of the reservations, as in the earlier Allotment movement, is to open up these resources to non-Indians. Thus, independence and freedom from government control and protection can be understood as fundamentally consistent with the desires of non-Indian economic interests which are always well represented in Congress. Black Americans and white ethnics as groups enjoy no such resource base or problematical legal status, which may explain the lag between the growth of the ideologies of freedom for native Americans and freedom for Black Americans and immigrants. As the energy crisis deepens we can expect that the fuel resources on western reservations will play a role in an intensified movement to end the "special status" of Indians and promote Indian freedom and independence.

The New Ethnicity

Half a decade after the "deliberate speed" in desegregation ordered by the Supreme Court in 1955, the movement toward integration of schools had become a slow, tortuous process. With the inauguration of President Kennedy, who was committed to active measures toward equality for American blacks, and the sit-ins and bus boycotts of the early 1960s, a veritable revolution in civil rights began. Led by black activists and supported by white political liberals, pressure mounted for new, broad legislation. Kennedy's early executive orders, extending those promulgated under Presidents Roosevelt and Truman, signaled a "new deal" for black Americans. After Kennedy's assassination, President Johnson led Congress in producing the historic civil rights acts of 1964 and 1965.

Neither the Civil Rights Act of 1964 nor the Voting Rights Act of 1965 provided for more than legal equality, and agitation continued for means to insure that black Americans would gain some degree of economic and political parity with whites as well. Once again, cultural nationalism, with its rallying cry of "Black is Beautiful," became attractive as a political strategy. The situation was much like that in many developing nations. Political action was stimulated by the difference between expectation and accomplishment (Makielski 1973:3), with ethnicity as an important principle of organization (for an example from the Third World, see Cohen 1969).

In the long hot urban summers of the late 1960s, it appeared that the frustration of black people had found a new and dangerous expression: violence. The response was to sharpen the definition of black urban ghettos as "problem areas," and to simultaneously contain and prevent violence while setting up programs of improved job opportunities and training. Continued agitation for political and economic power highlighted the disparity between legal equality and the failure of black Americans to achieve substantive equality during this time.

The social conflict of the 1960s, conducted at first with the tactics of nonviolence expressed by Dr. Martin Luther King and later by the less broadly based efforts of groups committed to violent tactics, seemed to many citizens a unique and unwarranted response to conditions that were gradually improving. Yet, in making their dissatisfaction louder and their demands more strident, argues Makielski

(1973:135), blacks were following an American tradition. Further, it is held that for "relatively powerless groups" conflict—at least below the level of rioting—is an effective political strategy (Rodgers and Bullock 1972:215).

"Affirmative action," a phrase first used by President Kennedy in 1961, had now become a keystone of federal policy. As federal guidelines developed, affirmative action replaced the older idea of equal opportunity in an effort to achieve economic parity for American minorities. While the Civil Rights Act of 1964 aimed to set American blacks free at last, the language of the legislation states the prohibitions more broadly. Title VII of the Act, for example, forbade discrimination in employment "because of such individual's color, religion, sex, or national origin."

"The greatest inroads on discrimination have followed paths blazed by black activists" (Rodgers and Bullock 1972:174).

White ethnics have been moving from a traditionally defensive and protective stance to an offensive and assertive one. Their encounters with black progress have been one of the primary causes for their assertion, another being their emergence into the middle class, . . . [and] their recent alienation from American institutions and way of life. They feel neglected and forgotten (Weed 1973:45).

As the federal and state governments increasingly made allocations of public monies contingent upon ethnic criteria, with special training and educational programs established for some but not all ethnic categories, the voices of those who felt "neglected and forgotten" grew louder. Native Americans, too, adopted strategies of cultural nationalism. The social divisiveness that appeared imminent in this varied chorus was quickly grasped by some social scientists and remarked upon for its pessimistic potential. Horowitz (1976:73), for example, labeled ethnicity as "a measure of disintegration in the American sociopolitical system."

Nathan Glazer sees the use of ethnic criteria by the national government as a distinct turn in a new direction. The attempt to provide substantive equality for American blacks, he contends, "turned into an effort to redress the inequality of all deprived groups" (Glazer 1975:31). This hope of making blacks the equal of other Americans "raised the question of who *are* the other Americans? How many of them can define their own group as *also* deprived?" (Glazer 1975:31)

Whether or not one agrees with Glazer's primary thesis that we have mistakenly slipped into "affirmative discrimination," public policy established in the decade of the 1960s laid the foundation for a sharpened pluralistic society. Glazer's opposition to current policy is based partly on his view that, in the United states, ethnicity is entirely voluntary, and "is part of the burden of freedom of all modern men who must choose what they are to be" (Glazer 1975:69). While there are numerous instances of voluntary ethnicity (see Hicks and Leis 1977 for case studies), there are still situations in which one is involuntarily treated as belonging to one or another ethnic category. Under some circumstances, at least, it appears that ethnicity is still a "stigmatic emblem" (De Vos and Romanucci-Ross 1975:389).

Anthropology and the "Great Society"

It has been widely assumed in social science literature, including studies produced by anthropologists, that there is a single, relatively homogeneous "American culture." Frequently referred to as "the standard American culture" (Mead 1955b:185), this monolithic creation is taken as the measure of various ethnic groups and deviants. This notion of *an* American culture has not, of course, included native Americans nor, except as variants, black Americans. That American anthropologists participate in the general consensus about an American culture can perhaps be laid to their dual role when they observe aspects of life in the United States as citizens and observers. Our inability to "come to terms with Afro-American life," as John Szwed suspects, "is merely a special case of a much larger problem" (1972:174). The larger problem hinges on our blind insistence that there is *an* American culture.

In the realm of ethnic studies, this view emerges as a refusal to consider white Protestants as an ethnic category. As Ulf Hannerz sees it, white Protestants "seem not to be considered an ethnic group at all; they are non-ethnic 'real Americans' . . . (1974:46)." This is, he suggests, an attitude "tainted . . . with white Protestant ethnocentrism . . ." (1974:46). In this aspect of the notion of an "American mainstream," we come perilously close to a reformulation of the foundation for Americanization programs designed to standardize immigrants into Americans.

Jules Henry, in remarking on de Tocqueville's observations about the America of the 1830s, was struck with the accuracy of the portrait for contemporary life (Henry 1973). Henry was, of course, referring to the aspects of de Tocqueville's work that show sameness and conformity among Americans. But de Tocqueville was too accurate an ethnographer to miss the other side of American life. His view of the relations among American Indians, Negroes, and Euro-Americans resembles in language and import the formulation Furnivall (1948) made of a plural society. De Tocqueville (1945:344) noted that "fortune has brought [the three 'races'] together on the same soil, where, although they are mixed, they do not amalgamate, and each race fulfills its destiny apart."

In anthropology, two reflections of the unitary culture view of the United States deserve special note. One is the somewhat outdated idea that, in the interests of effective professional training and greater objectivity, American anthropologists should not study America. While excellent investigations of American life have been made by anthropologists, the prevailing idea has been that such studies should not constitute one's major specialty. If one looks at the United States, at least the Euro-American part of it, as sharing a single culture, it is consistent to advise students not to study their "own cultural traditions." But if one sees America as diverse in cultural traditions, as constituting for some purposes a single society within which there are numerous cultural traditions, the admonition becomes less convincing. In recent years, this traditional view has been reversed in a resolution adopted by the American Anthropological Association which encourages more investigations in the United States.

Another important expression of the unitary view of America was perhaps best stated, although in exaggerated form, by W. Lloyd Warner in his foreword to the reissue of *Democracy in Jonesville:*

Borrowing from the Gospel of John, we can say that Jonesville is in all Americans and all Americans are in Jonesville, for he that dwelleth in America dwelleth in Jonesville, and Jonesville in him.

To study Jonesville is to study America; it is a laboratory, a clinic, a field study for finding out what we are as a people and for learning why we think and feel and do the things we do (1964:ix).

Long before Warner's restatement about Jonesville, however, anthropologists were cautioning each other to attend to the diversity of American life (Mason 1955), and to avoid mistaking the part for the whole (Steward 1950:20–94; Wolf 1956; Casagrande 1959).

Seeing in a single community, or even in a series of communities, the outlines of the entire nation—whether the United States or any other nation—was repeatedly criticized.

But the unitary view of American culture remained and is a salient feature of the "culture of poverty" advocates, particularly Oscar Lewis. First enunciated by him in 1959, the idea that there exist "cultures of poverty" received extended treatment in his study of Puerto Ricans in San Juan and New York. Lewis specifically noted that "the term 'subculture of poverty' is technically more accurate," and he used "culture of poverty." for convenience (1966a:xliii). The "culture of poverty" was frequently used to describe the lives of particular ethnic groups and neighborhoods. It was another way of labeling ways of living that appeared deviant from the "American mainstream."

Anthropologists have properly criticized sociological pronouncements that find urban black families enmeshed in "a tangle of pathology" (Moynihan 1965:47) or characterize the kinship behavior of Southern Appalachian people as "neurotic emotional entanglements" (Ball 1971:75). Yet, we betray the same tendency to conceive of the entire United States as encompassing a single cultural pattern by describing variations as "deviant" or "subcultural." Deviant from what? If subcultural, what constitutes the culture they are variants of? Wallace's (1961) demonstration of the *necessity* for nonsharing of certain elements of culture should caution us to expect our own society to be as problematic as others with respect to what is shared, by whom, and to what extent.

One of the most interesting features of the relationships between anthropology and public policy in the recent past has been the alacrity with which policy makers took up the idea of a "culture of poverty." It was broadcast in a number of simplified and popularized versions and is credited with much influence on national policy (Valentine 1971:193). The massive War on Poverty mounted by the federal government in the 1960s was based, according to Gladwin, "upon a definition of poverty as a way of life" (Gladwin 1967:26). The entire series of programs—VISTA, Job Corps, Head Start, and so on— aimed at changing attitudes, beliefs, and values, rather than on redistributing wealth and power. Lewis had indicated that poverty was probably easier to change than the *culture* of poverty, federal programs went for the tough goal: cultural retraining.

Anthropologists' conceptions of a unitary or mainstream culture for the United States were congruent with the assumptions that underlay these federal programs. The phrase "pockets of poverty" recognized poverty as a localized blight on an otherwise healthy and homogeneous cultural body. Subcultures of poverty, usually found in ethnic neighborhoods (Valentine 1968:125), were problems to be solved, deviants to be reconditioned and incorporated into standard American life. An alternative to the opinion that Lewis' "culture of poverty" idea was influential in itself is the suggestion that it served as a focal point for a view of the United states and its problems that was shared by government policy makers and many anthropologists.

As the anthropological study of the United States became more acceptable as a professional specialty, a new perspective emerged. With some exceptions (e.g., DeVos and Romanucci-Ross 1975), ethnicity came to be seen as not necessarily stigmatic, and heavy criticism of the "culture of poverty" idea made it less persuasive as an explanatory mechanism. Studies of black Americans treated them less as social problems than as distinctive cutural categories within American society. Linguistically, they were found to be different in very basic ways (Labov 1968). In Liebow's *Tally's Corner* (1967), Hannerz's *Soulside* (1969), and Stack's *All Our Kin* (1974), blacks are portrayed as acting rationally, given the constraints placed on their behavior. A new militancy among Native Americans led to greater appreciation of them as more than simply remnants from a disturbing imperialistic past. As litigation to reclaim tribal lands proceeded, a new recognition of Indians as citizens demanding their rights took hold, at least in some segments of the society.

Increasingly, the United States is now acceptable as a professional area for anthropological investigation; larger numbers of anthropologists strike out to mine this rich but formerly devalued lode. The changing perspective on anthropological study of the United States is partly derived from the social and cultural milieu in which the anthropologist is simultaneously researcher and citizen. Those roles being more sharply recognized and distinguished, the path is opened for scholarly study as distinct from citizen partisanship.

Conclusions

From this review of policy and anthropology and their relationship, several points emerge clearly and provide material for constructing guides for the future. The difficulty of bringing an anthropological perspective to bear on the problems of our own society, and in defining those problems, should not be underestimated.

If our goal is to contribute to the making of policy as anthropologists, our most productive course is to treat the United States as we have treated other societies. In doing so, we can produce descriptions and analyses of value to both anthropology and policy makers. From this perspective, the anthropologist could:

1. *Explicate the logic and consequences of public policy.* Rather than stand on the sidelines or steadfastly take up partisan positions, anthropologists should be equipped by their training to undertake a dispassionate analysis of the implications of proposed public policy, and that which is operative at present. As an example, let us consider current federal policy toward minorities. Anthropologists might examine the consequences of the federal definition of minority people, and draw out the implications for particular regions where minorities not officially recognized constitute a significant proportion of the local population. Policies toward minorities appear to have tendencies in two directions: toward insuring the maintenance of procedural equality (a policy of nondiscrimination) and toward bringing about substantive equality. The latter is operative in busing schoolchildren to achieve ethnic balance, in instituting programs of bilingual education, in establishing quotas for hiring and firing in federal contract work, and so forth. These two tendencies are sometimes congruent with each other—as in the affirmative action programs—and sometimes in conflict. There is a potential conflict, too, between busing schoolchildren and maintaining bilingual education: the achievement of appropriate ethnic balance could lead to distributing throughout an entire school system those most likely to benefit from bilingual classroom instruction. The well-known characteristic, whether by choice or not, for immigrants from the same country to belong to the same residential neighborhood seems to carry little weight in policy making. Strident calls for community control of local schools merely reveal another kind of partisanship. A cool-headed, ethnographically sound analysis could be more useful for policy and theory.

2. *Investigate the relationships between ideology and practice.* A task we have long been carrying out elsewhere, this kind of study

of ethnic policy is strongly needed. Glazer's contention, for example, that the nation is violating its sacred ideals of individual equality by the use of affirmative action programs deserves close attention (Glazer 1975). This apparent discrepancy between ideology and practice is at issue in a number of legal arenas. The California Supreme Court, for example, ruled in late 1976 that a medical school's policy of reserving a number of places for minority students in its entering class was unconstitutional (Anonymous 1976). What are the consequences of a policy of "reverse discrimination" for other aspects of American life? Should such a policy be limited to a particular period of time? Anthropologists are fit by training and outlook to examine these kinds of policy issues.

3. *Bring cross-cultural perspectives to bear on policy-related problems.* The application of public policy on ethnicity will doubtless increase the pluralistic features of American life. Anthropologists, in investigating such issues, can draw on an extensive body of data and theory developed in the Caribbean, Africa, and Southeast Asia. If the United States is headed toward either structural or cultural pluralism, then the experts in this kind of society are anthropologists. Just as we have performed as expert witnesses in the Indian land claims cases, we may also be called upon in the near future to play the same role in ethnic conflicts. If cultural differences become the criterion for such issues as federal aid, anthropologists are the obvious scholarly spokesmen.

In exploring for ourselves a larger role in public policy, the calm advice of Belshaw is appropriate as a conclusion:

The social scientist, then, should be reasonably modest in his claims; he should not go as far as many of my colleagues who say, for example, that since we don't know everything perhaps we know nothing, and that we should not use our knowledge as the basis for advice, since it is bound to be incomplete. Our responsibility, if we decide to enter this world, is to use our knowledge, give our advice, generate ideas, but never pretend that they have the kind of authority that can be provided in certain circumstances, in other fields, by physicists or engineers. (Belshaw 1976:275)

And if a deaf ear is all the response we get for our advice, take heart, for we are, historically speaking, in good company.

17

THE REORGANIZATION OF SCHOOLING: AN ANTHROPOLOGICAL CHALLENGE

Elizabeth M. Eddy

The evolution of public educational policy in America has occurred within the context of rapid social and cultural changes in American life. Historically, the organizational models of American schooling have been based on the production models of the factory. The emergent contemporary models for organizing the work of the school continue the custom of adapting industrial forms of organization to educational purposes and reflect changes in these. Here Elizabeth M. Eddy describes these models and discusses their significance for anthropologists.

Despite a growing body of anthropological research which is highly relevant to the organization of formal education, the empirical data of anthropology have been ignored in the formulation of educational policy. This problem is a critical one because the anthropological data suggest that schools are not adapting to the empirical realities of American cultural pluralism or the need to develop holistic approaches to knowledge in a world characterized by interdependent relationships with others and with the environment. Richardson, Hill-Burnett, and Miller have all underscored and further illustrated several of Eddy's major points. Viewed in juxtaposition with each other, all of these essays argue the need for major changes in current educational policies and for anthropologists to become actively involved in educational change.

EVER SINCE THE early days of American public education, the organizational models of formal schooling have reflected major phases of American history and cultural variations in the prevailing commumity systems of the nation. With the rise of industrialism and urbanization after 1865, it was only natural that the formal educational system was transformed from one which gave expression to the values of a rural America to one based on an urban world view and the business and industrial values which dominated American life at the turn of the century. Today, a similar transformation in schooling is appearing as a response to the emergence of a technological society and the human settlement patterns of metropolis and megalopolis.

The large bureaucratically organized school systems of contemporary America represent an application of business, industrial, and technological forms of organization to the problem of preparing children and youth for adult roles as citizens and workers in our society (Callahan 1962; Tyack 1974). Founded on a model of business efficiency, today's schools were originally an adaptation of the factory form of organization which existed during the latter half of the nineteenth century. The factory division of labor, chain of command, coordination, and mass production efficiency were viewed by many educators and others as the solution to the problem of transforming loosely structured village school systems into more centralized systems capable of responding to the economic and demographic transformations which were occurring in the cities (Tyack 1974:28–58). The movement towards greater centralization and mass education which began at that time continues to this day and affects all aspects of American formal education.

During the early twentieth century, the factory model yielded to the business corporation model. The major consequences of this change were greatly increased power for school superintendents, centralization of political power in comparatively small school boards who represented urban business and professional elites, and removal of power from decentralized ward-based school boards who represented local neighborhoods and citizens. School superintendents and their staffs became accepted as the experts in school management to whom almost total administrative power should be delegated, with the school board acting as a corporate board of directors who approved plans to be implemented by professional educators (Cronin 1973; Tyack 1974:126–176). During the last twenty years, similar trends have taken place in higher education where statewide coordinating agencies, responsible to a state board of citizens, have grown as a response to mass education at the post-secondary level (Halsted 1974:1–43).

For several decades, schools have been largely organized according to Taylor's *Principles of Scientific Management* (1911) for industrial efficiency. These stress the need for a managerial system to develop scientific understanding of each element of the work to be done, scientific selection and training of workers, and supervision of work to ensure that it is properly done according to scientific principles. Translated into the educational system, Taylor's principles provide the rationale for a standardized arrangement of pupils and teachers in space and time according to the work to be accomplished. While higher education has traditionally been exempt from the worst features of scientific management, it too has increasingly become subject to a managerially dominated system which is radically altering our colleges and universities (Halsted 1974).

What is the relationship between anthropological knowledge about the processes of education and the organizational models which have predominated formal schooling in America? Why is it important that anthropologists should become concerned with public policies which affect the formal educational settings in which children and youth are prepared for work and life in our society? These questions are the focus of this essay. Before turning to them, I present a general overview of the current social organization for the formal educational processing of pupils, the work of teaching and learning, and the management of the educational enterprise. Thus, the next several pages examine the following questions and provide essential background for the later discussion of the need for anthropologists to address themselves to issues of educational policy.

What is the world view of those who manage our educational system? How is it reflected in the organizational models utilized in operating the system? How do the models structure the patterns of interaction and relationships as these exist in time and space within the school and between school and community? What have been the changes in organizational models over time, and how are they related to technological change? What are the congruencies between the models and our society?

The Educational Production System

A major consequence of the application of business industrial forms of organization to our educational system has been the rise of a managerial ethos which views schools as factories and the educational process as a production system. Pupils are defined as human raw materials who are to be turned into products capable of meeting the needs of society for good citizens and specialized laborers. The burden of processing them through the educational system is the responsibility of teachers, working under the direction of a managerial elite who specifies production methods and goals and generally plans and controls classroom activities.

The mass production system of students relies heavily on small batch and unit production methods. Within industry, small batch production allows several items to be manufactured simultaneously (Whyte 1969:58). The educational version is the practice of batching students together who are of the same age and achievement level as measured by standardized tests. It is argued that homogeneous groupings provide greater individualization of instruction as pupils of varying abilities proceed at different rates through a lock step curriculum which divides knowledge into compartments according to subject and sequential levels of increasing difficulty. Each class of students is assigned to a separate teacher, working in a separate classroom, to provide them simultaneously with the same instruction, using the same books and materials. At the elementary level, one generalist teacher teaches all academic subjects to the same class throughout a school year. In the secondary school, pupils are assigned to a series of specialized teachers in each subject area—a pattern which continues in the more elaborately specialized and departmentalized college and university structure.

The unit production model wherein individual items are custom-made is common only at the advanced graduate level where students pursue independent individual work under the tutelage of a faculty member or committee. At the undergraduate and secondary levels, only talented honors students or those who need tutorial work, usually for remedial purposes, are likely to receive a custom-tailoring of the curriculum to meet individual needs and abilities.

The factory model, with its self-contained classrooms manned by solitary teachers and its compartmentalized levels and stages of pupil-processing, is based on large numbers of managerially standardized production units, classified according to the stage which the student product has reached at particular points in time. Over time, students are passed on to more advanced stages of processing along an educational assembly line designed to turn out a variety of human products who can fit into adult roles in our society. Yet, for 25 percent of our children and youth, the system as we have known it has been a factory for failure in attaining the minimal skills of communication and computation required for significant participation in American life today. This fact, together with the development of an educational technology more versatile than the standardized textbook, and the evolution of a world which is changing so rapidly that what is learned in school today is often dated tomorrow, has resulted in contemporary attempts to modify the social organization of pupil-processing.

The proposed new organizational model continues the practice of applying industrial organizational forms to the processing of pupils perceived as raw materials. But the industrial-business model is now that which has accompanied the technological revolution of the twentieth century. In the modern corporation, organization is no longer viewed as merely a human replica of a factory building containing a number of individual workers and their supervisors. Rather, the organization appears as "networks or patterns of sequential work operations that link production stages, staff and line personnel, and hourly workers. Work and systems are synonymous (Sayles 1964:22)." The individual's contribution is valuable only when made in the right place and time in a sequence. The purpose of organization is to ensure that this occurs, and lateral relations which tie together highly specialized and differentiated work units become equally or more important than traditional pyramidal relationships (Sayles and Chandler 1971:17–18).

A chief characteristic of technologically based industries is the continuous process operation in which activities must be constantly manned. These operations separate workers from physical contact with the product. Work flows through tubes and machines untouched by human hands; the worker's responsibility is to monitor it (Whyte 1969:58).

The replacement of the educational factory model with one based on more recent ways of organizing industrial production is taking several forms. The most important is the combination of nongraded classrooms, team teaching, and individualized instruction into an organizational model which operationalizes the continuous progress of every child in the school in an attempt to eliminate failure. A particular school may have all, some, or none of the above innovations, but an increasing number of schools are adopting one or more of these new approaches to the social organization of the classroom.

The emergent continuous progress movement alters the lockstep rigidities of past curricular sequences and homogeneous grouping of pupils according to age and ability. The small batch production model yields to a unit production model based on diagnostic testing and individualized learning treatments designed and monitored to enable pupils to master specified performance objectives. The production goal is the mastery of skills, irrespective of the time required. Students are measured against their own past performance rather than against the performance of others. The continuous progress of the individual pupil becomes important rather than his or her competitive standing vis-à-vis peers of the same age. Traditional ways of grading pupils and reporting grades are eliminated or supplemented by progress reports which describe what a pupil is able to do at a particular time and the progress made over time (Hillson and Hyman 1971:33–40).

Implementation of the continuous progress philosophy requires a reordering of pupils, teachers, and educational activities in space and time. The passing of the old compartmentalized ordering is visibly expressed by contemporary architectural designs for school buildings. As traditional walls separating classrooms come tumbling down and are no longer built, open, multipurpose flexible spaces designed for continuous learning appear. They are symbols that the educational factory system of the first industrial revolution is now obsolete.

Within both modern school buildings and many old ones, the new industrial pattern for educational organization is steadily evolving. It is especially evident in nongraded classrooms which bring together fifty to one hundred or more pupils of diverse age, achievement, and social background who are assigned to a team of two or more teachers who collaborate in planning their instructional program. Although team units of pupils and teachers are allocated specific space within the school, the traditional "home room" has now become a "home base"—a fixed point from which individuals disperse and to which they return, but it is no longer a self-contained classroom which is the exclusive territory of a single teacher.

A hallmark of the reorganized school is modular flexible scheduling in lieu of the rigid schedules of the past. Flexible scheduling allows both pupils and teachers greater mobility in space and time and a resultant diversity in the location and pacing of learning activities. Classrooms *per se* are no longer the sole center of educational activities, which now occur in a variety of differentiated physical settings, such as media centers, learning laboratories, and teacher workrooms, which are located throughout the school or even outside of it. Consequently, major organizational efforts are required to ensure that the right pupils are at the right place at the right time. The burden of this task falls upon the teaching team whose work arrangements represent significant alterations in the traditional flow of educational work and the nature of teaching itself. The details given below will further illustrate the impact that new industrial organizational models have had on our schools.

Work Flow and the Nature of Teaching

In the obsolete educational factory, work flow consisted of a sequence of patterned activities wherein students moved in compartmentalized units from primary and elementary phases of production through to final completion of the secondary stage or an optional post-secondary stage. In this model, teacher work flow comes in terms of classes of pupils for whom standardized educational activities are provided. When one teacher has performed his or her part of the educational processing, students are passed on to the next teacher in the work flow sequence, with the exception of those who are retained for reprocessing or allowed to skip one of the production stages. The pace of the work flow is largely controlled by management through curriculum guides and other supervisory activities which establish the general sequence of work, the amount of work to be done, the time to be allocated to it, and norms for achievement within the specified time limitations.

In the past, efficient functioning of the educational assembly line has depended on a smooth flow of students from point to point in space and time. While teachers can be briefly away from their positions without shutting the assembly line down, prolonged absence requires a substitute who can step in and keep the line moving. Mass prolonged absences, as in the case of a teacher strike, bring the line to a halt. Similarly, if a teacher moves more slowly than the norm by failing to dismiss pupils on time or by neglecting to prepare them for more advanced production stages, the fact will become evident to management and a source of complaint. Thus, teacher productivity and accountability has been a function of how quickly teachers accomplished the processing of pupils, as measured by the number of student products they turned out and whether or not they were slow, average, or advanced.

The traditional organizational structure of schools emphasizes the vertical relationships of those in the educational system. Through vertical transmission of knowledge and skills, mature teachers teach immature pupils by planning classroom activities which enable students to ascend to the next higher production level. Through vertical transmission also, the former first line supervisory teachers who have joined the managerial ranks pass on rules and regulations, rewards and punishments, and requests and demands that set the organizational boundaries within which teaching occurs. Pyramidal vertical relationships are also characteristic of relationships between schools and parents.

Remodeling of the school organization along the lines of more recent industrial work organizations alters both the customary work flow patterns and the nature of teaching. Team teaching necessitates abandonment of teacher autonomy and exclusive focus on vertical relationships between a single teacher and class of pupils. It requires that teachers work collaboratively in lateral relationships and share instructional responsibility for the same group of pupils. Team teaching also implies daily interdependent reciprocal working relationships between teachers, in contrast to teacher independence of others. The activities of one teacher are contingent upon those of one or more of the other members of the team, and teachers must jointly plan for coordination of activities in terms of space, time, materials, and instructional content. Crucial decisions must be made about the abilities, skills, and specialized knowledge that individual teachers can contribute to team efforts. Corollary decisions specify which pupils should be where, when, and with whom, for what kind of educational processing (Shaplin and Olds 1964; Smith and Keith 1971:209–234).

Essentially, team teaching entails the development of a taxonomy of teaching tasks as a basis for a division of labor and specialization among team members. At the same time, pupils and their learning needs are diagnosed and classified so that students may be grouped and regrouped according to their differential achievement within subject areas (Shaplin and Olds 1964; Smith and Keith 1971:209–234). Networks or patterns of sequential instructional and learning tasks are operationalized for each pupil, and it is these that link together the stages of the production process, the team members and auxiliary personnel who work with the team. While work flow continues to come in terms of pupils, they are no longer provided with standardized activities designed for those of their general class, but with individualized and specialized treatment of their particular learning problem.

Increased specialization of teaching roles and greater specificity of pupil learning needs are carried a step further when individualized instruction, with the aid of technological hardware and technologically programmed instructional materials, is utilized in a major way. Technological tools permit a diversity of pupil groupings and instructional materials which were unknown in the classrooms of a different era. For example, all pupils assigned to a team, or even to a single teacher in a self-contained classroom, may work towards the same goal using different materials and rates of progress, or pupils may work toward different goals with varying materials and rates of progress. In some cases, goals, materials, and rates of progress may be largely determined by the pupils themselves in consultation with the teacher (Smith and Keith 1971:330–331).

Whether within or outside of a team organization, technologically based individualized instruction is designed to transform the work of teachers. Teachers are no longer viewed as dispensers of knowledge but as "catalysts'" of inquiry and organizers of learning (Smith and Keith 1971:34; Gross et al. 1971:12–15). Their role is one of managing sequenced *systems* of learning with the aid of the rapidly developing educational technology provided by the private sector. In the fail-proof school envisioned by some educators, the reduction of knowledge to prespecified measurable behavioral objectives, performance criteria, and outcomes becomes the requisite first step to the technological production of educational programs which will guarantee results, even among chronic failures. Unlike their counterparts of today and yesterday, the future teachers of America will not be called on to "initiate untried proposals," but to take over the operation of programs that have already been tested by industry and found to be successful (Lessinger 1970:134). Freed from the burden of teaching as we have known it, the work of teachers will become diagnostic and managerial as they monitor the continuous progress of children linked to a work flow process which moves through technological learning systems untouched by their hands.

Contemporary Educational Management

The technologically based reorganization of pupil processing has been accompanied by the renascence of a vigorous emphasis on the technocratic scientific management of schools. Under the rubrics of planning–program–budgeting, accountability, performance based teacher education, behavioral objectives, and performance contracting, contemporary neo-Taylorites aspire to utilize the ideology, rationale, and methods of systems engineering to design and manage our educational system.

In professional engineering, the techniques of systems analysis provide ways of analyzing engineering systems as a whole and to discover the orderly interdependent relationships of the parts and the ways in which modifications in one of the parts affects other parts and the entire system. The use of systems analysis permits a more scientific analysis in order to maintain and effect technical control of physical systems. Although engineers have utilized these techniques in industry, the space program, and the military to design more effective complex engineering systems, their usefulness in resolving major social and educational problems has yet to be demonstrated (Hoos 1972; Smith 1975). Nevertheless, the "systems management" of education has become widespread during the 1970s.

The trends are evident in many state educational systems, the adoption by teacher training institutions of performance based programs of teacher education, the requirement of several state certification agencies that teachers be trained in this type of program as a condition of certification, the pressure to require that teachers use behavioral objectives, the adoption of program budgeting by several states, and the proliferation of techniques at all levels of government to continuously monitor educational activities and results. Throughout the country, consulting firms, interstate commissions, public officials and others are reducing the educational system to numbers which can be computerized and compiled into management information systems for use in cost-benefit analyses, predictive models of enrollment and manpower trends, and the development of systems for controlling, operating, planning, and evaluating educational institutions.

The current resurgence of educational scientific management reflects general citizen dissatisfaction with the cost and quality of services delivered by our public institutions and a demand that they become more accountable. With respect to schooling, vocal and angry minority groups in slum areas have for several years demanded a return of schools to local community control and a policy which would hold teachers and schools responsible for their massive failure to educate the children of the poor.[1] Within Congress and elsewhere, there has been dissatisfaction that the vast outpouring of federal funds to help disadvantaged pupils has not as yet made a significant change in their school achievement.[2] Others have attacked the schools for their bureaucratic oppression of the young and their insensitivity to the human needs of children.[3] Still other groups and individuals are concerned with the content of the curriculum and the types of values that it expresses.[4] For many, school desegregation has brought fears that the quality of education will deteriorate if substantial numbers of failing pupils are brought into schools attended by their children.[5] For educational administrators and legislators, the rising costs of educa-

[1] Kenneth B. Clark, for example, has proposed that teachers in schools in slum areas should be paid solely on the basis of their abilities to teach pupils fundamental computational and reading skills. (New York Times, July 26, 1970, p. 56). The most dramatic confrontation between those demanding community control of schools and school authorities occurred in New York City in 1968. For further details, see Levine (1969) and Maurice Berube and Marilyn Gittell (1968).

[2] See A. Harry Passow (1974) for a review of efforts that have been made since the early 1960s to provide compensatory education for the disadvantaged.

[3] See, for example, Henry (1963), Holt (1964), Goodman (1965), Kohl (1967), Denison (1969), Herndon (1968), Moore (1967), Eddy (1967), Kozol (1967), Leacock (1969), Rist (1973).

[4] A recent controversy of special interest to anthropologists revolves around Man: A Course of Study. Some of the issues have been recently described by Peter Woolfson (1974).

[5] This issue has been of special concern to educators who have attempted to introduce a number of educational innovations to cope with the problem of providing quality education for all children, including nongraded classrooms, team teaching, and individualized instruction. For a summary of some of these developments, see Francis Keppel (1966).

tion have resulted in political pressures to get more for the dollars spent.

Responding to these dissatisfactions, the educational engineers promise that the utilization of their techniques will provide a quality education for *all* students in the most efficient way possible. One statement on the subject (Lessinger 1970) argues that every child has the right to be taught what he needs to know in order to be a productive member of society, that taxpayers have a right to know what educational results are produced by a given expenditure, and that schools have a right to draw on resources from all sectors of society rather than being limited to their already overburdened resources. The achievement of the goal of "*guaranteed* acquisition of basic skills by *all* of our children" requires the definition of what we want and the bringing together of resources and technology to assure results. Thus, the well-engineered program in the schools will:

require educational planners to specify, in measurable terms, what they are trying to accomplish . . . provide for an independent audit of results . . . allow taxpayers and their representatives to judge the educational payoff of a given appropriation . . . stimulate a continuing process of innovation, not merely a one-shot reform . . . call forth educational ideas, talent, and technology from all sectors of our society . . . allow schools to experiment with new programs at limited risk and adopt the best of them promptly . . . Above all, it will guarantee results in terms of what students can actually do (Lessinger 1970:13).

The utopian vision of the educational engineers is that by applying systems analysis they will gain an understanding of the whole educational system and be able to rationally modify and control it according to agreed upon prespecified objectives. Viewing our schools, colleges, and universities as anachronistic mechanisms, the educational engineers aim to redesign them so that these institutions will become more productive. They recognize that the educational system is complex and human and that the application of engineering theory and methodology to the educational system is difficult because the educators themselves lack clear objectives, measurement techniques, and models for teaching–learning processes and situations. Yet, they do not question the appropriateness of applying the engineering world view to the complex problems entailed, nor do they hesitate to reduce the problems of educational management to technological ones. Consequently, the contemporary symbol of "scientific" and rational management of planned educational change is the planning department staffed by systems analysts trained in mathematics, econometrics, operations research, computer programming, model building and decision theory. These experts possess skills, techniques, and a terminology which few in the educational system understand, and they increasingly provide the data on which many educational decisions are made. Their hope is to achieve greater economy in the running of our schools, but they also promise to make "every kid a winner" and eliminate the losers in our schools (Lessinger 1970; Noar 1972). We turn now to the primary methods being used to fulfill the promise.

Planning-Programing-Budget System (PPBS)

An important expression of the systems management approach to public policy is the planning-programing-budget system which has been a forerunner of other management innovations that have recently appeared on the educational scene.[6] PPBS was initially developed by the Rand Corporation while studying Air Force deterrence strategies, and later incorporated into the Department of Defense under Robert McNamara. By executive order of President Johnson in 1965, it was mandated for use by all federal agencies, including the Department of Health, Education, and Welfare. While federal PPBS died in 1970, many of the emphases of PPBS continue to permeate public fiscal policy at all levels of government.

In the field of education, PPBS has come to imply centrally administered techniques for planning, performance evaluation, resource allocation, and budgeting. Unlike past budgeting systems based on the functions performed, such as teaching, school maintenance, and research, program budgeting is based on program outputs. Funds are allocated according to what they will buy—for example, a doctoral program in anthropology, an undergraduate major in music, a new reading program, or an improved program in social studies.

PPBS activities require that each administrative unit specify measurable objectives, alternate courses of action to achieve them,

---

[6] For full discussions of the pros and cons of PPBS see Novick (1965), *Public Administration Review* (1966:243–310 and 1969:111–202). Hoos (1972) documents many of the deleterious consequences which have resulted from the application of PPBS and other systems engineering approaches to many areas of public policy, including education.

and the cost of the several options. In essence, the program budget indicates how financial resources are to be applied to the accomplishment of stated measurable objectives—for instance, 10 doctoral degrees, 100 undergraduate majors, or 200 high school seniors who can pass college placement tests sufficiently well to qualify for admission to the state university. Subsequently, the measurable performance objectives provide a basis for accountability, demonstrated achievement or lack thereof, and evaluation of whether or not to continue programs.

Planners must show the demands that a program will generate over a period of time, usually five years, and reasons why the plan offered is superior to alternative ways of achieving the desired objectives. Proposed new programs and significant departures from previously approved appropriation patterns must be presented separately and justified. In practice, the preparation of budget requests in terms of PPBS concepts entails the identification and description of resource inputs and production outputs, in budgeting terms, for each major academic and service program or activity in the school or on the campus.

The Accountability Movement

The requirement that educators justify their existence in terms of achieved objectives, which began with PPBS, has now resulted in the rise of the accountability movement in public education. The term "accountability" made its first contemporary national debut in educational circles early in 1970. Addressing the American Association of School Administrators in February, James E. Allen, then the U.S. Commissioner of Education, explained that what has caused disillusionment and lack of confidence in public schooling is "in large measure our inability to substantiate results." Declaring that "the strengthening of the concept of accountability . . . is imperative," he called for research aimed at improving the ability to assess educational programs. (Lessinger 1970:134). On March 3, 1970, President Nixon sent a special message on educational reform to Congress, which urged school systems to "begin the responsible, open measurement of how well the educational process is working." He endorsed the concept of accountability, as follows: "School administrators and school teachers alike are responsible for their performance, and it is in their interest as well as in the interests of their pupils that they be held accountable. Success should be measured not by some fixed national norm but rather by the results achieved in relation to the actual situation of the particular school and the particular set of pupils'' (*New York Times,* March 4, 1970:28).

At the time these statements were issued, the concept of performance contracting and greater utilization of private educational firms for the teaching of reading and math skills was already being explored at the federal and state level. Based on the belief one of the difficulties with public schools is that teachers are overburdened and that schools lack competitors to spur them on to excellence, performance contracting opens up the public school system to educational resources in the private sector so that both teachers and pupils may learn from and about new technological learning systems. Of greater import to the accountability movement, however, is that private contractors are paid according to how well and how quickly they accomplish the task of improving the basic skills of pupils. With the aid of the United States Office of Education, the first performance contract of this nature was signed by the Texarkana school system in the fall of 1969 (Lessinger 1970:91–103 and 141–231). By 1970–71, performance contracts were operating in more than 170 school districts, and educational technology companies had increased tenfold to more than 100 (Chapman 1973:315).

The deepening national focus on teacher and school accountability has given impetus to the definition of classroom goals in terms of behavioral objectives. Rooted in behavioral psychology, the attempt is to define what must be taught, how to know when it has been taught, and the materials and procedures that will work best to teach what one wishes to teach. In a widely used book on the subject (Mager 1962), an instructional objective is defined as an *"intent* communicated by a statement describing a proposed change in a learner—a statement of what the learner is to be like when he has successfully completed a learning experience . . . a description of a pattern of behavior (performance) we want the learner to be able to demonstrate'' (Mager 1962:3). The emphasis is on measurable, observable attributes and on tests that measure performance in terms of goals. To be useful, objectives should be stated in terms of what learners must be able to do or perform in order to indicate mastery of the objective. Thus, ''to develop an appreciation for music'' may be a worthy objective, but it is stated so vaguely that it fails to com-

municate the intent of the teacher. Much better would be the statement, "to be able to correctly answer 95 multiple-choice questions
on the history of music," which describes an observable act that will
be accepted as evidence that the learner has achieved the objective.
Even better yet, would be a statement which includes a criterion of
acceptable performance by specifying the time limit within which the
task must be completed, the minimum number of correct answers that
will be required for acceptable performance, and so on, e.g., to be
able to correctly answer 80 out of 95 multiple-choice questions on the
history of music within an hour (Mager 1962).

Intimately related to the accountability movement and the emphasis on behavioral objectives is the recent demand for performance
or competence based teacher education. This is the name given to a
series of efforts to improve teacher training by focusing on explicit,
observable acts which teachers perform. Here, too, the sole emphasis
is on what can be measured, so as to achieve clarity of results and
precise standards for evaluating prospective teachers. The essential
elements are the public statement of specific behavioral objectives in
terms of teaching competencies to be demonstrated and the criteria
and standards to be used to assess competencies at prescribed mastery
levels. The primary evidence for assessment is based on the performance of the prospective teacher whose progress is rated according to
demonstrated competency. The instructional program for teachers in
training thus has as its major purpose the development and evaluation
of specific, measurable competencies (Arnstine 1975).

Anthropology and Educational Policy

Thus far, a description of the formal organizational models which are
dominant in American public education has formed the substance of
this essay. In retrospect, it seems that the cultural continuities of
present with past models threaten to bring us to the perpetuation of an
indiscriminate application of industrial-business values, with little or
no consideration of educational purposes. There is the continued perception of the child as a *tabula rasa* raw material who can be turned
into a useful product by expert diagnosis and treatment. There is the
perpetration of the emphasis on the teacher as a professional specialist whose work can be successfully separated from whatever human

and social realities exist on the job. There is the persistence of business efficiency as a central concern and the reduction of educational processes to the lowest common denominator of measurement and cost. In the name of equality and progress for all, there is the perennial growth of a centralized managerial programming and supervision of educational activities. Finally, there is the continuous preoccupation with individual differences and accomplishment which views the dyadic teacher-pupil relationship as the only significant one for educational purposes.

While the linkage of business–industrial ideologies and methods to the educational system is not new, the extent to which modern neo-Taylorites reduce formal schooling to a system of computational exercises and educational bookkeeping is unprecedented. This development is particularly amazing because, unlike the situation at the turn of the century when scientific management first appeared, there is now considerable knowledge within the social sciences to substantiate the erroneous assumptions of past and present scientific management approaches to human behavior and organization (Drucker 1954:273–288; Whyte 1969:3–24; Sofer 1972:21–42). The problem is not one of misusing anthropological and other social data but of failing to recognize that such data have any relevance whatsoever to the organization of schooling. Thus, the formulation of educational management and social organization within the highly abstract and static context of program-budgeting behaviorism and accountability, represents a new pinnacle in the low status accorded to the social and human dimensions of formal schooling—a cultural bias which is also reflected in the low priorities given to social studies, the social sciences, and social foundations of education within the formal curriculum.

Nonsocial in nature, anti-intellectual in practice, and antiscientific in conceptualization, the educational engineering approach reduces the school to an orchestrated system of behavioral modification, directed by technological experts whose primary concern is with the technicalities of education rather than its content. In the process, teaching and learning functions are shattered into so many fragments that they resemble Humpty Dumpty after his great fall. What is now obvious is that the formulation of educational policy must be regained from those who have committed themselves, the schools, and the preparation of teachers to a technocratic ideology which fails to do justice to the complexities of the educational enterprise and the society of which it is a part.[7] What then do anthropologists have to contribute? Why is it urgent that they do so?

Anthropological Perspectives on School Organization

Anthropological perspectives on the organization of formal schooling are in distinct contrast to those which have prevailed among American educators.[8] Whereas the organizational models described above define teaching and learning as the primary, if not exclusive, prerogative of the school, the anthropological model understands teaching and learning as processes which occur throughout life in a variety of interrelated social systems. Viewing education as the transmission of culture, anthropologists have long documented the thesis that formal schooling plays only a small part in the learning of the child or youth. In primitive societies where formal schooling does not exist, learning takes place entirely within a network of kin and other natural groupings. What has often been overlooked in complex societies is that kin, peers, and others outside of the school continue to play significant roles in teaching and learning.[9]

By the time children attend school, they already possess social identities within the significant groups of which they are members. They have learned modes of customary behavior, interaction, and communication with others which give expression to the values of family and community to which they belong. They come not as *tabulae rasae* but as human representatives and bearers of cultural variations within the human species. In complex societies, especially, the historical processes of immigration and migration have resulted in rich human diversities and traditions among the children of any given society. Thus, the "standard" child does not exist except in the eyes of ethnocentric dominant groups who seek to mold all children in their own image and define those who are different as deviants who must be made to conform to the standard model.

From the cross-cultural understandings of anthropology, we

[7] See Hoos (1972), Hostropp et al. (1973), and Smith (1975) for a sampling of recent critiques of the application of systems management to education.

[8] It is not my purpose to review the literature in the field of educational anthropology. Readers wishing to become acquainted with anthropological research in this area are referred to Burnett (1974), and Roberts and Akinsanya (1976).

[9] For discussions of the role of family and peers in the socialization of children for formal schooling in complex societies, see Seeley et al. (1956), Whiting (1963), Gans (1962), Howard (1970), Moore (1973).

learn the importance of specific social and cultural settings for transmitting to children wide varieties of life styles, world views, skills, and conceptual styles. Because learning is a total social process of growth and development, it cannot be reduced to a linear progression of isolated traits, nor can it be subjected to individualized mechanistic treatments. Individual differences are important, but they are intimately linked to the history of the child in social and cultural groupings. As a consequence, the social and cultural contexts of learning outside of the school are highly significant variables in the learning process within the school (Gay and Cole 1967; Cole et al. 1971; Cazden et al. 1972; Kimball and Burnett 1973).

What we have said about the child also applies to those whom a society formally designates as teachers and school administrators. They, too, are bearers of social and cultural traditions, customary behaviors, and values. These embrace not only the heritage of birth and upbringing, but also the professional legacy acquired after a prolonged period of specialized socialization into the educational career (Eddy 1969). Historically, the traditional training of educators has been comprised of a technical training directed toward the standardization of their qualifications, goals, and methods as well as their cultural behavior and values.

Yet, technical knowledge is only part of the job of teaching in and administering schools, and diversities of community and pupils require more than a standard response—a fact which is now clear in the massive failure of our schools among the contemporary urban poor. There is need to work effectively with pupils and adults in schools, school systems, and communities, and to recognize that the standardized version of human behavior described in the textbook is largely a totem of upper middle class America. In actual situations, school and community life create demands for flexibility and activities related to the intraorganizational needs of the school and the interorganizational arrangements which link school to community. Unfortunately, the professional training inculcates the view that these demands are "interruptions" to the "real" work of teaching and management.[10] On the contrary, these demands are the social warp and woof of establishing and maintaining the human networks and groups within which the formal processes of education succeed or fail.

[10] An emphasis on the nonhuman dimensions of the job is occurring in many fields of work. See Sayles (1964) for a discussion of this trend in the field of management.

If we accept the anthropological view that education is a process of cultural transmission which occurs in a variety of interdependent social systems and that learning is a total social process of growth and development, we come quickly to the understanding that the child is not a *tabula rasa* and that the work of professional educators cannot be separated from the human and social relationships which exist on the job and still remain viable as an educational rather than custodial enterprise. Corollary insights raise even further questions about the adequacy of the business-industrial organizational model for schooling and especially those aspects of it that are concerned with production management and quality control.

A host of misunderstandings about the school as a social system ensue from the definition of the pupil as the product of schooling. For one thing, it exaggerates the worth of schooling and implants among educators the presumptuous and erroneous belief that they are the only important socializers of children. Further, the definition of pupil as product ignores the fact that students are workers in the school. They combine within themselves not only the raw material and product elements of schooling but also the work element. The view that the work output of the school is essentially a teacher activity completely overlooks the work tasks performed by pupils and the interdependent reciprocal relationships between teacher and student work. It also neglects the significance of lateral cooperative relationships connected to school work that occur between students outside and within the formal classroom (Burnett 1968b).

The current insistence that teachers are solely responsible for classroom work output is so far removed from any understanding of the work organization of the school that it is no wonder that the American Federation of Teachers, the National Educational Association, and others have been outraged by the naïveté of the accountability movement and its crass attacks upon the teaching profession (Selden 1973; Bain 1973). The difficulty goes beyond the failure to recognize that the child is neither a *tabula rasa* nor a product. It also includes a blindness to the defects of the educational managerial system itself and the fact that both teachers and pupils work within an industrial model of education that is no longer functional for our society even when based on contemporary forms of industrial organization.

The critical fallacy of the industrial model for formal education is the intense reification of knowledge—the perception of it as a material "thing" that can be packaged into bits and pieces for individual consumption and bought and sold rather than learned through association with others. Equally serious is the confusion and equating of knowledge with technical performance skills. The isolated parochialism of American schools today and their monopoly of formal education is largely a reflection of an organizational structure which expresses this view of knowledge. It underlies the denigration of the knowledge the child acquires outside of the school, the failure to view family, peers, and community as important sources of knowledge, the obsessive preoccupation with developing taxonomies of knowledge and enshrining them within specialized departments, the reliance on continuous testing and grading of the child, the definition of the teacher as the central transmitter of knowledge, and the emergence of a consumer approach to education which defines the work of schools as producing goods which students may purchase so as to acquire saleable skills for the market place outside of school.

But the relationship of schooling to other aspects of our society is not limited to the economic sector, for the consequences of schooling also affect other social systems. For example, how does narrow specialized competitive training affect the abilities of people to work cooperatively in the solution of human and technical problems? Is failure of many of our large private and public institutions to meet human needs an unanticipated consequence of our educational system? Is the rampant anti-intellectualism in contemporary America a revolt against our educational system as well as a sign that schools have successfully transmitted the view that knowledge for its own sake is unimportant? Do the youth movements into communes, drugs, and protest groups suggest that for many youth formal schooling no longer offers significant human relationships? Does the abandonment of our aging to segregated institutions and communities removed from public life express the value that only those who can actively perform are worthy of significant inclusion in our society? Does the protest of blacks, Chicanos, native Americans, women and other minorities about their place in American life suggest that the industrial form of organization as we have known it, both in and outside of schools, perpetuates a now outmoded class system?

In posing the above questions, the intent is not to castigate the schools but rather to make the point that their interdependence with other aspects of our society makes what happens within them of vital concern to all Americans. It is precisely because schools do transmit the dominant values, customary behavior, and relationships between the peoples of a society that they are a rich source for understanding many aspects of social and cultural behavior. In America particularly, the centrality and importance of the educational system means that it often reflects the social and cultural disturbances of a rapidly changing society.[11] Thus, to talk about educational policy is to raise fundamental issues which go to the heart of our society. What are some of the critical issues being raised in schools today and how do they reflect changes in our society?

Toward the Future

The most basic question in contemporary American education is what we mean by formal schooling as we approach the twenty-first century. Do we mean a segregation of our young into educational institutions, beginning as soon after birth as they can toddle and continuing through the college years, as advocates of extending mass public education downwards and upwards would seem to suggest? Do we mean provision of a wide variety of formal education opportunities accompanied by a publicly financed consumer credit system which allows people to purchase the type of schooling they prefer, as suggested by proponents of an educational voucher system? Do we have in mind the design of a system which many people will drop in and out of according to changes in their life situations, as the attempt to provide special services for women who have raised their families, special occupational groups needing retreading, and senior citizens seem to indicate? Are we moving toward a national system of education, as the trends in federal funding and regulations appear to foreshadow? Do we intend to systematically develop alternate settings for formal schooling and contract out some aspects of formal schooling, as the performance contract movement is now doing? Are we committed to schools that represent all groups in the community or metropolitan area, as the movement away from the neighborhood school suggests?

---

[11] Among several anthropological discussions of the relationship between formal American schooling and culture, the following are especially noteworthy: Henry (1963), Kimball and McClellan (1962), Mead (1970a), Kimball (1974b).

Do we mean the development of organizational structures in which lateral cooperative relationships between school personnel and between school and community replace hierarchical competitive relationships, as the growth of team teaching and the community education movements imply? Do we intend the creation of technocratically managed institutions for children in which they primarily learn to manipulate and respond to machines, as the educational engineering movement seeks to implement?

As the twentieth century ebbs away, there is evidence to suggest that American educational institutions and the society they mirror are on the verge of a sea change. The century is ending as it began, with vocal minorities seeking to realize full participation in our society, widespread discontent with our public educational and other institutions, and the rise of new attempts to apply the principles of a narrowly conceived system of "scientific management" to the major problems and institutions of our society. But the situation is different now than it was in 1911 when Taylor's *Principles of Scientific Management* was first published. During the intervening years modern technology has made it possible for humans to destroy both themselves and their environment. As a consequence, the interdependence between the relationships of peoples to their physical environment and to each other must become the substance of major scientific endeavors to discover the new knowledge and the new forms of human organization that will enable the continued survival of humankind. Hence, the continual utilization of our schools, colleges, and universities to transmit only bits and pieces of knowledge without a holistic understanding of the interdependent relationships between parts and wholes is a potentially lethal strike against the welfare of peoples all over the world. Similarly, the perpetuation of an educational social organization based on a nonhuman mechanistic view of educational processes will become not just an American tragedy (Callahan 1962) but an American and world disaster.

What happens to formal schooling within American society is no longer a matter which can be ignored by anyone concerned with human dignity and freedom and the processes by which people learn to become responsible human beings. The answers to the questions posed above and others that might have been asked are of direct concern to all anthropologists and their students and indeed to all citizens. They represent a critical facet of the need and opportunities to develop an urgent anthropology related to the modern world—an anthropology which claims America and her educational institutions and problems as worthy of the best that anthropologists can offer.

18

USES AND NONUSES OF ANTHROPOLOGICAL DATA ON DRUG ABUSE

William L. Partridge

Similar to the case of education, the genesis and implementation of drug abuse policy is unrelated to the long history of scientific research on drugs, their uses, and their effects. Research activities of scientists may be stimulated by policy, but research does not seem to stimulate policy development or implementation.

William L. Partridge presents a carefully documented case study to illustrate the above points. His analysis reveals that, in the drug abuse field, policy makers have ignored not only the data of anthropologists but also those of other scientists. As a consequence, our policies have not been based on scientific evidence but rather have given expression to a wide range of social prejudices and fears. This is peculiar not only to America but is true in other cultures as well. Thus, effective work in changing public policies about drug use will necessitate more than undertaking research on the subject. Researchers must also be concerned with the development of strategies for the use of scientific data in the solution of problems.

DRUG USERS AND abusers have been studied by scientists since before the turn of the century, and in recent decades scientific work in this area has dramatically increased. During this entire time, public

I wish to thank Vera Rubin and Elizabeth M. Eddy for comments and suggestions on an earlier draft of this essay. Correspondence and conversations with Solon T. Kimball, Eliot D. Chapple, Brian M. du Toit, and William E. Carter regarding parts of it have been very helpful. The responsibility for the use I have made of their comments is entirely mine.

policies have also been devised to control drug abuse. Yet in the 1970s drug abuse was declared more prevalent than ever (Mitchell 1970:22), and policies and programs designed to control it were reported to be unsuccessful in the great majority of cases (Artinian 1975:13–35).[1] The paradox of vastly increased scientific knowledge, coupled with a rise in the severity of the problem and the failure of public policy to control drug abuse, leads me to ask: What is the relationship between scientific knowledge and public policy concerning drug abuse?

In this essay I expore possible answers to the above question. But more precisely, I raise the issue as it pertains to the anthropologist's contribution to scientific knowledge in this area and to public policy formulation and implementation. For anthropologists can bring to the study of drug use the comparative, holistic, and evolutionary perspective which illuminates customs that may appear strange or problematical to other Western scientists. Both the singularity of the data available from other societies where hallucinogens and narcotics are traditionally used, and the methods and theories of anthropology make the anthropological contribution to public policy valuable.

First, I describe some of the reasons drug use is defined as a social problem in most segments of Western society, especially our own. Next I present an anthropological approach to the problem based on my fieldwork in 1972 and 1973.[2] Following this, I compare the data and analysis stemming from this work to those of other scientists who have worked in the same area, thereby showing the significance of an anthropological approach. Finally, the relationship between scientific data and public policy is explored; conclusions are drawn and suggestions are made for further research.

[1] Medical rehabilitation programs, first developed by the U.S. Public Health Service at hospitals in Lexington, Kentucky and Fort Worth, Texas, have a very poor cure rate. The literature reveals that 13.5 percent remain abstinent for the first six months. This drops to 6.6 percent over the next four years, and by the fifth year less than 3 percent remain abstinent (Artinian 1975). Other rehabilitative approaches, such as therapeutic community residence programs, outpatient programs, rational authority programs, chemotherapy, and religious conversion claim higher rates of success, but evaluations of these claims are unclear. Only in the case of life-long incorporation into a therapeutic program (such as Synanon) can the rate be said to be high, and as Brecher et al (1972) note, if the patients leave, the relapse rate rises to 90 percent. The need for new approaches is clearly evident.

[2] Fieldwork from which material in this essay is drawn was supported by the National Institute of Mental Health Predoctoral Research Fellowship number 1F01MH54512-01 CUAN and the supplementary grant number 3F01DA54512-01S1 CUAN.

Throughout the drug cannabis or marihuana is used as my example.[3] But the conclusions reached are not restricted to this drug alone, for in our society cannabis has been treated in folk mythology and public policy as a lethal, socially dangerous substance, just as heroin, cocaine, and other narcotics and hallucinogens. My remarks about cannabis, therefore, apply to many other drugs, although the enthnohistory, pharmacology, and etiology of usage varies among these substances. It is unfortunate that public policy has not reflected this variance.

Who Defines the Drug Abuse Problem?

Considerable public concern about drug abuse in the United States is generated out of a traditional ignorance of drugs other than alcohol. La Barre (1972) has noted the paucity of Western knowledge of narcotics and hallucinogens: prior to the sixteenth century only six such substances were known in the Old World, but New World peoples sought out and identified over eighty such plants. This remarkable contrast in ethnobotanical knowledge is a product of a particularly Western tradition, since these plants occur in approximately the same numbers in both the Old World and New World.

Since the Inquisition in medieval Europe, the centralized Church and Nation-State have been concerned with prohibiting the use of selected drugs and establishing the deviant social status of some drug users, mainly because they were shamans or village herbalists whom the Church sought to supersede (Harner 1973). The Protestant Reformation crystallized the ethos of abstinence, further legitimizing the efforts of church and state to restrict usage of these substances. This negative tradition in our cultural heritage is peculiar to the West.

Hallucinogens and narcotics have played and continue to play major roles in religious rites in most of the rest of the world. In some cases the plant itself is perceived to be a deity: the Soma of the an-

---

[3] Schultes, Evans, Klein, Plowman, and Lockwood (1975) have proposed a reconsideration of the genus cannabis, and suggest a polytypic classification of *C. sativa, C. indica,* and *C. ruderalis.* On the basis of their key, it seems likely that Colombians are dealing with *C. sativa.* Attempts to take cannabis samples out of the country and transmit them to Dr. Schultes at the Harvard Botanical Museum failed. Since I am untrained in botany, I am unwilling to identify the plants in Colombia with a precise scientific name in the absence of corroboration, and have used only the generic name throughout.

cient Aryans or *Amanita muscaria* (Wasson 1968, 1972) and the peyote cactus of the Huichol and other native American groups or *Lophophora williamsii* (La Barre 1938; Aberle 1966; Furst 1972; Myerhoff 1974). In other cases, the plant is an instrument of ritualized communication with a deity: the *eboka* of the Bwiti cults among the Fang people or *Tabernanthe iboga* (Fernandez 1972); the *yáje* of the Tukano of Colombia or *Banisteriopsis caapi* (Reichel-Dolmatoff 1968, 1972); and the deadly nightshade or *Atropa belladonna,* mandrake or *Mandrabora,* henbane or *Hyoscyamus,* and thorn apple or *Datura* of the witches of medieval Europe (Harner 1973). In still other cases, the hallucinogen takes on curative powers and serves the related purposes of diagnosis and treatment of illness: the tobacco of the Warao of Venezuela (Wilbert 1972, 1975) and the Tenetehara of Brazil (Wagley and Galvão 1949) or *Nicotiana spp.*; the morning-glory seeds of the Zapatec, Mixtec, Chinanatecs, and Masatecs of the Oaxaca Valley of Mexico or *Rivea corymbosa* (Schultes 1969, 1972); and the San Pedro cactus or *Trichocereus pachanoi* of the mestizo farmers of the coast of Peru (Sharon 1972). The list is a lengthy one.

In contrast, Western religious life has traditionally valued altered states of consciousness unaided by narcotics or hallucinogens (e.g., dreams, possessions, etc.). As long ago as the Middle Ages, such substances have been suppressed, together with the herbalists who utilized them. Suppression from customary usage was accompanied by purge from the official mythology of the Church.[4] Some altered states of consciousness in Church mythology were probably aided by hallucinogenic or narcotic substances, but they were not interpreted this way; subsequent visionary experiences are generally attained in the West without the use of drugs. Thus the shamanistic trances of Moses, Aaron, Ezekiel, and other Hebrew shamans are interpreted as purely supernatural events unaided by drugs. The visions of the Greek Eleusis cults were probably produced by ingestion of some substances, but are also interpreted as supernatural communication. The raptures of St. Bernard and St. Francis would be interpreted as the ravings of intoxicated mystics only by the most heretical Westerner. The hallucinations of Joan of Arc, the fourteenth-century Saint

---

[4] The folk uses of cannabis survived in eastern Europe, where, apparently, the efforts to impose a single religion and to purge herbalists did not last. Benet (1975) describes the uses of cannabis in this area of the Old World.

Vitus dance mania, and the visionary savagery of the Flagellants are all traditionally viewed as unaided by narcotics or hallucinogens. In the West, altered states of consciousness in Church mythology are unaided by earthly substances.

In the United States and England, this cultural mythology is expressed in historical fact and contemporary experience. The prophetic trances of George Fox and other eighteenth-century Quakers, the violent convulsions of the "French Prophets" of eighteenth-century England, and the hysterical fits induced by Wesley's preaching were unaided by narcotics or hallucinogens. In America the "gift of tongues" of the Shakers of New York, the frenzied spasms called the "barks," the "jerks," and the "rolls" of the Kentucky Revival of 1800, the millennial dreams of the Millerites of 1843, the Beekmanites of 1875, the Wilderness Worshipers of 1889, and the hysteria of contemporary pentecostal sects are similarly unaided by hallucinogenic or narcotic substances.

Westerners have traditionally confined the use of such substances within what Durkheim called the profane or secular realm of social life (1947:38–42). The purge during the preceding centuries from the sacred realm removed a strong motive for seeking out and institutionalizing use of such substances. Even when non-Western drugs have been borrowed and institutionalized in the West, they have diffused to the profane or secular realm. Following the expansion of Europe throughout the world, a variety of previously unknown drug substances became popular in the West. Tobacco and cocaine were adopted from the Americas, and opium, caffeine, and cannabis were diffused immediately from the East. By the nineteenth century, these previously unknown or suppressed (in the case of cannabis, see Benet 1975) substances enjoyed widespread medical usage by physicians in England, France, the United States and other Western nations.

The rapid diffusion and adoption of these drugs was stimulated by the discovery of quinine in the seventeenth century. The product of a South American plant, quinine was the first drug unequivocally linked to a specific medical disorder (fever of malaria) and proven to be scientifically efficacious for its treatment. Western medical history was changed, for until that discovery there had been no empirical link established between various substances used in medicine (unicorn horn, fly specks, pigeon dung, etc.) and specific medical disorders

(Shapiro 1959). A period of conscious experimentation with the newly discovered drugs now began.

Sigmund Freud seized upon cocaine, the product of South American *Erythroxylon coca,* in an attempt to treat his own heart disease (Brecher et al. 1972:272). One of the founders of Johns Hopkins Medical School, William Stewart Halsted, who was himself addicted to cocaine, discovered the surgical use of cocaine as the first local anesthetic (Brecher et al. 1972:33–35). During the latter half of the nineteenth century, over one hundred scientific papers and books were published extolling the benefits of cannabis for use in treating menstrual cramps and excessive bleeding, treatment and prophylaxis of migraine headache, alleviation of withdrawal symptoms of opiate addiction, tetanus, insomnia, delirium tremens, muscle spasms, strychnine poisoning, asthma, cholera, dysentery, labor pains, psychosis, spasmodic cough, excess anxiety, gastrointestinal cramps, depression, nervous tremors, and bladder irritation (HEW 1971:53–54; Rubin and Comitas 1975:12).

This upsurge in drug use was not confined to the medical segment of the secular realm. Some drugs were adopted for recreational purposes, or spread from specialized medical use to general multiple-purpose use throughout society. Initially dispensed by doctors and druggists, opiates were eventually stocked by grocery and general stores in England and the United States during the nineteenth century, and trade in opiates was brisk (Brecher et al. 1972:3–7). In the United States domestically grown opium was common in folk remedies until 1914. In England, the widespread use of opiates in London, Manchester, and Liverpool led Karl Marx (1967:398) to condemn opium addiction as one of the effects of capitalistic exploitation of labor. Similarly, cocaine was used for folk remedy and recreational purposes. When Coca-Cola was first produced in the United States in 1885, one ingredient in it was cocaine (Brecher et al. 1972:270), later to be replaced by caffeine (Brown 1975). Cannabis, initially introduced into the Americas for fiber production, was not widely used in medicine until British research in Calcutta demonstrated its value (Fluckiger and Hanbury 1879:548). The recreational use of cannabis in the United States did not become popular until the prohibition of alcohol during the 1920s (Brecher et al. 1972:406–412).

In summary, after initially being purged from Western religious life, narcotics and hallucinogens became embedded in Western secular life following the expansion of European culture over the rest of the world. What is new to Westerners, as Furst (1972) observes, is not the knowledge that certain substances act powerfully on the mind and body. Rather, it is the widespread popularity of such substances in a society that has not traditionally valued them, and the medical, social, and legal consequences of extensive use.

A second purge of narcotics and hallucinogens, this time from the secular realm, began at the turn of the century in the United States and eventually spread to other countries. Today it is common to think of the health and social consequences of these substances, but this second purge did not originate because of such considerations. The first drug that concerned our government was opium. In 1875, San Francisco passed the first opium ordinance, mainly in reaction to its importation by Chinese immigrants (Brecher et al. 1972:42). As Otto Klineberg (Goodenough 1963:170) noted, the Chinese were initially perceived by whites in California as sober, thrifty, law-abiding workers, and in newspapers they were even described as "the most worthy of our newly-adopted citizens." During the economic depression of the 1860s, however, there was a dramatic change in the white stereotype of the Chinese. They were now described as being criminal, debased, vicious in addition to the fact that they smuggled opium into the country.

The efforts to control opium were unrelated to concern about health or social consequences of opium use. Congress joined the effort to control immigrant opium businesses by imposing a tariff on its importation in 1883, and by specifically exempting domestically grown opium in 1890. Public health was not yet the issue (Brecher et al 1972:42–44).

The United States convened an international opium conference in 1909 and again in 1911, producing the Hague Convention of 1912, aimed at restricting traffic in opium. The British were running cheap India opium to China, hurting the Chinese economy, and diverting Chinese silver bullion to Britain rather than to the United States. In this political climate, and with an eye to American investments in China, Secretary of State William Jennings Bryan urged that Congress fulfill its obligations under the Hague Convention of 1912. The Harrison Narcotic Act of 1914 was the result, and during congressional debate there was no mention of health or social considerations. All political talk was of restricting British dominance of the opium trade in China and implementation of the Hague Convention. The Act cut off opium supplies and now users were considered criminals. (Brecher et al. 1972:47–49).

Similarly, the origin of the prohibition of cannabis was not rooted in public health or social welfare concerns. Cannabis was neither taxed nor illegal until 1937, and the prohibition was due to the efforts of former Assistant Prohibition Commissioner Harry J. Anslinger, who had become director of the newly created Federal Bureau of Narcotics. Following the failure of the Eighteenth Amendment and the Volstead Act of 1919 to prohibit the use of alcohol, Anslinger turned to narcotics and hallucinogens. He had jurisdiction over opiates and cocaine, but he sought to extend government control also to cannabis (Brecher et al. 1972:419). An intense publicity campaign was waged to convince the public and Congress that cannabis was a "lethal" drug and fears were aroused through horror stories of axe-wielding, cannabis-crazed murderers reported in newspapers and magazines (Becker 1963).

The assertion that cannabis was lethal was unsupported by scientific evidence. As Snyder (1971:16–17) notes, the ratio between the effective dose of alcohol and the lethal dose is 1 to 10, whereas the ratio between the effective dose of cannabis and the lethal dose is 1 to 40,000, a dosage completely beyond the range of human imagination. No medical, psychiatric, or pharmacological testimony was presented at congressional hearings. All discussion was only of horror stories. The result was the Marihuana Tax Act of 1937. Since passage of that Act, federal and state penalties for possession, cultivation, or sale of cannabis have increased in severity, culminating by 1970 with sentences of life imprisonment for a first-possession offense in Missouri and the death sentence for sale to a minor under twenty-one in Missouri and Louisiana (Brecher et al. 1972:419–420).[5]

As Vera Rubin (1975:8) has noted, efforts to link cannibis to pathologies such as chromosomal defects, spontaneous abortions, and psychoses, as well as crime and antisocial behavior, have come about

---

[5] Penalties have been reduced in some states like California, where possession of less than an ounce of cannabis is sanctioned by a small fine. But it should be noted that law enforcement authorities continue to seek jail terms for other offenses. The work of undercover agents in high schools in Los Angeles recently resulted in the arrest of many teenagers for sales or gifts of cannabis. Such arrests initiated the process whereby teenagers are committed to institutions, to be trained there by older inmates for life as criminals (ACLU 1975). In contrast, large-scale importers and distributors are rarely arrested.

only after prohibition. Prohibition has never been a product of concern for individual or societal health or well-being. Had this been the case, Congress would have discovered a wealth of scientific data on hallucinogens and narcotics. Contrary to popular opinion, *much* is known (and was known in 1937) about cannabis (HEW 1971:53). Recent research during the 1960s has only capped over seventy years of scientific investigation, and as Hollister (1971) observed, very little has been added that was not already known.

In 1894 the Report of the Indian Hemp Drugs Commission was published by the government of Great Britain. It is the most thorough and complete study of cannabis ever undertaken (Rubin and Comitas 1975:16). The findings indicate cannabis to be essentially harmless. In 1929 a full-scale investigation of cannabis smoking by American military personnel in the Canal Zone of Panama was undertaken by the Army Medical Corps. These findings (Siler et al. 1933) supported those of the Indian Hemp Commission. But neither of these landmark studies, nor the hundreds of scientific articles and books published throughout the world, were considered relevant to congressional hearings.[6]

It can be concluded, therefore, that the scientific data and findings about drug use have been ignored by the federal government. Rather, prohibitive legislation has resulted from traditional ignorance of drugs and political and economic factors. The fact that scientific data and analysis have played no role in defining the drug abuse problem or in the policy-making process must be kept in mind as we turn to the contributions anthropology has made to an understanding of the drug abuse problem.

An Anthropological Perspective on Drug Use

From 1937 to the present, the Federal Bureau of Narcotics has insisted that drug users are criminals who support themselves by preying on society (Brecher et al. 1972:38). Though this assertion has never actually been demonstrated, a great deal of scientific research has been devoted to it since 1937. In spite of this, very little of this research is useful in either evaluating the claim made by the Bureau

[6] For an international bibliography of books and articles available at the time, see UNESCO 1965.

or for understanding the drug abuse problem. A major reason is that questions of social policy cannot be answered by laboratory and clinical experiments (Hollister 1971). Paradoxically, there has been almost no research on the use of cannabis in natural social settings (HEW 1971). Data collected in such facilities as laboratories, clinics, and prisons are not generally useful because of the placebo effect, where perceptions of drug effects and the social and psychological behavior of subjects are more the product of institutionalized expectations attached to the setting of the experiment rather than to the drug itself. Scientific researchers have continued to ignore the work of Wallace (1959), Becker (1963), and others who have demonstrated that the effects of drugs vary dramatically with social and cultural context.

In contrast to the studies of captive inmate populations, recent studies sponsored by the National Institute of Mental Health have recognized that the relationship between man and drugs is not merely chemical.[7] It is this type of study which can usefully evaluate the assertion that the use of cannabis is related to deviancy, parasitism, and marginality (HEW 1971:53).

Anthropologists were hired to carry out basic research on cannabis in naturally occurring human communities in several different cultures. These observers have long noted that the behavior of individuals in groups is a product of cultural conditioning, that patterned social life, results from "conditioning influences from the organization of one's fellows about the individual" (Arensberg and Kimball 1965:45). Values and perceptions develop out of these systems of interaction (Kimball 1966). Thus, cannabis use must be understood within the community context of family life and replication of society, economic production, distribution and consumption activities, systems of belief and perception, and so on. In much the same way as anthropologists have described the natural history of shell neck-

---

[7] Multidisciplinary studies including anthropologists as well as anthropological investigations which were sponsored by the National Institute of Mental Health, have been located in Jamaica (Rubin and Comitas 1975), South Africa (du Toit 1975, 1976), Costa Rica (Carter, Coggins and Doughty 1976), Greece (Stefanis, Ballas and Madianou 1975), and Colombia (Partridge 1974). In 1973, the National Institute of Mental Health brought together specialists in botany, chemistry, psychology, anthropology, sociology, law, and other fields for a conference on cannabis at the ninth International Congress of Anthropological and Ethnological Sciences. *Cannabis and Culture* (Rubin 1975) contains the proceedings of that conference, the first such compilation on the subject by an international group of scholars.

laces, cattle, and corn, we must ask "what is the natural history of cannabis in community life?"

With this objective in mind, I undertook research in 1972 and 1973 in an agro-pastoral community on the north coast of Colombia, where cannabis has been customarily used for generations.[8] Cannabis is illegal in Colombia, but enforcement of the laws restricting its cultivation, use, and sale has been lax to the point of nonobservance. The drug is accepted and positively valued among estate workers, peasants, and artisans in a community I have called Majagua (Partridge 1974, 1975a,b, 1977). The community is characterized by two distinct subcultures, the highland and the coastal subcultures, which are differentially related to some aspect of the production, distribution, and consumption of cannabis. I will briefly describe the entire process, and then give attention to a comparison of cannabis users vis-à-vis nonusers.

The highland subculture, transmitted by migrants from the interior of Colombia in the 1950s (Fals Borda 1955), includes peasants who colonized land in the foothills of the Sierra Nevada de Santa Marta above the town of Majagua, and shopkeepers from the interior who opened general stores in town at about the same time. The two groups are linked through an elaborate system of exchange relationships involving ritual coparenthood, crops, credit, labor, sharecropping arrangements, and patron–client relations involving small cash gifts and loans. Only the peasants are involved in cannabis production, and each March they plant from one to ten hectares of cannabis for sale to middlemen.

The middlemen are not highland shopkeepers, but upper sector wealthy townspeople of the coastal subculture; landowners of large estates, politicians, and professionals. They handle the international traffic in cannabis for which Colombia has become notorious. The coastal subculture is comprised of an upper sector of large landowners, politicians, and professionals and a lower sector of estate workers, peasants, and artisans. These two sectors are linked through distinctive but equally elaborate exchange relationships, just as the two sectors of the highland subculture are.

---

[8] I chose Colombia for research because of my training in Latin American culture history, and because I was intrigued by rumors of electro-shock therapy being used on cannabis offenders during my visits to José M. Valverde, M.D. Antonio Guerra G., M.D. in Cali, Colombia, in the summer of 1971. These reports were later confirmed by William E. Carter and Raphael Elejalde, M.D.

Significantly, neither the highland growers nor the upper sector middlemen smoke cannabis. On the contrary, such smoking is confined to the lower sector of the coastal subculture. This pattern of usage is unrelated to the huge commercial traffic which links the highland peasants and coastal elite. (For a more detailed description, see Partridge 1975a.)

In summary, there are two patterns of production–distribution–consumption of cannabis in Majagua. One involves commercial exchanges among highland peasants, coastal elites, and foreign buyers. The other is a local, traditional system of exchanges involving estate workers, peasants, and artisans of the coastal subculture. It is the latter system which is of interest here.

If we are to understand the role of cannabis in social life, our focus must be upon the typical interaction patterns of cannabis users. For it is social interaction which defines and gives meaning to individual behavior. We are learning that just as patterns of interaction vary widely between cultures, so too does the significance of cannabis use (Rubin 1975; du Toit 1975; Comitas 1975; Partridge 1975a,b; Carter, Coggins, and Doughty 1976).

In Majagua, the interaction form characterized by the name *chagua* provides the setting and conditions of cannabis use and is the structure of interaction which gives meaning to it. Historically, the Spanish grafted onto the native cultures of Colombia's north coast the cattle estate system and the *encomienda,* the labor recruiting device of the great estates. Immediately adjacent to the estate stood indigenous communities which were taxed for the support of the Spanish cities. In native communities, in the cities, and on the great estates, the *chagua* or communal work party was the vehicle by which labor tributes and taxes were met. Ordinances were passed to permit the natives to continue conducting "their drunken feasts upon occasion of the collective planting, on the condition that there not be excess" (Patiño 1965:392), my translation). Although the *chagua* persists today, it was modified by the presence of the United Fruit Company between 1896 and 1964, which brought wage labor and a migratory agricultural laboring class to the coast (Bernal 1971). Thus, today work gangs are composed of nonkin whereas traditionally they were made up of kinsmen.

The *chagua* form of work organization, called the *minga* or *mita* elsewhere in the Andean region, traditionally involved the exchange of labor, food, and drink among the participants. Indians of a community gathered at the garden plot of one of their fellows or of an estate owner to cut brush and trees and burn off the plot. The owner was obligated to provide maize beer and food, and to reciprocate with his own labor another time. The *chagua* of today is a mechanism of labor organization among coastal peasants, estate workers and artisans. As we have noted, ties of social cooperation were cemented in earlier times through ritual exchanges of valued items. During the heyday of banana production in Majagua, an industrial mode of organization was introduced and, though exchanges linking workers were rescheduled to take place after work and on weekends, they continued to be important elements of life in the coastal subculture (Partridge 1977). With the departure of United Fruit in 1964, however, the region became economically depressed, and a large labor surplus resulted. The exchange relationships which knit these nonkin members of work gangs into cohesive units now became even more important.

Cannabis smoking has become a part of this exchange ritual of the work gang only during the last sixty years (Ardila Rodriguez 1965; Patiño 1969). Cannabis diffused to Colombia's north coast from the Antilles following the completion of the Panama Canal and the vast human interchange among Circumcaribbean countries during its construction (Ardila Rodriguez 1965). Smoking of cannabis diffused only to work groups of the coastal subculture. Life histories of workers reveal that cannabis smoking begins when adolescent males adopt adult work patterns between the ages of twelve and twenty-two. Initiation into cannabis smoking invariably takes place in the context of work out in the fields and pastures, not in leisure activity locations. Informants report between eleven and thirty-one years of smoking experience, and no informant reports that his father used the drug. The neophyte is initiated by members of the nonkin-based work gang.

Gathering for work in the morning, and rest breaks throughout the day, are the occasions for sharing cannabis, alcohol, and tobacco. Not all workers can provide these items for others or for themselves on all days, since wages are extremely low (25 pesos a day or US$1.05). There exists, therefore, an unstated rule that these items are to be shared among work group members with the tacit assumption that others will reciprocate this favor. These exchanges are viewed as important among workers, for there exists a putative superiority of worker values embodied in them, such as generosity, reciprocity, fairness, and the like. Workers feel that the values which have always been associated with work in the *chagua* distinguish them from the elite and highland peasants and shopkeepers. Through the manifestations of these values in behavior, reciprocal relationships of some stability emerge (Partridge 1975b).

Conversely, the breach of the implicit exchange contract brings explicit condemnation from one's fellows. Those who do not honor the subtle obligations to reciprocate soon find themselves ostracized by the label *vivo*. To be *vivo* in this community is to be considered intelligent and active of mind, but unscrupulous and untrustworthy. Such a man takes advantage of gifts from others, a mark of intelligence, but refuses to repay such gifts, which is a sign of untrustworthiness. *Vivo* men are ejected from the work gang.

The meaning of cannabis use in this community, therefore, is threefold. These can be called the exegetic significance, the operational significance, and the positional significance (Turner 1966). The exegetic meaning is displayed by cannabis smokers through verbal statements among themselves and in response to questions, which describe cannabis as an energizer. The smokers say that cannabis reduces fatigue (*quita el cansancio*), provides energy for hard work (*fuerza*), and gives a worker spirit (*ánimo*) for working well. Some men use cannabis in a daily program of health maintenance, believing it to have a prophylactic effect for a variety of illnesses (Fabrega and Manning 1972). Others use the crushed leaves to relieve pain, and some say it can be brewed into a tea to calm a crying infant. But the most common and important meaning is that cannabis energizes workers (see also Rubin and Comitas 1975).

We have seen that cannabis also carries meaning at an operational level, which is reflected in the many ways people use the drug in various settings. Exchanges of the drug are ritualized and highly valued, and failure to honor the obligations to participate in such customs means exclusion from the work gang. Adolescent neophytes continually seek admission to work gangs, and part of the process through which they are selected involves the cannabis ritual.

The positional meaning of cannabis use lies in its relation to a specific cluster or *gestalt* of symbols, and here we find cannabis to be related to some of life's most important goals. Attaining adult status involves not only winning a position on a work gang, but also beginning a family of procreation, building a house, and performing one's religious roles in family and community. These form a cluster of symbols which infuse cannabis smoking with meaning beyond the context in which it occurs. Cannabis is smoked out in the fields and pastures, but the display of cannabis smoking is of wider importance. Its meaning is transferred from the context of work to other domains of coastal life; two of these domains are housebuilding and assembling alcohol for religious purposes.

Housebuilding occurs at the dispersal stage of the developmental cycle of the domestic unit (Fortes 1958). This is the time when children marry and establish a separate residence. Many young men and their mates spend a few years residing with parents before a separate house can be started, during which time the man accumulates wood, palm leaves, bricks, and cement. Houses grow by accretion, first as a mud-and-stick *bareque*, then a brick and concrete wall is constructed around it, and finally a brick and concrete house replaces the *bareque,* perhaps with a zinc roof. The process may take a decade to complete; at each stage the male depends upon nonkin members of his work gang for weekend and evening labor, the loan of tools, materials, and advice. Of course he will spend much of his time also working on the slowly developing homes of his co-workers.

Similarly, all men of the work gang stand at one time or another as godparents to the children of co-workers. Acceptance of this honor means sponsorship of a feast, paying fees to the Catholic priest, and assembling great quantities of alcohol. Food for the meal is not lavish, and fees to the priest are minimal. But alcohol is expensive (15 pesos for a six-ounce bottle), and low wages do not permit a man to save very much toward purchases of large amounts. Moreover, workers do not often enjoy the services of a wealthy patron. Thus, saving money for such large expenses is not a realistic goal, but maintaining a wide range of nonkin reciprocal ties of obligation is. Such ties can be had by investing a few pesos a week in cannabis, alcohol, and tobacco. When religious obligations culminate in a huge purchase of alcohol, a man turns to a number of co-workers from whom he seeks small loans to meet these.

To be called *vivo,* therefore, is a matter of consequence. It means to be denied assistance in achieving the status of *padre de familia,* literally, father of a family. But this means more than mere paternity; it also means holding a full-time job, procreating children, living in one's own home, and meeting one's religious obligations. For most men, achievement of this status is possible only through winning a position on a work gang.

In conclusion, the role of cannabis in social life is not to be understood in conditions which create deviancy, parasitism, and marginality, but rather in those which produce conformity, social alliance, and productivity. The rituals of cannabis use are linked to some of the more elementary processes of social life in the community: labor recruitment, the maturation process, and achievement of adulthood. Those who smoke cannabis produce the food eaten by all others who live in the community. Cannabis is thereby linked to essential economic activities upon which the community depends.

Drug Policy and Programs in Colombia

Since I have shown that, in Colombia, cannabis smokers are not deviant, parasitic, or marginal, it might be expected that differences would be found between United States and Colombian scientific literature and government policy regarding cannabis. This is not the case. Scientific research published in Spanish followed prohibition of cannabis. Laws against cannabis have been in effect since 1928 (Patiño 1967). It is to this literature that the nonspecialist in the government bureaucracy will turn in an effort to understand the drug abuse problem in Colombia, so it is useful here to briefly review it.[9]

Scientific literature on cannabis in Spanish is scant and what exists is not of high quality.[10] Colombian researchers have confined their work to laboratories, clinics, and prisons. No studies of the natural community in which cannabis is customarily used existed prior to 1974. The few studies which are available discuss four kinds of evidence: testimonials of violators, mythological reports, clinical, autopsy and physiological data, and sociological interviews. Examples will be presented of each.

---

[9] For purposes of this discussion it is assumed that bureaucratic functionaries in Colombia are monolingual in Spanish and unaware of literature in other languages. This is not true of Colombian scientists, many of whom are fluent in several languages.

[10] This is not to say that high quality scientific work does not exist at this time, for example, that of Elejalde (1975). But this has been the case only recently.

Testimonials of Violators

Peon del Valle (1933) considered the confessions of prison inmates in Mexico City between 1932 and 1933 to be valid scientific evidence. Prisoners described the effects of cannabis which drove them to commit crimes, and he accepted their explanations. Ortiz Velasquez (1947) accepted the testimony of a Medellín shopkeeper who reported that a single cannabis cigarette drove him to a state of semiconsciousness in which he sold all of the goods in his store for only 800 pesos. Most typical of this kind of evidence is the testimony of a naïve experimenter. Ortiz Velasquez (1947) in Colombia cites the descriptions of cannabis effects of Gautier and Baudelaire in order to demonstrate that an artificial world is created by smoking, as does Bard (1941) in Argentina, Jardines Carrion (1951) in Cuba, and Wolff (1949) in Argentina. Also often cited is Marco Polo's testimony that cannabis drove the religious sect which attacked his caravan to commit atrocities (Ortiz Velasquez 1947; Wolff 1949). One writer, Bard (1941), goes so far as to consider valid the testimonies of "two artists, one musician, and two newspaper reporters" who experimented with the drug in the United States, Mexico, and Cuba respectively. Such colorful testimony may be usefully employed to illustrate scientific data, but in the articles reviewed here they are treated as data.

Mythological Reports

Esquival Medina and Gonsalez (1938) provide one of the most curious kinds of evidence. This is the earliest report of what I call the "iguana legend." No source is given, yet later writers have included it in their official reports (Wolff 1949). The story goes that it is the custom in Central America to smoke cannabis while sitting in a circle around an iguana. Each participant inhales the smoke, passes the cigarette on to the next person, and then blows smoke over the iguana. When the iguana falls over unconscious, the participants know they have smoked enough. Such myths share with the testimonies cited above the common property of being impossible to verify or replicate.

Clinical, Autopsy, or Physical Data

Barbero Carnicero and Flores Marco (1944), Bernath and Martini Herrar (1943), Peñuelas Heras (1946), Wolff (1949), and Perez

(1952) each provide data collected through clinical examinations. Thes studies devote little attention to social and cultural variables, and those subjects which are studied are inadequately identified, so it is impossible to generalize the findings. As a result we know that six psychiatric patients in Medellín reported feelings of euphoria after smoking cannabis (Perez 1952), but since we learn nothing of the social and cultural backgrounds of the subjects nor the social and cultural contexts in which they used cannabis we learn nothing about cannabis or cannabis users.

Sociological Interviews
The assertion that cannabis leads to deviancy, parasitism, and marginality may be usefully evaluated with sociological data. Of the four kinds of evidence available in the Spanish literature, this kind alone could be directly useful. Unfortunately, Peon del Valle (1933), Ardila Rodriguez (1965), and others have relied exclusively upon studies of inmates of prisons, hospitals, and psychiatric wards. The link between deviancy and cannabis in these populations is slight, and such findings are quite useless. Since sociological data are potentially useful, I will compare data collected among prison inmates by Ardila Rodriguez (1965) with those I collected in 1972 and 1973 in Majagua. The problems with studies of captive populations can thereby be illustrated.

Ardila Rodriguez examined the records of hundreds of interviews conducted by prison officials with subjects arrested in Colombia who were cannabis users. From these interviews, he abstracted the following characteristics of cannabis users: migration, single civil status, marginality, unemployment, concubinage, criminality, lack of housing, lack of children, low wages, low productivity, illiteracy, family disintegration, and segregation from society.

About half of all coastal workers, peasants, and artisans live in concubinage, as do about half of the highland peasants who do not use cannabis. Coastal people of this social sector have from one to three years of primary schooling, but the highlanders have no schooling at all and are functionally illiterate. All estate workers, peasants, and artisans of the coast earn very low wages and have no other sources of economic productivity except their physical labor. Highlanders have colonized land and as a result they have more resources, but even so they live at a level of poverty comparable to that of coastal lower sector families. Each group works quite hard in agriculture, cattle ranching and the trades, and these provide the food and daily material necessities consumed in the community. Unemployment in both subcultures is confined to the elderly and adolescents. Criminality is more common among highlanders since they are continually arrested for carrying firearms in violation of Colombian law. Lack of housing is atypical of both subcultures; single civil status (lack of mate) is equally rare; and a lack of children is unheard of in both subcultures. Highlanders are more segregated from the larger society, since they are foreign to the coast and live up in the mountains away from the coastal towns. "Family disintegration" is a concept that is difficult to compare across cultural boundaries, but if Ardila Rodriguez refers to some family form other than that which was typical of parental and grandparental generations, there is no difference. Similarly, "marginality" demands careful definition. Clearly, both users and nonusers are playing an integral role in community life, and cannot be considered marginal by any definition.

Of the thirteen characteristics, only one appears to significantly distinguish between the subcultures. That factor is migration. A migratory phase of the life cycle is typical of the coastal male during adolescence, and it is at this time that cannabis smoking is initiated. Yet, the mere fact of migration cannot be considered a precondition for cannabis use, since all highlanders are migrants into this region. It is apparent that when the problem is conceptualized as a simple matter of matching traits statistically which have been extracted from captive populations, as Ardila Rodriguez has done, very little useful data emerges.

The paucity of reliable scientific data available to nonspecialist government employees and the public in Colombia has not deterred the development of policies which prohibit cannabis. New legislation has recently been introduced which stiffens penalties for cannabis violations (Escobar Mendes 1973). No new research, medical discoveries, or publications in Spanish language scientific journals have stimulated this move. However, considerable amounts of American dollars are being given to Colombian government agencies by the United States government to stimulate increased enforcement of Colombian prohibition laws, as described in the national newspaper *El Tiempo* (June 13, 1973, page 1). In 1971 the U.S. Congress implemented the Foreign Assistance Act, which links continued foreign aid to vigorous prosecution of prohibition laws.[11] One result is that Colombian law enforcement officials are now interested in increasing prohibition activities, for much the same reason that highland peasants in Majagua grow cannabis as a cash crop.

The Role of Anthropologists in Policy Formulation

We have seen that anthropologists, with the support of the National Institute of Mental Health, are making a unique contribution to drug abuse research. I will summarize the major elements of this contribution, and then will point out their significance for policy formulation.

Anthropologists' unique contribution lies in the long-term study of community-level processes, and the description and analysis of the natural history of drug abuse. Earlier, I stated that sociological data would be the most useful for evaluating the assertions of the federal agencies concerned with prohibition of cannabis. But sociological studies of institutionalized inmate populations can be a fruitless approach. Anthropologists, who normally base their studies in human communities typical of identifiable cultural traditions, can broaden the data base to include social processes which produce captive populations as well as other groups within the full round of community life. Such research cannot be conducted in comfortable offices with calculators nor through short interviews, but they must take place in the field of social relationships where drug users and nonusers live out their daily lives.

But changing the location of data collection and analysis from prison to natural community is not sufficient. Anthropological theory and methods direct attention to a specific constellation of variables within the community, namely those which are related to constraints and incentives that surround the choice to either use or not to use drugs. Some of those which have been reported by anthropologists are as follows. The locus of institutionalized connections among spheres of experience (domestic, economic, political, religious, etc.) within a population provides the social sanctions and controls which

[11] I wish to thank Roderick Burchard for calling my attention to these provisions of the Foreign Assistance Act of 1971. See Burchard (1976) and Craig (1976) for descriptions of some results of this policy in Peru and Mexico respectively.

delimit drug use. The networks, corporate groupings, and semiautonomous social fields through which individuals live out their life cycles are patterned into a structure of interindividual relations that constitute conditioning influences. Choice is canalized by such structures (Comitas 1975; Partridge 1975a). Understanding the meanings which attach to such choices entails a concomitant study of the cultural and subcultural traditions which legitimize behavioral choices, providing systems of symbolic logics that not only provide significance but also narrow the field of choice by differentially ranking elements of the cultural universe according to notions of prestige, health, and other aspects of world view (Rubin 1975; Myerhoff 1974; 1975; Agar 1973; Partridge 1973). Beyond these kinds of data, there must also be a recognition that choice among differentially ranked elements of a cultural universe occurs within sequences of fluctuating and shifting interaction patterns characteristic of individual life cycles, the developmental cycle of the domestic unit, and the daily, weekly, seasonal and yearly cycles of community life. The rituals which mark and regulate such transitions and transformations, wherein choices are formally displayed for public sanction, are a part of the temporarily sequenced interplay of symbolic logic and elementary behavioral processes which may be easily compared cross-culturally. Through such comparisons a theoretical model may emerge which will assist us in understanding drug abuse (Partridge 1975b, 1977).

In addition to the unique contributions furthered by anthropological research, there are others we can make which overlap those of other social scientists. An obvious example is in the epidemiology of drug use, the extent and distribution of drug use in defined social and cultural population units. With some exceptions (du Toit 1975, 1976) such studies are usually confined to the United States (McGlothlin 1975) or other industrial societies. Here anthropologists can work with sociologists and statisticians in perfecting the tools of epidemiological survey, many of which are unworkable in societies other than the industrial West where they were first developed. Such studies can lead to an understanding of the true dimensions and character of drug abuse in the West.

There is another kind of cooperative research which can have impact upon policy making. This is the evaluation of the effects of current public policy. To continue with the Colombian example, it has been seen that cannabis is not linked to deviancy, parasitism or marginality in Majagua. The use of drugs was not so linked in the United States prior to 1914. It was only following vigorous enforcement of prohibition policy by federal agencies that drug users were arrested, stripped of their possessions, separated from their communities, made unemployable and destitute, and then defined as criminals (Brecher et al. 1972; Becker 1963; Lindesmith 1940). Through harrassment, drug users were turned into drug abusers. Spradley (1970) has described in detail how this process works. This has not been the case in Colombia, where law enforcement has permitted drug users to remain productive members of their communities. But there is every indication that continuing pressure from the United States will alter this situation. The role of the applied scientist would be to chart the progress of events now taking place, to study the effects on human lives of repressive policy, and to publicize the results. Our task at this level is to distinguish between the facts and the fictions of public policy implementation.

The research contribution of anthropologists, therefore, is one area where we can attempt to affect public policy. But this is not sufficient. As Willner has said:

The Pentagon Papers provide more dramatic evidence than any I could offer of the limited role knowledge may have in the making of political decisions. Politicians and the policy makers they appoint are not likely to be influenced by knowledge unless it is politically convenient or personally congenial. And politically convenient information can always be found to buttress political decisions (1973:550).

In both Colombia and the United States we have seen that drug abuse policies are not the products of scientific investigation or a concern with public or individual welfare. The formulation of policy is a political process, and this fact represents special problems for the applied anthropologist. Many scientists fall prey to the belief that bad public policy is based on bad data and that good data will generate good public policy. This view overlooks the fact that scientific data are rarely a part of the political decision making process.

The first steps toward an anthropological contribution to drug abuse policy formulation, basic research, have been taken.[12] But it is

[12] Anthropological data have been included in recent government reports on cannabis (HEW 1971, 1972, 1973).

clear that this may not necessarily lead to wiser public policy. Kimball (1974b:276) has raised a challenge for anthropologists working in educational research and administration that can well be extended to all of us: "Anthropologists must join with the practitioners in the formulation of the goals and in the strategies of their achievement." If we accept this challenge in the field of drug abuse, it seems clear that we must increasingly become involved in the practical problems of government. At present, no anthropologists are directly involved in policy formulation, and publication of our research findings remains one of the most effective ways in which to attempt to affect policy makers. We must recognize the limits of the utility of research and publication, however, and we must seek to become involved in political decision making. It is not likely that anthropologists will be invited into the process of policy formulation. If we are to assist at all in the development of goals and the strategies for their achievement, the initial impetus must come from ourselves and our continuing responsibility to our profession, our informants, our friends, and the public at large.

19

POPULATION POLICY FOR THE UNITED STATES:
THE ROLE OF APPLIED ANTHROPOLOGY

Sally Kimball Makielski

Sally K. Makielski presents an analysis of population policy in the United States and the contributions of anthropology to it. Her review shows that American population policy is not explicit but rather a series of reactions to needs of the moment based on an awareness of population changes. She points out that, although population growth in America is currently approaching zero, major population issues still confront the nation because of the consequences of earlier growth patterns for housing, jobs, health care, education, crime, and other problem areas.

Makielski notes that anthropologists are newcomers to the field of population studies and that thus far very little of their work has contributed to studies of American population trends or policies. She challenges anthropologists to become engaged in the analysis of population problems in the United States, and suggests the types of contributions that they might make.

JUDGING FROM THE scarcity of activity by anthropologists in the population area, the role of the applied anthropologist vis-à-vis U.S.

Sally K. Makielski (Ph.D., Columbia) is special assistant to the director for Urban Energy Studies, Loyola University of the South in New Orleans. Her past research has included studies of sexual isolation in Drosophila, fine structural analysis of the sperm of a fungus gnat, the maintenance of mimicry in the swallowtail butterfly, a survey of the ecology and pollution of the James River Basin and, more recently, public health problems in New Orleans. Dr. Makielski has taught biology at Loyola University, worked as an environmental specialist for the New Orleans Area Health Planning Council, and served as special lecturer in demography at the University of New Orleans.

population policy is in its infancy and offers a challenging new area of endeavor. Although the United States does not have an explicit population policy, many policies are in effect which indirectly affect the demographic behavior of the American public, thus providing a wide area of choice for future work. This essay is concerned with several facets of this question: the nature of population policy itself; present U.S. policies that affect population; the population movement and the events which gave it thrust; the present policy areas of major importance; and the role that anthropology can play in both the formulation and implementation of this policy.

Population Policy

In its simplest terms, population policy is designed to directly affect the demographic variables of fertility, mortality, and migration (international immigration and internal distribution).[1] More generally, population policy is concerned with population size, growth, and structure (Berelson 1973:145). Such direct policies are usually formulated when there is a clear disparity between the overall good of society and the effect of specific activities of individuals (Westoff 1973:176). When the birth rate is low, official pronatalistic policies result from marked interest in such matters as the need for economic growth and manpower for armies. When the reverse situation holds (too rapid population growth), policies become antinatalistic.

    Because birth, death, and migration rates of a country are only a concern when they disrupt societal processes and goals, population policy directed toward demographic processes attempts to achieve some end and is, thus, a policy of means, the ends being resource conservation, economic well being, and so on (Berelson 1971:177). For this reason most population policies are tied to social and political programs (Berelson 1971:173) and may be either directive or responsive, depending on the circumstances (Berelson 1974:785; National Academy of Sciencies 1974:86). Policies responding to the age and sex structure of the population are an example of the latter.

    Policies designed to influence housing or transportation, for ex-

---

[1] Anderson (1975:3) defines a policy as: "A purposive course of action followed by an actor or set of actors in dealing with a problem or matter of concern." Public policies are those developed by governmental bodies and officials.

ample, have an indirect but sometimes considerable effect on population variables and therefore these policies must also be considered when examining population policy. In other words, population policy, both direct and indirect, can be viewed in a broad context as any policy which affects the health, housing, economics, environment (natural and man-made) and mobility of the society (National Academy of Sciences 1971:70).

Although the United States does not have an explicit population policy, there is a general, unwritten policy to reduce mortality that is found in such programs as Medicaid and Medicare, public health, support for medical research, and speed limits, among others.

On the other hand, while the overall trend in policy appears to be toward a national antinatalistic posture, a myriad of laws and regulations currently exists that both promote and discourage fertility. Laws regulating age of marriage and ease of divorce, for example, are state rather than federally enacted and vary widely from locale to locale (Driver 1972:96).

Only two major positions on fertitity have been taken by the federal government: the Comstock Law, prohibiting the interstate transport of contraceptive devices, which was enacted in 1873 and repealed in 1971; and the 1973 Supreme Court Decision on abortion.

The federally sponsored family planning programs express an implicit national concern with high birth rates in low income groups. These programs, which primarily affect blacks, provide information about and access to contraceptives. While the premise for these programs has been criticized (Blake 1969:522–529),[2] the availability of and access to oral contraceptives and intrauterine devices has brought about a decline in unwanted children among both whites and blacks (Westoff 1976:38–41).

The many child welfare programs (Aid to Families with Dependent Children, day care centers, school lunches) may be considered pronatalistic, but only in the sense that provision is made for children; other similar legislation has also had very little pronatalistic effect (Berelson 1974:785)[3].

[2] See Davis (1967:730–739) for an earlier discussion of the faults of the family planning program.

[3] See the Commission on Population Growth and the American Future (1972) for evidence that these programs have very little effect in encouraging fertility in those receiving the benefits.

The first official U.S. stance on immigration was taken in 1882 when Chinese immigrants were excluded from the country. Later, an increasing concern with the number of immigrants entering the country, especially from non-northern European countries, was formally enacted into government policy with the Immigration Act of 1924. This law limited the total number of immigrants to 150,000 annually and also limited the number that could be admitted from each country.

The Immigration Act of 1924 remained in effect until a new act was passed in 1965. This most recent act sets priorities for family reunification, asylum for refugees, and needed skills and professions (Commission on Population Growth and the American Future 1972:200). The most conspicuous effect of federal policies on the American populace, however, has resulted from policies with some purpose other than that of regulating population.

Viewed in broad context, the United States has adopted a series of policies which affect the population. The most crucial of these, in terms of effect on demographic processes, have been those which affect internal distribution. The only unifying characteristic of these policies is that they have been formulated to accomplish some other end: economic development, improved transportation, better housing (Berelson 1974). Their effect on population processes has been inadvertent and sometimes even conflicting in result.

Of particular interest for the present discussion are those federal policies which have indirectly influenced population distribution. In the nineteenth century, for example, the Homestead Act of 1862 and federal support for the development of the railroads during the late 1800s had profound effect on the development and population of the lands west of the Mississippi River. During the twentieth century, particularly after the end of World War II, the following policies have affected the location of people: transportation, especially development of the interstate highway system started under Eisenhower; government contracts and the location of military installations; agricultural policy that has had the effect of supporting agriculture as a massive business enterprise, thereby driving the small farmer off the land; housing programs; a tax structure favoring ownership of single-family dwellings, thus supporting the move to the suburbs; urban renewal, which has affected the location of inner city residents; and the Economic Development Administration.

Should it occur, the passage of a national Land Use Policy in the future will further affect where people may and may not live; again with the intent of protecting certain types of land (agricultural, forest, coastal) without any direct intent of influencing the location of people. In addition, presently existing zoning ordinances, flood plain zoning, and density controls are examples of local actions where population location is controlled.

The programs operating under the Department of Health, Education and Welfare in conjunction with those of the Environmental Protection Agency, are the ones which, in various ways, affect the quality of life in the United States. While these programs may play some part in individual demographic decisions—where to move, how many children to have—they are undefinably indirect in effect and will not be considered further.

Having taken a brief look at the nature of population policy and the types of policies which have affected demographic processes in this country, it is now necessary to look at population growth in the United States, which sets the stage for the development of the population movement. It is in this arena that anthropologists make a tardy appearance.

United States Population Growth

In the territorial area that is now incorporated into the United States, the 1745 population is estimated to have been approximately 1 million. By the time the first census was made in 1790, it had quadrupled to 4 million persons.

The crude birth rate (number of births per 1,000 persons) which was about 55 per 1,000 in 1800, had dropped to 40 per 1,000 by 1860 and declined further to 27 per 1,000 in 1900. By this time, the population was 76 million.

Also during the nineteenth century, the crude death rate (number of deaths per 1,000 persons) declined from 25 per 1,000 in the early 1800s to approximately 21 per 1,000 by 1900. This century experienced successive waves of immigration, occurring primarily in the 1845–60 and 1865–1915 spans. About 10 million immigrants entered the United States between 1905 and 1915.

Meanwhile, the death rate continued to decline during the twentieth century until it stabilized at about 9 per 1,000 in the 1940s. The birth rate dropped to a low 18 per 1,000 in the 1930s, but unlike the death rate, it began to increase in 1940, hit a high of 26.5 per 1,000 in 1945 and remained at about 25 per 1,000 until 1957. It turned sharply downward in 1965 (19.4 per 1,000), reached 18.4 per 1,000 in 1970, and has since fluctuated around that level (Bogue 1969:127–141).

Between 1950 and 1960 the population increased by 30 million people (11 percent of this increase was due to net immigration) and reached 179.3 million persons in 1960. The 1970 population reached 205 million and is projected, providing the immigration rate continues at its present level, to reach 271 million by the year 2000 (a 66 million increase in thirty years) if the families have only two children on the average, and 322 million (a 117 million increase in thirty years) if the average number of children per family is three (Commission on Population Growth and the American Future 1972:19).

The Population Movement

The population movement came to the fore in the late 1960s partly as a result of the baby boom in the United States following World War II, partly as a result of concern over rapid population growth in the developing countries, and partly with concern for environmental deterioration[4] and resource depletion (Berelson 1974:773; Elliot et al., 1971:186). The movement was composed of persons representing three main interests: planned parenthood, environmental protection, and full equality for women.

The origins of the population movement stem from nineteenth century England (1823), where birth control measures were advocated for working class groups because of their high birth rates (Bogue 1969:18). The birth control movement in the United States began with the efforts of Margaret Sanger in the 1920s and 1930s. Her efforts met with little success, however, (see discussion in Piotrow 1973) and whatever concern had been aroused about birth control dimmed when the birth rate declined during the depression years

---

[4] A companion to this concern is the concern for the deterioration of the quality of life in urban areas (The Commission on Population Growth and the American Future 1965:320).

to such an extent that even demographers were alarmed (Bogue 1969:137; Piotrow 1973:121).

The interest in slow population growth in the United States dates to the 1930s. The National Resource Committee, appointed under the presidency of Franklin Delano Roosevelt, issued a report on *The Problems of a Changing Population*. In this report, the members of the committee expressed the opinion that a stabilized or slowly decreasing population would be desirable in view of the use of the nation's resources (Westoff 1973:169).

The momentum for some type of population policy, especially toward the developing countries, grew gradually through the Eisenhower, Kennedy, and Johnson administrations.[5] A Committee on Population and Family Planning was established in 1968; Public Law 91-572, the Family Planning Services and Population Research Act of 1970, were signed into law by Johnson (Westoff 1973:170).

During the same period, concern was growing in the country over increased pollution and resource depletion and its relationship to uncontrolled population growth. The most outspoken group was Zero Population Growth, Inc., formed in 1968 by Paul Ehrlich, an ecologist and author of the popular *Population Bomb* (Westoff 1973:171). At the same time, the issue of women's rights was growing in force (Piotrow 1973).

In June 1970 a National Congress on Optimum Population and Environment was held in Chicago. This was the first concerted attempt to explore policy issues that could unite birth controllers, conservationists, youths, blacks, and women. Also in 1970, a bill to establish a Commission on Population Growth and the American Future became law (Westoff 1973:170).

Anthropologists, meanwhile, showed little interest in the population movement during its growth and gradual rise to national attention. For example, of nineteen papers given in a discussion devoted to new horizons in anthropology (Tax 1964), none were concerned with the population question. Applied anthropologists, in particular, were notably disinterested in the area, perhaps because of their negative reactions to the federal government following World War II (Mead 1973:8). Macfarlane published an article in 1968 critical of anthropologists for not becoming involved with the population issue.

[5] See Piotrow (1973) for a detailed discussion and Westoff, (1973) and Elliot et al. (1971) for shorter reviews of this period.

He was especially critical that while demography is concerned with changes over time in the structure of a population, most anthropological studies are static cross-sectional analyses. His suggestions for contributions that anthropologists could make include: further research on the effects of various factors on fertility; the effects of improved methods of fertility control on changes in fertility; comparative analyses of the effect of various age structures (number of living generations in a particular population) on attitudes and institutions; and, the effect of population density and speed of population growth on shaping personality and perception.

Expression of active interest on the part of anthropologists appears in publications starting in 1971. Since that time, this interest has continued to grow and, in the following pages, I will summarize the subject in relation to a discussion of suggestions that have been made for U.S. population policy and those policy areas that will be of foremost concern for the remainder of the century.

The Commission on Population Growth and the American Future

The report of the Population Commission issued in March 1972, is the closest the United States has come to having an explicit population policy (Westoff 1974:732). The report received little government attention at the time because two of its many recommendations were considered too controversial. One of these favored removing legal impediments to minors' access to contraceptives, and the other recommended:

. . . with the admonition that abortion not be considered a primary means of fertility control, . . . present state laws restricting abortion be liberalized along the lines of the New York State statute, such abortions to be performed on request by duly licensed physicians under conditions of medical safety (1972:178).

The Commission, composed of representatives of a spectrum of interests, was primarily concerned with the future quality of national life as affected by two major factors: unlimited population growth and an increasing maldistribution of the population resulting in urban congestion and rural depletion.

The general position of the Commission was that the goals of population policies should create ". . . social conditions wherein the desired values of individuals, families, and communities can be realized; equalizing social and economic opportunities for women and members of disadvantaged minorities; and enhancing the potential for improving the quality of life" (1972:112).

The Commission examined the effect and demands of a future average of two- versus three-child families in such areas as the economy, resources and the environment, government, public policy, and education, and concluded that a stabilizing population growth (an average two-child family) would create a better quality of life for the American public.

The second major area of concern was the distribution of population which by 1970 had become 70 percent urban; the Commission saw the role of the federal government as formulator of overall policies relating to the distribution of population and economic activity.

The Commission called for the coordination of a set of national population distribution guidelines with the national urban growth policy provided for in Title VII of the Housing and Urban Development Act of 1970. It recommended, in addition, that the federal government, while in the process of formulating such guidelines, should:

1. Develop goals, objectives, and criteria for shaping national population distribution guidelines.

2. Anticipate, monitor, and appraise the distribution and migration effects of governmental activities that influence urban growth—defense procurement, housing and transportation programs, zoning and tax laws, and so forth.

3. Develop a national land-use policy which would establish criteria for the proper use of land consistent with national population distribution objectives and guidelines.

4. Provide technical and financial assistance to regional, state, metropolitan, and local governmental agencies concerned with planning and development.

5. Coordinate the development and implementation of a growth center policy (1972:226).

Two other concerns stand out in the Commission Report which are of interest to the present discussion. One is with the effect of the baby boom generation moving through the age structure of the population. The other is the increasing segregation of one suburban development from another on socioeconomic, ethnic bases.

The Commission's main concern with immigration was with the

problem of illegal aliens, despite the fact that if native births and deaths had been balanced during the 1960–70 period, immigration would have accounted for 100 percent of the population growth. The Commission felt that for humanitarian and historical reasons, the present level of immigration should remain the same. It recommended, therefore, that "immigration levels not be increased and that immigration policy be reviewed periodically to reflect demographic conditions and considerations" (1972:206).

Population Policy—the Future

At present, the only direct national policies (in the sense of influencing demographic processes) are provision of family planning information and techniques to those who cannot afford them and the Immigration Act of 1965. All other policies, while perhaps having greater influence, are directed toward other goals.

Present indications are that the birth rate will remain relatively low despite the predictions of Sklar and Berkov (1975:693–700) because of the increasing costs of rearing children. As previously mentioned, unwanted births have declined (Westoff 1976:41).

There is, however, a clear need for a national policy on fertility in the future because of the unpredictable fluctuations which occur in the birth rate and their consequent effect on the society. The policy will need to be formulated in the context of the effect of the increase or decrease in the number of births on such sectors as the economy and the environment, and will have to await the development of social science techniques with reliable predictive value.[6]

Various suggestions have been made for the type of population policy that is needed for the United States. These include, for the most part, the already mentioned problem of population distribution—urban growth, rural and small town depletion, and the formation of regional megalopoli (Driver 1970:379; Commission on Population Growth and the American Future 1972:207–227; Spengler 1975:192). Some of the suggested approaches for solving the problem are the following: growth center strategies supporting small towns and cities which have demonstrated a potential for growth

---

[6] See Blake (1969) for a discussion of the criteria for a policy designed to influence reproductive behavior.

(Westoff 1974:752); an urban homesteading act, establishing criteria for optimum population size and/or distribution (Spengler 1975:167);[7] new towns; preparation of citizens to live in any part of the United States (Commission on Population Growth and the American Future 1965:321); subsidized dispersal of industry; and support to disadvantaged areas (Berelson 1974:785). Most of these strategies, which have been tried by the United States as well as by other developed nations suffering from the same problems, have been generally unsuccessful (Berelson 1974:785; Westoff 1974:752). In essence, policies to control the distribution of population are basically nonexistent (Berelson 1973:158), are not easily amenable to government policy, and may be the wrong approach to solve the problems associated with maldistribution (Westoff 1974:755).

It seems unlikely, then, that explicit policies will be developed at the federal level to directly influence either the fertility rate or the distribution of population. It also seems clear that the major population problems will continue to be those associated with distribution—the problems of continued urbanization, economic differences between regions, pollution "hot spots," overcrowding—and those associated with the uneven age composition of the population created by the baby boom.

I would now like to make a few comments about the baby boom. The problems created by the baby boom bulge in the population structure have already begun and will continue to be a national issue throughout the lifetime of this generation. The leading edge of the bulge is now thirty. Having already strained the school system and increased the rate of juvenile delinquency, accidents, and crimes, the baby boom is now contributing to unemployment, housing shortages, and in due course will create a disproportionately large elderly population (Commission on Population Growth and the American Future 1972:17–18).

Given the present circumstances, it would seem desirable that the policies at the federal level governing resource use, land use, urban rehabilitation, economic opportunities, and pollution control be coordinated to provide an overall direction to the indirect demographic consequences of these policies. This will require a detailed analysis of the indirect effects of each policy and reformulation of the

[7] Also see Singer (1971) for a discussion of optimal levels of population.

policy to accomplish the desired goal. A policy or set of policies is also needed to provide flexibility in the society in order to minimize the effects of the baby boom bulge as it moves through the age structure of the population.

Given the broad definition of population policy and the many facets of population problems, the anthropologist has many contributions to make to both the formulation and the implementation of policy. Because of the recent interest in population, there is an obvious need for anthropological research and application. The concluding section of this discussion will briefly review the present status of anthropology in relation to the population issue, will point to some areas of needed research, and will explore the role of the applied anthropologist in national population policy.

Population Policy and Anthropology

Active interest in population problems emerged among anthropologists in the 1970s with the publication of a number of articles and books.[8] In overall terms, the interest was in the long-term history of population dynamics, demographic processes in primitive and peasant societies and cultures, and population size, density and pressure (Nag 1973). More specifically, the vast majority of these publications are devoted to such topics as population aspects of hunter-gatherers, primitive societies, paleodemography, and the relationship between population size and density and social and political organization. Papers have appeared on: the demography of small-scale societies (Turnbull 1972); the relationship between demography, ecology, social structure and settlement patterns (Kunstadter 1972); sexual practices and human fertility (Nag 1972); population size and degree of sociocultural complexity (Carneiro 1967); and a discussion of Pleistocene population size and infanticide, infant transport, and food as a limiting factor (Denham 1974).

The basic premise of the demographic transition theory—that

[8] See (1) an extensive bibliography of prior publications compiled by Marshall et al. (1972), *Current Anthropology* 13:268–277, as well as the series of articles on "Anthropology and Population Problems" also in Volume 13 of *Current Anthropology;* (2) books edited by Polgar (1971 and 1975); Harrison and Boyce (1972); Spooner (1972); Nag (1975); and Marshall and Polgar (1976); (3) a review of demography and anthropology by Baker and Sanders (1972.

human populations increase in number to the limits of the carrying capacity of the system only to have family size lowered by norms created in industrial societies—has been challenged by anthropologists (e.g., Polgar 1972:204–206; Cowgill 1975:513) as well as by others (Teitelbaum 1975:420–425).[9] In addition to recent research interest in population, including interest in developing methodologies and research areas, a number of anthropologists have also become active in the population issue. This concern has been primarily directed toward the developing countries.

Suggestions for future research areas have been, among others, cross-cultural studies of natality differences, inclusion of demographic data in ethnographic studies,[10] analysis of family structure or economic relationships on rates of population growth, and population dynamics among isolated hunter-gatherers and agriculturists (Shea and Emmons 1972:279–283).

Methodological aspects of anthropological demography that should be developed are divided into four major categories: fundamentals of population study, methods of population study, aspects of descriptive data, and data processing (for details, see Shea and Emmons 1972:279–283).

The 1974 World Population Conference held in Bucharest, Rumania marked the first time anthropologists gathered as an international group to confer with population experts (Nag 1975:265).[11] Continued active interest in population issues is evidenced by the participation of anthropologists in the fall 1975 meetings of the World Population Society and the spring 1976 meetings of the American Association for the Advancement of Science.

There have been a few statements on national population problems. For example, Polgar views the primary problems in metropolitan industrial countries as follows:

the maldistribution of the population (including segregation of poor and minority people in urban ghettos); the continued prevalence of unwanted births (but see Westoff, 1976); the ominous deterioration of resources brought

---

[9] See Polgar (1972) or Tietelbaum (1975) for a description of the theory, and Hall (1972) for a discussion of a fourth stage of the theory for industrialized countries.

[10] See Petersen's (1975) discussion of anthropologists' need to know more about demographic techniques.

[11] See this article for a review of anthropologists actively involved in the population issue.

about by the economic system; and resistance to eliminating the remaining obstacles to female equality (1972:210).

However, as should be evident from the preceding paragraphs, anthropologists have shown little interest in United States population problems or policies.[12]

Anthropology, Government Policy, and the Future

Anthropologists have a valuable contribution to make to the formulation as well as the implementation of United States population policy, and in many respects, the formulation of policy is the more critical of the two. In order to be effective, policy should be formulated with an understanding of the interaction of culture with population processes (AAAS 1974:69), the sociocultural determinants of fertility as well as the sociocultural consequences of fertility (Nag 1973:63), and of those other variables—economic and political—which affect these processes and are in turn affected by them.

Policy makers must have an understanding of the set of interactions that produced the present demographic conditions in order to know how to devise programs which will achieve future policy goals. As previously noted, the major areas of policy concern in the United States today are population distribution and the effect of the baby boom bulge on the age structure of the population. These are the areas to which anthropologists could most fruitfully address their attention.

Another area in which anthropologists can constructively direct their efforts is the modification and redefinition of research techniques and problems for urban societies,[13] since United States policy must necessarily be concerned with an urban population. While anthropologists have shown little interest in the use of demographic data (Baker and Sanders 1972:152), they can contribute to expanding the base of demographic data gathering by filling in the gaps in demo-

---

[12] See Shea and Emmons (1972) for a report on anthropologists involved with environmental concerns.

[13] See an extensive and useful discussion by Weaver and White (1972).

graphic information about determinants and consequences of population phenomena. More specifically, it has been suggested that:

The familial and socio-cultural aspects of these phenomena, at all levels of industrial development, may be best understood through coordinated studies of small communities using participant observation, informed interviews, historical research, tests of cognitive and affectual dispositions (Nag 1975).[14]

Specific areas of research are suggested from anthropological population studies of less complex societies. Some of these are: the effect of population size and density on the degree of sociocultural complexity in urban areas (e.g. Carneiro 1967:234–243); the relationship between culture and residential and regional locational preferences (e.g. Kunstadter 1972:313–351); the impact of family size (enlarged or reduced) on culture, kinship, economics, social stratification, political organization, and ideology (Nag 1973:64); and, age and residence as major factors in social organization (e.g., Turnbull 1972:281–312).

While the United States is not crowded on a per square mile basis, this is a frequent complaint of Americans (Wattenberg 1971:97). Anthropological analysis of Americans' sense of space and the effects of the offense of that sense could be another area of inquiry.

A related area in which the anthropologist can make contributions is the study and interpretation for policy makers of the present and future effects on the society as Americans adapt from rural to metropolitan (urban and suburban) living. To cite some examples: Is the kinship system affected and if so, how? In what way are these relationships replaced? Is the move to the suburbs an expression of a rural outlook, or are other factors involved?[15] Is the polarization of suburbs along socioeconomic lines a cause for concern (as expressed by the Population Commission) or is this a continuation of a pattern common to urban areas?

Several authors (Cowgill 1975:515, Dumond 1975:715) have

[14] Quoted in Nag (1975), from a document entitled *Comments and Proposals Formulated at the Seminar on the Draft World Population Plan of Action.*

[15] Many Americans would prefer to live in a rural area close to a metropolitan center (Fuguitt and Zuiches 1975:491).

suggested that one of the primary motivating forces in limiting family size in industrialized countries is self-interest, since the effect of overprocreation is felt immediately. Others (Benedict 1972:83; Westoff 1973:173) have pointed to the fact that low income people in industrialized as well as developing countries see no advantage to family regulation and therefore tend to view family planning programs with hostility. Both sets of attitudes deserve further investigation because future family planning policy may have to concern itself with middle income behavior (in the event of another baby boom) as well as with low income views.

Anthropologists could examine, in addition, the effectiveness of population policies in relation to the American ideals of 'life, liberty and the pursuit of happiness,' especially as expressed in strongly held values of property.

Presently existing family planning programs could benefit from the cultural understanding of anthropology, and anthropologists could play an important role in delineating the cultural constraints under which the programs operate. Moreover, they can suggest approaches for successful implementation of these programs within the cultural context of the target group. As Polgar pointed out:

Anthropologists would exercise their skills most usefully if they were to analyze the social and cultural settings from which the inadequacies of present population programs derive. What cultural blocks exist on the level of government bureaucracies, medical personnel or top decision-makers? (1971:7).

Finally, in those areas of policy which bear indirectly on population behavior, the anthropologist can also act as a cultural diplomat between those implementing federal policy and those affected by the policy. Accustomed as he or she is to working within the context of both cultural systems and complex policy making and policy implementing organizations, the anthropologist is in the unique position of being able to act as an interpreter of the hidden consequences of policy on population problems. Much like the international diplomat, who represents one nation but ideally grasps the needs and purposes of other nations and is thereby able to mediate conflicts, the anthropologist as cultural diplomat can seek out the middle areas between policy goals and cultural values. To be able to do so, however, the anthropologist must understand the powerful short-run pressures on policy makers, pressures that frequently mean making and carrying out decisions with little reference to long-term consequences. And, at least as important, there must be available to him or her a full grasp of the directions, implications, and values which underly population growth and change.

Summary

For the most part, population policy is a policy of means. In other words, policies designed to influence the demographic processes of birth, death, and migration are formulated when population growth is either too little or too great to satisfy economic needs, environmental quality, and availability of housing.

The United States has no explicit population policy, although the statements of the Commission on Population and the American Future approximate an explicit position. Many federal policies directed toward such areas as transportation or agriculture, however, cause population processes, especially the internal migration of the populace.

The major population issues at present are the distribution of the population and the effect of the baby boom bulge on the age structure of the country. These areas would bear the most fruitful involvement by anthropologists.

Other potential areas of activity for anthropologists include, among those discussed, expanding demographic techniques, acting as cultural diplomats between policy implementors and policy recipients, and examining the changing American culture as the country evolves from a rural to an urban population.

20

APPLYING THE ANTHROPOLOGICAL
PERSPECTIVE TO SOCIAL POLICY

Robert H. Heighton, Jr. and Christy Heighton

Based on their experiences as employees of the Southern Regional Education Board, Robert and Christy Heighton consider specific contributions that anthropologists can make to deliberate social planning processes and the evaluation of them. They see the major contributions of anthropology in the discipline's breadth of view, theories of change, study of systemic relationships within the context of an organic whole, means of controlling for value judgments, and use of inductive reasoning. They note that the models and theoretical models of anthropology are only mirrors of reality which must be tested in applied situations.

The Heightons share the conviction of Kimball and other contributors to this volume that, if anthropologists are to effectively contribute to nonacademic roles and institutional settings, applied work and contributions will have to become as valued as academic ones. It is only as this occurs that anthropologists will be enabled to make significant contributions to social policy.

Robert H. Heighton, Jr., (Ph.D., Hawaii) is currently an environmental education specialist in California where he is also a student at the Starr-King Unitarian-Universalist School for the Ministry in Berkeley. He has done fieldwork in Hawaii, the Caribbean, rural and urban southern United States, and state and federal mental health agencies. He has served as director of the Mental Health Program Evaluation Project for the Southern Regional Education Board in Atlanta, Ga. He previously taught at the University of Florida, where he also served as associate director of the Urban and Regional Development Center.

Christy Heighton (B.A., University of Florida) is currently a marketing media specialist working with the Berkeley Consumer Coop, and is associate editor of *Ecology and Religion,* a monthly newspaper. She is a professional journalist and writer with undergraduate training in anthropology.

SOCIAL SCIENTISTS ARE increasingly involved in the formulation of social policy intended to improve the sociopsychological and physical environments of communities. Contemporary problems of population growth, environmental destruction, limited natural resources, food production and distribution, and technological change are all coming to a head in modern forms of urban settlement. Local urban or rural communities throughout the world provide the settings in which people engage in those activities which either worsen or improve the human physical and environmental dilemmas posed by rapid and uncontrolled growth amid a situation of limited resources. Using methods and findings of social research, policy scientists engage in the development and implementation of governmental actions directed towards the solution of these and related problems.

This essay examines social policy planning from the perspectives of sociocultural anthropology. Past contributions of anthropological theory to social policy planning have been largely limited to the concept of cultural relativity (Mann 1972:354). Thus, comparative cultural impacts related to early childhood experience are central to much of the social and educational planning thought that emerged during the 1960s. Planners are also aware of participant observation as a research method, although they seldom use it. However, basic concepts and methods of anthropology (e.g., the concept of culture, the community study method, the present-day concept of functionalism, holism, the natural history method, pluralism, and theories of innovation and change) have yet to contribute to social policy thought and practice.

Our purpose here is to examine the planning component of social policy in light of anthropological perspectives. We summarize some of the key concepts and issues in planning today, and suggest ways in which anthropologists may begin to meet the challenges posed by social policy planning. In discussing issues, we describe each one and then examine possible anthropological contributions to it.

Social Policy and Planning

The policy sciences study the process of deciding or choosing, and evaluate the relevance of available knowledge for the solution of particular problems. Rein (1971:297) outlined the scope of social policy as the "integration of values, the principles by which these values are translated into policies and programs, assessments of the outcomes of implementing these principles in terms of the values asserted, and the search for strategies of feasible change which promise a better fit between values, principles and outcomes." Policy scientists use methods (e.g., economic, sociological, and quantitative) and findings of social research in the development and implementation of governmental actions intended to improve the sociopsychological and physical environments of communities and to meet their dependency needs.

The term *social policy* defies simple definition, and there are at least four different ways in which it is commonly used.[1] First, the term can be used as a *philosophical concept* which refers to the collective searching and actions of communities, organizations, and political agencies for solutions to mutual problems. A second definition views social policy as a *product* consisting of either documents or conclusions drawn by persons who are responsible for improving community living conditions and for the amelioration of social problems. A third definition emphasizes a fundamental *process* through which communities and agencies provide an element of stability (ordered change through time) and improve their social and physical environments by planning for desired future goals. Finally, social policy can be defined as a *framework for action*—as both the product and the process which, if clearly delineated, can serve as a guide for action to effect desirable changes in a community.

Five intellectual tasks involving planning are performed in social policy at varying levels of insight and understanding: clarification of goals; description of trends; analysis of conditions; projection of future developments; and invention, evaluation, and selection of alternatives (Lasswell 1968:181–182). In dealing with matters of social policy, there are no boundaries which divide problems into the disciplinary realms of economics, sociology, or psychology, because problems usually contain components that need to be addressed by several disciplines. Moreover, one cannot avoid working with a problem simply because it falls outside one's own field of knowledge. In principle, the anthropological perspective has always been one of dealing with a total cultural situation.

---

[1] The discussion in this paragraph is based upon Freeman and Sherwood (1970:2–3).

According to Lasswell (1968), as the globe shrinks into inter-dependence, relying more fully on science and technology, social policy will continue to gain significance. Interdependence implies that each participant and item in the social process is affected by the context in which it exists; the future structure of the context is in turn influenced by the changing pattern of detail. To work with this inter-dependence, we need information which is capable of providing rational guidance for attempts to maximize values (Lasswell 1968:184). Analyses of culture and personality have deepened and widened our relevant knowledge, but the examination of policy requires additional types of information about both economic and noneconomic factors, such as the following: educational and health facilities; the distribution of power in society; economic, social, and political stratification; institutions and attitudes; and intentionally induced policy measures designed to change one or several of these factors.

If anthropologists are to play a more active and vital part in social policy, they need to understand the practical operation of government so as to be better able to formulate policy questions, identify problems, produce information on problems, and provide specific situational information (Goodenough 1963). Anthropologists with this knowledge are in a better position to help policy makers examine and understand the daily interactions between the policy process and the systems of programmatic, systemic, and personal values which operate within it.

Social policy is essentially concerned with moral and ethical concepts. Thus, anthropologists who work as policy scientists must deal with two elements in decision making: selection of a set of alternatives to choose from; and selection of a set of preferences against which to rank the alternatives. Bauer and Gergen (1968) note that any optimized model for decision making is based upon a set of preferences (values) that indicate an optimal solution; however, there is no such thing as an optimal public policy, since the optimum varies according to political philosophies and cultural groups.

The value system in which a particular program originates and that evolves during program development influences both program goals and the means of attaining them. When programmatic values differ from those of the society at large, they may impede the optimal solution of the problem. In this situation, anthropologists can assist an administrator to specify program values, to discover the values of recipient populations, and perhaps to reconcile the two.

Because a program, with its associated value system, operates within a larger political system with its attendant values, administrators often need help in identifying what these political values are and who holds them. Anthropologists can help make explicit the values behind pertinent legislation and the possible compromises that can be reached among the political value systems of various power and pressure groups. Anthropologists also can help clarify intentional and unintentional vagueness in political value systems so that administrators can structure program priorities within the constraints of political reality. Policy makers themselves are influenced by hidden personal and professional values which affect their perspectives, priority setting, and interpretations of outcomes and their implications. Anthropologists can help administrators become sensitive to their own values and their resulting impact on actions so that these influences do not strongly distort policy decisions.

Traditionally, planning has been defined as a process of identifying alternatives, discussing the advantages and disadvantages of each, and then making a decision based on this information. Social planning involves the drawing up of plans for future action in regard to social institutions and resources (Madge 1968:125). The major distinction between traditional and newer schools of thought within the planning profession lies in the difference between a ''rational'' model and a ''participatory'' one. The rational model emphasizes planning as an intellectual activity divorced from its environment, and considers the collection and analysis of facts as the major planning activity. The participatory model underscores the importance of planning as a political and social process carried out by, or in consultation with, those affected. These two previously distinct models are now merging under the rubric of social policy planning (Littlestone 1973:4, 9).

As a process, planning is neither plans nor forecasting. Plans outline a specific course of action, while forecasting is an attempt to predict future events. In contrast, planning is a dynamic series of guides to aid present decisions aimed at shaping the future to desired ends.

Evaluation is an integral part of the planning process, and must be mentioned in any complete discussion of planning. Full discussion of evaluation is beyond the scope of this chapter.[2] However, it is im-

[2] For a more complete discussion, see Van Maanen (1973).

portant to note that the cycle of planning and evaluation ideally operates in a continuous feedback pattern that modifies plans as a program "rolls" toward its goals. Thus, planning should be constantly reviewed and updated by evaluation throughout a project. This ideal situation has been described as follows:

. . . evaluation begins during the planning phase of program development and usually involves such things as an analysis of the problem, the formulation of program goals and an appraisal of existing or alternative programs. Program implementation calls for another evaluation phase which, in turn, feeds back valuable information for the revision of plans and programs. This planning, implementing, and refining process to which evaluation is inherently connected may be repeated indefinitely until the goals are realized or discarded. Evaluation must be seen as an unfolding and cyclical process, for "good" programs may take years to develop (Van Maanen 1973:12).

Evaluation of a program attempts to determine if it is meeting the goals set out in its plans. Theoretically, program evaluation is concerned with outcomes and impacts, but it also deals with the effort and activity designed to lead to desired outcomes. During the implementation of a program, evaluation monitors program operations for the purpose of providing information to planners and administrators which can be used for correcting procedures and revising objectives. Ideally, the evaluation process involves "determining the program components and operations requiring study, selecting the appropriate techniques for gathering data, and collecting, analyzing, and presenting the information in the most useful way for the administrator" (Heighton and McPheeters 1976:3).

There are two major categories of evaluation: formative and summative (Scriven 1972). Summative evaluation, which is usually conducted by evaluators not actually associated with a program, is supposed to determine whether a planned program is ameliorating a targeted social problem; it is related to decisions for program continuance or future program planning. Persons not familiar with evaluation generally consider summative evaluation to be the only or major type of evaluation.

The lesser known but more prevalent formative or "in-house" evaluation provides monitoring data for administrators during the life of the program. It appears to be more useful than summative evaluation because it provides specific information for immediate program correction and improvement. This type of evaluation can best be defined as "the process of making reasonable judgments in effort, adequacy, effectiveness, and efficiency based on systematic data collection and analysis that is integrated into management" (personal communication, Clifford C. Attkinsson).

Issues in Planning

The contemporary movement toward planning social policy has raised a number of significant questions related to the nature of social problems and the needs and expectations of both planning professionals and the public about the ways to reduce them. Fundamental changes are occurring that affect the ways social problems are defined and approached. During the past decade, numerous issues have emerged as matters of substantial debate among members of the planning profession. Three of these are discussed here: (1) the meaning of comprehensiveness; (2) the extent to which planning can and should entail democratic choices in contrast to authoritarian controls; and (3) the appropriate role for each level of planning.

Comprehensiveness

Planners have traditionally used the term "comprehensive" to mean a general plan that is "the finished official statement of a municipal legislative body which sets forth its major policies concerning desirable future physical development" (Black 1968:349). For some individuals in the planning profession, comprehensive means encompassing "all geographical parts of the community and all functional elements which bear on physical development" (Black 1968:349), while other planners argue that a comprehensive plan must encompass physical, social, economic, administrative, and fiscal elements (Kain 1970:221–223; Gans 1970:223–225).

Related to the definition of comprehensive is the question of the separation of physical and social planning. Traditionally, planners have been concerned with physical planning, which is based upon land use and physical design. The assumption has been that, if a good physical environment exists, social problems will be reduced in number or eliminated. Some planners have juxtaposed physical planning with social planning because of this assumption. The majority of planners consider these two distinctly different types of planning, although some (Gans 1970:223–225) are now calling for a union of the two to produce a humanistically oriented planning.

For anthropologists, the debates over the meaning of "comprehensive" and the question of the separation of physical and social planning are artificial. Planners who approach these questions from the holistic perspective of sociocultural anthropology would agree that there are no physical or social or economic problems, only problems composed of physical, social, and economic elements. The anthropological perspective would consider a plan comprehensive if it included all the important variables (human, social, environmental, economic, etc.) and the relationships among them that contribute to the definition and examination of the problem.

Studying cultural and statistical data in context by using the community study method (Arensberg and Kimball 1965), anthropologists learn that some interrelationships and subsystems are more important to the system than others and limit detailed study to these crucial areas. Planners who employ this method may avoid the problem of concentrating too much on unnecessary detail. Initially, the entire system should be studied as though one were looking in at it while standing outside in a larger system. Arensberg and Kimball state, "the most important point is not the exhaustion of detail, but the breadth of view" (1965:32).

The concepts of holism and community can also help planners to adopt a more useful form of the concept of functionalism than that which they generally use. Since the days of Radcliffe-Brown and Malinowski, this concept has evolved from the elemental definition of functions as reasons or purposes to mean the network of variable relationships between elements and patterns of a system, which cannot be understood without experiencing the culture in which they are found. The concept of community centers on these relationships as they are structured by the interaction of individuals, groups, functions, space and time in a community, and can be used to determine their contributions to group welfare and the extent to which modification in any element affects others.

Data derived from the community study method are often vital to building a context within which to place statistical data for interpretation, especially when multiple interpretations are possible. For example, planners may discover that a particular area has a large number of households with no resident adult male acting as head.

These data could reflect a system of plural marriage in which co-wives reside separately and husbands live with one wife at a time, or a community organization in which all adult males reside together and apart from their wives and children, or a family form in which support for the household comes from kinsmen by blood, with no such position as resident husband, or the males may be migrant workers for long periods of time while their families remain in their home community. Thus, statistical data alone cannot describe a culture but require further investigation and additional cultural data in order to derive meaning (Valentine 1968:6–7).

In anthropological study, "the empirical fit between attitude and behavior, a belief and culture pattern, an institutional norm and a custom or sanction, is of more interest than the number of persons who express the attitude or practice the behavior on the average or other statistically representative quality of these things" (Arensberg and Kimball 1965:33). By studying cultural data and statistics in context through the community study method, anthropologists can add a living dimension to the planning process, which may help to improve the reception of plans and avoid accusations that planners are more concerned with figures and physical arrangements than with people (Fromm 1972:67–71).

Authoritarian Control versus Democratic Choice

Planning seems to be boiling with issues, but the majority are symptoms and manifestations of the major issue of authoritarian control versus democratic choice, which reflects the American value of individualism and general distrust of governmental authority. In discussing this issue, we will examine the use of planning for change or maintenance of the *status quo,* ordering society, and elitism.

During the turmoil and fragmentation of the 1960s, various factions such as racial, ethnic, and radical political groups, struggling first for a voice in the process of governance and then control, began to see planning as a change mechanism to achieve their ends. Current turbulence in the planning profession is a symptom of the struggle to either change American society or preserve the *status quo.* Proponents of social change insist that in order to make substantial changes in American society, the nature of contemporary planning itself must first change. They maintain that modern planning has become change-resistant, because much of it is done by government and is designed to keep the country stable and calm. In an attempt to know everything in advance and to strictly control every outcome, planning homogenizes the environment and leaves no room for unplanned change, unanticipated events, or changes other than those desired by the group in control, thereby replacing innovation with stability. Governments and other bureaucracies, rather than encouraging innovation at a time when we need new answers to old problems, attempt to stabilize the rate and type of change. However, historically significant change has always been unique and unpredictable, and often arose from innovation and instability (Grabow and Heskin 1973:108).

In attempting to order society, government sometimes unintentionally creates greater chaos. Although it is possible to create order in a subsystem while the rest of the system is in chaos, there comes a point when the more order one tries to introduce into a subsystem, the greater disorder one produces in the total system; the interdependence of subsystems may cause a directed change in one to create unanticipated events in another. Further, government's attempt to create order, thereby decreasing the diversity that can cause conflicts, may reduce the flexibility of the system.

In nature, the survival of a community is correlated with the diversity of that community. When faced with a crisis, the diversified community has the flexibility to adapt to conditions that may cause the homogeneous community to die. Governments, with their penchant for ordering social and physical things, potentially create nonadaptive, homogenous human communities. Their policies may seek to continue the *status quo,* or perhaps attempt to move all social levels to a new order. In either case, the governmental role is usually prescriptive, and planners generally base their plans on what *will* be according to the government in power rather than on what *should* be. Far from serving the diverse sectors of society, some planners feel that their profession is increasingly beholden to one master, the government (Barr 1972:155–159).

Traditionally, planners have served in advisory positions to governmental units and elites who have wanted particular social reforms implemented or scuttled. Because they have worked for power elites, planners are often viewed as members of these elites, an impression which some of them help foster. Some critics contend that planning is elitist because it separates planners from those for whom they plan;

planning requires the use or manipulation *of* persons, nature, and the world; it foregoes meaningful relationships *with* them.

The anthropological perspective, using concepts such as culture, cultural relativism, the community study method, participant observation, pluralism, and theories of innovation and change, can offer some possible directions for the resolution of the controversy over authoritarian control and democratic choice. Charges of elitism in planning might be reduced if the concepts of cultural relativism, the natural history or inductive approach used in the community study method, and participant observation were used to sensitize planners to the sources of their biases and to keep them in contact with the citizens they serve. To guard against elitism, planners must understand the values and customs of diverse populations, the external values and influences at work in the larger culture within which these groups exist, and their own personal values.

Firsthand knowledge of the target population, gained through participant observation performed by planners or anthropologists, can provide baseline data; and the questioning of pressure groups and governmental units can help discover and specify the values that affect relationships between the target group and outsiders. By examining the values of their discipline, planners will become more sensitive to assumptions which may distort their perception. For example, if those for whom the planning is being done are conceived in terms of a deficiency model which defines them as "culturally disadvantaged," planning and action will likely be poor and inappropriate. The concept of "cultural disadvantage" is based on an assumption that everyone should be like middle class America (Howard 1970:169). On the other hand, extreme relativism can also be biased because it leads the planner to equate any recognition of differences with discrimination and to fail to consider differences when necessary.

The natural history or inductive method of reasoning makes no assumptions about the group under study, nor does it begin research with the intention of proving a specific hypothesis. It is not hampered, as the deductive approach occasionally is, by an incorrect model, but discerns the natural model of the community as the study proceeds. Its use can help planners avoid problems related to implicit biases because it does not start with value assumptions, but discovers the values of the community.

Acceptance of cultures as different rather than as better or worse, could lead planners to the acceptance of heterogeneity (also known as cultural pluralism) and away from the concept of the "melting pot", which assumes that all Americans want to lose their ethnic identity and conform to the stereotypic image of middle class behavior and values. The anthropological concept of pluralism can be used to support the idea that uniformity is not a viable option but that heterogeneity can be a beneficial alternative, allowing diverse communities and/or cultures to work together creatively and still maintain their individual identities. Rubin (1961) has discussed how cultural groups which maintain separate identities on the local level cooperate with each other at higher levels. It is where diverse groups come together that heterogeneity produces its greatest flowering of creativity, as witnessed by the exhilaration in such cosmopolitan centers as San Francisco, Paris, and similar cities.

Heterogeneity, or the diversity of cultural pluralism, offers a community or culture a wide variety of adaptive possibilities in a time of rapid change. Anthropological concepts and theories of change can facilitate a general understanding of change and ease people's fear of it. Anthropologists working in developmental programs have produced theories and research methodologies dealing with the process of change that could be vitally important to planners and administrators (Smith and Fischer 1970:82). Some of these change concepts include the effects of urbanization, cultural borrowing and diffusion, acculturation and forced acculturation, innovation, and the influence of nonhuman factors such as environmental change. These theories are potentially useful in helping planners to guide change and to better understand how stability or maintenance of the *status quo* may lead to nonadaptive effects, as, for example, when ecological, social, or technological change has so altered the community's pattern of living that some or all of its current values and customs work against continued survival.

The Levels of Planning

Planning today exists in the national, regional, state, and local levels of government. We agree with Galloway (1941:29) that there should be three levels of planning: directive, administrative, and operative. At issue are the appropriate roles for each level and citizen participation. Ideally, policy making and guidance should be centered in

Washington; administration should be decentralized in the states and regions; and operation should be localized. Thus, the farther the level of planning from the actual operations, the more generalized its activities. Detailed planning would be done only at the scene, where the planner could best understand the peculiarities of local situations.

According to Perloff, local planning is generally concerned with aesthetics, engineering, land use, governmental procedures, social welfare, and the functioning and development of the community (Coke 1968:27). However, numerous localities lack viable planning departments and the financial or technical ability to plan for themselves. Furthermore, local areas have been so constrained by state, regional, and federal regulations that many have lost the ability to innovate and initiate (Rondinelli 1973:19).

In recent federal legislation such as that for the Urban Planning Assistance "701" Program and the Professional Standards Review Organizations, the National Health Planning and Resource Development Act of 1974, and the Community Mental Health Centers Amendments of 1975, the federal government has emphasized the participation of citizens in the allocation and uses of power. At present, when have-not blacks, Mexican-Americans, Puerto Ricans, Eskimos, native Americans, and whites try to act, they usually encounter elaborate ruses to reduce or eliminate their participation and influence.

Two examples from San Francisco point out what citizen participation in planning can accomplish. In the first, residents of Chinatown designed and proposed housing projects with a high number of occupants per square foot and with senior citizens near younger generations, in accordance with Chinese cultural values. The city initially turned down the proposal but accepted it when a large number of residents supported the plan. In the second example, black architects incorporated features congruent with black tradition in the United States by designing units with a shower and bath attached directly to a large living room that could be used to accommodate transient guests (Maruyama 1973:355).

However, some groups of citizens are unable to participate in the planning process because they do not share the necessary knowledge or technical sophistication. For these persons, advocacy planning is the only hope of representation. The advocate planner is their voice and represents their views to the decision makers. Advocate planners differ from most planners in their primary concern for low income or otherwise disadvantaged groups.

Some plans, such as those for environmental quality and transportation, must necessarily transcend local political boundaries and must therefore be handled on a state or regional basis. For example, comprehensive state planning is now under way in many states and is frequently accompanied by state-level activities involving supervision of local planning, coordination of local and intrastate regional planning, and occasionally, the institution of local planning.

Interstate regions are commonly composed of a group of states or parts of several states, which band together to work out a common problem or plan for a common resource or goal. Smaller intrastate regions may consist of several counties or municipalities. Thus, a river basin region may encompass all or parts of several states, while an environmental or sewage treatment problem may be common to several cities, towns, or counties. Acting alone, each could only partially solve the problem, but acting together, they can perhaps pool their resources to arrive at a better solution. In part, regional planning groups are a response to the impact of metropolitan growth on the rural areas, the need for resource and environmental planning, and the presence of regional needs such as transportation, and economic market areas.

The formation of regional planning organizations is frequently resisted by citizens who perceive regional bodies as one more layer of government in which they have no choice. Consequently, regional organizations are purposely limited in scope and advisory in activity. This problem will continue to haunt regional planning as federal pressure for planning increases and socioenvironmental problems worsen, unless the planning profession can educate the public so that they understand and participate in the planning process.

Regional planning has usually been based on political regions or physical-geographical ones having a common problem. We agree with Fisher (1969) that there is a need for more attention to human desires and patterns of living as compared to concern for land forms and political jurisdictions. In 1939, Howard W. Odum, a founder of the Department of City and Regional Planning at the University of North Carolina, proposed that governmental policy should include programs of regional planning based on *cultural* regions. According to Odum:

a region has organic unity not only in its natural landscape, but in that cultural evolution in which the age-long quartette of elements are at work—namely, the land and the people, culturally conditioned through time and spatial relationships. Thus, Professor Aronovici defines regionalism as "the study of the relation of man to geographic areas, and the potentialities which this relation represents in terms of human welfare and progress. The history of tribes, nations and races is one long record of regional realism, in terms of expansion and contraction of regional boundaries (1964:156).

Because cultures, peoples, and nations grow from regional bases, it is impossible to understand or direct society except through a regional approach (Odum 1964:153). Regional delineations should take into consideration the organic human-culture regional areas, the geographical factors of situation and climate, the political factors of organization and control, and the technological aspects (Odum 1964:308–309).

Odum found that, in order for the characterization of one region to be useful in planning, it had to be contrasted to and compared with other regions in the nation. In this way, the regional approach could become a dynamic tool in the attempt to understand the living geography of a nation and the relation of each region to the whole; it could have a valuable application in the testing of proposed national policies on a regional scale.

National planning and regional planning generally go together, and ideally both should act to develop the concepts of constructive, farsighted management (Gillie 1967:9). The Appalachian Regional Development Program which was initiated by the United States Congress in 1965, the Tennessee Valley Authority, and the Mississippi and Ohio Valley Committees are examples of coordinated national and regional planning (Newman 1972; Odum 1964).

Various federal agencies have been engaged in planning for the economy, employment, international economic relations, social planning for public health, housing, education, recreation, manpower, social security, interstate migration, and rural and urban rehabilitation. A major part of the federal level's present involvement in planning consists of granting funds to state and local governments for transportation planning, urban beautification, urban planning and renewal, and economic development.

At present, federal planning policy is formulated and implemented by a multitude of middle level bureaucratic offices with highly specialized personnel, information, technical expertise, and influence, each of which can carve spheres of dominion in policy implementation (Rondinelli 1973:15). Examples include the Model Cities program, antipoverty legislation (Donovan 1967), the Public Works and Economic Development Act (Rondinelli 1969), and Federal Highway Assistance (Morehouse 1969; Levin and Abend 1971).

Although federal level planning is currently fragmented into operative and policy setting roles, its ideal role is directive or guiding. In other words, the top level of social policy should be involved with comprehensive and coordinated policy making and the directions in which the country should move. The local governments should then implement the directives, with state and regional governments guiding and coordinating local efforts. In some instances, such as desegregation and energy planning, the federal level cannot simply be involved with policy making, but must also plan policy since the program must be implemented in all areas of the country.

When the federal level engages in planning and passes instructions to the states and local governments, the process is termed centralized and is described as planning from the top down. The public, states, and localities may or may not be given a chance to comment on the plans before they are implemented. Although this form of planning "for" a community may make the mechanics of planning more efficient, there is no proof that the result of the plan is better. Typically, the public views the entire process as dictatorial, elitist, and paternalistic. Advocates of community control criticize this approach for taking away the freedom of self-control. Many planners oppose the top down approach because it forces the profession to fight through a growing jungle of rules, regulations, standards, guidelines, and paperwork.

The decentralized process of planning from the bottom up, on the other hand, allows the community to make its own decisions and plans, while the planner handles the technical end of the process. Although this approach is more difficult to achieve because of the larger number of persons involved, plans are generally more readily accepted by community members who feel the plans are theirs. This closer touch with the community aids the development of plans which are more responsive to the problems, needs, and desires of community members.

Anthropologists can work as planners on all four levels of planning: national, regional, state, and local. At every level, however, they must remember that they are operating within a political system and must work within values which at times may run counter to their own. They must reconcile their values, the values of their discipline, and the values of the political system so that they can effectively fight within the system rather than flee from it. Anthropologists in planning must be committed to planning and must be willing to live on a battle line; they should realize they are going to win some of the issues and lose others.

Planning on a national scale offers opportunities for anthropologists in administrative and staff positions, particularly in the federal agencies of Health, Education and Welfare, and the Department of Housing and Urban Development, because national plans must recognize the human component. In 1934, the now-defunct National Planning Board said that the application of anthropology to national planning would have enormous significance if the study of man were used to obtain a clear view of the structure, interests, and activities of human beings, and that, in any plan concerning human activities, anthropology could contribute valuable insight on the conditions and states of mind of the people (National Planning Board 1934:52). While contributions to national policy have been and will continue to be important, anthropology's impact on this level will be necessarily limited because there are fewer jobs available than on regional, state, and local levels.

On the regional level, the community study method is potentially useful in planning because it can provide a living cultural snapshot of a relatively large geographical area by examining the relational systems, values, and customary behavior of people in time and space. The natural history, or inductive, approach of the community study method allows for the study of communities, relationships, systems, and subsystems, so that they may be compared and contrasted to discover what is typical and varying in the structure and process of a cultural region. This method of comparing and contrasting regions could be used to determine necessary regional modifications in national policy and to facilitate the use of regions as testing grounds for various proposed federal plans and policies.

On the state and local levels, there are opportunities for anthropologists to work closely with state and local officials and citizens in planning. In line with this they may effectively consult with state legislative staff in preparing legislation, or with local planners or officials in drafting new ordinances. Particularly in local planning, we see anthropologists' most important roles to be those of facilitating and initiating community planning efforts, and training and consulting with community members.[3] For example, when we were involved in planning in a rural Florida county, we first had to convince community members and local officials that planning was necessary because state level planners and legislators were considering laws requiring local planning. A key aspect of convincing the persons involved was a knowledge of the community through firsthand observation and participation. During the planning process, we not only taught local officials and community members to plan for themselves, but we also continuously fed information to the county commission (the organization that was responsible for the plan), and held regular meetings with citizens.

When aiding a community to plan for itself, it is extremely important for anthropologists to remember that the primary planners are those in the community. Consequently, anthropologists should *not* make themselves indispensable. We have found that the most successful approach for anthropologists to take is that of the midwife, because people are usually wary of "experts."

As consultant planners on the community and state levels, anthropologists, through studying relational systems, can point out potential barriers such as racial or educational discrimination to citizen participation; can locate resources and the gatekeepers who control access to these resources in the system; and can identify the various groups within a system and help develop a plan that will include a voice for all. In promoting participation, anthropologists frequently will operate as mediators among community groups.

When acting as planning advocates, anthropologists may serve as cultural translators. Anthropologists have a long history of speaking up for "their" tribes or people, particularly in the South Pacific (Piddington 1970) and Latin America (Peattie 1968b), and more recently as advocates in the United States (Schensul 1974; Jacobs 1974). Anthropological skill in translating ideas and values cross-culturally will prove useful in pleading the cases of the disadvantaged before the power holders.

[3] For further discussion, see Peterson (1974b).

Conclusion

Anthropologists can make valid and valuable contributions working in policy analysis and planning, even though they, like other social scientists, sometimes have exaggerated doubts or make overly ambitious claims about their contributions to the solution of social problems. The perspectives of anthropology are particularly appropriate to combine with the skills of planning, because anthropology has what planning has always lacked: a greater connection with and understanding of the diversity of human wants expressed in the reality of life. We see anthropology's major contributions in the discipline's breadth of view, theories of change, study of systematic relationships in the context of an organic whole, means of controlling for value judgments, and use of inductive reasoning.

Anthropological research methods are usually broad, flexible, relatively unstructured, and based on the holistic perspective and the practice of continually testing data and hypotheses. In studying real life situations, each element or subsystem is placed within the context of its culture, and compared and contrasted with all other elements to gain a picture of the organic whole. This perspective allows anthropologists to view organizations and cultures as natural systems, and to recognize that problems of social policy planning may require the collaboration of several disciplines. While research for policy purposes often requires anthropologists to function as members of multidisciplinary teams, one of the major complaints of administrators is the general lack of teamwork skills among anthropologists. Mead (1973:5,7) has pointed out that the last twenty-five years have been dominated by massive individual enterprises in the discipline which are notable for the style of the individual integrating intelligence but not for teamwork.

A key to the success of any endeavor is the inclusion of all pertinent data, but, rather than attempting an eclectic approach to collecting sociocultural data, anthropologists weigh the importance of each item within the system and then focus on the crucial ones. Systemic relationships can be elicited through the use of the community study method and other methods that emphasize induction and the discovery of the interrelationships of elements within the context of systems. The concept of systems proves valuable to anthropologists in action settings where a major part of their tasks as researchers and policy makers involves defining the boundaries of the system affected by a problem, determining the conceptual or theoretical levels on which the actors of the system are operating, and eliciting values through interaction patterns. However, anthropologists may need to communicate to nonanthropologists their understanding of systems, and facilitate communications among persons in various parts of the social policy process. Their ability to compare and contrast, by shifting levels of abstraction and conceptualization within and among systems, can allow them to act as facilitators and communicators, for example, between levels of government, between government and private interests, and among citizens, governmental representatives, and the private sector.

Nonetheless, since most plans and policies are intended to change the environment, citizens and some planning professionals may view anthropologists not as facilitators/translators, but as manipulators (Peattie 1968a). In one sense this is correct, since the power to conceptualize is the power to manipulate. Also, there are still some vestiges of paternalism among anthropologists, left over from the days of working in colonial administration. Perhaps if anthropologists approach action work with the attitude of the assisting midwife rather than the prescribing doctor, they can allay fears of manipulation and elitism.

The United States currently appears to be moving toward more planning, in an attempt to reduce conflict, improve efficiency, cut costs, and regulate society. Although planning may make American interactions and government more predictable, a healthy human society depends on the presence and stimulation of heterogeneity and some ongoing conflict. Anthropological research has demonstrated the viability of heterogeneity in human culture (Rubin 1961), and could be used to illustrate that too much concern with order may lead to an inability to adapt to change. Frequently, directed change is resisted either to vindicate the *status quo* or because of fear of the unknown. Yet, once the processes of change are more fully understood, they often become something people can use rather than fear. Thus, anthropological theories and research methodologies dealing with the process of change can be vitally important to planners and administrators (Smith and Fischer 1970:82). Perhaps one of anthropology's greatest contributions is helping individuals to view change as growth and to understand its roots, processes, and outcomes.

The conditions which foster fruitful and productive change and cultural adaptations to change can be examined by using anthropological methods. Change can be planned to take place in one large jump, with consequently large unanticipated effects, or to occur incrementally through smaller changes directed to reach a goal over a period of time. Plans and policies are often best approached incrementally through achievable short and medium range goals that can be examined and understood before further change is planned, thus allowing the achievement of major goals through reaching successive subgoals. This organic approach to planned change uses the same method of thinking as Rothman, Erlich, and Teresa (1976) propose in their manual for planning social change.

The use of inductive reasoning in planning social policy and anthropology's means of controlling for value judgments are two further contributions of the discipline. Inductive reasoning allows the policy planner to explore situations and alternatives, unencumbered by preconceived models, and leaves him or her free to follow the natural logic and structure of a particular system. Cross-cultural knowledge and experience with value systems helps anthropologists to contribute to social policy planning in a number of areas: when there is a need to identify values which are to be satisfied; when a project implies that people will be making decisions and choices in the light of cultural values and cultural, economic, and social resources; when plans entail the interaction of individuals within a social structure or social organization and the ramifications of social networks for the passage of concepts, ideas, goods, and action; when it is necessary to analyze whether a strategy or project will have the desired effects upon the social system; when it is necessary to analyze the valuational and cultural components in the skill-resources available for development; and when it is necessary to evaluate the success of particular programs in light of their objectives (Belshaw 1972).

But, if anthropologists wish to have greater impact upon and apply their cross-cultural pool of knowledge to American institutions and policies, they must first change their popular image from that of a group of eccentrics working with bones and exotic cultures (Piddington 1970:128) to one of a practical profession which offers effective, comprehensive, sensitive, and workable solutions to current problems. As a beginning, they must realize that their models and theoretical constructs are not reality but only mirrors of reality which must be tested in applied situations. Anthropologists will have to learn to work within the constraints of American society and to make recommendations and accept responsibility for them. Finally, the discipline which concerns itself with the study of human beings must come to value applied contributions to human welfare as highly as it does academic contributions to the discipline. Then, perhaps, anthropologists with their holistic and dynamic approach to the understanding of peoples and the interactions of culture and biology will take their place as important contributors to social policy.

Part IV

EDUCATIONAL AND ETHICAL IMPLICATIONS

Thus far, this volume has been largely concerned with the work applied anthropologists have undertaken in the past, are presently engaged in, or might undertake in the future. The issues of formal preparation for applied roles in nonacademic settings and the ethical considerations which must be taken into account in applied work have been discussed in passing, but they have not been the primary focus for discussion. Yet both issues are major ones confronting the discipline of anthropology today.

This section examines these issues, brings together what has been previously said about them, and adds new ideas to each subject. How does the formal training of anthropologists need to be altered for the rapidly changing world? What are the contributions of applied anthropology to a better understanding of our ethical dilemmas as anthropologists and to the resolution of these dilemmas? These are the questions that concern us here.

21

TRAINING FOR APPLIED ANTHROPOLOGY

Elizabeth M. Eddy and William L. Partridge

The rapid expansion of the discipline of anthropology in America since World War II has occurred within the bureaucratic structures of higher education. Increased departmentalization and specialization have often resulted in arbitrary boundaries between anthropologists and those in other disciplines and professions which are no longer useful for educational purposes.

Eddy and Partridge candidly discuss some of the shortcomings of traditional training and suggest the need for new types of interorganizational relationships within academe for the preparation of applied anthropologists. They call for the development of professional area studies and a restructuring of graduate departments to provide the new type of training needed for applied work.

THE PROFESSIONALIZATION OF American anthropology has occurred within the context of higher education. In the United States, the establishment of the department as the basic unit of academic work and administration first appeared in the late nineteenth century during the same period that anthropological and other national learned societies were formed and graduate work became an integral part of American higher education (Jenks and Riesman 1968: 13). Formal university training of American anthropologists began in 1887 when Franz Boas founded the first academic department of anthropology at Clark University in Worcester, Massachusetts. Learned societies of anthropologists in existence at the time included the American

Ethnological Society, the Anthropological Society of Washington, the Archeological Institute of America, and the American Folklore Society. By 1902, the year the American Anthropological Association was founded with eighty-seven members, academic departments had already been established at Columbia, Berkeley, and Harvard.

Ever since these early beginnings, the institutional context of anthropology has reflected the cultural patterning of American higher education. The proliferation of departments and specialization has been a major characteristic of American academe, and anthropology has been no exception to this major trend. The first departments of anthropology were closely associated with museums, which hired most of those who acquired doctoral degrees. During the 1930s, as social and cultural anthropology began to develop as social sciences, the centers of anthropological research shifted to universities. Joint departments of anthropology and sociology, or occasionally with other disciplines, were common as graduate departments emerged in many state and private universities (Eggan 1963). Today, nearly all anthropologists are in separate departments, and there are 314 institutions of higher education in the United States and Canada which have academic departments of anthropology (American Anthropological Association 1976b).

The continuous growth of professional anthropology is further reflected in the increased strength of professional associations. As of January 31, 1976, the membership of the American Anthropological Association totaled 9,881 (excluding institutional members). Currently there are thirty-two professional anthropological associations listed by the Executive Office of the American Anthropological Association; thirteen of them have been organized since the 1950s (American Anthropological Association 1976a).

Contemporary anthropologists and their students tend to take the expansion of academic departments and professional anthropology for granted. The abnormal period of rapid growth in higher education following World War II created an acute need for teachers of anthropology to staff new departments and older departments that were under pressure to serve larger numbers of students. Of necessity, primary attention was given to building departments. For example, in November 1958, a Ph.D. Curricula Conference was held in Washington, D.C., to recommend guidelines for graduate education (Foster 1958). Two years later, in 1960–61, a special Education Resources in

Anthropology project, supported by the National Science Foundation, was undertaken by the Department of Anthropology at Berkeley. This project sponsored ten symposia throughout the country to discuss the teaching of anthropology. The papers presented were published by the American Anthropological Association, together with an extensive listing of teaching resources (Mandelbaum, Lasker, and Albert 1963a; 1963b). The topics encompassed both undergraduate and graduate teaching and all of the major subfields of the discipline, including applied anthropology and the teaching of anthropology to professional students in the fields of education, public health, law, and government.

In a paper prepared for one of the symposia, Eggan (1963) succinctly expressed the tenor of this period by stating that "current prospects for expansion in anthropology suggest that we do not need to worry about an overproduction of Ph.D.'s for some time to come." In less than a decade, however, the time for concern had arrived. An historic downward shift in birthrates combined with the accelerated departmental growth rate of the post-World War II years to create a situation in which the expansion of positions in higher education can no longer absorb all of the Ph.D. graduates who are being produced. It is estimated that by 1982 at the latest, the majority of new Ph.D.'s will be unable to find academic positions (D'Andrade et al. 1975).

This new situation means that professional anthropology, which began in the museums and then moved into the universities, is now entering a third stage of development in which applied anthropology must play a central role. With the founding of the Society of Professional Anthropologists in Tucson, Arizona, in 1974, this emphasis has already been expressed in organizational form. Comprised of 180 members, SOPA began as a local regional group of professional anthropologists employed in nonacademic settings. Their purpose is "to provide a forum wherein scientist and practitioner can meet as equals; where the search for new knowledge can be tempered by the cold water of practical application" (SOPA *Newsletter,* October 1976). Recently, an organization similar to SOPA has been organized in the Washington, D.C., area (Washington Association of Professional Anthropologists).

Today, the future of American anthropology largely depends on restructuring its present institutional context, essentially the graduate department, so that it may become a chrysalis rather than a coffin (Hymes 1969:9) for the preparation of significant numbers of applied anthropologists who will work outside of academe. Within a decade, the response of academicians to the opportunity to incorporate as equals those who search for new knowledge "tempered by the cold water of application" will likely determine whether or not applied anthropologists will become fully integrated into the anthropological mainstream or divorce themselves from it in much the same way that social workers and public administrators historically separated from sociology and political science as distinct areas of professional applied endeavor. What is entailed if the latter rather than the former course of events is to occur?

Faculty Development

The reorganization of departmental activity and the resocialization of anthropologists for expanded roles in our society will not be easy. Kimball (essay 15) has earlier described the monastic retreat of many anthropologists from the world around them. As a consequence, only a handful of faculty have had experience working as anthropologists outside of academe or applying their training to practical problems. Most have had no contact with the basic literature in the field of applied anthropology. Their knowledge of or interest in American institutions is typically limited. While traditional field work in other cultures has been a valuable part of anthropological training, the cross-cultural aspects have frequently been overlooked in practice. The knowledge base about American culture, necessary for cross-cultural understanding, was neither there to start with nor subsequently attained. A major result of these and other factors is that many faculty today are unable to be wise mentors of students who will not replicate themselves in academic life.

Miller (essay 7) has earlier pointed out the lack of faculty development in higher education generally. Within anthropology, it seems that we will continue this neglect only at the risk of perpetuating departments which retreat into the past. Given the structure of academe, such departments may endure for a long time as feudal baronies beyond the reach of even the most courageous of academic deans. But is this what anthropology departments should become (or remain) in the future? Or do we want vibrant departments that reach out to the university and the world at large?

The choice of the latter alternative requires concerted efforts to broaden the horizons of a critical mass of current faculty members beyond the parochialisms of daily departmental life and the intense competition of narrowly trained specialists whose relationships primarily preserve the *status quo* and prevent departmental adaptation to the new environment in which anthropology finds itself. The old belief that once trained in anthropology, one is prepared for anything, is a false one. Most faculty are ill-prepared for teaching students about the relevance of anthropology to American life and problems, and many students learn of it for the first time only when Margaret Mead visits the campus.

Preparation for this new field of endeavor must be as carefully undertaken as would be plans for a sabbatical leave in an unfamiliar society. This does not mean that faculty need to "go native" but that they should apply their anthropological skills in crossing the bureaucratic and cultural boundaries of the campus. It is a matter of claiming those in other disciplines and professions as worthy of anthropological efforts and as those from whom anthropologists can learn about problems in professional areas for which anthropological training is appropriate. Such transdisciplinary learning is already occurring in medical anthropology and educational anthropology, and is potentially possible in many other fields also.

We join Hymes (1969:7) in suggesting the need for departmental faculty to seriously consider the question of "how much of what goes on in departments today is for the sake of mankind's self-knowledge (let alone liberation), and how much for the sake of perpetuating, extending, and proliferating departments?" We suggest, too, that imaginative attention to this question, supported by careful ethnographic studies of departmental activities, may well lead to an internal restructuring of this basic disciplinary unit which will enable it to more fruitfully adapt to present needs of the discipline to move into the modern world in expanded ways. The task ahead is to restructure our departments to provide a forum "wherein scientist and practitioner can meet as equals" to set new goals for the study of mankind and the role of anthropology in our world.

Professional Area Studies

In difficult times of transition, some departments will doubtless cling tenaciously to customary patterns of training in the name of "standards" or other shibboleths which promote an elitest *status quo* vis-à-vis other disciplines and nonacademic professions. Others are already choosing a different route by seeking to train anthropologists for entry into the modern world of work outside of academe (Cochrane 1971; Leacock, Gonzalez, and Kushner 1974). All departments will do well to seriously examine the context and the content of their activities. Students seeking a career in anthropology also will do well to evaluate departments in order to find out which will train them to become engaged in new professional roles and problem areas and which will train them to replicate past activities.

We noted earlier that anthropologists tend to take for granted the departmental organization of anthropology inherited from the past. Nevertheless, there is nothing sacrosanct about the contemporary organization of anthropology departments, and their form reflects an early twentieth century factory model of educational processing (Eddy, essay 17). The binding together of the traditional four subfields which arose at a time when anthropology was limited to the study of peoples of the past is no longer appropriate. A dose of linguistics, a dose of cultural anthropology, a dose of physical anthropology, and a dose of archeology intended to train fieldworkers among nonliterate peoples often result in teachers and students who vary the fourfold prescription very little. We agree with Hymes (1969:44) that there is no compelling reason for departments to continue the traditional fourfold scheme. One or more components might be dropped, according to the strengths within or outside a department or the needs of individual students to pursue more intellectually and professionally relevant subject matter in terms of their career goals. We also believe that the lockstep rigidities of the factory form of academic organization are disadvantageous for both students and faculty, although some are able to escape its limitations. Anthropologists should become activists in breaking down the bureaucratic barriers to transdisciplinary academic work.

Training anthropologists to meet both today's needs and those of the future requires flexible academic programs. The broad outlines of these are reflected in the experiences which the contributors to this

volume have reported. For students planning to work in nonacademic institutions, such programs should include: (1) theoretical and
methodological training in the analysis of complex societies and institutions and of the processes of adaptation and change; (2) transdisciplinary problem orientation; and (3) the innovation of systematic
field training in collaboration with other scientists and professionals.

Academic training can be more or less relevant to practical problems depending upon its content. There is no reason, as Kimball
(essay 15) states, to believe that intellectual talent is sufficient qualifi-
cation to justify pronouncements regarding contemporary issues and
problems. Anthropologists must have as a primary goal the engagement of students in research into contemporary social life, so that intellectual training takes place in the field of ongoing social and cultural change. Low level talent in manipulating abstract categories in
the absence of data gathering and processing is of little value. Training in the analysis of interaction and social systems provides the
student of human behavior with essential tools for empirical study,
tools which generate explanatory theory through practice. Only in
this manner is structure seen to emerge from behavior and the continuing situational manipulations, adjustments, negotiations, and adaptation to changing conditions of social life. The elaborate patterns
of interaction described by Arensberg (essay 2) do not disappear at
some evolutionary stage but continue to shape responses to stimuli.
The complex patterning of perceptions described by Goodenough
(essay 3) become more significant as society becomes more complex.
The two are linked in an ongoing process of adaptation as described
by Hill-Burnett (essay 5). If a department would train students to deal
skillfully with practical problems, a theoretical and methodological
grounding in the study of these and other processes of adaptation and
change is a basic and initial step.

A second critical ingredient in the training of applied anthropology professionals is a multidisciplinary problem orientation. Archeologists, biological anthropologists, and linguists have long since discovered the interdependency of their science with other sciences, a
wide range of methodologies, and practical problems. Such interdependence also holds for genuine competence in the sociocultural
field (cf. Cochrane 1971; Hymes 1969). As Whyte, Miller, Peterson,
Medicine, Neville, Sayles, Taylor, Gardner, Dobyns, and Heighton
and Heighton each have pointed out, problems in the real world of

social theory building and application do not come in disciplinary compartments. Rather, they are multiplex, often requiring a team of specialists for more adequate formulation and solution but always involving interested parties with numerous and varied perspectives on the problem. While there still may be a legitimate case to be made for including all of the four subfields in the educational training of an abstract anthropologist, the problems of applied anthropology are somewhat different. For this reason, we suggest that applied anthropologists be trained to develop specialized knowledge of areas outside of anthropology in lieu of one or more of the traditional subfields within the discipline. In view of the experiences reported by contributors to this volume, it seems important that applied anthropologists gain knowledge of modern institutions, legal systems, political systems, and sociological, economic, and political science insights into the social changes which form the context of our times (cf. Little 1963; Hammel 1976; Spicer 1976). Both the work of social anthropologists and that of other social scientists in complex societies should be a major component of the academic preparation for applied anthropology.

Third, we urge that careful consideration be given to a reappraisal of the types of fieldwork experience appropriate for applied anthropologists in training. Experience as a solitary anthropologist undertaking an ethnographic study in a remote setting is not the best preparation for applied research. More appropriate is a study undertaken within a complex organizational setting, or as a member of a team project, which provides direct experience in the social context of work on practical problems. As Richardson (essay 4) points out, intellectual intelligence, unaccompanied by behavioral intelligence, is really problematical when practical problem definition and solution necessarily involve the skills of interacting with others. All of the roles described in this book depend upon such skills, and it is no accident that they have been highlighted by individuals who have adapted to institutional work settings. As Whyte (essay 6) notes, such experience will place proper emphasis upon the innovation of approaches that are grounded in theoretical and methodological priorities of anthropology, yet are responsive to the specialized needs of other scientists, co-workers, the communities served, and agencies for which work is undertaken. This is particularly clear in the policy research areas explored by Hicks and Handler, Eddy, Partridge, Makielski, and Heighton and Heighton. In these areas, the need for collaboration between professionals from the fields of planning, evaluation, health, nutrition, education, political organization, and the like is evident. Historically, the capacity of American higher education to incorporate academic and professional training within the university structure is a social invention of the first order. We believe that the modern university offers unique opportunities for collaboration with these and other fields, and that preparation for applied work should incorporate course work and other educational experiences in a professional field outside of anthropology.

In summary, we advocate that for applied anthropology the area studies of the post-World War II years must yield to professional area studies based on the following three factors: a thorough grounding in social anthropological theory and research methods suitable to the analysis of ongoing community and organizational change and adaptation; the specific transdisciplinary professional concerns of those outside of anthropology involved in problem oriented research; and innovative research training and involvement in complex social organizations with professional personnel trained in ameliorating human problems. Just as anthropology has drawn on disciplines outside of itself for cultural area studies, so now it must draw on resources that lie beyond the four-field department for professional area studies. The other social sciences and professional colleges offer rich opportunities for the development of training programs which will give students experience with those who have other world views and knowledge. Emphasis should also be given to the formulation of problems and findings in ways that communicate to practitioners as well as scientists. Obviously such training programs must be carefully developed and only the best of our students should be recruited for them. These students should be broadly interested in the multiple tasks which lie ahead and the involvement with others which these tasks demand.

The human and scientific needs to which anthropologists can speak transcend departmental and disciplinary boundaries (cf. Hymes 1969:6). Our own self-imposed arbitrary boundaries which have in the past declared American society, applied anthropology, and training in other disciplines as "off bounds" for serious scholarly work, must be dissolved, and the scope and depth of our ethical commitment to human well-being must be broadened. When these artificial boundaries are removed, a most important step will have been taken to improve the intellectual life of our departments and the educational and vocational opportunities for our students. The future of applied anthropology as a profession, and the vitality of anthropology as a field of inquiry will depend upon the resources which we bring to these new frontiers of professional development.

22

THE EVOLVING ETHICS OF
APPLIED ANTHROPOLOGY

Margaret Mead

Margaret Mead reminds us that the ethical considerations which govern and guide the work of applied anthropologists are those of all anthropologists. Our ethics are based in individual commitment to the principles of scientific responsibility. The special circumstances in which applied anthropologists work, however, involve purposeful intervention in the lives of people and therefore demand that special thought be devoted to ethical dilemmas. The founders of the Society for Applied Anthropology recognized this and formulated the first ethics statement of any professional anthropology association.

Here Dr. Mead elaborates the three general principles of anthropological responsibility which have evolved since the founding of the Society. She stresses, as did Eddy and Partridge earlier, that ethical behavioral and intellectual intelligence must be forged early in professional careers through systematic training and involvement in the value dilemmas which characterize our work and our world. It is here, in the process of individual development of values in response to persis-

Margaret Mead (Ph.D., Columbia) is curator emeritus of ethnology at the American Museum of Natural History and adjunct professor of anthropology at Columbia University. Dr. Mead has received twenty honorary degrees as well as many prizes and awards in recognition of her pioneering role in American anthropology and in science. Dr. Mead's fieldwork in industrial and pre-industrial societies has resulted in twenty-four books she has authored, in addition to eighteen she has co-authored with other scientists. She has held offices in many scholarly organizations, and is a past president of the World Federation for Mental Health, the Society for Applied Anthropology, the American Anthropological Association, the Scientists' Institute for Public Information, the Society for General Systems Research, and the American Association for the Advancement of Science. Dr. Mead's many interests include childhood socialization, social organization, culture building, culture change, ekistics, personality and culture, cultural aspects of nutrition, national character, ecology, and family life.

tent problems and newer issues of the day, that the outlines of an emerging professional "code" of ethics will evolve. If involvement in value dilemmas is part of the training of applied anthropologists we can also be certain that we will retain that professional flexibility which permits us to struggle with new dilemmas and adapt to the changing conditions of anthropological work.

OUR UNDERSTANDING OF the special ethical requirements of the practice of applied anthropology has evolved as the discipline of anthropology itself has grown and changed within a rapidly changing world (Schwartz 1975). When I entered anthropology in 1922, our ethical problems were primarily concerned with the degree to which we became involved in the protection of primitive peoples and their cultures which were being eroded and destroyed by contacts with technologically, politically, and ideologically more organized societies whenever they came in contact with them. Whether we were working among Eskimos or Australian Aborigines, North American Indians or Todas, as members of living societies, or whether we were seeking to reconstruct the past histories or the vanished cultures of peoples who had disappeared under the impact of conquest, disease, and decimation, the vulnerability of primitive groups who maintained their culture through oral transmission without script, to societies with the kinds of organization which script made possible, was very clear to us (Mead 1956a, 1959).

Primitive cultures—in the sense of preliterate cultures—were vanishing, as ways of life, if not as societies of living human beings. The central scientific ethic of cultural or social anthropology (we did not discriminate between the terms then) was to preserve a record of the precious and vanishing fabric of ancient customary behavior in whatever ways were open to us. This responsibility carried with it a respect for the dignity of the contemporary members of a culture; we valued every manifestation in folklore and myth, in the distinctiveness of the language spoken, in art and ritual, kinship and political organization, and the technologies of making a living. In turn, the value that we placed on vanishing custom gave us a different relationship to the peoples we studied and gave them a different relation to us who came as strangers among them and won their trust (Mead 1970b).

Ethical questions revolved around the obligation, with limited equipment and limited funds, to preserve as much as each one of us could of the small scraps of old beliefs and practices that remained among acculturated, but identifiable peoples, and of the whole range of cultural behavior. From this obligation several other ethical imperatives flowed: we had to get as good a record as we could; we had to record all the aspects of a culture because a culture was a whole and no part was less essential than any other; and because we ourselves, individually or in twos or threes, were running a race against time and were likely to be the only trained ethnologists who would ever study that particular people at that particular period in their history. There was an obligation to the people themselves because we had means which they lacked of studying their cultures that merged with our scientific conceptions of what needed to be studied; and there was an obligation to colleagues in the field who were interested in aspects of the culture which concerned us less—cat's cradles, perhaps, or the fastening of canoes or outriggers, or the variations in the decoration of everyday objects.

These were the imperatives of the discipline that combined the kinds of preoccupations that have become crystallized and stereotyped within the contrasting concerns of the humanities, the social sciences and the natural sciences. The conscientious field worker dealt, at least in some slight degree, with the ecological setting, the physique, the history, the arts and industries, the beliefs and practices of all peoples seen from the perspective of the concentration on preserving and learning about those cultures which were least likely to survive. Respect for the members of primitive cultures also carried with it respect for all the members of our own societies, whether they were immigrants or outcasts, aristocrats or members of small little-known cults or great religions. Because we emphasized the psychic unity of all mankind, and valued what others undervalued—the unwritten languages, oral traditions, primitive and archaic customs—we inevitably become champions of the dispossessed, defenders of the despised and neglected, pleaders for a wider view and a greater tolerance (Boas 1928; Herskovits 1972; Lewis 1966a; Valentine 1972).

We also became involved in the material and psychological well-being of the peoples we studied. We were sensitive to the impact of heartless or well-meaning regulations imposed by those in power, and alert to the destructiveness of most culture contact. We used to say that the young fieldworker on his or her first field trip who did not become involved in some argument with the authorities over some stupidity or insensitivity was not worth much as a human being, but that those who continued to become too involved were not likely to be good anthropologists (Mead 1970b). Ethical problems revolved around the ways in which we reported our findings, respect and protection for individuals, caution in reporting practices which might bring individuals and communities into conflict with the laws of the superordinate colonial and colonizing powers, and the extent to which we should engage in struggles dictated by our knowledge of the culture and our human concern for the peoples whom we came to know better and differently than did other outsiders. How actively we became engaged in battles over land, hunting, or mineral rights, or the kinds of education and citizenship that were being offered or withheld from primitive peoples, therefore, became a matter of ethical commitment. Activism, which ended in an inability to do any more work in an area, was poor scientific strategy; concentrating on the specific interests of the disciplines of anthropology to the exclusion of a given people's hunger and need was poor performance on the part of members of the human race that embraced us all (Tax 1952).

All of these issues are very much alive today (Adams 1970) in the extraordinarily changed climate of opinion of the 1970s. It is sterile to discuss the ethics of applied anthropology without taking the ethics of the entire discipline into account; the quarrels over the respect for ancient graveyards, the collection of artifacts once valued slightly and now valued intensely, the protection of individuals now called "human subjects" (Graubard 1969), the rights of members of a group to their own artistic products—their music and art style (Lomax 1977)—are all current versions of these perennial considerations. Where we once argued for the careful preservation of artifacts in museums, and won the trust of the old custodians of cultural remains, so that medicine bundles and fetiches were preserved from deterioration, now we are embattled by the demands of the descendants of those same people, who want to reclaim those artifacts (Fenton 1971). Where we once tried to widen the general public's understanding of the culturally specific traditions of peoples whom they had not learned to respect, today we are accused of stealing these same people's secrets or exposing their mysteries for our own gain.

Too much concentration on the subject matter of our science, or too little publication in a form accessible to a newly literate people, is branded as inhumane and selfish, but too much publication about the past of newly arrived nation-states brands us as attackers, if not outright maligners, of those who are prouder of modernization than of their histories. The applied anthropologist, a scientist who is first of all an anthropologist, cannot escape from the current phrasing of these perennial concerns of our discipline (American Anthropological Association 1970; Beals 1967; Silvert 1965; Thompson 1976).

It was those anthropologists who believed that anthropology could become a profession devoted to the well-being of some segment of the population or some institutional form, to changing patterns of agriculture, health care, education, political organization, and social participation, who founded the Society for Applied Anthropology in 1941, and who, after the experience of World War II, began to struggle explicitly with a code of ethics (Brown, Chapple, and Mead 1949). The story of these earlier involvements has been discussed in earlier essays of this volume (Partridge and Eddy, Arensberg, and Eddy and Partridge) and in a growing literature (Casagrande and Gladwin 1956; Mead and Metraux 1957, 1965; A. Metraux 1953; Spicer 1977).

I wish to concentrate here on the specific ethics of applied anthropologists in our roles as interventionists and as practitioners whose work can be expected to have identifiable consequences in the lives of human communities. As interventionists we became practitioners and needed professional ethics, just as the medical or legal professions need professional ethics. As practitioners we have clients who invoke our aid or retain us for a fee, or demand our participation in some wider issues. The extent of our involvement may be very special, such as the introduction of some new agricultural or health practice among a modernizing people. It may be much larger, as consultants in the educational policy of an American state or an African country. It may be wider still, as we are asked to participate in deliberations which affect the future of the global community (Laszlo 1977), as we did during World War II in decisions about Japan (Benedict 1946; Mead and Metraux 1965).

These involvements differ in degree: whether involvement is full time and a principal source of livelihood and professional identification, whether it is invoked in terms of some voluntary association

(Opler 1959) or by some bureaucratic demands, whether one is involved in times of total crisis like World War II, or in times of great political polarization—like the Vietnam War in the United States, the Cyprus question in England, the South African question in the Netherlands, the Algerian question in France, the treatment of pastoral peoples in Iran and Afghanistan, Ethiopia, and Kenya, the mining of uranium in Australia, or the opening up of the Amazon in Brazil.

Within these different climates of national (Coleman 1966, Mead in press b) and international (Mead 1963; Textor 1966) concerns, the involvement of anthropologists in matters which have immediate political, social, or economic consequences may differ very sharply (Mead, Dobzhansky, Tobach and Light 1968; Division of Church and Society 1975). In some situations, governments may seek the services of anthropologists, while in others they might expel them from the country, or even imprison them for inappropriate partisanship or interference in the country's internal affairs (Rozen 1976; Smith, Hicks, and Wicke 1976). But we should not, I believe, let such extreme differences in the importance of particular applications of anthropology blind us to the core of our ethical responsibilities. If we choose to act as full-time practitioners, as consultants, or as members of voluntary concerned associations (Carothers 1972; Opler 1959), we are being applied anthropologists. If we have the knowledge and the skill which makes us capable of applying anthropology, then we cannot divest ourselves of the responsibility that goes with that knowledge. A priest who loses his faith may be defrocked, a physician who has violated medical ethics may be barred from the operating room, a teacher may leave the school and stop teaching, but applied anthropologists cannot divest themselves of their anthropological skills. They may publicly announce their withdrawal from the profession and so, to some extent, protect their colleagues from the repercussions of their behavior. But ethically, a skill based on an understanding of culture remains, and wherever two or three human beings are gathered together, that knowledge will matter (Mead 1942b).

But if applied anthropology is to become a profession and not simply a collection of random activities in which anthropologists interest themselves idiosyncratically and expedientially (Bernard and Sibley 1975), then it is necessary to explore in which ways it resembles other professions, how it can learn from the ethical struggles of other professions and, because of profession-specific considerations, why it has to develop specific ethics.

Immediately after World War II, when practically every anthropologist in the country had been active as an applied anthropologist, the Society for Applied Anthropology began to struggle with a code of ethics which was eventually passed in 1962 as the Statement on Ethics. As a member of the original committee, I took medical ethics as a provisional model, and asked about analogous requirements: What was to be the overriding value within which applied anthropologists would act, as the physician was faithful to life and the judge to the law (Mead 1962)? What were our obligations to our clients? What were our responsibilities as a profession to train and certify the fitness of our members to act as applied anthropologists? What were our obligations to one another as fellow practitioners?

These questions remain, and they have not been embodied in any recognized set of institutional practices which provide for them and protect both practitioners and those who invoke their help. Our ability to certify fitness has become weaker because the old status of a Fellow of the American Anthropological Association, which assured at least the amount of knowledge necessary for a Ph.D. or its equivalent, is gone with the relaxed standards for membership. The Society for Applied Anthropology is simply a group of interested human scientists who enjoy working in an anthropological framework, but membership in the society carries no professional certification. We are still subject to the efforts of anthropologists as a whole to define the limits of their responsibilities, to their efforts to punish, discredit, or disproportionately protect their colleagues (Barth 1974; Dobzhansky 1963; Mead 1963b,c; Turnbull 1974), and to their refusal to set any standards for membership and responsibility within the profession. Correspondingly, applied anthropologists who have problems with clients—a government agency obsessed by accountability, an institution whose leadership repudiates the help it has invoked, a political party that goes out of power, an educational system that wants to economize—have no recourse (Rynkiewich and Spradley, 1976)! There is no standard by which they can be judged as competent or incompetent, well or poorly trained, in "good standing" or not.

The question of becoming a recognized profession has many complications. How are the overriding values of anthropology to be defined, so that an anthropologist might indeed take an oath of loyalty to them, and so that they might become the basis on which his or her loyalty could be attested by colleagues? Under the influence of the group who worked with the Harvard School of Business, the early discussions at the Society for Applied Anthropology centered on the matter of wholes (Bateson and Mead 1941). Anthropologists, we said, dealt with wholes—whole systems, whole institutions, whole societies, ultimately the whole world. Our task, in any particular case, was to define the whole within which we were working—a factory, a school system, a hospital, a political unit, an ecological unit—and then act in terms of the good of the whole. That good was defined as the preservation of a dynamic equilibrium which contained the idea of potentialities for adaptation and constructive change. It was criticized as being too cold and uncommitted by the advocates of Sol Tax's Action Anthropology (Tax 1952) in the 1950s, by those who felt that dynamic equilibrium was a characteristic of closed systems during the expansionist days of early space exploration, when the emphasis was on space as an open system (at the Pittsburgh meeting of the SfAA in 1961), and as lacking political partisanship during the polarizations of the late 1960s and early 1970s. Practically, it meant that an applied anthropologist would refuse to be retained by management without the consent of labor, by a colonial bureaucracy without the involvement of the people being governed, by a hospital administration without taking the patients' feelings and wishes into account. This is, of course, unacceptable to any group who feels that their cause or position is right and that those of others—management, labor, the establishment, the hierarchy, the agitators, the prison population—are either negligible or wrong.

An insistence upon dealing with a whole system, taking into account the place of any given system in larger systems, presents many problems of responsibility and competency. In medicine, surgery on the poorest, least valued member of a society carries the same ethical imperatives as surgery on a ruling potentate or prime minister. It also requires skill of the same kind. The throats of the mighty who address an audience of millions do not, as far as we know, develop a different kind of cancer from the throats of hawkers who shout at country fairs. But the difference between advising the local department of health or the local agricultural extension service on how to get some practice accepted within some set of traditional cultural attitudes on one hand, and on the other hand advising the Chiefs of Staff on the probable consequences of retaining or deposing the Japanese emperor after World War II, conducting the Nuremberg trials, or refusing to let the Concorde land in New York, or advising on the selection of "volunteers" to maintain a watch in the Sinai Desert, is enormous. The amount of knowledge and imagination required for tasks of such different scale is not measurable by any known test. Yet if we are to have professional ethics on which a client could count, on which a government demanding accountability could call, by which a young member of the profession can be guided, some way of dealing with the question of scale is essential.

During the discussions at the Society for Applied Anthropology immediately following World War II, we tried to deal with responsibility for the longest time perspective and widest repercussions that any given anthropologist was capable of thinking of; a very young and inexperienced anthropologist would not be expected to have the foresight of a more experienced one. If anthropologists knew enough to gauge the effect on legislation in Australia of legislation about immigration or reservation policy in the United States, it would be their responsibility to include that knowledge in any recommendations they made. At the meeting of the Preparatory Committee for the World Congress on Mental Health in 1948 (International Preparatory Committee 1948, Opler 1959), we tried to include these concerns under the heading of "foreseeable effects," so that the practitioner who was intervening in human affairs would only be held responsible for what he or she was able to foresee. But the capacity for foresight, like the definition of a whole system within a series of levels (Miller 1975), is still very much more ambiguous and resistant to codification than is the responsibility for appropriate training for a surgeon and appropriate precautions by the operating room staff.

The best that we can do at present, I believe, is to try to design new types of graduate training (Mead 1972b), since one of the principal difficulties of young anthropologists at present is orienting themselves and their specific skills and research interests within the framework of national and international institutions.

When the American Academy of Arts and Sciences convened a conference, consisting largely of anthropologists, to consider man's progress (Hoagland and Burhoe 1962), most of them were only too willing to refuse to consider larger problems and instead to leave such problems to economists or political scientists. Yet anthropologists, with their knowledge of how to work with wholes, have a great deal to contribute to the thinking about larger wholes—nations, continents, the planet, the solar system, the whole biosphere, and the surrounding atmosphere. But they need experience in moving from the microscale, where our discipline's competence lies, to the macroscale, in devising macroscopes (Mead and Heyman 1975) which will both preserve the precious detail of living human groups and yet include them systematically in larger wholes at higher levels.

Students therefore need exposure to discussions of these large-scale problems of war and peace (Fried, Harris, and Murphy 1968), protection of the environment (Commoner 1971; Mead and Kellogg in press), proliferation of nuclear economies (Division of Church and Society 1975), exploration of space (Mead, Michael, Lasswell and Frank 1958), as well as the more familiar issues of opposition to scientific racism (Coleman 1966; Comas 1961; Dobzhansky 1963; Wade 1976), vigilance against the use of information about communities which could be used against them as in the discussions about Thailand (American Anthropological Association 1971; Mead 1972c), and wariness about neo-colonialism (Gough 1968; Horowitz 1965).

Students also need exposure to cybernetics and general systems theory, and to the way our traditional script-bound type of linear thinking determines our attempts to escape Euro-American ethnocentrism (G. Bateson 1972; M. C. Bateson 1972; Chapple in press; Foerster 1950–1956). If they plan to become applied anthropologists, students need practice as part of their graduate work, and systematic contacts with the fields in which they expect to specialize: nutrition (Burgess and Dean 1962; Greene 1977; National Research Council 1943, 1945), education (Landes 1965; Vanderbilt 1952; Wax, Diamond and Gearing 1971), health (Jarvik 1975; Macgregor 1960), urban planning (Gans 1965; Doxiadis 1974; Mead 1975b), foreign affairs (Maday 1975), and international organizations (A. Metraux 1953; Mead 1976a; Torre 1963). We can see to it that these students are well acquainted with all the possibilities of instrumentation (Hockings 1975; Mead 1976c) and the related issue of protection of privacy and consent (Mead 1961, 1970b).

We can encourage students' participation in interdisciplinary and international organizations where they will be exposed not only to the best practice and most recent theoretical developments, but also to the points of ambiguity and current controversy in their chosen areas of interest. Here they will take part in the wider discussions about scientific responsibilities and some of the proposed solutions (AAAS Committee on Science in the Promotion of Human Welfare 1964; Boffey 1969; Edsall 1975; Kantrowitz 1967; Land 1973; Laszlo 1973, 1977; Waddington 1972). Proof of such active participation can be made a criteria for search committees and personnel departments, and funds can be sought to make such participation possible (Maday 1976).

We can work for the inclusion of groups previously excluded by sex, age, color, or ethnic identity, and so increase our anthropological competency. We can encourage the publication of books like *Ethics and Anthropology* (Rynkiewich and Spradley 1976) and Walter Goldschmidt's forthcoming volume on anthropology before and during World War II. We could set up some kind of council of advisers that would not be an ethics committee intent on disciplining those with whom they disagree, but a group to help young practitioners think out knotty problems, especially those where all possible solutions seem to be a choice between evils, as so many problems of long culture contact tend to be.

Young anthropologists at present are in a position similar to that of the isolated worker-priests in France who went, one by one, to work in industry and were either abandoned by or themselves abandoned the Church in the end, because they had no one to consult or talk with in the course of their upsetting experiences. For the anthropological fieldworker this is almost always the case: the letter which answers an inquiry arrives on the boat on which he or she quits the field. But there is no need to carry over these unfortunate conditions of isolation in most fieldwork to applied anthropologists who work where other applied anthropologists or other applied human scientists are within reach. The essence of ethics is a human group struggling with new dilemmas (Rynkiewich and Spradley 1976). As anthropologists who specialize in the diverse dilemmas of culture-specific situations, we should at least be able to provide for consultation and discussion among ourselves. Realizing the difficulty of the task is at least a step toward better solutions.

In summary, the discussions of ethics in applied anthropology have been concerned with practice and with task-oriented participation of anthropologists as practitioners; the discussions of ethics within the wider anthropological community have been concerned primarily with the fate of primitive peoples, minorities, just or unjust wars, and racial or biological determinism versus economic determinism. When discussing these issues, anthropologists have shown themselves to be extraordinarily incapable of applying the principles of their own discipline to themselves. Blind political partisanship has been, if anything, more rampant among anthropologists than in the other human sciences. This may at least partly be attributed to the greater degree of involvement of fieldworkers with the people they study. Other human scientists work regular hours, keep appointments in offices, or deal with data that others have gathered (Mead 1955a). Each anthropological fieldworker tends to rediscover culture all over again, and to make a deep emotional commitment to those aspects of the discipline's central paradigm that can be reexperienced. (Mead 1970b). I believe that we should be able to look at our own culture (Mead and Metraux 1957) and the polarizations that arise within it, with the same degree of sophistication that we use in analyzing primitive systems. But, those who are quickest to denounce their fellow anthropologists for ethnocentrism and imperialism (Weaver 1973) are also the least likely to be sophisticated about their own cultural biases. So, I regard the uproar that has gone on and continues to go on within the anthropological community primarily as a sign of a lack of sophistication and an inability to establish any real group solidarity.

It is true that almost every American anthropologist of my generation was actively involved in World War II, but that involvement was one of individual choice. One of our occupational diseases is a high degree of individualistic anarchy. Since World War II, every meeting of the American Anthropological Association has been marred by impassioned, ill-considered, unsophisticated debates, and there is usually very little difference in rationality on either side of any argument.

In spite of, rather than because of, the heatedness of the argument, I think we have made some progress, as we have moved from the obligation to protect the identity of individual informants, to the obligation to protect the identification of the group being studied—both well recognized before World War II—to the obligation to protect the culture when publication might provide material for those with the power and intention of destroying it, to the obligation not to publish material on specific communities which might become the targets of military or political attack. We have also made some advances in describing our specific obligations to attend to the rights of preliterate, or ethnically subordinated peoples, because of our greater knowledge and experience of how destructive certain activities—like forcible resettlement, the clearing of a jungle or forest, the intrusion of tourists on a large scale, or the introduction of new kinds of communication—can be (Carpenter 1973; Carpenter and Heyman 1970). This type of obligation is called, by the Society of Friends, the obligation of the "weighty friend" (the one who has more knowledge) to speak up. But within the procedures of the Society of Friends, there is also an obligation not to repeat what others have said and to remain silent when one has nothing substantive to say.

I think we have been successful when it comes to the ethics of practice, when an anthropologist acts to change conditions in some way, either as a commentator on the social scene, as an expert witness (Mead 1965, 1976b), or as a consultant to a government agency (Mead 1969), a tribal council, or a voluntary association. The principal issues have been the identification of an overriding value—a whole—the attempt to identify the nature of such wholes through cybernetics and general systems theories, and the attempt to define responsibility in terms of the extent to which a practitioner is capable of foresight. Other ethical issues which have been fruitfully explored are the obligation to tell the truth—a technical as well as an ethical imperative, where trust is an essential condition of research (Mead 1961)—and a distinction between the manipulation of individuals, the manipulation of groups, and the attempts to change a culture so that individuals or groups can function better (Mead 1942b, 1967). Recent emphasis in wider social science circles on "the quality of life" should involve applied anthropologists in another round of critical self-examination of that part of our discipline whose members believe that anthropology can make constructive contributions to the emerging global order (Laszlo 1977; Maruyama and Dator 1971).

BIBLIOGRAPHY OF WORKS CITED

Abegglen, James
  1958.   *The Japanese Factory System*. Glencoe, Ill.: Free Press.

Aberle, David
  1966.   *The Peyote Religion Among the Navajo*. New York: Wenner-Gren.

Adams, Richard N.
  1970.   *Crucifixion by Power: Essays on Guatemalan National Social Structure 1944–1966*. Austin: University of Texas Press.

Agar, Michael
  1973.   *Ripping and Running: A Formal Ethnography of Urban Heroin Addicts*. New York: Seminar Press.

American Anthropological Association
  1970.   "Principles of Professional Responsibility." *Newsletter* of the American Anthropological Association 11 (9).
  1971.   "Charge to the Ad Hoc Committee to Evaluate the Controversy Concerning Anthropological Activities in Relation to Thailand." *Newsletter* of the American Anthropological Association 12 (3).
  1976a. *Annual Report 1975*. Washington, D.C.: American Anthropological Association.
  1976b. *Guide to Departments of Anthropology 1976–77*. Washington, D.C.: American Anthropological Association.

American Association for the Advancement of Science
          Committee on Science in the Promotion of Human Welfare (Barry Commoner, Robert B. Brode, T. C. Byerly, Ansley J. Coale, John T. Edsall, Lawrence K. Frank, Margaret Mead, Walter Orr Roberts, Dael Wolfle.) 1964. "Reply to Science and the Race Problem." *Science* 143: 915.
  1974.   *Culture and Population Change*. Washington, D.C.: American Association for the Advancement of Science.

American Civil Liberties Union—Southern California
1975.   "No Police in Schools Without Court Order." *Open Forum* 53(1):1–2.

Anderson, James E.
1975.   *Public Policy-Making*. New York: Praeger.

Anthropology and the American Indian
1973.   San Francisco, Calif.: Indian Historian Press.

Ardila Rodriguez, Francisco
1965.   *Aspectos médico legales y médico sociales de la Marihuana*. Doctoral dissertation, University of Madrid.

Arensberg, Conrad M.
1941.   "Toward a 'Control' System for Industrial Relations. A Review of *Management and the Worker*." *Applied Anthropology* 1:54–57.
1942.   "Report on a Developing Community, Poston, Arizona." *Applied Anthropology* 2:2–21.
1947.   "Prospect and Retrospect." *Applied Anthropology* 6:1–7.
1951.   "Behavior and Organization: Industrial Studies." In John Rohrer and Muzafer Sherif, eds., *Social Psychology at the Crossroads*, pp. 324–352. New York: Harper and Row.
1955.   "American Communities." *American Anthropologist* 57:1143–60.
1967.   "Upgrading Peasant Agriculture: Is Tradition the Snag?" *Columbia Journal of World Business* 2(1):68–71.
1972.   "Culture as Behavior: Structure and Emergence." In Bernard J. Siegal, ed., *Annual Review of Anthropology* 1:1–26. Palo Alto, Calif.: Annual Reviews.
1975.   "Discussion of C. Steward Sheppard, The Role of Anthropology in Business Administration." In Bela C. Maday, ed., *Anthropology and Society*, pp. 71–75. Washington, D.C.: Anthropological Society of Washington.

Arensberg, Conrad M. and Solon T. Kimball
1938.   *Family and Community in Ireland*. Cambridge, Mass.: Harvard University Press.
1965.   *Culture and Community*. New York: Harcourt Brace and World.

Arensberg, Conrad M. and Arthur H. Niehoff
1964.   *Introducing Social Change: A Manual for Americans Overseas*. Chicago, Ill.: Aldine.

Armstrong, A. J.
1882–85. "Crow Agency Report." Washington, D.C.: U.S. Department of Interior Annual Report, 4 vols.

Arnstine, Donald
1975.   "PBTE and Measurement: A Program Based on a Mistake." In Ralph A. Smith, ed., *Regaining Educational Leadership: Critical Essays on PBTE/CBTE, Behavioral Objectives and Accountability*, pp. 165–175. New York: Wiley.

Artinian, Barbara M.
1975.   *Identity Change in a Therapeutic Community*. Ph.D. dissertation, University of Southern California.

Ashby, Sir Eric
1959.   *Technology and the Academics*. London: Macmillan.

Bain, Helen
1973.   "Self Governance Must Come First, Then Accountability." In R. W. Hostrop, J. A. Mecklenburger, and J. A. Wilson, eds., *Accountability for Educational Results*, pp. 357–359. Hamden, Conn.: Linnet Books.

Baker, Paul T. and William T. Sanders
1972.   "Demographic Studies in Anthropology." In Bernard J. Siegal, ed., *Annual Review of Anthropology*, 1:151–178. Palo Alto, Calif.: Annual Reviews.

Ball, Richard A.
1971.   "The Southern Appalachian Folk Subculture as a Tension-Reducing Way of Life." In John D. Photiadis and Harry K. Schwarzweller, eds., *Change in Rural Appalachia: Implications for Action Programs*, pp. 69–79. Philadelphia: University of Pennsylvania Press.

Baltzell, E. Digby
1964.   *The Protestant Establishment: Aristocracy and Caste in America*. New York: Vintage Books.

Barbero Carnicero, A. and R. Flores Marco
1944.   "Enfermedad del Cáñamo." *Revista Clínica Española* 13:395–399.

Bard, L.
1941.   "Algunas observaciones clínicas sobre la intoxicación crónica por la marihuana." *La Prensa Médica Argentina* 2(3):171–179.

Barker, Roger B.
1963.   *The Stream of Behavior*. New York: Meredith.

Barnard, Chester I.
1938.   *The Functions of the Executive*. Cambridge, Mass.: Harvard University Press.

Barnett, Homer G.
1956.   *Anthropology in Administration*. Evanston, Ill.: Row, Peterson.

Barr, Donald A.
1972.   "The Professional Urban Planner." *Journal of the American Institute of Planners* 38:155–159.

Barth, Fredrick
1974.   "On Responsibility and Humanity: Calling a Colleague to Account." *Current Anthropology* 15(1):99–102.

Bastide, Roger
1973.   *Applied Anthropology*. Alice L. Morton, trans. New York: Harper and Row.

Bateson, Gregory
1935.   "Culture Contact and Schismogenesis." *Man* 35:178–183.
1942.   "Morale and National Character." In Goodwin Watson, ed., *Civilian Morale*, pp. 71–91. New York and Boston, Mass.: Houghton Mifflin.
1972.   *Steps to an Ecology of Mind*. San Francisco, Calif.: Chandler.

Bateson, Gregory and Margaret Mead
1941.   "Principles of Morale Building." *Journal of Educational Sociology* 15:206–220.

Bateson, M. C.
1972.   *Our Own Metaphor.* New York: Knopf.

Bauer, R. and K. Gergen
1968.   *The Study of Policy Formation.* New York: Free Press.

Beals, Ralph L.
1945.   *Cheran: A Sierra Tarascan Village.* Washington, D.C.: Smithsonian Institution, Institute of Social Anthropology, Publication 2.
1969.   *Politics of Social Research: An Inquiry into the Ethics and Responsibilities of Social Scientists.* Chicago, Ill.: Aldine.

Beals, Ralph L. et al.
1967.   "Background Information on Problems of Anthropological Research and Ethics." *Newsletter* of the American Anthropological Association 8:1–13.

Becker, Howard S.
1963.   *Outsiders: Studies in the Sociology of Deviance.* New York: Free Press.

Bell, Daniel
1976.   *The Cultural Contradictions of Capitalism.* New York: Basic Books.

Belshaw, Cyril
1966.   "Project Evaluation." *International Development Review* 8(2):2–6.
1972.   "Anthropology." *International Social Science Journal* 24:80–94.
1976.   *The Sorcerer's Apprentice: An Anthropology of Public Policy.* New York: Pergamon.

Benedict, Burton
1972.   "Social Regulation of Fertility." In G. A. Harrison and A. J. Boyce, eds., *The Structure of Human Populations,* pp. 73–89. Oxford: Clarendon Press.

Benedict, Ruth
1935.   *Zuni Mythology.* 2 vols. Columbia University Contributions to Anthropology, 21. New York: Columbia University Press.
1946.   *The Chrysanthemum and the Sword.* Boston, Mass.: Houghton Mifflin.
1947.   *Race: Science and Politics.* New York: Viking.

Benet, Sula
1975.   "Early Diffusion and Folk Uses of Hemp." In Vera Rubin, ed., *Cannabis and Culture,* pp. 81–116. The Hague: Mouton.

Bennett, John W. and Iwao Ishino
1963.   *Paternalism in the Japanese Economy.* Minneapolis: University of Minnesota Press.

Berelson, Bernard
1971.   "Population Policy: Personal Notes." *Population Studies* 25:173–182.
1973.   "Population Growth Policy in Developed Countries." In Charles F. Westoff et al., eds., *Toward the End of Growth,* pp. 145–160. Englewood Cliffs, N.J.: Prentice-Hall.

1974.   "Summary." In Bernard Berelson, ed., *Population Policy in Developed Countries,* pp. 771–789. New York: McGraw-Hill.

Bernal, Segundo
1971.   "Algunos aspectos sociológicos de la migración en Colombia." In R. Cardona Gutierres, ed., *Las Migraciones Internas,* pp. 51–101. Bogotá: Editorial Andes.

Bernard, H. Russell and Willis E. Sibley
1975.   *Anthropology and Jobs.* Washington, D.C.: American Anthropological Association.

Bernath, Z. V. and P. Martini Herrar
1943.   "Estudio sobre la patogenía de la enfermedad del Cáñamo." *Revista Chilena de Higiene y Medicina Preventiva* 6:11–20.

Berube, Maurice and Marilyn Gittell
1968.   *Confrontation at Ocean Hill-Brownsville.* New York: Praeger.

Bieder, Robert E. and Thomas G. Tax
1976.   "From Ethnologists to Anthropologists: A Brief History of the American Ethnological Society." In John V. Murra, ed., *American Anthropology: The Early Years,* pp. 11–22. New York: West.

Black, Alan
1968.   "The Comprehensive Plan." In William I. Goodman and Eric C. Freund, eds., *Principles and Practice of Urban Planning,* pp. 349–378. Washington, D.C.: International City Managers Association.

Blake, Judith
1969.   "Population Policy for Americans: Is the Government Being Misled?" *Science* 164:522–529.

Blau, Peter M.
1974.   "Parameters of Social Structures." *American Sociological Review* 39:615–635.

Boas, Franz
1898.   "Growth of Toronto Children." *Report of the U.S. Commissioner of Education for 1896–1897,* pp. 1541–1599. Washington, D.C.
1910.   "Changes in Bodily Form of Descendants of Immigrants." Partial report on the results of an anthropological investigation for the U.S. Immigration Commission. Washington, D.C.: Government Printing Office. (Senate Document no. 208, 61st Cong., 2d Sess.)
1911.   *The Mind of Primitive Man.* Rev. ed. New York: Free Press, 1963. (Orig. pub. New York: Macmillan).
1928.   *Anthropology and Modern Life.* New York: Norton.

Boas, Franz and Ella Deloria
1941.   *Dakota Grammar.* Memoirs of the National Academy of Sciences, vol. 33. Washington, D.C.: U.S. Government Printing Office.

Boffey, Philip M.
1969.   "Defense Research: Pressure on Social Sciences." *Science* 164:1037–1039.

Bogue, Donald J.
1969.   *Principles of Demography.* New York: Wiley.

Boissevain, Jeremy and John C. Mitchell
1973. *Network Analysis: Studies in Human Interaction.* The Hague: Mouton.

Brace, C. Loring and M. F. Ashley Montagu
1965. *Man's Evolution: An Introduction to Physical Anthropology.* New York: Macmillan.

Bradford, Leland P., Jack R. Gibb, and Kenneth D. Benne, eds.
1964. *T-Group Theory and Laboratory Method: Innovation in Reeducation.* New York: Wiley.

Brecher, Edward M. and Editors of Consumer Reports
1972. *Licit and Illicit Drugs.* Boston: Little, Brown.

Brown, Antoinette B.
1975. "The Etiology of Caffeine Usage Among the Creek." Paper presented at the symposium: Secular Ritual and Altered States of Consciousness, Society for Applied Anthropology, Amsterdam. (Files of the Author).

Brown, Gordon G., Eliot D. Chapple, and Margaret Mead
1949. "Report of the Committee on Ethics." *Human Organization* 8:20–21.

Bunzel, Ruth
1962. "Introduction." In Franz Boas, *Anthropology and Modern Life,* pp. 4–10. New York: Norton. (Orig. pub. 1928.)

Burchard, Roderick
1976. "The Peruvian Dilemma: Coca, Cocaine, and International Politics." Paper presented at the symposium: The U.S. Connection, Latin American Studies Association, Atlanta, Ga. (Files of the Author).

Burgess, Anne and R. F. A. Dean, eds.
1962. *Malnutrition and Food Habits: Report of an International and Interprofessional Conference.* London: Tavistock.

Burnett, Jacquetta Hill
1968a. "Anthropological Study of Disability from Educational Problems of Puerto Ricans." Application for Research Grant, DHEW Social and Rehabilitation Service. Urbana, Ill.: Bureau of Educational Research. (Files of the author).
1968b. "Workflow versus Classroom Models of Academic Work." *Michigan Journal of Secondary Education* 9:14–24.
1969. "Event Description and Analysis in the Micro-ethnography of Urban Classrooms." Urbana, Ill.: Bureau of Educational Research. (Files of the author.)
1970. "Culture of the School." *Council on Anthropology and Education Newsletter* 1:4–13.
1972. "Event Analysis as a Methodology for Urban Anthropology." Anthropological Study of Disability from Educational Problems of Puerto Rican Youth. Final Report: DHEW, SRS, Grant no. RD 2969 G69, vol. 2, part 2. Urbana, Ill.: Bureau of Educational Research. (Files of the Author.)
1973. "Event Description and Analysis in the Microethnography of the Classroom." In F. A. Ianni and E. Storey, eds., *Cultural Relevance and*

Educational Issues: Readings in Anthropology and Education, pp. 287–303. Boston, Mass.: Little, Brown.

1974a. *Anthropology and Education: An Annotated Bibliographic Guide*. New Haven, Conn.: HRAF Press.

1974b. "Social Structures, Ideologies, and Culture Codes in Occupational Development of Puerto Rican Youths. Anthropological Study of Disability from Educational Problems of Puerto Rican Youths." Final Report: DHEW, SRS Grant no. RD 2969 G69. vol. 1. Urbana, Ill.: Bureau of Educational Research. (Files of the Author.)

Burns, Tom
1954. "The Directions of Activity and Communication in a Departmental Executive Group." *Human Relations* 7:73–97.

California
1976. "California High Court Rules on Davis Minority Program." *Forum*, October 6. Berkeley: University of California School of Law.

Callahan, Raymond E.
1962. *Education and the Cult of Efficiency*. Chicago, Ill.: University of Chicago Press.

Campbell, Joan
1971. *Agricultural Development in East Africa: A Problem in Cultural Ecology*. Ph.D. dissertation, Anthropology Department, Columbia University.

Carnegie Commission on Higher Education
1973. *Priorities for Action: Final Report*. New York: McGraw-Hill.

Carneiro, Robert L.
1967. "On the Relationship Between Size of Population and Complexity of Social Organization." *Southwestern Journal of Anthropology* 23:234–243.

Carothers, E. et al.
1972. *To Love or to Perish: The Technological Crisis and the Church*. New York: Friendship Press.

Carpenter, Edmund
1973. *Oh, What a Blow that Phantom Gave Me*. New York: Holt, Rinehart & Winston.

Carpenter, E. and K. Heyman
1970. *They Became What They Beheld*. New York: Outerbridge and Dienstfrey.

Carter, William E., Wilber J. Coggins, and Paul L. Doughty
1976. *Chronic Cannabis Use in Costa Rica*. A Report by the Center for Latin American Studies of the University of Florida to the National Institute on Drug Abuse. Contract Number NO1-MH3-1233 (ND).

Casagrande, Joseph B.
1959. "Some Observations on the Study of Intermediate Societies." In Verne F. Ray, ed., *Intermediate Societies, Social Mobility, and Communication*. Proceedings of 1959 Meeting of the American Ethnological Society. Seattle: University of Washington Press.

Casagrande, J. B. and T. Gladwin, eds.
  1956. *Some Uses of Anthropology: Theoretical and Applied.* Washington, D.C.: Anthropological Society of Washington.

Caudill, William
  1953. "Applied Anthropology in Medicine." In A. L. Kroeber, ed., *Anthropology Today,* pp. 771–806. Chicago, Ill.: University of Chicago Press.

Cazden, Courtney B., Vera P. John, and Dell Hymes, eds.
  1972. *Functions of Language in the Classroom.* New York: Teachers College Press.

Chapman, Paul
  1973. "Comparison of Historical and Contemporary Movements for Accountability." In R. W. Hostrop, J. A. Mecklenburger, and J. A. Wilson, eds., *Accountability for Educational Results,* pp. 307–318. Hamden, Conn.: Linnet Books.

Chapple, Eliot D.
  1941. "Organization Problems in Industry." *Applied Anthropology* 1:2–9.
  1942. "The Analysis of Industrial Morale." *Journal of Industrial Hygiene and Toxicology* 24(7):163–172.
  1949. "The Interaction Chronograph: Its Evolution and Present Application." *Personnel* 25(4):295–307.
  1953a. "Applied Anthropology in Industry." In A. L. Kroeber, ed., *Anthropology Today,* pp. 819–831. Chicago, Ill.: University of Chicago Press.
  1953b. "The Standard Experimental (Stress) Interview as Used in Interaction Chronograph Investigations." *Human Organization* 12:23–32.
  1970. *Culture and Biological Man: Explorations in Behavioral Anthropology.* New York: Holt, Rinehart, and Winston.
  In press. "Populations of Coupled Non-Linear Oscillators in Anthropological Biology Systems." Paper presented at the IEEE Systems, Man and Cybernetics Society, November 1976.

Chapple, Eliot D. and Conrad M. Arensberg
  1940. "Measuring Human Relations: An Introduction to the Study of the Interaction of Individuals." *Genetic Psychology Monographs* 22:3–147.

Chapple, Eliot D. and Carleton S. Coon
  1942. *Principles of Anthropology.* New York: Holt.

Chapple, Eliot D. and Gordon Donald
  1946. "A Method for Evaluating Supervisory Personnel." *Harvard Business Review* 24:197–214.
  1947. "An Evaluation of Department Store Salespeople by the Interaction Chronograph." *Journal of Marketing* 12:173–185.

Chapple, Eliot D. and Erich Lindemann
  1941. "Clinical Implications of Measurements of Interaction Rates in Psychiatric Patients," *Applied Anthropology* 1:1–10.

Chapple, Eliot D. and Leonard R. Sayles
  1961. *The Measure of Management.* New York: Macmillan.

Clifton, James A., ed.
1970.   *Applied Anthropology: Readings in the Uses of the Science of Man*. Boston, Mass.: Houghton Mifflin.

Clinton, Charles A.
1975.   "The Anthropologist as Hired Hand." *Human Organization* 34:197–204.

Cochrane, Glynn
1971.   *Development Anthropology*. New York: Oxford University Press.

Cohen, Abner
1969.   *Custom and Politics in Urban Africa: A Study of Hausa Migrants in Yoruba Towns*. Berkeley: University of California Press.
1974.   *Two-Dimensional Man: An Essay on the Anthropology of Power and Symbolism in Complex Society*. Berkeley: University of California Press.

Coke, James G.
1968.   "Antecedents of Local Planning." In William I. Goodman and Eric C. Freund, eds., *Principles and Practice of Urban Planning*, pp. 7–28. Washington, D.C.: International City Managers Association.

Cole, Michael, John Gay, J. A. Glick, and D. W. Sharp
1971.   *The Cultural Context of Learning and Thinking*. New York: Basic Books

Coleman, J. S. et al.
1966.   *Equality of Educational Opportunity*. Washington, D.C.: Government Printing Office.

Collins, Orvis and June Collins
1973.   *Interaction and Social Structure*. The Hague: Mouton.

Comas, Juan
1961.   " 'Scientific' Racism Again?" *Current Anthropology*, 2(4):303–340.

Comitas, Lambros
1975.   "The Social Nexus of Ganja in Jamaica." In Vera Rubin, ed., *Cannabis and Culture*, pp. 119–132. The Hague: Mouton.

Commission on Population Growth and the American Future
1965.   "Final Report on 'The Population Dilemma'." In Larry K. Y. Ng, ed., *The Population Crisis, Implications and Plans for Action*, pp. 317–322. Bloomington: Indiana University Press.
1972.   *Population and the American Future*. New York: Signet. The 23d American Assembly.

Commoner, Barry
1971.   *The Closing Circle*. New York: Knopf.

Coser, Lewis A., ed.
1963.   *Sociology Through Literature*. Englewood Cliffs, N.J.: Prentice-Hall.

Cowgill, George L.
1975.   "On Causes and Consequences of Ancient and Modern Population Changes." *American Anthropologist* 77:505–525.

Craf, John R.
1958.   *Junior Boards of Executives*. New York: Harper.

448   Bibliography

Craig, Richard B.
1976.   "La Campaña Permanente: Mexico's Anti-Drug Campaign." Paper presented at the symposium: The U.S. Connection, Latin American Studies Association, Atlanta, Ga. (Files of the Author.)

Cronin, Joseph M.
1973.   *The Control of Urban Schools: Perspectives on the Power of Educational Reformers.* New York: Free Press.

Cruz, Maria
1974.   *Social Factors and Self-Esteem Among Puerto Rican and Non-Puerto Rican Students.* Ph.D. dissertation, University of Illinois.

D'Andrade, Roy G. et al.
1975.   "Academic Opportunity in Anthropology, 1974–90." *American Anthropologist* 77:753–773.

Davis, Allison W.
1948.   "The Measurement of Mental Systems." *Scientific Monthly* 66:301–316.

Davis, Allison W. and John Dollard
1940.   *Children of Bondage.* Washington, D.C.: American Council on Education.

Davis, Allison W., Burleigh B. Gardner, and Mary R. Gardner
1941.   *Deep South: A Social-Anthropological Study of Caste and Class.* Chicago, Ill.: University of Chicago Press.

Davis, Kingsley
1967.   "Population Policy: Will Current Programs Succeed?" *Science* 158:730–739.

DeLaguna, Frederica
1960.   "Method and Theory of Ethnology." In F. DeLaguna, ed., *Selected Papers from the American Anthropologist (1888–1920)*, pp. 782–792. Evanston, Ill.: Row, Peterson.

Deloria, Ella
1944.   *Speaking of Indians.* New York: Friendship Press.

Deloria, Vine, Jr.
1969.   *Custer Died for Your Sins.* New York: Macmillan.

Denham, Woodrow W.
1974.   "Population Structure, Infant Transport, and Infanticide among Pleistocene and Modern Hunter-Gatherers." *Journal of Anthropological Research* 30:191–198.

Denison, George
1969.   *The Lives of Children.* New York: Random House.

Densmore, Frances
1929.   *Chippewa Customs.* Washington, D.C.: Bureau of American Ethnology, Bulletin 86.

De Vos, George and Lola Romanucci-Ross, eds.
1975.   *Ethnic Identity: Cultural Continuities and Change.* Palo Alto, Calif.: Mayfield.

Dickson, William J. and F. J. Roethlisberger
  1966.   *Counseling in an Organization.* Boston, Mass.: Harvard University, Graduate School of Business Administration.

Division of Church and Society
  1975.   *The Plutonium Economy: A Statement of Concern.* New York: National Council of the Churches of Christ.

Dobyns, Henry F.
  1971.   "On the Economic Anthropology of Postcolonial National Development." *Current Anthropology* 12:393–394.
  1974.   *Hualapai Indians. Prehistoric Indian Occupation within the Eastern Area of the Yuman Complex: A Study in Applied Archaeology.* 3 vols. New York: Garland.

Dobyns, Henry F., Paul L. Doughty, and Harold D. Lasswell
  1971.   *Peasants, Power, and Applied Social Change: Vicos as a Model.* Beverly Hills, Calif.: Sage.

Dobzhansky, Theodosius
  1963.   "A Debatable Account of the Origin of Races." Review of *The Origin of Races* by Carleton S. Coon. *Scientific American* 208(2):169–172.

Dollard, John
  1937.   *Caste and Class in a Southern Town.* New Haven, Conn.: Yale University Press.

Donovan, John C.
  1967.   *The Politics of Poverty.* New York: Pegasus.

Doxiadis, C. A., ed.
  1974.   *Anthropopolis: City for Human Development.* Athens: Athens Publishing Center.

Dozier, Edward P.
  1966.   *Hano: A Tewa Indian Community in Arizona.* New York: Holt, Rinehart, and Winston.

Drake, St. Clair and Horace R. Cayton
  1945.   *Black Metropolis.* New York: Harcourt, Brace.

Driver, Edwin D.
  1970.   "Summary of the Social Sciences and Population Policy: A Survey." *Demography* 7:379–392.
  1972.   *Essays on Population Policy.* Lexington, Mass.: Lexington Books.

Drucker, Peter F.
  1954.   *The Practice of Management.* New York: Harper and Row.

Dumond, D. E.
  1975.   "The Limitation of Human Population: A Natural History." *Science* 187:713–721.

Durkheim, Emile
  1947.   *The Elementary Forms of Religious Life: A Study in Religious Sociology.* J. W. Swain, trans. Glencoe, Ill.: Free Press. (Orig. pub. in 1915.)

450   Bibliography

du Toit, Brian M.
1975.   "Dagga: The History and Ethnographic Setting of Cannabis Sativa in Southern Africa." In Vera Rubin, ed., *Cannabis and Culture*, pp. 81–116. The Hague: Mouton.
1976.   "Ethnicity and Patterning in South African Drug Use." In Brian M. du Toit, ed., *Drugs, Rituals, and Altered States of Consciousness*, pp. 75–99. Rotterdam: A. A. Balkema.

Eaton, G. Gray
1976.   "The Social Order of Japanese Macaques." *Scientific American* 235: 96–106.

Eddy, Elizabeth M.
1967.   *Walk the White Line: A Profile of Urban Education*. Garden City, N.Y.: Doubleday.
1969.   *Becoming a Teacher: The Passage to Professional Status*. New York: Teachers College Press.

Edsall, John T.
1975.   *Scientific Freedom and Responsibility*. Washington, D.C.: American Association for the Advancement of Science.

Eggan, Fred
1963.   "The Graduate Program." In David G. Mandelbaum, Gabriel W. Lasker, and Ethel M. Albert, eds., *The Teaching of Anthropology*, pp. 409–419. Washington, D.C.: American Anthropological Association.

Ehrlich, Paul R.
1968.   *The Population Bomb*. New York: Ballantine.

Elejalde, B. R.
1975.   "Marihuana and Genetic Studies in Colombia." In Vera Rubin, ed., *Cannabis and Culture*, pp. 327–343. The Hague: Mouton.

Elliot, Robin, Lynn C. Landman, Richard Lincoln, and Theodore Tsuruoka
1971.   "United States Population Growth and Family Planning: A Review of the Literature." In D. Callahan, ed., *The American Population Debate*, pp. 185–226. New York: Doubleday.

Ellison, Ralph
1966.   *"An American Dilemma:* A Review." In *Shadow and Act*, pp. 290–302. New York: Signet Books.

Embree, John
1943.   "Dealing with Japanese." *Applied Anthropology* 2:37–41.

Erasmus, Charles J.
1961.   *Man Takes Control: Cultural Development and American Aid*. Minneapolis: University of Minnesota Press.

Escobar Mendes, Miguel
1973.   Realizaciones y perspectivas de la lucha contra la drogadicción en Colombia. II Seminario Nacional Sobre Farmacodependedcias. Ms. (Files of the Author.)

Esquival Medina, R. and G. Gonsalez
1938.   "Marijuana: estudio especial de las problemas planteados por la marijuana." *Revista Médica de Yucatán* 19:265–274.

Etzioni, Amitai
1972. "The Search for Political Meaning." *The Center Magazine* 5(2):2–11.

Evans-Pritchard, E. E.
1946. "Applied Anthropology." *Africa* 16:92–98.

Fabrega, Horacio Jr. and Peter K. Manning
1972. "Health Maintenance Among Peruvian Peasants." *Human Organization* 31:243–256.

Fallers, Leonard A.
1974. *The Social Anthropology of the Nation-State.* Chicago, Ill.: Aldine.

Fals Borda, Orlando
1955. *Peasant Society in the Colombian Andes.* Gainesville: University of Florida Press.

Fenton, William N.
1971. "The New York State Wampum Collection: The Case for the Integrity of Cultural Treasures." *Proceedings of the American Philosophical Society,* 115(6):437–461.

Fernandez, James
1972. *"Tabernanthe Iboga:* Narcotic Ecstasis and the Work of the Ancestors." In Peter Furst, ed., *Flesh of the Gods,* pp. 237–260. New York: Praeger.

Fisher, Joseph
1969. "Regional Planning: Determining the Public Interest." In Maynard M. Hufschmidt, ed., *Regional Planning: Challenge and Prospects,* pp. 3–27. New York: Praeger.

Fluckiger, Friedrich A. and Daniel Hanbury
1879. *Pharmacographia: A History of the Principal Drugs of Vegetable Origin Met with in Great Britain and British India.* London: Macmillan.

Foerster, Heinz von, ed.
1950–56. *Cybernetics.* 5 vols. New York: Josiah Macy Jr. Foundation.

Forde, Daryll
1953. "Applied Anthropology in Government: British Africa." In A. L. Kroeber, ed., *Anthropology Today,* pp. 841–865. Chicago, Ill.: University of Chicago Press.

Fortes, Meyer
1958. "Introduction." In Jack Goody, ed., *The Developmental Cycle of Domestic Groups,* Cambridge Papers in Social Anthropology, No. 1.

Foster, George M.
1948. *Empire's Children: The People of Tzintzuntzan.* Washington, D.C. Smithsonian Institution, Institute of Social Anthropology Publication No. 6.
1952. "Relationships Between Theoretical and Applied Anthropology: A Public Health Program Analysis." *Human Organization* 11:5–16.
1958. *Summary Report.* Wenner-Gren-American Anthropological Association Ph.D. Curricula Conference, Washington, D.C., November 23–24 (mimeographed).
1962. *Traditional Cultures and the Impact of Technological Change.* New York: Harper and Row.
1969. *Applied Anthropology.* Boston: Little, Brown.

Franklin, S. H.
1969. *The European Peasantry: The Final Phase*. London: Methuen.

Frazier, E. Franklin
1939. *The Negro Family in the United States*. Chicago, Ill.: University of Chicago Press.

Freeman, Howard E. and Clarence C. Sherwood
1970. *Social Research and Social Policy*. Englewood Cliffs, N.J.: Prentice-Hall.

Freilich, Morris, ed.
1970. *Marginal Natives: Anthropologists at Work*. New York: Harper and Row.

Fried, Morton H.
1953. *The Fabric of Chinese Society*. New York: Praeger.

Fried, Morton, Marvin Harris, and Robert Murphy, eds.
1968. *War: The Anthropology of Armed Conflict and Aggression*. Garden City, N.Y.: Natural History Press.

Fromm, Erich
1972. "Humanistic Planning." *Journal of the American Institute of Planners* 38:67–71.

Fuchs, Estelle and Robert J. Havighurst
1972. *To Live on This Earth: American Indian Education*. Garden City, N.Y.: Doubleday.

Fuguitt, Glen V. and James J. Zuiches
1975. "Residential Preferences and Population Distribution." *Demography* 12:491–504.

Furnivall, John S.
1948. *Colonial Policy and Practice*. Cambridge: Cambridge University Press.

Furst, Peter, ed.
1972. *Flesh of the Gods: Ritual Use of Hallucinogens*. New York: Praeger.

Galloway, George B. and Associates
1941. *Planning for America*. New York: Holt.

Gans, Herbert J.
1962. *The Urban Villagers: Group and Class in the Life of Italian Americans*. New York: Free Press.
1965. "The Failure of Urban Renewal." *Commentary* (April), 39:29–37.
1970. "From Urbanism to Policy-Planning." *Journal of the American Institute of Planners* 36:223–225.

Gardner, Burleigh B.
1945. *Human Relations in Industry*. Chicago, Ill.: R. D. Irwin.

Gay, John and Michael Cole
1967. *The New Mathematics and an Old Culture: A Study of Learning among the Kpelle of Liberia*. New York: Holt, Rinehart, and Winston.

Gearing, Fred
1970. "The Strategy of the Fox Project." In James A. Clifton, ed., *Applied Anthropology*, pp. 113–120. New York: Houghton Mifflin, reprinted

from Fred Gearing, R. McC. Netting, and L. R. Peattie, *Documentary History of the Fox Project: 1949–1959*, pp. 294–300. Chicago, Ill.: University of Chicago, Department of Anthropology.

Gillie, F. B.
1967.   *Basic Thinking in Regional Planning.* The Hague: Mouton.

Gillin, John
1947.   *Moche: A Peruvian Coastal Community.* Washington, D.C.: Smithsonian Institution, Institute of Social Anthropology Publication No. 3.

Gladwin, Thomas
1967.   *Poverty U.S.A.* Boston: Little, Brown.

Glaser, Barney G. and Anselm L. Strauss
1967.   *The Discovery of Grounded Theory: Strategies for Qualitative Research.* Chicago, Ill.: Aldine.

Glazer, Nathan
1975.   *Affirmative Discrimination: Ethnic Inequality and Public Policy.* New York: Basic Books.

Goldfrank, Esther
1943.   "Historic Change and Social Character: A Study of the Teton Dakota." *American Anthropologist* 45:67–83.

Gonzalez, Nancy S.
1972.   "The Sociology of a Dam." *Human Organization* 31:353–60.

Goodenough, Ward H.
1956.   "Componential Analysis and the Study of Meaning." *Language* 32:195–216.
1963.   *Cooperation in Change.* New York: Russell Sage Foundation.
1969.   "Re-thinking Role and Status: Toward a General Model of Relationships." In Stephen A. Tyler, ed., *Cognitive Anthropology,* pp. 311–330. New York: Holt, Rinehart and Winston.
1971.   *Culture, Language, and Society.* Reading, Mass.: Addison-Wesley Modular Publications No. 7.

Goodman, Paul
1965.   *Compulsory Mis-Education.* New York: Horizon Press.

Gottlieb, David
1974.   "Work and Families." *The Journal of Higher Education.* 45:535–544.

Gough, Kathleen
1968.   "Anthropology and Imperialism." *Monthly Review* 19:12–27.

Gouldner, Alvin W.
1959.   "Organizational Analysis." In R. K. Merton, L. Broom, L. S. Cottrell, Jr., eds., *Sociology Today,* pp. 400–428. New York: Basic Books.

Grabow, Stephen and Alan Heskin
1973.   "Foundations for a Radical Concept of Planning." *Journal of the American Institute of Planners* 39:106–114.

Graubard, S. R., ed.
1969.   "Ethical Aspects of Experimentation with Human Subjects." *Daedalus* (Spring), 98(2):v–603.

454   Bibliography

Green, Wayne E.
1975.   "Inept Advocates? Lawyers' Competence at Courtroom Work Stirs Growing Debate." *Wall Street Journal,* February 24, 55(92):1, 17.

Greene, Lawrence, ed.
1977.   *Malnutrition, Behavior, and Social Organization.* New York: Academic Press.

Gross, Neal, Joseph B. Giacquinta, and Marilyn Bernstein
1971.   *Implementing Organizational Innovations: A Sociological Analysis of Planned Educational Change.* New York: Basic Books.

Guest, Robert A.
1962.   *Organizational Change: The Effect of Successful Leadership.* Homewood, Ill.: Irwin and Dorsey Press.

Haas, Theodore H.
1957.   "The Legal Aspects of Indian Affairs from 1887–1957." *Annals American Academy of Political and Social Sciencies.* 311:12–22.

Halbwachs, Maurice
1930.   *Les Causes du Suicide.* Paris: Librairie Felix Alcan. (Reprinted New York: Arno Press, 1975.)

Hall, Edward T.
1966.   *The Hidden Dimension.* Garden City, N.Y.: Doubleday.
1976.   *Beyond Culture.* Garden City, N.Y.: Doubleday.

Hall, Roberta L.
1972.   "The Demographic Transition: Stage Four." *Current Anthropology* 13:212–215.

Halsted, D. Kent
1974.   *Statewide Planning in Higher Education.* Washington, D.C.: Government Printing Office.

Hammel, E. A.
1976.   "Training Anthropologists for Effective Roles in Public Policy." In Peggy R. Sanday, ed., *Anthropology and the Public Interest,* pp. 29–33. New York: Academic Press.

Hannerz, Ulf
1969.   *Soulside: Inquiries into Ghetto Culture and Community.* New York: Columbia University Press.
1974.   "Ethnicity and Opportunity in Urban America." In Abner Cohen, ed., *Urban Ethnicity,* pp. 37–76. ASA Monograph 12. London: Tavistock.

Hansen, Asael T.
1976.   "Robert Redfield, The Yucatan Project, and I." In John V. Murra, ed., *American Anthropology: The Early Years,* pp. 167–186. New York: West.

Harner, Michael J.
1973.   "The Role of Hallucinogenic Plants in European Witchcraft." In Michael J. Harner, ed., *Hallucinogens and Shamanism,* pp. 125–150. London: Oxford University Press.

Harris, Marvin
    1964.   *The Nature of Cultural Things.* New York: Random House.
    1968.   *The Rise of Anthropological Theory.* New York: Thomas Y. Crowell.

Harrison, G. A. and A. J. Boyce
    1972.   "Introduction, The Framework of Population Studies." In G. A. Harrison and A. J. Boyce, eds., *The Structure of Human Populations,* pp. 1–16. Oxford: Clarendon Press.

Haskell, Edward F.
    1972.   *Full Circle: The Moral Force of Unified Science.* New York: Gordon and Breach.

Heighton, Robert H., Jr. and Harold L. McPheeters
    1976.   *Program Evaluation in the State Mental Health Agency: Activities, Functions, and Management Uses.* Washington, D.C.: Department of Health, Education, and Welfare. Doc. No. (ADM) 76:310.

Henry, Jules
    1963.   *Culture Against Man.* New York: Random House.
    1973.   "A Theory for an Anthropological Analysis of American Culture." In Jules Henry, ed., *On Sham, Vulnerability, and Other Forms of Self-Destruction,* pp. 59–81. New York: Random House.

Herndon, James
    1968.   *The Way It Spozed To Be.* New York: Simon and Schuster.

Herskovits, Melville J.
    1941.   *The Myth of the Negro Past.* New York: Harper.
    1953.   *Franz Boas: The Science of Man in the Making.* New York: Scribner's.
    1972.   *Cultural Relativism.* Frances Herskovits, ed. New York: Random House.

Hessler, Richard M. and Peter Kong-Ming New
    1972.   "Toward a Research Commune?" *Human Organization* 31:449–451.

Hicks, George L. and Philip E. Leis, eds.
    1977.   *Ethnic Encounters: Identities and Contexts.* North Scituate, Mass.: Duxbury Press.

Higham, John
    1974.   *Strangers in the Land: Patterns of American Nativism 1860–1925.* 2d ed. New York: Atheneum.

Hill-Burnett, Jacquetta
    1976.   "The Joking Relationship Between Teachers and Puerto Rican and Non-Puerto Rican Youths in School." Urbana, Ill. Bureau of Educational Research. (Files of the author.)

Hillson, Maurie and Ronald T. Hyman, eds.
    1971.   *Change and Innovation in Elementary and Secondary Organization.* 2d ed. New York: Holt, Rinehart, and Winston.

Hinsley, Curtis M.
    1976.   "Amateurs and Professionals in Washington Anthropology, 1879–1903." In John V. Murra, ed., *American Anthropology: The Early Years,* pp. 36–68. New York: West.

Hoagland, Hudson and Ralph W. Burhoe, eds.
    1962.   *Evolution and Man's Progress*. New York: Columbia University
        Press.

Hockings, Paul, ed.
    1975.   *Principles of Visual Anthropology*. The Hague: Mouton.

Hodgkinson, Harold
    1974.   "Adult Development: Implications for Faculty and Administrators." *Ed-
        ucational Record*. 55:263–274.

Hollister, Leo E.
    1971.   "Marihuana in Man: Three Years Later." *Science* 172:21–29.

Holmberg, Allan R.
    1958.   "The Research and Development Approach to the Study of Change."
        Human Organization 17:12–16.

Holmberg, Allan R. et al.
    1962.   "Community and Regional Development: The Joint Cornell-Peru Experi-
        ment." *Human Organization* 21:107–124.

Holt, John
    1964.   *How Children Fail*. New York: Pitman.

Homans, George C.
    1950.   *The Human Group*. New York: Harcourt Brace.

Homans, George C. and David M. Schneider
    1955.   *Marriage, Authority, and Final Causes: A Study of Unilateral Cross-
        Cousin Marriage*. New York: Free Press.

Hoos, Ida R.
    1972.   *Systems Analysis in Public Policy: A Critique*. Berkeley: University of
        California Press.

Horowitz, Irving L.
    1965.   "The Life and Death of Project Camelot." *Trans-action* 3(1):3–7,
        44–47.
    1976.   *Ideology and Utopia in the United States, 1956–1976*. London: Oxford
        University Press.

Horowitz, Irving L., ed.
    1974.   *The Rise and Fall of Project Camelot*. Rev. ed. Cambridge, Mass.: MIT
        Press. (Orig. publ. 1967.)

Horsfall, Alexander and Conrad M. Arensberg
    1949.   "Teamwork and Productivity in a Shoe Factory." *Human Organization*
        8:13–26.

Hostetler, John
    1968.   *Amish Society*. Baltimore, Md.: Johns Hopkins University Press.

Hostetler, John and Gertrude Enders Huntington
    1971.   *Children in Amish Society*. New York: Holt, Rinehart, and Winston.

Hostrop, R. W., J. A. Meklenburger, and J. A. Wilson, eds.
    1973.   *Accountability for Educational Results*. Hamden, Conn.: Linnet Books.

Howard, Alan
  1970.   *Learning To Be Rotuman: Enculturation in the South Pacific.* New York: Teachers College Press.

Huse, Edgar
  1975.   *Organization Development and Change.* New York: West.

Hymes, Dell, ed.
  1964.   *Language, Culture and Society.* New York: Harcourt and Brace.
  1969.   *Reinventing Anthropology.* New York: Random House.
  1972.   "Introduction." In Courtney B. Cazden, Vera P. John, and Dell Hymes, eds., *Functions of Language in the Classroom,* pp. xi–lvii. New York: Teachers College Press.

International Preparatory Committee
  1948.   "Statement for International Congress on Mental Health, London, August 1948." *Psyche* 11(3):235–261.

Jacobs, Sue-Ellen
  1974.   "Action and Advocacy Anthropology." *Human Organization* 33:209–215.

Jacobs, Wilbur R.
  1950.   *Diplomacy and Indian Gifts: Anglo-French Rivalry Along the Ohio and Northwest Frontiers, 1748–1763.* Stanford, Calif.: Stanford University Press.
  1954.   *The Appalachian Frontier: The Edmond Atkin Report and Plan of 1755.* Columbia: University of South Carolina Press.
  1972.   *Dispossessing the American Indian.* New York: Scribner's.
  1974.   "The Tip of an Iceberg: Pre-Columbian Indian Demography and Some Implications for Revisionism." *William and Mary Quarterly* 31:123–132.
  1975.   "Native American History: How It Illuminates Our Past." *The American Historical Review* 80(3):593.

James, Bernard J.
  1971.   "Niche Defense Among Learned Gentlemen: Notes on Organizational Inertia in Universities." *Human Organization* 30:223–228.

Jardines Carrion, H.
  1951.   "La Marihuana en America." *Revista Farmacéutica de Cuba* 29:34–44.

Jarvik, Lissy F.
  1975.   "Thoughts on the Psychobiology of Aging." *American Psychologist* 30:576–583.

Jenks, Albert E.
  1921.   "The Relations of Anthropology to Americanization." *Scientific Monthly* 12:240–245.

Jenks, Christopher and David Riesman
  1968.   *The Academic Revolution.* Garden City, N.Y.: Doubleday.

Johnson, Lyndon B.
  1964.   Speech at the University of California, Irvine.

Johnson, Wendell
1953. "The Fateful Process of Mr. A Talking to Mr. B." *Harvard Business Review* 31(1):49–56.

Jones, Delmos J.
1970. "Towards a Native Anthropology." *Human Organization* 29:251–259.
1971. "Social Responsibility and the Belief in Basic Research: An Example from Thailand." *Current Anthropology* 12:347–350.

Jorgensen, Joseph G.
1971. "Indians and the Metropolis." In Jack Waddell and O. M. Watson, eds., *The American Indian in Urban Society,* pp. 66–113. Boston, Mass.: Little, Brown.

Kain, John F.
1970. "Rampant Schizophrenia: The Case of City and Regional Planning." *Journal of American Institute of Planners* 36:221–223.

Kantrowitz, Arthur
1967. "Proposal for an Institution for Scientific Judgment." *Science* 156:763–764.

Kaplan, David
1974. "The Anthropology of 'Authenticity'; Everyman His Own Anthropologist: An Essay Review." *American Anthropologist* 76:824–839.

Kardiner, Abram and Edward Preble
1961. *They Studied Man.* Cleveland, Ohio: World.

Keesing, Roger
1970. "Toward a Model of Role Analysis." In Raoul Narroll and Ronald Cohen, eds., *A Handbook of Method in Cultural Anthropology,* pp. 423–454. Garden City: The Natural History Press.

Keller, A. R.
1881. "Crow Agency Report." Washington, D.C.: Department of the Interior Annual Report.

Kelly, Lawrence C.
1977. "Anthropology and Anthropologists in the Indian New Deal." Paper presented at the Organization of American Historians, April, 1977, Atlanta, Ga. (Files of the author.)

Kendon, Adam
1963. *Temporal Aspects of the Social Performance in Two-Person Encounters.* Dissertation, Oxford University.

Kennard, Edward A. and Gordon Macgregor
1953. "Applied Anthropology in Government: United States." In A. L. Kroeber, ed., *Anthropology Today,* pp. 832–840. Chicago, Ill.: University of Chicago Press.

Keppel, Francis
1966. *The Necessary Revolution in American Education.* New York: Harper and Row.

Kimball, Solon T.
1946. "The Crisis in Colonial Administration." *Applied Anthropology* 5:8–16.

1960.   "Cultural Influences Shaping the Role of the Child." In *The National Elementary Principal: Those First School Years* 40:8–32.
1966.   "Individualism and the Formation of Values." *Journal of Applied Behavioral Sciences* 2:465–482.
1974a. "Comment." *Impact of Science on Society* 24:109–117. Paris: UNESCO.
1974b. *Culture and the Educative Process*. New York: Teachers College Press.

Kimball, Solon T. and Jacquetta H. Burnett, eds.
1973.   *Learning and Culture*. Seattle: University of Washington Press.

Kimball, Solon T. and James McClellan, Jr.
1962.   *Education and the New America*. New York: Random House.

Kimball, Solon T. and Marion Pearsall
1954.   *The Talladega Story*. University: University of Alabama Press.

Kimball, Solon T. and John H. Provinse
1942.   "Navajo Social Organization in Land Use Planning." *Applied Anthropology* 1:18–25.

Kluckhohn, Clyde and Robert A. Hackenberg
1954.   "Social Science Principles and the Indian Reorganization Act." In William H. Kelly, ed., *Indian Affairs and the Indian Reorganization Act: The Twenty Year Record*, pp. 29–34. Tucson: University of Arizona Press.

Kluckhohn, Clyde and Olaf Prufer
1959.   "Influences During the Formative Years." In Walter Goldschmidt, ed., *The Anthropology of Franz Boas*, pp. 4–28. American Anthropological Association Memoir 89.

Koestler, Arthur
1967.   *The Act of Creation*. New York: Macmillan.

Kohl, Herbert
1967.   *36 Children*. New York: New American Library.

Kozol, Jonathan
1967.   *Death at an Early Age*. Boston, Mass.: Houghton Mifflin.

Kroeber, Alfred L.
1959.   "Preface." In Walter Goldschmidt, ed., *The Anthropology of Franz Boas*, pp. v-vii. American Anthropological Association Memoir 89.

Kuhn, Thomas S.
1962.   *The Structure of Scientific Revolutions*. Chicago, Ill.: University of Chicago Press.

Kunstadter, Peter
1972.   "Demography, Ecology, Social Structure and Settlement Patterns." In G. A. Harrison and A. J. Boyce, eds., *The Structure of Human Populations*, pp. 313–351. Oxford: Clarendon Press.

La Barre, Weston
1938.   *The Peyote Cult*. Yale University Publications in Anthropology No. 19.
1972.   "Hallucinogens and the Shamanic Origins of Religion." In Peter Furst, ed., *Flesh of the Gods*, pp. 261–278. New York: Praeger.

Labov, William
1968. *A Study of the Non-Standard English of Negro and Puerto Rican Speakers in New York City.* Vol. 2: Final Report, Cooperative Research Project No. 3288. Washington, D.C.: Office of Education.

Land, George
1973. *Grow or Die.* New York: Random House.

Landes, Ruth
1965. *Culture in American Education.* New York: Wiley.

Lantis, Margaret
1945. "Applied Anthropology as a Public Service." *Applied Anthropology* 4:20–32.

Lasch, Christopher
1975. "The Democratization of Culture." *Change: The Magazine of Higher Learning* 7(Summer): 14–23.

Lasswell, Harold D.
1968. "Policy Sciences." In *International Encyclopedia of the Social Sciences* 12:181–188. New York: Macmillan.

Laszlo, Ervin, ed.
1973. *The World System: Models, Norms, Applications.* New York: Braziller.

Laszlo, Ervin et al.
1977. *Goals for Mankind: A Report to the Club of Rome on the New Horizons of Global Community.* New York: Dutton.

Lauria, Anthony
1964. "Respeto, Ralajo, and Interpersonal Relations in Puerto Rico." *Anthropological Quarterly* 37:53–67.

Lawler, Edward E.
1973. *Motivation in Organization.* Monterrey, Calif.: Brooks-Cole.

Leacock, Eleanor
1969. *Teaching and Learning in City Schools.* New York: Basic Books.
1973. "The Concept of Culture and Its Significance for School Counselors." In F. A. Ianni and E. Storey, eds., *Cultural Relevance and Educational Issues: Readings in Anthropology and Education,* pp. 189–200. Boston, Mass.: Little, Brown.

Leacock, Eleanor, ed.
1971. *The Culture of Poverty: A Critique.* New York: Simon and Schuster.

Leacock, Eleanor, Nancie L. Gonzalez, and Gilbert Kushner
1974. *Training Programs for New Opportunities in Applied Anthropology.* Washington, D.C.: American Anthropological Association.

Leighton, Alexander H.
1945. *The Governing of Men.* Princeton, N.J.: Princeton University Press.

Lesieur, Frederick, ed.
1958. *The Scanlon Plan: A Frontier in Labor-Management Cooperation.* Cambridge, Mass.: Technology Press of MIT.

Lesser, Alexander
1968. "Franz Boas." *International Encyclopedia of the Social Sciences.* 2:99–110. New York: Macmillan.

1976.   "The American Ethnological Society: The Columbia Phase, 1906–1946." In John V. Murra, ed., *American Anthropology: The Early Years,* pp. 126–135. New York: West.

Lessinger, Leon
1970.   *Every Kid a Winner: Accountability in Education.* New York: Simon and Schuster.

Levin, M. and N. Abend
1971.   *Bureaucrats in Collision: Case Studies in Area Transportation.* Cambridge, Mass.: MIT Press.

Levine, Naomi
1969.   *Ocean Hill-Brownsville: A Case History of Schools in Crisis.* New York: Popular Library.

Lévi-Strauss, Claude
1963.   *Structural Anthropology.* C. Jacobson and B. Schoepf, trans. New York: Basic Books. (Orig. publ. 1958.)
1969.   *The Elementary Structures of Kinship.* Boston, Mass.: Beacon Press. (Orig. publ. Paris: Presses Universitaires de France, 1949.)

Lewis, Hylan
1955.   *Blackways of Kent.* Chapel Hill: University of North Carolina Press.

Lewis, John P.
1964.   *Quiet Crisis in India: Economic Development and American Policy.* Garden City, N.Y.: Doubleday.

Lewis, Oscar
1966a. *La Vida: A Puerto Rican Family in the Culture of Poverty—San Juan and New York.* New York: Random House.
1966b. "The Culture of Poverty." *Scientific American* 215:19–25.

Liebow, Eliot
1967.   *Tally's Corner: A Study of Negro Streetcorner Men.* Boston, Mass.: Little, Brown.

Lindesmith, Alfred R.
1940.   "Dope Fiend Mythology." *Journal of the American Institute of Criminal Law and Criminology* 31:207–208.

Linton, Adelin and Charles Wagley
1971.   *Ralph Linton.* New York: Columbia University Press.

Linton, Ralph
1936.   *The Study of Man.* New York: Appleton.

Linton, Ralph, ed.
1945.   *The Science of Man in the World Crisis.* New York: Columbia University Press.

Little, Kenneth
1963.   "The Context of Social Change." In David G. Mandelbaum, Gabriel W. Lasker, and Ethel M. Albert, eds., *The Teaching of Anthropology,* pp. 363–371. Washington, D.C.: American Anthropological Association.

Littlestone, Ralph
1973.   "Planning in Mental Health." In Saul Feldman, ed., *The Administration*

of Mental Health Services, pp. 3–28. Springfield, Ill.: Charles C. Thomas.

Livingston, Robert Teviot and Stanley H. Milberg
1957.   *Human Relations in Industrial Research Management.* New York: Columbia University Press.

Lomax, Alan
1977.   "An Appeal for Cultural Equity." *Journal of Communication* 27(2):125–138.

Lorenz, Konrad
1966.   *On Aggression.* New York: Harcourt Brace and World.

Lowie, Robert H.
1912.   "Some Problems in Ethnology of the Crow and Village Indians." *American Anthropologist* 14:60–71.
1922.   "Material Culture of the Crow Indians." *Anthropological Papers of the Museum of Natural History* 225:201–270.
1935.   *The Crow Indians.* New York: Rinehart.
1937a.   "Introduction." In W. Lloyd Warner, ed., *A Black Civilization,* pp. xv–xix. New York: Harper.
1937b.   *The History of Ethnological Theory.* New York: Farrar and Rinehart.

Loy, Artha Sue
1974.   Appendix B: "Language Study." In J. Hill Burnett, ed., *Social Structures, Ideologies, and Culture Codes in Occupational Development of Puerto Rican Youths: Anthropological Study of Disability from Educational Problems of Puerto Rican Youths,* pp. 315–325. Urbana, Ill.: Bureau of Educational Research. (Files of the Author).

Lurie, Nancy Oestreich
1955.   "Problems, Opportunities, and Recommendations." *Ethnohistory,* 2:357–375.
1956.   "A Reply to 'The Land Claims Cases.' Anthropologists in Conflict." *Ethnohistory* 3:256–279.
1957.   "The Indian Claims Commission Act." *Annals of the American Academy of Political and Social Science* 311:56–70.
1968.   "Historical Background." In Stuart Levine and Nancy Lurie, eds., *The American Indian Today,* pp. 49–81. Deland, Fla.: Everett Edwards.
1970.   "Anthropologists in the U.S. and the Indian Claims Commission." Paper presented at the American Ethnological Society–Northeastern Anthropological Society, Ottawa, May 7–9, 1970.

Lynd, Robert S. and Helen M. Lynd
1929.   *Middletown: A Study in Contemporary American Culture.* New York: Harcourt, Brace.

Macfarlane, Alan
1968.   "Population Crisis: Anthropology's Failure." *New Society* 12:519–521.

Macgregor, Frances C.
1960.   *Social Science and Nursing.* New York: Russell Sage Foundation.

Macgregor, Gordon
1946.   *Warriors Without Weapons: A Study of the Society and Personality of the Pine Ridge Sioux.* Chicago, Ill.: University of Chicago Press.

MacLean, Paul D.
1968. "Alternative Neural Pathways to Violence." In Larry Ng, ed., *Alternatives to Violence*, pp. 24–34. New York: Time-Life Books.

Maday, Bela C.
1976. "Individual Research Training Support in Anthropology 1964–1976." *Newsletter* of the American Anthropological Association 17:7–9.
1977. "Anthropologists in the United States Government." *Human Organization* 36:89–97.

Maday, Bela C., ed.
1975. *Anthropology and Society*. Washington, D.C.: Washington Anthropological Society.

Madge, Charles
1968. "Planning, Social: Introduction." In *The International Encyclopedia of the Social Sciences*. 12:125–129. New York: Macmillan.

Mager, Robert F.
1962. *Preparing Instructional Objectives*. Belmont, Calif.: Fearon.

Makielski, S. J., Jr.
1973. *Beleaguered Minorities: Cultural Politics in America*. San Francisco: W. H. Freeman.

Malinowski, Bronislaw
1922. *Argonauts of the Western Pacific*. New York: Dutton.
1929. "Practical Anthropology." *Africa* 2:23–38.

Mandelbaum, David G., Gabriel W. Lasker, and Ethel M. Albert
1963a. *The Teaching of Anthropology*. Washington, D.C.: American Anthropological Association Memoir 94.
1963b. *Resources for the Teaching of Anthropology*. Washington, D.C.: American Anthropological Association Memoir 95.

Mann, Lawrence
1972. "Social Science Advances and Planning Applications: 1900–1965." *Journal of the American Institute of Planners* 39:346–358.

Manners, Robert A.
1974. "Introduction to the Ethnohistorical Reports on the Land Claims Cases." In H. F. Dobyns, *Hualapai Indians*, pp. 17–19. New York: Garland.

Marcson, Simon
1960. *The Scientist in American Industry*. New York: Harper and Row.

Marshall, John F., Susan Morris, and Steven Polgar
1972. "Culture and Natality: A Preliminary Classified Bibliography." *Current Anthropology* 13:268–277.

Marshall, John F. and Steven Polgar, eds.
1976. *Culture, Natality, and Family Planning*. Monograph 21, Carolina Population Center. Chapel Hill: University of North Carolina.

Martin, Phillip, John H. Peterson, Jr., and Jan P. Peterson
1975. "Choctaw on-Campus Intensive Education Program at Mississippi State University." *BIA Education Research Bulletin* 3:1–9.

Maruyama, Magoroh
  1973.   "Human Futuristics and Urban Planning." *Journal of the American Institute of Planners* 39:346–358.

Maruyama, Magoroh and James A. Dator, eds.
  1971.   *Human Futuristics*. Honolulu: Social Science Research Institute, University of Hawaii.

Marx, Karl
  1967.   *Capital: A Critique of Political Economy*. Vol. 1. Samuel Moore and Edward Aveling, trans. New York: International. (Orig. pub. 1867.)

Mason, Leonard
  1955.   "The Characterization of American Culture in Studies of Acculturation." *American Anthropologist* 57:1264–1279.

Mayo, Elton
  1940.   *The Human Problems of an Industrial Civilization*. New York: Viking. (Orig. pub. New York: Macmillan, 1933.)
  1945.   *The Social Problems of an Industrial Civilization*. Boston, Mass.: Harvard University, Graduate School of Business Administration.

McGlothlin, William H.
  1975.   "Sociocultural factors in Marihuana Use in the United States." In Vera Rubin, ed., *Cannabis and Culture*, pp. 531–547. The Hague: Mouton.

Mead, George H.
  1934.   *Mind, Self, and Society*. Chicago, Ill.: University of Chicago Press.

Mead, Margaret
  1928.   *Coming of Age in Samoa*. New York: William Morrow.
  1942a.   *And Keep Your Powder Dry*. New York: William Morrow.
  1942b.   "The Comparative Study of Culture and the Purposive Cultivation of Democratic Values." In Lyman Bryson and Louis Finkelstein, eds., *Science, Philosophy, and Religion*, Second Symposium, pp. 56–69. New York: Conference on Science, Philosophy, and Religion in Their Relation to the Democratic Way of Life.
  1953a.   "National Character." In A. L. Kroeber, ed., *Anthropology Today*, pp. 642–667. Chicago, Ill.: University of Chicago Press.
  1953b.   *Cultural Patterns and Technical Change*. Paris: UNESCO.
  1955a.   "Effects of Anthropological Field Work Models on Interdisciplinary Communication in the Study of National Character." *Journal of Social Issues* 11:3–11.
  1955b.   *Male and Female*. New York: Mentor Books. (Orig. pub. New York: Morrow, 1949).
  1956a.   "Commitment to Field Work." In *Gladys A. Reichard, 1893–1955*, pp. 22–27. New York: Barnard College.
  1956b.   *New Lives for Old: Cultural Transformation-Manus*. New York: New American Library.
  1959.   "Apprenticeship Under Boas." In Walter Goldschmidt, ed., *The Anthropology of Franz Boas*. pp. 29–45. American Anthropological Association Memoir 89.
  1961.   "The Human Study of Human Beings." *Science* 133:163.
  1962.   "The Social Responsibility of the Anthropologist." *Journal of Higher Education* 33:1–12.

1963a.   "Clocking the Timetable of Man." Review of *The Origin of Races* by Carleton S. Coon. *Saturday Review* 46(25):41.

1963b.   "Geneva: Helping the Less Developed Nations—Lessons from the U.N. Conference." *International Science and Technology* 16:86–87.

1963c.   "Scientist Reviewers Beware." *Science* 141:312–313.

1964a.   *Continuities in Cultural Evolution.* New Haven, Conn.: Yale University Press.

1964b.   *Food Habits Research: Problems of the 1960s.* National Academy of Sciences, National Research Council Publication No. 1225.

1965.   "The Future as the Basis for Establishing a Shared Culture." *Daedalus* (Winter), 94:135–155.

1966.   *The Changing Culture of an Indian Tribe.* New York: Putnam. (Orig. pub. New York: Columbia University Press, 1932.)

1967.   "Anthropologists, Scientists and Laity." *The Sciences* 7:10–13.

1969.   "Statement," U.S. Senate, 91st Cong., 1st sess., *Competitive Problems in the Drug Industry. Hearings before the Subcommittee on Monopoly of the Select Committee on Small Business on Present Status of Competition in the Pharmaceutical Industry, Part 13, Psychotropic Drugs, July 16, 29, 30 and October 27, 1969,* pp. 5456–5477. Washington, D.C.: U.S. Government Printing Office.

1970a.   *Culture and Commitment: A Study of the Generation Gap.* Garden City, N.Y.: Natural History Press.

1970b.   "The Art and Technology of Field Work." In Raoul Naroll and Ronald Cohen, eds., *A Handbook of Method in Cultural Anthropology,* pp. 246–265. Garden City, N.Y.: Natural History Press.

1972a.   *Blackberry Winter.* New York: Simon and Schuster.

1972b.   "Changing the Requirements in Anthropological Education." *Western Canadian Journal of Anthropology* 3:19–23.

1972c.   "Thailand Controversy: Response to the Board's Response to the Discussion." *Newsletter* of the American Anthropological Association 13(2):1, 6.

1973.   "Changing Styles of Anthropological Work." In Bernard J. Siegel, ed., *Annual Review of Anthropology,* 2:1–26. Palo Alto: Annual Reviews.

1975a.   "Discussion." In Bela Maday, ed., *Anthropology and Society,* pp. 13–18. Washington, D.C.: Anthropological Society of Washington.

1975b.   "Statement." In Alexander B. Leman and Ingrid A. Leman, eds., *Great Lakes Megalopolis,* p. 12. Symposium, Toronto, March 24–27, 1975. Ottawa: Ministry of State for Urban Affairs.

1976a.   "A Comment on the Role of Women in Agriculture." In Irene Tinker and Michele Bo Bramson, eds., *Women and World Development,* pp. 9–11. Washington, D.C.: Overseas Development Council (AAAS).

1976b.   "Statement." In U.S. Senate, 94th Cong., 2d Sess., *National Science Foundation Authorization Legislation, 1976. Hearings Before the Special Subcommittee on the National Science Foundation of the Committee on Labor and Public Welfare, on S. 3202, March 1 and 3, 1976,* pp. 184–197. Washington, D.C.: Government Printing Office.

1976c.   "Toward a Human Science." *Science* 191:903–909.

1977.   "Applied Anthropology: The State of the Art." In Anthony F. C. Wallace et al., eds., *Perspectives on Anthropology 1976.* Washington, D.C.: American Anthropological Association.

In press.
>   "Anthropology and the Climate of Opinion." *Annals of the New York Academy of Sciences.*

Mead, Margaret, Theodosius Dobzhansky, Ethel Tobach, and Robert E. Light, eds.
>   1968.   *Science and the Concept of Race.* New York: Columbia University Press.

Mead, Margaret and Ken Heyman
>   1975.   *World Enough: Rethinking the Future.* Boston: Little, Brown.

Mead, Margaret and William Kellogg, eds.
In press.
>   *The Atmosphere: Endangered and Endangering.* Baltimore, Md.: National Institute of Health, Fogarty International Center.

Mead, Margaret and Rhoda Metraux
>   1957.   "Image of the Scientist among High School Students: A Pilot Study." *Science* 126:384–390.
>   1965.   "The Anthropology of Human Conflict." In Elton B. McNeil, ed., *The Nature of Human Conflict,* pp. 116–138. Englewood Cliffs, N.J.: Prentice-Hall.

Mead, Margaret and Rhoda Metraux, eds.
>   1953.   *The Study of Culture at a Distance.* Chicago, Ill.: University of Chicago Press.

Mead, Margaret, Donald N. Michael, Harold D. Lasswell, and Lawrence K. Frank
>   1958.   "Man in Space: A Tool and Program for the Study of Social Change." *Annals of the New York Academy of Sciences* 72(4):165–214.

MeKeel, Scudder
>   1936.   *The Economy of a Modern Teton Dakota Community.* New Haven, Conn.: Yale University Publications in Anthropology, No. 6:1–14.

Mellor, John W.
>   1962.   "The Process of Agricultural Development." *Journal of Farm Economics* 44:700–716.

Mendras, Henri
>   1970.   *The Vanishing Peasant: Innovation and Change in French Agriculture.* Jean Lerner, trans. Cambridge, Mass.: MIT Press.

Merton, Robert K.
>   1957.   *Social Theory and Social Structure.* New York: Free Press.

Metraux, Alfred
>   1953.   "Applied Anthropology in Government: United Nations." In A. L. Kroeber, ed., *Anthropology Today,* pp. 880–894. Chicago, Ill.: University of Chicago Press.

Miller, James G.
>   1975.   "The Nature of Living Systems." *Behavioral Science* 20(6):343–365.

Miller, Paul A.
>   1973.   *The Cooperative Extension Service: Paradoxical Servant. The Rural Precedent in Continuing Education.* A. A. Liveright Memorial Series, Landmarks and New Horizons in Continuing Education 2. Syracuse, N.Y.: Syracuse University.

Mintz, Sidney
  1970. "Foreword." In Norman Whitten and John Szwed, eds., *Afro-American Anthropology,* pp. 1–16. New York: Free Press.

Mintzberg, Henry
  1973. *The Nature of Managerial Work.* New York: Harper and Row.

Mirsky, Jeanette
  1937. "The Dakota." In Margaret Mead, ed., *Cooperation and Competition Among Primitive People,* pp. 382–427. New York: McGraw-Hill. (Reprinted Boston: Beacon Press, 1961.)

Mississippi Band of Choctaw Indians
  1972– *Accelerated Progress through Self-Determination.* 2 vols. Philadelphia,
  73.   Miss.

Mitchell, John
  1970. "John Mitchell on Marihuana." *Newsweek,* September 7, p. 22.

Montagu, Ashley
  1964. *Man's Most Dangerous Myth: The Fallacy of Race.* 4th ed. Cleveland, Ohio: World.

Moore, G. Alexander
  1967. *Realities of the Urban Classroom.* Garden City, N.Y.: Doubleday Anchor.
  1973. *Life Cycles in Atchalán: The Diverse Careers of Certain Guatemalans.* New York: Teachers College Press.

Moravcsik, M. J. and J. M. Ziman
  1975. "Paradisia and Dominatia: Science and the Developing World." *Foreign Affairs* 53:699–724.

Morehouse, T. A.
  1969. "The 1962 Highway Act: A Study in Artful Interpretation." *Journal of the American Institute of Planners* 35:160–168.

Morgan, Lewis Henry
  1851. *League of the Ho-de-no-sau-nee, or Iroquois.* Rochester, N.Y.: Sage.
  1871. Systems of Consanguinity and Affinity of the Human Family. Smithsonian Institution Contributions to Knowledge No. 17, article 2. Washington, D.C.: Government Printing Office.
  1877. *Ancient Society.* New York: Holt.

Morland, John Kenneth
  1958. *Millways of Kent.* Chapel Hill: University of North Carolina Press.

Moynihan, Daniel P.
  1965. *The Negro Family: The Case for National Action.* Washington, D.C.: Government Printing Office.

Mulhauser, Frederick
  1975. "Ethnography and Policymaking: The Case of Education." *Human Organization* 34:311–314.

Murdock, George P.
  1936. *Rank and Potlach among the Haida.* New Haven, Conn.: Yale University Publications in Anthropology No. 13:1–20.

468   Bibliography

Murray, Albert
1973. "White Norms, Black Deviation." In J. A. Ladner, ed., *The Death of White Sociology*, pp. 96–113. New York: Random House.

Myerhoff, Barbara G.
1974. *The Peyote Hunt*. Ithaca, N.Y.: Cornell University Press.
1975. "Peyote and Huichol Worldview: The Structure of a Mystic Vision." In Vera Rubin, ed., *Cannabis and Culture*, pp. 417–438. The Hague: Mouton.

Myrdal, Gunnar
1944. *An American Dilemma*. 2 vols. New York: Harper.

Nag, Moni
1972. "Sex, Culture and Human Fertility: India and the United States." *Current Anthropology* 13:231–237.
1973. "Anthropology and Population: Problems and Perspectives." *Population Studies* 27:59–68.
1975. "Population Anthropologists at Work." *Current Anthropology* 16:264–266.

Nag, Moni, ed.
1975. *Population and Social Organization*. The Hague: Mouton.

Nakane, Chie
1970. *Japanese Society*. Berkeley: University of California Press.

Naroll, Raoul and R. G. Sipes
1973. "A Standard Ethnographic Sample: Second Edition." *Current Anthropology* 15:1–2, 111–140.

Nash, Philleo
1973. "Applied Anthropology and the Concept of Guided Acculturation." In *Anthropology and the American Indian*, pp. 23–31. San Francisco, Calif.: Indian Historian Press.

National Academy of Sciences
1971. *Rapid Population Growth: Consequences and Policy Implications*. Baltimore, Md.: Johns Hopkins University Press.
1974. *In Search of Population Policy: Views from the Developing World*. Washington, D.C.: National Academy of Sciences.

National Planning Board
1934. *National Planning Board Final Report 1933–1934*. Washington, D.C.: Government Printing Office.

National Research Council
1943. Report of the Committee on Food Habits 1941–1943. Bulletin No. 108. Washington, D.C.
1945. Report of the Committee on Food Habits. *Manual for the Study of Food Habits*. Bulletin No. 111. Washington, D.C.

Naylor, Larry L.
1973. "Applied Anthropology: Approaches to the Using of Anthropology." *Human Organization* 32:363–370.

Neville, Gwen Kennedy
1971. *Annual Assemblages as Related to the Persistence of Culture Patterns:*

An Anthropological Study of a Summer Community. Ph.D. dissertation, University of Florida.

1975. "Kinfolks and the Covenant: Ethnic Community Among Southern Presbyterians." In John W. Bennett, ed., *The New Ethnicity: Perspectives from Ethnology,* pp. 258–274. 1973 Proceedings of the American Ethnological Society. New York: West.

Newman, Monroe
1972. *The Political Economy of Appalachia.* Lexington, Mass.: D. S. Heath.

Niehoff, Arthur H.
1964. "The Primary Variables in Directed Culture Change." Paper presented at the Annual Meeting, American Anthropological Association, Detroit, Mich. Mimeographed. (Files of the author.)

1966. *A Casebook of Social Change.* Chicago, Ill.: Aldine.

Niehoff, Arthur H. and J. Charnel Anderson
1964. *A Selected Bibliography of Culture Change Projects.* Alexandria, Va.: George Washington University Human Resources Research Office.

Noar, Gertrude
1972. *Individualized Instruction: Every Child a Winner.* New York: Wiley.

Norman, J. T.
1954. "Now They Stand Up under Pressure." *Sales Management* 73:36–37 ff.

Northrup, F. S. C.
1953. "Cultural Values." In A. L. Kroeber, ed., *Anthropology Today,* ed. pp. 668–681. Chicago: University of Chicago Press.

Novick, David, ed.
1965. *Program Budgeting: Program Analysis and the Federal Budget.* Cambridge, Mass.: Harvard University Press.

Oberg, Kalervo
1956. "Community Center Project at Chonin, Brazil." In Arthur Niehoff, ed., *A Casebook of Social Change,* pp. 78–90. Chicago, Ill.: Aldine.

Oberg, Kalervo and Jose Arthur Rios
1955. "A Community Improvement Project in Brazil." In B. Paul, ed., *Health, Culture, and Community,* pp. 349–376. New York: Russell Sage Foundation.

Odum, Howard W.
1964. *Folk, Region, and Society: Selected Papers.* Chapel Hill: University of North Carolina Press.

Officer, James
1971. "The American Indian and Federal Policy." In Jack Waddell and O. M. Watson, eds., *The American Indian in Urban Society,* pp. 8–65. Boston, Mass.: Little, Brown.

Opler, Marvin K., ed.
1959. *Culture and Mental Health.* New York: Macmillan.

Opler, Morris E.
1952. "The Creek 'Town' and the Problem of Creek Indian Political Reorgani-

zation.'' In Edward Spicer, ed., *Human Problems in Technological Change*, pp. 165–180. New York: Russell Sage Foundation.

Ortiz Velasquez, J.
1947.   ''Marihuana y sus efectos.'' *Anales de la Academia de Medellín* 3:498–510.

Panday, Triloki Nath
1972.   ''Anthropologists at Zuñi.'' *Proceedings of the American Philosophical Society* 116(4):321–336.

Panel on Youth (of the President's Science Advisory Committee)
1974.   James Coleman, ed., *Youth: Transition to Adulthood*. Chicago, Ill.: University of Chicago Press.

Partridge, William L.
1973.   *The Hippie Ghetto: The Natural History of a Subculture*. New York: Holt, Rinehart, and Winston.
1974.   *Exchange Relationships in a Community on the North Coast of Colombia with Special Reference to Cannabis*. Ph.D. dissertation, University of Florida.
1975a.   ''Cannabis and Cultural Groups in a Colombian Municipio.'' In Vera Rubin, ed., *Cannabis and Culture*, pp. 147–172. The Hague: Mouton.
1975b.   ''Ritual Mediation of Access to Human Resources.'' Paper presented at the symposium: The Work of Ritual, American Anthropological Association, San Francisco, Calif.
1977.   ''Transformation and Redundancy in Ritual: A Case from Colombia.'' In Brian M. du Toit, ed., *Drugs, Ritual and Altered States of Consciousness*, pp. 59–73. Rotterdam: A. A. Balkema.

Passow, A. Harry
1974.   ''Contemporary Instructional Intervention.'' In Fred N. Kerlinger and John B. Carroll, eds., *Review of Research in Education*, 2:145–175. Itasca, Ill.: F. E. Peacock.

Patiño, Victor Manuel
1965.   *Historia de la actividad agropecuario en América Equinoccial*. Cali: Imprenta Departamental.
1967.   *Plantas cultivadas y animales domésticos en América Equinoccial: plantas miscelaneas*. Vol. 3. Cali: Imprenta Departmental.
1969.   *Plantas cultivadas y animales domésticos en América Equinoccial: plantas introducidas*. Vol. 4. Cali: Imprenta Departamental.

Paul, Benjamin, ed.
1955.   *Health, Culture, and Community*. New York: Russell Sage Foundation.

Peattie, Lisa Redfield
1958.   ''Interventionism and Applied Science in Anthropology.'' *Human Organization* 17:4–8.
1968a.   ''Reflections on Advocacy Planning.'' *Journal of the American Institute of Planners* 34:80–88.
1968b.   *The View from the Barrio*. Ann Arbor: University of Michigan Press.

Peñuelas Heras, E.
1946.   ''Nota histórica sobre la Cannabosis.'' *Revista Clínica Española* 22:124–128.

Peon del Valle, J.
    1933.   "Algunos aspectos de la actual lucha contra la toxicomanía en Mexico."
            Boletin de la Oficina Sanitaria Panamericana 12:347–355.

Perez, Juan B.
    1952.   "Intoxicación por la Marihuana." *Antioquia Médica.* July.

Petersen, William
    1975.   "A Demographer's View of Prehistoric Demography." *Current Anthro-
            pology* 16:227–245.

Peterson, John H., Jr.
    1970a.   *Socio-Economic Characteristics of the Mississippi Choctaw Indians.* So-
            cial Science Research Center Report No. 34. State College: Mississippi
            State University.
    1970b.   *The Mississippi Band of Choctaw Indians: Their Recent History and
            Current Social Relations.* Ph.D. dissertation, University of Georgia.
    1972.   "Assimilation, Separation and Out-Migration in an American Indian
            Community." *American Anthropologist* 74:1286–1295.
    1973a.   "A Very Applied Anthropologist's Report from the Field." Paper pre-
            sented at the annual meeting of the Southern Anthropological Associa-
            tion. (Files of the author.)
    1973b.   "Working for a Tribal Government." Paper presented at the annual
            meeting of the Central States Anthropological Association. (Files of the
            author.)
    1974a.   "The Operation of a Tribal Planning Center." Paper presented at the an-
            nual meeting of the Society for Applied Anthropology. (Files of the au-
            thor.)
    1974b.   "The Anthropologist as Advocate." *Human Organization* 33:311–318.

Peterson, John H., Jr., Barbara G. Spencer, and Choong S. Kim
    1974.   *Choctaw Demographic Survey.* Philadelphia, Miss.: Mississippi Band of
            Choctaw Indians.

Piddington, Ralph
    1970.   "Action Anthropology." In James A. Clifton, ed., *Applied Anthropol-
            ogy: Readings in the Uses of the Science of Man,* pp. 127–143. Boston,
            Mass.: Houghton Mifflin.

Piehler, Henry F., Aaron D. Twerski, A. S. Weinstein and W. A. Donaher
    1974.   "Product Liability and the Technical Expert." *Science* 186:1089–1093.

Piotrow, Phyllis Tilson
    1973.   *World Population Crisis: The United States Response.* New York:
            Praeger.

Polgar, Steven
    1972.   "Population History and Population Policies from an Anthropological
            Perspective." *Current Anthropology* 13:203–211.

Polgar, Steven, ed.
    1971.   *Culture and Population: A Collection of Current Studies.* Cambridge,
            Mass.: Schenkman.
    1975.   *Population, Ecology, and Social Evolution.* The Hague: Mouton.

Posposil, Leopold
    1963.   *The Kapauku Papuans of West New Guinea.* New York: Holt, Rinehart,
            and Winston.

Powdermaker, Hortense
1939.   *After Freedom: A Cultural Study in the Deep South*. New York: Viking.
1966.   *Stranger and Friend: The Way of an Anthropologist*. New York: Norton.

Provinse, John H.
1942.   "Cultural Factors in Land Use Planning." In Oliver La Farge, ed., *The Changing Indian*, pp. 55–71. Norman: University of Oklahoma Press.

Provinse, John H. and Solon T. Kimball
1946.   "Building New Communities During Wartime." *American Sociological Review* 11:396–410.

Public Administration Review
1966.   "Planning-Programming-Budgeting System Symposium." 26:243–310.
1969.   "Planning-Programming-Budgeting System Reexamined: Development, Analysis and Criticism." 29:111–202.

Rachlin, Carol K.
1968.   "Tight Shoe Night: Oklahoma Indians Today." In Stuart Levine and Nancy O. Lurie, eds., *The American Indian Today*, pp. 99–114. De-Land, Fla.: Everett Edwards Press.

Radcliffe-Brown, A. R.
1922.   *The Andaman Islanders*. Cambridge: Cambridge University Press.

Raia, Anthony P.
1974.   *Managing by Objectives*. Glenview, Ill.: Scott, Foresman.

Rappaport, Roy A.
1968.   *Pigs for the Ancestors*. New Haven, Conn.: Yale University Press.

Redfield, Robert
1930.   *Tepoztlán, A Mexican Village: A Study of Folk Life*. Chicago, Ill.: University of Chicago Press.
1950.   *A Village that Chose Progress: Chan Kom Revisited*. Chicago, Ill.: University of Chicago Press.
1955.   *The Little Community*. Chicago, Ill.: University of Chicago Press.
1956.   *Peasant Society and Culture*. Chicago, Ill.: University of Chicago Press.

Redfield, Robert, Ralph Linton, and Melville Herskovits
1936.   "Memorandum for the Study of Acculturation." *American Anthropologist* 38:149–152.

Redfield, Robert and Alfonso Villa Rojas
1934.   *Chan Kom: A Maya Village*. Carnegie Institution of Washington Publication No. 448.

Redfield, Robert and Milton Singer
1954.   "The Cultural Role of Cities." *Economic Development and Cultural Change*, 3:53–73.

Reichel-Dolmatoff, Gerardo
1968.   *Desana: simbolismo de los Indios Tukano del Vaupés*. Bogotá: University of the Andes.
1972.   "The Cultural Context of an Aboriginal Hallucinogen: *Bannisteriopsis Caapi*." In Peter Furst, ed., *Flesh of the Gods*, pp. 84–113. New York: Praeger.

Rein, Martin
1971.   "Social Policy Analysis as the Interpretation of Beliefs." *Journal of the* *American Institute of Planners* 37:297–310.

Richardson, Frederick L. W.
1941.   "Community Resettlement in a Depressed Coal Region." *Applied Anthropology* 1:24–53.
1961.   *Talk, Work, and Action.* Monograph No. 3. Ithaca, N.Y.: Society for Applied Anthropology.
1965.   "Executive Action—Stimulating Others to Greater Performance." Document 8426, American Documentation Institute, Library of Congress, Washington, D.C.
1966.   "Recollecting vs. 'Live' Recording: Organizational Relationships of a Surgeon." *Human Organization* 25:163–179.
1975.   "Organizational Evolutions from Mating Pairs to Trading Nations." In Steven Polgar, ed., *Population, Ecology, and Social Evolution,* pp. 305–335. The Hague: Mouton.

Richardson, F. L. W. and Charles R. Walker
1948.   *Human Relations in an Expanding Company.* New Haven, Conn.: Yale Labor and Management Center.

Richardson, F. L. W. and Kenneth White
1965.   "Technical Supplement" to "Executive Action," Document 8425, American Documentation Institute, Library of Congress.

Richardson, F. L. W. et al.
1972.   "Committee Meetings—The Non-Rational Process of Conference Discussion." Ms. (Files of the author.)

Rist, Ray C.
1973.   *The Urban School: A Factory for Failure.* Cambridge, Mass.: MIT Press.

Roberts, Joan I. and Sherrie K. Akinsanya
1976a.   *Educational Patterns and Cultural Configurations: The Anthropology of Education.* New York: David McKay.
1976b.   *Schooling in the Cultural Context: Anthropological Studies of Education.* New York: David McKay.

Roberts, John M.
1951.   *Three Navajo Households.* Cambridge, Mass.: Papers of the Peabody Museum of Archaeology and Ethnology, 40(3).

Rodgers, Harrell R., Jr. and Charles S. Bullock III
1972.   *Law and Social Change: Civil Rights and Their Consequences.* New York: McGraw-Hill.

Roethlisberger, Fritz J. and William J. Dickson.
1939.   *Management and the Worker.* Cambridge, Mass.: Harvard University Press.

Rondinelli, Dennis A.
1969.   *Policy Analysis and Planning Administration: Toward Adjunctive Planning for Regional Development.* Ph.D. dissertation. Cornell University.
1973.   "Urban Planning as Policy Analysis: Management of Urban Change." *Journal of the American Institute of Planners* 39:13–22.

Rothman, Jack, John L. Erlich and Joseph G. Teresa
1976. *Promoting Innovation and Change in Organizations and Communities: A Planning Manual*. New York: Wiley.

Rozen, David
1976. "Tax, Mead, Goldschmidt—Where Are You?" *Newsletter* of the American Anthropological Association 17(5):2.

Rubin, Morton
1951. *Plantation County*. Chapel Hill: University of North Carolina Press.

Rubin, Vera
1961. "The Anthropology of Development." In Bernard J. Siegel, ed., *The Biennial Review of Anthropology*, pp. 120–172. Stanford, Calif.: Stanford University Press.

Rubin, Vera and Lambros Comitas
1975. *Ganja in Jamaica*. The Hague: Mouton.

Rubin, Vera, ed.
1975. *Cannabis and Culture*. The Hague: Mouton.

Rynkiewich, Michael A. and James P. Spradley, eds.
1976. *Ethics and Anthropology*. New York: Wiley.

Sainsbury, Peter
1955. *Suicide in London: An Ecological Study*. Maudsley Monographs No. 1. London: Chapman and Hall.

Sayles, Leonard
1964. *Managerial Behavior*. New York: McGraw-Hill.

Sayles, Leonard and Margaret K. Chandler
1971. *Managing Large Systems: Organization for the Future*. New York: Harper and Row.

Schensul, Stephen L.
1974. "Skills Needed in Action Anthropology: Lessons Learned from El Centro de la Causa." *Human Organization* 33:203–209.

Schoolcraft, Henry R.
1852–57.*Information Respecting the History, Condition, and Prospects of the Indian Tribes of the United States*. 6 vols. Philadelphia, Pa.: Lippincott.

Schultes, Richard Evans
1969. "Hallucinogens of Plant Origin." *Science* 163:245–254.
1972. "An Overview of Hallucinogens in the Western Hemisphere." In Peter Furst, ed., *Flesh of the Gods*, pp. 3–54. New York: Praeger.

Schultes, Richard Evans, William M. Klein, Timothy Plowman, and Tom E. Lockwood
1975. "Cannabis: An Example of Taxonomic Neglect." In Vera Rubin, ed., *Cannabis and Culture*, pp. 21–38. The Hague: Mouton.

Schwartz, Theodore
1975. "Introduction." *Ethos* 3(2):93–96.

Science for the People
1972. *China: Science Walks on Two Legs*. New York: Avon.

Scriven, Michael
1972. "The Methodology of Evaluation." In Carol H. Weiss, ed., *Evaluating Action Programs,* pp. 123–136. Boston, Mass.: Allyn and Bacon.

Seeley, John R., Alexander Sim, and Eleanor Loosley
1956. *Crestwood Heights.* New York: Basic Books.

Selden, Davis
1973. "Productivity Yes. Accountability No." In R. W. Hostrop, J. A. Mecklenburger, and J. A. Wilson, eds., *Accountability for Educational Results,* pp. 352–356. Hamden, Conn.: Linnet Books.

Shapiro, Arthur K.
1959. "The Placebo Effect in the History of Medical Treatment: Implications for Psychiatry." *American Journal of Psychiatry* 116:298–304.

Shaplin, Justin T. and Henry F. Olds, Jr., eds.
1964. *Team Teaching.* New York: Harper and Row.

Sharon, Douglas
1972. "The San Pedro Cactus in Peruvian Folk Healing." In Peter Furst, ed., *Flesh of the Gods,* pp. 114–135. New York: Praeger.

Shea, Mary Beth and Mary E. Emmons
1972. "Report on Seminar on Anthropology and Social Problems: Population; Environment; Education." *Current Anthropology* 13:279–283.

Shipek, Florence C.
1974. "Anthropologists Shortchanged as Consultants." *Newsletter* of the American Anthropological Association 15(8):2.

Siler, J. F. et al.
1933. "Marihuana Smoking in Panama." *Military Surgeon* 73:269–280.

Silvert, Kalman H.
1965. "American Academic Ethics and Social Research Abroad." *American Universities Field Staff Reports,* pp. 1–21. West Coast South America Series 12(3).

Simon, Herbert
1973. "Hierarchy and Organization." In Howard Pattee, ed., *Hierarchy Theory: The Challenge of Complex Systems,* pp. 3–27. New York: Brazillier.

Singer, Fred S., ed.
1971. *Is There an Optimum Level of Population?* New York: McGraw-Hill.

Singer, Milton
1976. "Robert Redfield's Development of a Social Anthropology of Civilizations." In John V. Murra, ed., *American Anthropology: The Early Years,* pp. 187–260. New York: West.

Sjoberg, Gideon, ed.
1967. *Ethics, Politics, and Social Research.* Cambridge, Mass.: Schenkman.

Sklar, June and Beth Berkov
1975. "The American Birth Rate: Evidences of a Coming Rise." *Science* 189:693–700.

Sloan, Alfred P., Jr.
1964.   *My Years with General Motors.* Garden City, N.Y.: Doubleday.

Smith, Allan H. and John L. Fischer
1970.   *Anthropology.* Englewood Cliffs, N.J.: Prentice-Hall.

Smith, Louis M. and Pat M. Keith
1971.   *Anatomy of Educational Innovation: An Organizational Analysis of an Elementary School.* New York: Wiley.

Smith, Marion
1959.   "Boas' Natural History Approach to Field Method." In Walter Goldschmidt, ed., *The Anthropology of Franz Boas,* pp. 46–60. American Anthropological Association Memoir 89.

Smith, Ralph A., ed.
1975.   *Regaining Educational Leadership: Critical Essays on PBTE/CBTE, Behavioral Objectives and Accountability.* New York: Wiley.

Smith, Robert, Frederic Hicks, and Charles Wicke
1976.   "Paraguayan Anthropologist Jailed—Association Action Sought." *Newsletter* of the American Anthropological Association 17(2):18.

Snyder, Solomon H.
1971.   *Uses of Marihuana.* New York: Oxford University Press.

Society of Professional Anthropologists
1976.   *Newsletter,* October 1976. Tucson, Ariz.: Society of Professional Anthropologists.

Sofer, Cyril
1972.   *Organizations in Theory and Practice.* New York: Basic Books.

Spengler, Joseph J.
1975.   *Population and America's Future.* San Francisco, Calif.: W. H. Freeman.

Spicer, Edward H.
1940.   *Pascua: A Yaqui Village in Arizona.* Chicago, Ill.: University of Chicago Press.
1946.   "The Uses of Social Scientists by the War Relocation Authority." *Applied Anthropology* 5:16–36.
1954.   *Potam: A Yaqui Village in Sonora.* American Anthropological Association Memoir 77.
1976.   "Beyond Analysis and Explanation? Notes on the Life and Times of the Society for Applied Anthropology." *Human Organization* 35:335–343.
1977.   "A History of Application of Anthropology in North America: 1915–1955." In Anthony F. C. Wallace, et al., *Perspectives on Anthropology 1976.* Washington, D.C.: American Anthropological Association.

Spicer, Edward H., ed.
1952.   *Human Problems in Technological Change.* New York: Russell Sage Foundation.

Spicer, Edward H., et al.
1969.   *Impounded People: Japanese-Americans in Relocation Centers.* Tucson: University of Arizona Press (Orig. pub. Washington, D.C.: Government Printing Office, 1946.)

Spindler, George, ed.
 1955.   *Education and Anthropology*. Stanford, Calif.: Stanford University
         Press.
 1963.   *Education and Culture: Anthropological Approaches*. New York: Holt,
         Rinehart, and Winston.

Spiro, Melford E.
 1955.   "The Acculturation of American Ethnic Groups." *American Anthropol-
         ogist* 57:1240–1252.

Spitz, Rene A.
 1945.   "Hospitalism: An Inquiry into the Genesis of Psychiatric Conditions in
         Early Childhood." In *Psychoanalytic Study of the Child*. 1:53–74. New
         York: International Universities Press.
 1946.   "Hospitalism: A Followup Report on Investigation Described in Volume
         I, 1945"; "Anaclitic Depression: An Inquiry into the Genesis of Psychi-
         atric Conditions in Early Childhood II." In *Psychoanalytic Study of the
         Child*, 2:113–117, 312–342. New York: International Universities Press.

Spooner, Brian, ed.
 1972.   *Population Growth: Anthropological Implications*. Cambridge, Mass.:
         MIT Press.

Spradley, James P.
 1970.   *You Owe Yourself a Drunk: An Ethnography of Urban Nomads*. Boston,
         Mass.: Little, Brown.

Stack, Carol
 1974.   *All Our Kin: Strategies for Survival in the Black Community*. New York:
         Harper and Row.

Stavenhagen, Rodolfo
 1971.   "Decolonizing Applied Social Sciences." *Human Organization*
         30:333–344.

Stavis, Benedict
 1975.   *Making Green Revolution: The Politics of Agricultural Development in
         China*. Ithaca, N.Y.: Cornell University, Center for International Stud-
         ies.

Stefanis, C., C. Ballas and D. Madianou
 1975.   "Sociocultural and Epidemiological Aspects of Hashish Use in Greece."
         In Vera Rubin, ed., *Cannabis and Culture*, pp. 301–326. The Hague:
         Mouton.

Steward, Julian H.
 1933.   *Ethnography of the Owens Valley Paiute*. University of California Publi-
         cations in American Archeology and Ethnology 33:233–350.
 1938.   *Basin-Plateau Aboriginal Socio-Political Groups*. Washington, D.C.:
         Bureau of American Ethnology Bulletin No. 120.
 1950.   *Area Research: Theory and Practice*. Social Science Research Council
         Bulletin No. 63.
 1955.   *Theory of Culture Change: The Methodology of Multilinear Evolution*.
         Urbana: University of Illinois Press.
 1956.   *The People of Puerto Rico*. Urbana: University of Illinois Press.

478   Bibliography

1969.   "The Limitations of Applied Anthropology: The Case of the Indian New Deal." *Journal of the Steward Society* 1(1):1–17.

Stewart, Omer C.
1961a.   "The Native American Church and the Law with Description of Peyote Religious Services." Westerners Brand Book, 17:3–47.
1961b.   "Memorandum of Examples of Dr. Omer C. Stewart Respecting Defendant's Exhibit 113: (1) Non-Southern Paiute References; (2) Titles for Which No Defendant's Exhibit Offered; (3) Secondary Sources by Popular Writer; (4) Scholarly Reports Not Evaluated; and (5) Works Listed in Bibliography Not Cited in Report." U.S. Indian Claims Commission, Dockets 88 and 130. Typescript.
1970.   "Symposium: Academics, Humanism and the Ethics of Involvement." Paper presented at the Society for Applied Anthropology, Annual Meeting, Boulder, Colo., April 2, 1970. (Files of the author.)
1973.   "Anthropologists as Expert Witnesses for Indians: Claims and Peyote Cases." In *Anthropology and the American Indian*, pp. 35–42. San Francisco, Calif.: Indian Historian Press.

Stewart, Rosemary
1967.   *Managers and Their Jobs*. New York: Macmillan.

Stocking, George W., Jr.
1968.   *Race, Culture, and Evolution: Essays in the History of Anthropology*. New York: Free Press.

Swanton, John R.
1922.   *Early History of the Creek Indians and Their Neighbors*. Washington, D.C.: Bureau of American Ethnology Bulletin No. 73.

Szwed, John F.
1972.   "An American Anthropological Dilemma: The Politics of Afro-American Culture." In Dell Hymes, ed., *Reinventing Anthropology*, pp. 153–181. New York: Vintage.

Talbert, Carol
1974.   "Experiences at Wounded Knee." *Human Organization* 33:215–217.

Taylor, Carol
1970.   *In Horizontal Orbit: Hospitals and the Cult of Efficiency*. New York: Holt, Rinehart, and Winston.

Taylor, Frederick W.
1911.   *The Principles of Scientific Management*. New York: Harper and Row.

Tax, Sol
1937.   "The Social Organization of the Fox Indians." In Fred Eggan, ed., *The Social Anthropology of North American Tribes*, pp. 242–282. Chicago, Ill.: University of Chicago Press.
1942.   "Ethnic Relations in Guatemala." *América Indígena* 2:43–48.
1945.   "Anthropology and Administration." *América Indígena* 4:21–33.
1951.   *Penny Capitalism: A Guatemalan Indian Economy*. Smithsonian Institution, Institute of Social Anthropology Publication 16.
1952.   "Action Anthropology." *América Indígena* 12:103–109.
1958.   "The Fox Project." *Human Organization* 17:17–19.
1964.   "The Uses of Anthropology." In Sol Tax, ed., *Horizons of Anthropology*, pp. 248–258. Chicago, Ill.: Aldine.

Teitelbaum, Michael S.
1975.   "Relevance of Demographic Transition Theory for Developing Countries." *Science* 188:420–425.

Textor, Robert B., ed.
1966.   *Cultural Frontiers of the Peace Corps.* Cambridge, Mass.: MIT Press.

Thompson, Bobby and John H. Peterson, Jr.
1975.   "Mississippi Choctaw Identity: Genesis and Change." In John W. Bennett, ed., *The New Ethnicity: Perspectives from Ethnology,* pp. 179–196. 1973 Proceedings of the American Ethnological Society. New York: West.

Thompson, Laura
1951.   *Personality and Government: Findings and Recommendations of the Indian Administration Research.* Mexico City: Instituto Indigenista Interamericano.

1956.   "U.S. Indian Reorganization Viewed as an Experiment in Social Action." In *Estudios Antropológicos publicados en homenaje al doctor Manual Gamio,* pp. 514–522. Mexico City: National Autonomous University of Mexico, Mexican Anthropological Society.

1970.   "Is Applied Anthropology Helping to Develop a Science of Man?" In James A. Clifton, ed., *Applied Anthropology: Readings in the Uses of the Science of Man,* pp. 225–245. Boston, Mass.: Houghton Mifflin.

1976.   "An Appropriate Role for Postcolonial Applied Anthropologists." *Human Organization* 35:1–7.

Tocqueville, Alexis de
1945.   *Democracy in America.* 2 vols. New York: Vintage Books. (Orig. pub. Paris: vol. 1, 1834; vol. 2, 1840.)

Torre, Mottran, ed.
1963.   *The Selection of Personnel for International Service.* Geneva and New York: World Federation for Mental Health.

Trow, Martin
1969.   "Elite and Popular Functions in American Higher Education." In W. R. Niblett, ed., *Higher Education: Demand and Response,* pp. 181–202. London: Tavistock.

1973.   *Problems in the Transition from Elite to Mass Higher Education.* Carnegie Commission on Higher Education. Ann Arbor, Mich.: University Microfilms, Inc., reprint.

Turnbull, Colin M.
1972.   "Demography of Small-Scale Societies." In G. A. Harrison and A. J. Boyce, eds., *The Structure of Human Populations,* pp. 281–312. Oxford: Clarendon Press.

1974.   "Reply." *Current Anthropology* 15(1):103.

Turner, Victor
1958.   "Betwixt and Between the Liminal Period in Rites of Passage." In W. A. Lessa and Evon Z. Vogt, eds., *Reader in Comparative Religion,* pp. 338–347. New York: Harper and Row.

1966.   "The Syntax of Symbolism in an African Religion." *Philosophical Transactions of the Royal Society of London,* Series B., Biological Sciences 251:295–303.

1969.   *The Ritual Process: Structure and Anti-Structure.* Chicago, Ill.: Aldine.

Tyack, David B.
1974.   *The One Best System: A History of American Urban Education.* Cambridge, Mass.: Harvard University Press.

Tyler, Stephen A., ed.
1969.   *Cognitive Anthropology.* New York: Holt, Rinehart, and Winston.

Tyler, S. Lyman
1964.   *Indian Affairs: A Study of the Changes in the Policy of the United States Toward Indians.* Provo, Utah: Brigham Young University Press, Institute of American Indian Studies.

UNESCO
1965.   *The Question of Cannabis: Cannabis Bibliography.* New York: United Nations.

U.S. Department of Health, Education, and Welfare. National Institute of Mental Health
1971.   *Marihuana and Health: A Report to the Congress from the Secretary.* Washington, D.C.: Government Printing Office.
1972.   *Marihuana and Health: Second Annual Report to Congress from the Secretary.* Washington, D.C.: Government Printing Office.
1973.   *Marihuana and Health: Third Annual Report to Congress from the Secretary.* Washington, D.C.: Government Printing Office.

U.S. Department of the Interior
1946.   *Community Government in War Relocation Centers.* U.S. Department of the Interior, War Relocation Authority. Washington, D.C.: Government Printing Office. (Prepared by Solon T. Kimball.)

Valentine, Charles A.
1968.   *Culture and Poverty: Critique and Counter-Proposals.* Chicago, Ill.: University of Chicago Press.
1971.   "The 'Culture of Poverty': Its Scientific Significance and Its Implications for Action." In Eleanor Burke Leacock, ed., *The Culture of Poverty: A Critique,* pp. 193–225. New York: Simon and Schuster.
1972.   *Black Studies and Anthropology: Scholarly and Political Interests in Afro-American Culture.* Reading, Mass.: Modular Publications.

Vance, John T.
1969.   "The Congressional Mandate and the Indian Claims Commission." *North Dakota Law Review* 45:325–336.

Vanderbilt, Arthur et al., eds.
1952.   *Modern Education and Human Values.* Pittsburgh, Pa.: University of Pittsburgh Press.

Van Lawick-Goodall, Jane
1971.   *In the Shadow of Man.* Boston: Houghton Mifflin.

Van Maanen, John
1973.   *The Process of Program Evaluation: A Guide for Managers.* Washington, D.C.: National Training and Development Service Press.

Vayda, Andrew P., ed.
1969.   *Environment and Cultural Behavior: Ecological Studies in Cultural Anthropology.* New York: Natural History Press.

Veblen, Thorstein
1921.   *Engineers and the Price System.* New York: B. W. Huebsch.

Voget, Fred W.
1975.   *A History of Ethnology.* New York: Holt, Rinehart, and Winston.

Wachman, Marvin
1974.   "Needed: An Urban-Grant Approach to Higher Education." *Educational Record* 55(4):242–247.

Waddington, C. H., ed.
1972.   *Biology and the History of the Future.* Chicago, Ill.: Aldine–Atherton.

Wade, Nicholas
1976.   "Sociobiology: Troubled   Birth   for   New   Discipline," *Science* 191:1151–1155.

Wagley, Charles
1941.   *The Economics of a Guatemalan Village.* American Anthropological Association Memoir 58.
1949.   *Social and Religious Life of a Guatemalan Community.* American Anthropological Association Memoir 71.
1953.   *Amazon Town: A Study of Man in the Tropics.* New York: Macmillan.

Wagley, Charles and Eduardo Galvão
1949.   *The Tenetehara Indians of Brazil.* New York: Columbia University Press.

Wagley, Charles and Marvin Harris
1955.   "A Typology of Latin American Subcultures." *American Anthropologist* 57:428–451.

Walker, Charles R.
1962.   *Modern Technology and Civilization.* New York: McGraw-Hill.

Walker, Charles R. and Robert A. Guest
1952.   *The Man on the Assembly Line.* Cambridge, Mass.: Harvard University Press.

Walker, Charles R., Robert Guest, and Arthur Turner
1956.   *The Foreman on the Assembly Line.* Cambridge, Mass.: Harvard University Press.

Wallace, Anthony F. C.
1959.   "Cultural Determinants of Response to Hallucinatory Experience." *American Medical Association Archives of General Psychiatry* 1:58–69.
1961.   *Culture and Personality.* New York: Random House.
1965.   "James Mooney (1861–1921) and the Study of the Ghost-Dance Religion." In James Mooney, ed., *The Ghost-Dance Religion and the Sioux Outbreak of 1890,* pp. v–x. Chicago, Ill., University of Chicago Press.
1969.   *The Death and Rebirth of the Seneca.* New York: Random House.

Warner, W. Lloyd
1937.   *A Black Civilization.* New York: Harper.
1941.   "Social Anthropology and the Modern Community." *American Journal of Sociology* 46:785–796.
1962.   *The Corporation in the Emergent American Society.* New York: Harper.

Warner, W. Lloyd and Josiah Low
1947. *The Social System of the Modern Factory.* New Haven, Conn.: Yale University Press.

Warner, W. Lloyd and Paul S. Lunt
1941. *The Social Life of a Modern Community.* New Haven, Conn.: Yale University Press.

Warner, W. Lloyd et al.
1964. *Democracy in Jonesville: A Study in Quality and Inequality.* New York: Harper and Row, Harper Torchbooks.

Wasson, Gordon R.
1968. *Soma: Divine Mushroom of Immortality.* New York: Harcourt Brace Jovanovich.
1972. "What was the Soma of the Aryans?" In Peter Furst, ed., *Flesh of the Gods,* pp. 55–83. New York: Praeger.

Wattenberg, Ben
1971. "The Nonsense Explosion." In D. Callahan, ed., *The American Population Debate,* pp. 69–109. Garden City, N.Y.: Doubleday.

Wax, Murray
1956. "The Limitations of Boas' Anthropology." *American Anthropologist* 58:46–63.

Wax, Murray, Stanley Diamond, and Fred O. Gearing, eds.
1971. *Anthropological Perspectives on Education.* New York: Basic Books.

Weaver, Thomas and Douglas White
1972. "Anthropological Approaches to Urban and Complex Society." In Thomas Weaver and Douglas White, eds., *The Anthropology of Urban Environments,* pp. 109–125. The Society for Applied Anthropology Monograph Series—Monograph No. 11, Boulder, Colo.

Weaver, Thomas, ed.
1973. *To See Ourselves.* Glenview, Ill.: Scott, Foresman.

Weber, Max
1964. *The Theory of Social and Economic Organization.* Trans. by A. M. Henderson and T. Parsons. New York: Free Press.

Weed, Perry L.
1973. *The White Ethnic Movement and Ethnic Politics.* New York: Praeger.

Westerhoff, John H. and Gwen Kennedy Neville
1974. *Generation to Generation: Conversations on Religious Education and Culture.* Philadelphia, Pa.: Pilgrim Press.

Westerman, Floyd
1969. "Custer Died for Your Sins" (album). New York: Perception Records.

Westoff, Charles F.
1973. "Recent Developments in Population Growth Policy in the United States." In Charles F. Westoff et al., eds., *Toward the End of Growth,* pp. 166–177. Englewood Cliffs, N.J.: Prentice-Hall.
1974. "United States." In Bernard Berelson, ed., *Population Policy in Developed Countries,* pp. 731–759. New York: McGraw-Hill.

1976. "The Decline of Unplanned Births in the United States." *Science* 191:38–41.

White, Leslie
1932. *The People of San Felipe*. American Anthropological Association Memoir 38.
1943. "Energy and the Evolution of Culture." *American Anthropologist* 45:335–356.
1951. "Lewis H. Morgan's Western Field Trips." *American Anthropologist* 53:11–17.
1959a. "Lewis Henry Morgan: His Life and Researches." In Lewis H. Morgan, *The Indian Journals, 1859–1862*, Leslie White, ed., pp. 3–12. Ann Arbor: University of Michigan Press.
1959b. *The Evolution of Culture*. New York: McGraw-Hill.

Whiting, Beatrice B.
1963. *Six Cultures: Studies of Child Rearing*. New York: Wiley.

Whitten, Norman and John Szwed
1970. "Introduction." In Norman Whitten and John Szwed, eds., *Afro-American Anthropology*, pp. 23–60. New York: Free Press.

Whyte, William Foote
1943. *Street Corner Society*. Chicago, Ill.: University of Chicago Press.
1955. *Money and Motivation*. New York: Harper and Row.
1969. *Organizational Behavior: Theory and Application*. Homewood, Ill.: Richard D. Irwin and the Dorsey Press.
1975. *Organizing for Agricultural Development*. New Brunswick, N.J.: Transaction Books.

Wilbert, Johannes
1972. "Tobacco and Shamanistic Ecstacy Among the Warao Indians of Venezuela." In Peter Furst, ed., *Flesh of the Gods*, pp. 201–213. New York: Praeger.
1975. "Magico-Religious Use of Tobacco Among South American Indians." In Vera Rubin, ed., *Cannabis and Culture*, pp. 439–461. The Hague: Mouton.

Wilke, Philip J., Thomas F. King, and Stephen Hammond
1975. "Aboriginal Occupation at Tahquitz Canyon: Ethnohistory and Archaeology." In Lowell J. Bean, ed., *The Cahuilla Indians of the Colorado Desert: Ethnohistory and Prehistory*, Ramona: Ballena Press Anthropological Papers No. 3.

Willis, William S., Jr.
1970. "Anthropology and Negroes on the Southern Colonial Frontier." In James Curtis and L. Gould, eds., *The Black Experience in America*, pp. 33–50. Austin: University of Texas Press.
1975. "Franz Boas and the Study of Black Folklore." In John W. Bennett, ed., *The New Ethnicity: Perspectives from Ethnology*, pp. 307–334. 1973 Proceedings of the American Ethnological Society. New York: West.

Willner, Dorothy
1973. "Anthropology: Vocation or Commodity." *Current Anthropology* 14:547–555.

Wissler, Clark
  1920. "Opportunities for Coordination in Anthropological and Psychological Research." *American Anthropologist* 22:1–12.

Witt, Shirley Hill
  1968. "Nationalistic Trends Among American Indians." In Stuart Levine and Nancy O. Lurie, eds., *The American Indian Today,* pp. 53–75. Deland, Fla.: Everett Edwards Press.

Wolf, Eric R.
  1955. "Types of Latin American Peasantry: A Preliminary Discussion." *American Anthropologist* 57:452–459.
  1956. "Aspects of Group Relations in a Complex Society: Mexico." *American Anthropologist* 58:1065–1078.
  1972. "American Anthropologists and American Society." In Dell Hymes, ed., *Reinventing Anthropology,* pp. 251–263. New York: Vintage.

Wolf, Eric and Joseph Jorgensen
  1970. "Anthropology on the Warpath in Thailand." *New York Review of Books,* November 19, pp. 26–35.

Wolff, Kurt H., trans. and ed.
  1950. *The Sociology of Georg Simmel.* Glencoe, Ill.: Free Press.

Wolff, Pablo Osvaldo
  1949. *Marihuana in Latin America: The Threat It Constitutes.* New York: Linacre Press. (Orig. pub. Buenos Aires: 1948.)

Woodward, C. Vann
  1957. *The Strange Career of Jim Crow.* New York: Oxford University Press.

Woodward, Joan
  1965. *Industrial Organization: Theory and Practice.* London: Oxford University Press.

Woolfson, Peter
  1974. "The Fight Over Macos: An Ideological Conflict in Vermont." *Council on Anthropology and Education Quarterly* 5(3):27–30.

Yang, Martin C.
  1945. *A Chinese Village.* New York: Columbia University Press.

Yankelovich, Daniel
  1974. "Turbulence in the Working World: Angry Workers, Happy Grads." *Psychology Today* 8(7):80–87.

Zimmerman, William J.
  1957. "The Role of the Bureau of Indian Affairs since 1933." *Annals,* American Academy of Political and Social Sciences 311:31–40.

Zorbaugh, Harvey W.
  1929. *Gold Coast and Slum: A Sociological Study of Chicago's Near North Side.* Chicago, Ill.: University of Chicago Press.